D1000229

IRIS MURDOCH: THE SAINT AND THE ARTIST

823
MURdoch
C

IRIS MURDOCH:
THE SAINT AND THE ARTIST

Peter J. Conradi

St. Martin's Press   New York

© Peter J. Conradi 1986

All rights reserved. For information, write:
St. Martin's Press, Inc., 175 Fifth Avenue, New York, NY 10010
Printed in Hong Kong
Published in the United Kingdom by The Macmillan Press Ltd.
First published in the United States of America in 1986

ISBN 0–312–43614–9

Library of Congress Cataloging in Publication Data
Conradi, Peter J., 1945–
Iris Murdoch: the saint and the artist.
Bibliography: p.
Includes index.
1. Murdoch, Iris – Criticism and interpretation.
I. Title
PR6063.U7Z63   1985   823'914   85–12000
ISBN 0–312–43614–9

For my parents

PLATO: . . . our home is elsewhere and it draws us like a magnet

SOCRATES: . . . Our home may be elsewhere, but we are condemned to exile, to live here with our fellow exiles

(Iris Murdoch, 'Art and Eros', a Platonic dialogue on some themes from *The Fire and the Sun*)

Contents

Contents

Preface

This is not a chronological survey of Iris Murdoch's work nor, strictly speaking, of the changes in thinking that underlie it. It is an extended essay in three parts. It has always been a problem for the critic to know how far to relate her work both to her theorising about the craft of fiction and also to her moral philosophy. How close is this relation and, where it seems distant, is this a matter for praise or blame? It is a tribute to the power and fascination of Murdoch's theoretical work that critics have returned to it with such baffled piety. Indeed the received approach to her work has been to ask what is marvellous in the theory, and then to look to the books to find the shortfall. However apt this seemed at the start of her career, it seems less so today. Brecht, James, Lawrence, Wordsworth, Woolf, Chaucer, Ben Jonson: the list of writers whom we do not praise for the virtues they hoped they had incarnated in their work is as long as literary history itself. It might indeed almost be taken as the defining characteristic of any writer at all worth notice that there is some disjunction between theory and practice, a disjunction recently seized on alike by deconstructionist critics, who show how the work dissipates and undoes its own premises and, very differently and more sympathetically, by John Bayley in *The Uses of Division*. Speaking to Harold Hobson in 1962 Iris Murdoch said, 'Eliot implies somewhere that Dante is greater than Shakespeare because Dante has a richer and more coherent philosophy behind him. But Eliot must be wrong ... Shakespeare is greater than Dante so it can't be essential for a writer to have a coherent philosophy behind him.'

The critic wishing to register his pleasure normally begins by asking what is marvellous in his subject and where it is to be found, before casting around for a means of describing it. I would argue that with *A Fairly Honourable Defeat* in 1970 a mature phase began in Murdoch's art and that the books which follow are the work of a very considerable artist indeed. They provide the yardstick by which the early work and theory may be judged, and which alter our view of both. We now need to read the earlier work *through* the later work.

This study therefore has three parts. In the first I look at the early work and at what she has termed her 'moral psychology'. This seems a more useful term for the critic than 'philosophy' since it suggests how much her thinking takes thrust from the simple and perplexing fact of human difference. For this reason, and because it holds the idea of conceptual mastery in such suspicion, her philosophy is in a sense an 'anti-philosophy'. The broad movement of her thought is from an uneasy flirtation with existentialism towards a more religious picture which shares much with Buddhism. In this process a Neoplatonic view of Eros, which brilliantly marries Freud to Plato, is central. Her views on the unconscious have been neglected. The idea of the purification of undifferentiated desire lies at the heart of her moral psychology and of her view of the artist's endeavour alike. I aim to show that a tension between a spiritual and a secular or worldly view of the moral agent animates her work from the beginning.

In the second part I look at four novels from the period 1957–68 which oscillate between being 'open' and 'closed', as she has termed the distinction: that is between a mythic and poetic intensity which the characters on occasion subserve, and a more open, airy and centrifugal structure. In the third part I examine the flowering of her talents in the books of the 1970s, which combine the formerly warring virtues of 'open' and 'closed', and marry myth with psychology.

In the conclusion I touch on the recent work, the question of 'Romanticism' and the ambiguous role of 'gentlemanliness' in her novels.

Acknowledgements

In writing this book I have incurred many debts. Without Priscilla Martin's inspiration and encouragement I should not have begun; and without Jim O'Neill's patient support I would never have finished. I would like to thank Mr Frank Paluka, head of Special Collections at the University of Iowa, and colleagues at the University of Colorado where I taught from 1978 to 1980, for enabling me to study drafts of Miss Murdoch's novels held at Iowa; and my colleagues at Kingston Polytechnic for their generosity in lightening my load, in giving me leave during the spring term of 1983, and in enabling me to visit Edinburgh for the fortnight of Miss Murdoch's Gifford lectures 'Metaphysics as a Guide to Morals' in November 1982. Miss Jane Turner of Chatto and Windus gave me access to reviews of and articles on Miss Murdoch's fiction; Oxford University Press and Routledge & Kegan Paul were similarly helpful with reviews of her philosophy. The middle chapters of this book, in particular, are adapted from a PhD at London University, 'Iris Murdoch and the Purification of Eros' (1984). This dealt more fully with Miss Murdoch's Platonism and less amply with her fiction; only six novels were considered in detail. Antonia Byatt was a most kindly and encouraging supervisor. Some other material first appeared in *Critical Quarterly, ELH* and *New Statesman* to whose editors I am indebted for permission to reprint.

For their help with background reading, discussion of early drafts, or for other comments I should like to thank Miriam Allott, Tim Cook, Martin Corner, Simon Edwards, Inga-Stina Ewbank, Ian Gregor, Jane Hope, Karl Miller, D. Z. Phillips and Lorna Sage. John Fletcher and Ann Loades gave invaluable bibliographical help. Students of Murdoch's work will owe much to John Fletcher's *Iris Murdoch: Her Work and her Critics 1933–1983* (Garland, NY; forthcoming). Michael Kustow generously supplied a transcript of the unpublished Platonic dialogue 'Art and Eros' which Miss Murdoch wrote for platform performance at the National Theatre in 1980; the BBC helped with transcripts of interviews; the University of East Anglia gave permission to quote from an unpublished 1976 interview between Miss Murdoch, Lorna Sage and Malcolm Bradbury. From these, as from other unpublished sources, Miss Murdoch kindly gave me permission to use specific quotations. The typescript was read by Martin Corner and by Lorna Sage, both of whom commented valuably. Sandra Philpotts helped me greatly with permissions, and with proofs, as did Daphne Turner. Miss Murdoch answered queries with the patient kindness for which she is known, and commented most usefully on early drafts for two chapters.

Responsibility for views expressed here remains, of course, solely my own.

I wish to thank Chatto and Windus Ltd and Viking Penguin Inc., for permission to reproduce the extracts from Miss Murdoch's novels; Oxford University Press, for permission to quote from *The Fire and the Sun: Why Plato Banished the Artists* (1977); and Routledge & Kegan Paul PLC, for permission to quote from *The Sovereignty of Good* (1970).

Kingston Polytechnic   P. J. C.

List of Abbreviations

The following abbreviations and editions have been used:

1. NOVELS

AM	*An Accidental Man*, 1971 (London: Triad/Panther, 1979)
B	*The Bell*, 1958 (Harmondsworth: Penguin, 1962)
BD	*Bruno's Dream*, 1969 (Harmondsworth: Penguin, 1970)
BP	*The Black Prince*, 1973 (Harmondsworth: Penguin, 1975)
FE	*The Flight from the Enchanter*, 1956 (Harmondsworth: Penguin, 1962)
FHD	*A Fairly Honourable Defeat*, 1970 (Harmondsworth: Penguin, 1972)
HC	*Henry and Cato*, 1976 (Harmondsworth: Penguin, 1977)
IG	*The Italian Girl*, 1964 (Harmondsworth: Penguin, 1967)
NG	*The Nice and the Good*, 1968 (London: Triad/Panther, 1977)
NS	*Nuns and Soldiers*, 1980 (London: Chatto & Windus, 1980)
PP	*The Philosopher's Pupil*, 1983 (London: Chatto & Windus, 1983)
RG	*The Red and the Green*, 1965 (London: Triad/Panther, 1978)
S	*The Sandcastle*, 1957 (Harmondsworth: Penguin, 1960)
SH	*A Severed Head*, 1961 (Harmondsworth: Penguin, 1963)
SPLM	*The Sacred and Profane Love Machine*, 1974 (Harmondsworth: Penguin, 1975)
SS	*The Sea, The Sea*, 1978 (London: Triad/Granada, 1980)
TA	*The Time of the Angels*, 1966 (London: Triad/Panther, 1978)
U	*The Unicorn*, 1963 (London: Triad/Panther, 1977)
UN	*Under the Net*, 1954 (Harmondsworth: Penguin, 1960)
UR	*An Unofficial Rose*, 1962 (London: Triad/Panther, 1977)
WC	*A Word Child*, 1975 (Harmondsworth: Penguin, 1976)

2. PHILOSOPHY

FS   *The Fire and the Sun*, 1977 (Oxford University Press, 1977)

SG   *The Sovereignty of Good*, 1970 (London: Routledge & Kegan Paul, 1970)

SRR   *Sartre: Romantic Rationalist*, 1953 (London: Bowes & Bowes, 1953)

3. INTERVIEWS

These are identified in the text by the name of the interviewer and the date when given, except for 'Caen'. For further details see the Select Bibliography.

4. ARTICLES

ad   'Against Dryness', *Encounter*, XVI (Jan. 1961) 16–20.

an   'Art is the Imitation of Nature', *Cahiers du Centre de Recherches sur les Pays du Nord et du Nord-Ouest*, l'Université de Caen, 1978.

eh   'The Existentialist Hero', *Listener*, 23 Mar. 1950, 523–4.

em   'Existentialists and Mystics', in W. Robson (ed.), *Essays and Poems Presented to Lord David Cecil* (London, 1970).

ht   'A House of Theory', *Partisan Review*, XXVI (1959) 17–31.

kv   'Knowing the Void', *Spectator*, CXCVII (2 Nov. 1956) 613–14.

me   'Metaphysics and Ethics', in D. F. Pears (ed.), *The Nature of Metaphysics* (London, 1957).

mmm 'Mass, Might and Myth', *Spectator*, CCIX (7 Sep. 1962) 337–8.

sbr   'The Sublime and the Beautiful Revisited', *Yale Review*, XLIX (Winter 1959) 247–71.

sg   'The Sublime and the Good', *Chicago Review*, XIII (Autumn 1959) 42–55.

sw   'Salvation by Words', *New York Review of Books*, 15 June 1972, 4.

vc   'Vision and Choice in Morality', *Aristotelian Society Supplementary Volume*, XXX (1956) 32–58.

Chronology

1974   *The Sacred and Profane Love Machine* published
1975   *A Word Child* published
1976   *Henry and Cato* published
1977   *The Fire and the Sun: Why Plato Banished the Artists**
        (based on the 1976 Romanes Lectures) published
1978   *The Sea, The Sea* and *A Year of Birds: Poems* published
1980   'Art and Eros', an unpublished Platonic Dialogue
        on some themes from *The Fire and the Sun* for platform
        performance at the National Theatre (February and
        March); libretto (unpublished) for *The Servants*, an
        opera by William Mathias, first performed on 15
        September at the New Theatre, Cardiff; *Nuns and
        Soldiers* published
1982   26 October–9 November: Gifford Lectures in Natu-
        ral Theology at University of Edinburgh entitled
        'Metaphysics as a Guide to Morals'
1983   *The Philosopher's Pupil* published
1985   *The Good Apprentice* published

* = philosophy.

Part I
'A Kind of Moral Psychology'

> The novel itself, of course, the whole world of the novel, is the expression of a world outlook. And one can't avoid doing this. Any novelist produces a moral world and there's a kind of world outlook which can be deduced from each of the novels. And of course I have my own philosophy in a very general sense, a kind of moral psychology one might call it rather than philosophy.
>
> (Iris Murdoch speaking at the University of Caen, 1978)

1 Introductory: 'Existentialist and Mystic'

Iris Murdoch is the author of some twenty-one novels, a handful of plays and poems, a number of influential articles, a book on Sartre, a book of her own moral philosophy, and a book on Plato's theory of art. She is a writer of international reputation. Apart from monographs there has been no full-length study of her work by a British critic since A. S. Byatt's valuable, pioneering study *Degrees of Freedom* twenty years ago. Despite the honours that the later work has won – *The Black Prince* won the James Tait Black Memorial prize in 1973, *The Sacred and Profane Love Machine* won the Whitbread prize in 1974, *The Sea, The Sea* the coveted Booker prize in 1978 – it has not been properly celebrated. I believe that the early theory, and also the real but limited success of the early apprentice fiction, have obscured the enormous, disorderly merits of the recent work. The later work in its turn must alter the way we view the earlier.

Few writers divide their audiences as radically. Between her advocates and her detractors there is a gulf fixed. Elizabeth Dipple's useful missionary *Work for the Spirit* (1982) sought to bridge this gap and to convert the latter into the former. This study is not, by contrast, a proselytising one. It seeks to persuade no one who does not already enjoy her work, but to describe some of the pleasures which an excessively narrow critical focus has neglected. This is a celebratory study whose aim is to try to illuminate her best work and to give some account of why she is found both entertaining, and also serious and important.

'Most artists understand their own weaknesses far better than the critics do', says Arnold Baffin in *The Black Prince*, a writer unflatteringly parodied, as his creator has been, for emptying himself in his books over the world 'like scented bath-water', and as living 'in a sort of rosy haze with Jesus and Mary and Buddha and Shiva and the Fisher King all chasing round and round

dressed up as people in Chelsea' (*BP* 137). Iris Murdoch is her
own best critic and best defendant. She gives the prolific Baffin
an eloquent self-defence too – 'The years pass and one has only
one life. If one has a thing at all one must do it and keep on and
on trying to do it better. And one aspect of this is that any artist
has to *decide* how fast to work. I do not believe that I would
improve if I wrote less. The only result of that would be that
there would be less of whatever there is' (172).

Murdoch's frailties are by now well chronicled. Borrowing her
own lofty criteria and sometimes drawing on her *Peccavis*, reviewers
have sometimes been content to issue bulletins of high-minded
reproof and adopt a tone of puritanical strictness. In what follows
I do not seek to whisk her away into academic irreproachability.
It is in some sense her human quality that seems to me engaging –
her quality of, in the best sense, 'stubborn imperfection'.[1] She
can be uneven, over-intellectual or romantic. There is some
unfinished and repetitive writing. The books can seem contrived
or over-plotted, the characters sometimes insufficiently imagined.
Her social range is not huge, she says little about work and often
appears to take money for granted. She can seem to be playing
a complex game with the reader. There is, as early reviewers
noted, 'too much' in the books.

The objections are by now well canvassed. Her virtues need
cataloguing too. She writes spell-binding stories in beautiful prose.
She knows how to master paragraphs and sentences and at her
best achieves an extraordinary, luminous, lyrical accuracy. She
has an intensely visual imagination and can use it to evoke things,
people, the activity of thinking, feeling, places, cars and dogs too.
In each novel are things that no other British writer has the
power to describe. Her empirical curiosity and moral energy seem
endless. Few other writers are as full of the naked pleasures of
looking and describing. She can tackle happiness, 'that deep,
confiding slow relationship to time' (*SPLM* 16), the subject-
matter for great writers. (Every fool can write about misery.)
London is a real presence in the books, indeed seems to figure
sometimes as an extra character, and even when her people are
having a hellish time there, which is often, the author's loving
and patient apprehension of the city comes through. This is the
more noticeable in that, Dickens and Woolf apart, London has
lacked distinguished celebrants. There is no touch of neurotic
agrarianism in Murdoch, and if London had its Samuel Palmer

it might well be her. But she can of course evoke the inner world, the world of fantasies, projections, demonic illusions too. No one writes better today about the urgencies and illusions of the moral life. She is our most intelligent novelist since George Eliot, and like George Eliot she was a mature thinker before she wrote her first novel. Her technique alters significantly as the novels progress. Many of her leading ideas are already there in her first work.

Does our sense that the novels feel 'contrived' damage the illusion that the characters are free? Decreasingly, I think. The point has too often been argued in a simple-minded manner. Even in the most Gothic of her novels the characters seem alive. What she writes owes much to 'romance'[2] and romance is both the most conventional and yet the least 'literary', most immediate of forms.[3] It is a form which demands a certain latitude in the matter of probabilities. All art is contrived, and in great art truth can be purchased at the expense of improbability; yet the absurdities vanish under the force of the art. This is clear in the case of Restoration comedy, or opera, both of which her work can resemble[4] or indeed in the case of Shakespearian drama, which her work increasingly contemplates and is nourished by. The plots of *King Lear* or *Much Ado about Nothing* are not 'realistic', and at the end of *Twelfth Night* we share in a 'triumph of the improbable'. These are plots which can grip you in the theatre and mock your attempts to recount them outside. You put up with the contrivance and conscious stylisation for the sake of the illumination they offer, and the degree of trust you show depends on the good will you bear the author, and the reward her illusions purchase. As Murdoch put this in the 1982 Gifford lectures – 'in good art we do not ask for realism; we ask for truth.'

Truth, of course, has had a bad press recently, and thus the question of stylisation has a way of returning. One reviewer recorded how his feeling on opening a Murdoch novel 'But surely human beings are not like this' can be swiftly followed by the feeling 'Perhaps this is just what human beings are in fact like, and it is precisely our delusion to imagine that we are not.'[5] I believe that one source of positive pleasure in the *bizarrerie* offered by her plots comes from our sense that, as Murdoch has often averred, people are secretly much odder, less rational, more often powered by obsession and passion than they outwardly pretend or know, and that the novelist is revealing such secrets in creating her (imaginary) people. Recent accounts of Bloomsbury – for example Angelica Garnett's *Deceived with Kindness* – make most Murdoch plots look models of understatement. 'Murdochian' has justly joined Dickensian and Swiftian as a way of pointing to certain aspects of the world. I think her characters are recognisable. These vain bookish civil servants, morally squeamish men whose sheer egoism is driving them mad, emotionally greedy women, precocious adolescents, isolated and awkward good characters, all involved in the great, lonely hunt for love and consolation and power: it is not a bad image of the world. It has universality too.

There are related points to be made about contrivance. Her best work is quiveringly real/unreal in its texture. What can be perplexing is not that she fails to convince, but that she can describe with an extraordinary hallucinatory validating detail and power the most 'unlikely' situations, so that, before you have time to decide whether or not you believe in them, you find yourself forced to imagine them. Her ingenious style of realism, in combining fantasy with a meticulous naturalistic rendering of detail, shares something with surrealism. It can drive a wedge between reason and imagination, so that we concur imaginatively, against reason's good advice; reason is dulled in something like awe at her sheer aesthetic nerve and inventiveness. In Chapter 5 I discuss how the limits to rationalism become for her a great theme. Her use of contrivance seems to relate to this, a deliberate and shameless affront, 'unbelievable' in a way that mimics and parodies the frequently unbelievable quality of life too. Unreality, in other words, can be a potent aesthetic device. The task of classifying, as her work often asserts, can perhaps never be more than a (serious) game; but visionary or 'magical' realism seems to get closer than most descriptive terms to the special and disturbing pleasure her work can afford. The question of artifice has too often been divorced from the question of pleasure.

She can create mystery and magic. In the least of her work there is something alive and interesting, an atmosphere which haunts and stays with you. The Dorset sea-scape of *The Nice and the Good*, the fog-bound rectory in *The Time of the Angels*, the various different Londons of *A Severed Head*, or *A Fairly Honourable Defeat* – these are real imaginative creations. The creation of a strong 'atmosphere' can be at odds with the creation of character and I think critics can be too puritan here. Even Shakespeare and Tolstoi do not always create 'memorable' characters. Like any other writer's, her characters can sometimes be memorable, sometimes merely believable, sometimes interesting without being persuasive, sometimes 'far too individual to remember'.[6] In the most idea-bound of her romances we have persons and not merely personifications. A disservice is done by critics awed by the cold prestige of 'philosophy', and mindful that Iris Murdoch is a philosopher as well as a novelist, who treat the novels as though their inhabitants must therefore be no more than symposiasts at a disputation. The books are full of ideas, of course, but are also about life, feed off life, feed back into life.

Murdoch clearly understands a great deal about people, with a quality of understanding I can best describe as 'animal intelligence', a Keatsian ability to encounter the sensuousness of the activity of thinking, in all its immediacy. She is interested in power, a subject largely ignored by critics. 'No question can be more important than "Who is the boss?" ', says Julius in *A Fairly Honourable Defeat*. The question 'Who is the boss?' links in her books, as in life, with sex and with spirit. There is a large other range of mixed emotion she is adept at evoking, especially, of course, love, her subject *par excellence*. If she is the Gilbert White of the sensations and the emotions, she is also love's natural historian.

She can appear to be playing a sophisticated game with the reader and the critic should beware of complaining that she is simply more intelligent than he is. If you enjoy her, her intelligence is part of what you are enjoying. I shall try to explain in Chapter 5 how the frustration of the reader's natural desire to make the world of the book transparent is a task she takes seriously. She is, I think, in Isaiah Berlin's famous dichotomy, much more of a fox than a hedgehog – one who knows many things before she knows one. Knowing many things is in a sense her premise for knowing one. Despite the fact that she has declared that she inclines, temperamentally, to monism (*SG* 50), she sees the world's variousness and multiplicity as art's opportunity, as well as its foe.

Her social range deserves comment. Often the novels will concern a central 'court' of relatives and friends, some of whom will have met at university, and whose older women-folk have sacrificed careers for those of their husbands. Such in-bred courts feed off Shakespeare, as she has often acknowledged, as well as off life. The British professional classes often lead such in-bred coterie lives, and she will be remembered, I am sure, partly as a chronicler of today's chattering classes. 'One can only write well about what one thoroughly understands' (Bradbury, 1976) she has noted, pointing out that any account of 'intelligent people who are interested in their society' will carry some general interest. One might gloss this by saying that a close account of those assumed by society to be 'the Great and the Good' is likely – as in the toughly satirical *A Severed Head* – to tell us something important about society itself, even though satire as such in the other novels is muted into a more general irony. Moreover, contrary to the superficial view that her social range has merely shrunk, a close look shows that it has polarised. There were always in her work deracinated intellectuals of various backgrounds, ambitious girls on the make (Madge in *Under the Net*, Miss Casement in *The Flight from the Enchanter*), working-class recruits to the intelligentsia, delinquents, Bohemians and refugees. Latterly there has been a polarisation of the cast into the possessing and the dispossessed, so that in *Henry and Cato* the two ends of Ladbroke Grove, one wealthy, the other derelict, act as an image of social contrast and inequality. In *A Word Child* the orphan and bastard Hilary Burde's seedy life contrasts with that of his rival Gunnar Jopling's 'casually gorgeous' milieu. And in *Nuns and Soldiers* Tim Reede moves from the class that raids other people's fridges to the class that owns the well-supplied fridge. It is certainly true that she animates well those characters who have had some sort of higher education. This is not quite the same as claiming she can deal only with the *Bourgeoisie*. To put the matter another way, it accurately reflects one of the ways in which, under the Welfare State, Britain's class structure tended to alter. Before the last war the inheritance of privilege did not necessarily involve attending university, though it did depend on attending 'Public school'. Since the war, whether or not you received higher education became, for some decades, important in a novel way. As Murdoch noted in 1959:

> Equality of opportunity produces, not a society of equals, but a society in which the class division is made more sinister by the removal of intelligent persons into the bureaucracy and the destruction of their roots and characteristics as members of the mass. (ht)

This middle-class intelligentsia broadly provides her material. 'Barkers people not Harrods people' as one of her characters notes (*AM* 27), though the spread moves upward on occasion. Murdoch's father was a civil servant, and during the war years so was she. As in so many Russian novels, bureaucrats abound, though tempered with members of genteel and other professions – school-teachers, wine-merchants, printers, rose-growers. Just as Britain has recently become more socially divided, so the world she has addressed has appeared more beleaguered and isolated. The loftiest apology for this social range is made by Bradley Pearson in *The Black Prince* when he points out that a truly enlightened person might perhaps be known by his sympathy's extending even as far as the rich (*BP* 348). Pearson himself, like Burde in *A Word Child* and Arrowby in *The Sea, The Sea*, is the child of a poor family.

Perhaps in the end – and this will be truer of contemporary writers than of any others – 'a philosopher's thought either suits you or it doesn't. It's only deep in that sense. Like a novel', as the dying Guy puts it in *Nuns and Soldiers* (2). Qualities such as facility, the capacity to re-work a few themes, and conscious stylisation, can be as characteristic of great as of small writers – it is as proper to speak of the facility of a Shakespeare as of a Wodehouse. I'd like to end this section by emphasising two faculties which seem to me to have been unfairly separated, when one of them has not been ignored. It has not been enough repeated that she is, as well as a very witty writer, also a consistently funny one, and that this humour is linked to her moral passion. Taine remarked of Dickens that his whole work might be reduced to the phrase 'Be good, and love'.[7] So might Murdoch's *oeuvre*. Both attack human self-centredness. That human beings are powered by egoism is not by itself, however, exciting news. The problem for the critic is in describing not just this message, but how it gets 'dissolved in the purr of beatitude'[8] the work promotes in us, and in describing the comic tension between that message, and everything in the work which resists and complicates it. She has admired in Shakespeare's plays not merely their 'tremendous moral charge' but also that 'it is morality at its most refined, and at the same time it is not dogmatic, it has got an element of extraordinary openness in it' (Bigsby, 1982). The author of these twenty-one novels seems to see life with one eye warm if not wet, one dry and distant, and perhaps narrates by two positives. There is in her mediation between these a sanity, a cheerful common sense, a gift for openness and for comedy, that need emphasising at the outset.

*

Iris Murdoch was born in Dublin in 1919, of Anglo-Irish parents. Her mother's family were from Dublin, her father's were County Down sheep-farming stock. Her mother gave up a career as a singer to marry at eighteen. Her gentle bookish father had survived the war partly through the good luck of being a cavalry officer – the cavalry missed the holocaust of the trenches. Further back her ancestors were mainly Irish farmers and soldiers. She had a very happy childhood, and was brought up in London, to which her parents moved when she was a baby, but with holidays in Ireland, and seeing Ireland as 'a very romantic land, a land I wanted to get to and discover' (Caen, 1978). Her father's family were 'admirable people, but Protestants of a very strict kind, and I think he wanted to get away' (Haffenden, 1983). The Anglo-Irish are a peculiar people, from whose stock some most gifted writers have come, but also a people with a dual identity, seeing themselves in some sense as both the true Irish *and* the true English, while being regarded by everyone else as neither, and as outsiders. About growing up in London Murdoch commented 'I feel as I grow older that we were wanderers, and I've only recently realised that I'm a kind of exile, a displaced person. I identify with exiles'(Haffenden, 1983). Perhaps Ireland provided her in her imagination with an absent, alternative identity. She has spoken often of her distress at the continuing violence there and Ireland has figured in only two novels – *The Unicorn*, which is a Gothic romance set on the West coast, and *The Red and the Green*, an account of the 1916 Easter rising which combines detailed research into the period with an intricate plot, and where the sexual imbroglio within an extended Anglo-Irish family partly mirrors the political tensions. The political viewpoint of the book, in so far as it commits itself to one, is that of the liberal Irish patriotism of the Anglo-Irish, who have of course often been zealots in that cause.

She was an only child and has related her writing drive to the search for imaginary brothers and sisters, as she has also seen in this a reason for her (and Sartre's) fascination with twins – 'the lost, the other person one is looking for' (Caen, 1978). She was educated at the Froebel Educational Institute, at Badminton College, then at Somerville College, Oxford, where she read 'Greats' (ancient history, classics, philosophy). Her knowledge and love of the classics, and of classical mythology, are evident throughout the novels, where such myths are sometimes played with and made to help yield decoration for the plot. From 1942 to 1944 she worked as temporary wartime civil servant (Assistant Principal) in the Treasury, and then for the following two years with the United Nations Relief and Rehabilitation Administration, first in Belgium and then in Austria, where she worked in a camp for displaced persons.

Her period with UNRRA seems to have been important for two reasons. In Brussels she encountered existentialism, which excited her about the possibilities, hitherto unconsidered, of philosophy. In 1947 she was to hold the Sarah Smithson Studentship in philosophy at Newnham College, Cambridge. She also saw a 'total breakdown of human society' which she has said it was instructive to witness (Haffenden, 1983). These two encounters now seem less far apart than might appear. This breakdown of society produced the refugees and homeless persons who figure in Murdoch's novels, as in history, and Sartrian existentialism was a philosophy that privileged the cultureless outsider hero. I don't think the role of existentialism in her thinking has been well focused. It has sometimes been said that she has moved from existentialism towards a religious position. This makes for a difficulty in discerning her right relation to existentialism, by which I mean Sartrian existentialism throughout, since that was the form which most interested her. In interview with Bigsby (1982) she suggested that her objections went right back to her first encounter with it in 1945. Her scepticism as well as her interest is quite apparent before her first novel was published in 1954, and her book on Sartre the previous year though respectful is scarcely uncritical. What excited her about it was the primary place it gave to a consideration and depiction of *experience*, a subject then absent from Anglo-Saxon philosophy, and its comparative willingness to tackle problems of value and morality. It was the phenomenological and moral bias of the existentialists that excited her, and she was one of the few English philosophers to have read them. In Britain there had been a disastrous shrinking of the field of moral philosophy to, for example, discussions of the ontological status of moral assertions, and an abdication of the responsibility to guide and instruct.

Philosophy seems to have come to matter to her, for all its clear difference from literature, for comparable reasons, because 'a dominant philosophy pictures the consciousness of the age' (sbr), and because man is the creature who 'makes pictures of himself and then comes to resemble the pictures' (me). She came to distrust Sartrian existentialism and British philosophy equally, and to see them as sharing a common ground in offering no barrier to romantic self-assertion. In a radio talk in 1950 she criticised both Sartre and Camus for presenting worlds which were simultaneously too intelligible and transparent, and also too lacking (unlike the world of Gabriel Marcel) in mystery – in which category she included nightmarish mystery – and magic. 'This fact alone, that there is no mystery, would falsify their claims to be true pictures of the situation of man . . . . We are not yet resigned to absurdity and our only salvation lies in not becoming resigned' (eh). The same year she asked, *à propos* Simone de Beauvoir's championing of T. E. Lawrence as an existentialist hero, 'Should he be taken as the model of the "good man" for this age?'9 In a sense this question resonates throughout her writing and its very subversive simplicity rightly disturbs us. What man are we being asked to admire in this novel or in that philosophy? And are the reasons just? By 1957 in a *Spectator* review she noted that the appeal of existentialism was its dramatic, solipsistic, romantic and anti-social exaltation of the individual.10 If the central question she was later to ask in *The Sovereignty of Good* – what is it that might 'lead to unselfish behaviour in the concentration camp?' (73) – has any answer, it is not the 'instantaneous' values of the existentialist hero or of his Anglo-Saxon voluntarist counterpart. I think it is no accident that the plot of her novels until 1970 often concerns the disruption of a court of settled, rooted English *Grands Bourgeois* by displaced persons and refugees. The theme is of course as old as Jane Austen, but Murdoch makes her own special use of it. Murdoch has written both of the 'phenomenal *luck* of our English-speaking societies' and, in the same article (sbr) of how such luck may obscure deep truth. These outsiders – the Luciewicz twins and Mischa Fox in *The Flight from the Enchanter*, the Levkins in *The Italian Girl*, Honor Klein and Palmer Anderson in *A Severed Head*, Julius King in *A Fairly Honourable Defeat* – may sometimes appear as twentieth-century versions of the sentimental or demonic egoists whose irruption into the innocent provincial redoubt Austen chronicled.[11] They as often, however, reveal the 'deep truth' hidden behind polite English manners.

The exact moment at which her disaffection with existentialism began may now be hard to determine. The spiritual claim that quarrels with it is present as early as *Under the Net*; and in a sense this argument has continued.

In the 1950s Murdoch began to read the great French mystic Simone Weil, whose influence on the novels A. S. Byatt has discussed in *Degrees of Freedom*. It is Weil's strength that she does not, unlike Sartre, sentimentalise the position of being radically denuded and outside society. Murdoch has called Simone Weil's *Need for Roots* 'one of the very few profound and original political treatises of our time'(kv). It argues that the most terrible deprivation possible is the destruction of one's past and one's culture. Weil's argument is that the affliction and degradation caused by the destruction of roots was such that it deprived all but the saintly person of the capacity to change or 'unself' from inside. The uprooted hurt and uproot others. Only for the saintly can virtue have no fixed address, in Weil's philosophy and in Murdoch's fiction. Morality depends, for Weil, on the slow attenuation or destruction of the ego, which itself requires a quiet environment. Sudden or violent deracination can mean complete or demonic demoralisation.

It is not, I think, that existentialism (or formalism) is wrong to attack the substantial self. It is rather that their attack is for Murdoch in bad faith. In pretending that the essential self does not exist the existentialist may behave like an 'egotist-without-an-I'. The Buddhist attack on the fictionality of the ego is more profound, for both Weil and Murdoch, because it is based on a realistic assessment of the limited capacity of the ego to decentre itself, and because it is nonetheless designed to alter perception and behaviour. The originality of Murdoch's novels is that they are full of a sense of what it means to come from one of the luckier, stabler societies or sections within that society, in an unlucky century, but avoid false piety about either that luck or that misfortune. The make-believe of ordinary life and the painful destruction of ordinary human illusion can be carried out anywhere, in a refugee camp or at a tea-table. Nowhere is privileged.

Just as her recoil from existentialism begins early, so I think does her attraction to a countervailing soul-picture which is, though absorbing much from Freud, religious yet (like Buddhism) atheist (and hence scandalous both to some Christians and to many humanists). Apart from a polemical letter to *The New Statesman* in 1941 defending the fellow-travelling Oxford Labour Group against J. W. Joad's 'liberal ethics of the nineteenth century' and his facile invocation to 'truth, beauty, goodness and love',[12] Murdoch's earliest prose publications are three reviews of books with Christian topics, written during the war for the *Adelphi*. They already prefigure her developed 'philosophy' of the 1960s, which she has pertinently called not so much a philosophy as a moral psychology (Caen, 1978) in its interest in the differences between people, and in 'how conduct is changed and how consciousness is changed' (Bellamy, 1977). These reviews, while making clear that she is non-Christian, also show that she is prepared calmly and sympathetically to consider the claim that 'science and philosophy may come to rest afresh upon a specifically religious exposition of the nature of reality.' Two other passages seem relevant to later preoccupations. The first concerns her interest in the dualism of worldliness and unworldliness, and the problem of the contemplative's 'return to the Cave'. 'One may sympathise with this horror that turns its face utterly from this world as a place of unrelieved filth and corruption – but the problem of the return to the Cave remains a very real one for Christianity.' In the second she compares the detachment of the artist with that of the saint. The artist, she argues, is not 'apart' as the saint is. 'He sees the earth freshly and strangely but he is ultimately part of it, he is inside the things he sees and speaks of as well as outside them. He is of their substance, he suffers with them. Of saints I know nothing . . . .'[13] That collocation of 'fresh' with 'strange' prefigures many of the effects of her novels. The 'odd' for her is often close to being or to revealing the beautiful.

From 1948 to 1963, when she gave up full-time teaching, she was Tutor in Philosophy and Fellow of St Anne's College, Oxford. In 1956 she married John Bayley, currently Thomas Warton Professor of English Literature at Oxford. John Fletcher has called theirs 'one of the most fruitful literary and critical partnerships of our time, and remarkable in any time'.[14] While Murdoch shows the novels to nobody until they are absolutely finished, they share a common humanism and an admiration for Shakespeare and

Tolstoi as the writers who best succeed in creating the illusion that their characters are free. I shall pursue some other connexions in reading the novels.

It is rare to find someone who has excelled, as has Murdoch, both as a novelist and as a moral philosopher. The precedent at which she glances at various points is the founder of European philosophy, Plato. In 1968 Murdoch called herself a Platonist (Rose, 1968). As well as philosophy, Plato is rumoured to have written poetry which he later tore up, and I think that in her we may intuit what she saw in Plato in *The Sovereignty of Good* – some version of 'the peculiarly distressing struggle between artist and saint' (88). She has spoken of this as a theme in her work in numerous interviews. She has described the division between would-be saint – Belfounder, Tayper-Pace, Ann Peronett – who have the certainty and power which come as gifts of faith, and possess a mysterious radiance beneath their ordinariness, and the would-be artist – Donaghue, Meade, Randall Peronett – who are imposing form onto essentially uncontrollable nature. The saint is unconsciously good, silent, and for him it is action that counts. The artist is consciously, aesthetically creating his life. To Bellamy she suggested that the importance of this conflict had to do with the ways in which the temptation to impose form existed in life as much as in art: the value of truth must pull at both.[15]

Thus the 'ancient quarrel' vivifies the novels themselves at the level of the moral psychology of the characters. Her depiction of artists – Miles in *Bruno's Dream*, Bradley in *The Black Prince* – is always suspicious; not, as the critic Dipple has too simply argued, that they are necessarily bad artists – in *The Fire and the Sun* Murdoch makes perfectly clear her view that 'Good artists can be bad men' (84) – but because 'art' itself is an analogue of the process by which we create in life a self-serving world view in which other people figure merely as subsidiary characters. This can be the only sense in which she refers, for example, to Michael Meade in *The Bell* as an artist – a man who has no strictly artistic ambitions.

Meeting Iris Murdoch in 1960 Ved Mehta wrote 'Among her friends and students Miss Murdoch has the reputation of being a saint, and she has no enemies' (Mehta, 1961).

*

A received view of the post-war British novel treats it as in slow retreat from a simple-minded and 'reactionary' social realism, and moving towards an embrace of the purportedly 'radical' virtues of fantasy, Gothic, and romance. A new generation of writers, beneficiaries of the 1944 Butler Education Act which enabled children from poorer homes to enjoy higher education, reacted in the 1950s against the canons of Modernism. They perceived it as a metropolitan and *rentier* mode, the writing of a privileged group typified often by Virginia Woolf. The new realism, championed by Amis and C. P. Snow, was resolutely provincial – anxious to celebrate the regions and to return, against the stylistic narcissism and self-consciousness of London and international Modernism, to the liberal conscience of Trollope, Wells, or George Eliot. The new realism, however, showed signs of strain. According to both Marxist and some liberal commentators this was because realism was underpinned by 'liberal humanism', an outmoded or inadequate 'ideology' whose superannuation cleared the way for more self-conscious, specula-tive and ironic forms. Social realism came to be seen as a naive or inauthentic mode, relying on a false view of the unified self, of perception and the innocent eye, and a falsely optimistic estimate of human history. And just as 'realism' came to be seen as a form of whiggish romancing, so 'romance' was to be the new realism. The novel thus acts out a Miltonic fall myth, first innocent and unselfknowing, later fallen, recessive, and wickedly selfconscious.

Murdoch's career strikingly belies this consoling map. She did criticise Modernism – or its symbolist legacy – in her early and influential essays, whose hostilities were very much of their time, and which have been plundered by critics for too few ideas. She did not start as a liberal and a social realist and move towards more 'apocalyptic' and Gothic forms. Instead she starts her work with a devastating critique of liberalism which resembles a systematic purgation, and begins her career in *Under the Net* where others of her generation look like ending theirs, with a work which is witty and anxious about art-as-lies, but one which also scorns the banal play which might have called its own illusionism into doubt. Such self-conscious play with the form, even in the later perplexing *The Black Prince*, is peripheral.

It might unkindly be said that liberal humanists in Britain have sometimes seemed to resemble Murdoch's character Eric in Australia where, ever since he arrived, 'people have disappointed me and deceived me and let me down' (*NG* 42) – either worrying away at the code like a game of Patience that seems unlikely to come out, or, in the case of the more prophetically inclined, as if it were just about to give way to some novel and more modish system of obligations whose name they were anxious to be the first to learn. For Murdoch the faults of liberalism are to a large extent the faults of existentialism. Both oppose, too simply, an innocent self to a guilty society, an inheritance they share from Romanticism. For her the question is posed not in terms of the mischievous default of history to make us secure and happy, but in terms of our own deep unacknowledged unfreedom and irrationality, our complicity in 'life-myths' we unknowingly construct and live by, and our deep defencelessness, which we wrap up in various ways, to history, chance and contingency. She has of course political concerns. She has campaigned among many other things against American involvement in Vietnam, and for homosexual law reform, and the novels obliquely discuss many public themes.[16] But, for her, man is not innately rational, good or free. 'Reason' has to be earned, unendingly struggled for, and her world is not inertly comprehensible, as in 'naïve' realism, but inexhaustibly mysterious and energetic beyond our easy grasp. An intense lyricism about this mystery marked her out from the first. To put her critique another way: there is in her work only ever the limited, very messy, imperfect and unperfectible task of love, and its failure. Society is not merely there outside us as a system of vulgar privations. Its nastinesses begin in our heads.

In both French and English novels of the mid-century the hero can appear as a potentially absolute individual unfairly circumscribed by a world of mere types. Although Amis's is a comic existentialism, both *Lucky Jim* and *Roquentin* seem similarly to dramatise their predicaments as those of 'freedoms caught in a trap' (*SRR* 36). It is the others who are irrational or falsely rational. The hero may, like Meurseult, be the only person who knows that he is powered by unreason and may thereby be 'authentic' in a way denied the less self-conscious; or like Bernard Sands in *Hemlock and After* may have his one moment of cruelty, an aberrance that must be neutralised before it destroys him.

Murdoch has attacked both 'self-knowledge' and 'sincerity' as second-rate and often delusive virtues. She has argued that both French existentialism and English linguistic philosophy are heirs of Romanticism and share a common voluntarism, a romantic

over-emphasis on the will. Both separate the moral agent from
all that surrounds him and, in speaking of the will as if it were
or could easily be free, wholly ignore the personality and the
huge and daunting power of its secret, fragmentary, opaque and
obsessive inner life. The unenlightened self is mechanical, and
escape from it is hard. 'Self-examination' strengthens its power.
Willed acts of imaginative attention to what lies outside it can
help erode it. In the important essay 'Existentialists and Mystics'
in 1970 she attacked the hero of much contemporary fiction as

> the lonely brave man, defiant without optimism, proud without
> pretension, always an exposer of shams, whose mode of being
> is a deep criticism of society. He is an adventurer. He is godless.
> He does not suffer from guilt. He thinks of himself as free. He
> may have faults, he may be self-assertive or even violent, but
> he has sincerity and courage, and for this we forgive him . . . .
> He *might* do anything.

She has called this hero 'existentialist' and noted that he already
looks a little out of date. He is the hero of novels by Hemingway,
Lawrence, Sartre, Camus, Amis . . . . It is typical of existentialism
that it 'either makes his responsibility absolute or abolishes it'
(Bigsby, 1982). Existentialism's promise of total human freedom
is a bogus one. Much of Murdoch's moral psychology boils down
to a criticism of the idea of fast moral change as romantic and
false, and a defence of slow moral change as something difficult,
piece-meal, and always incomplete.

'Existentialists and Mystics' is a meditation on various themes –
on the existentialist novel, on the novel which contains an
alternative 'mystical' hero, and the place of literature in the new
moral and political scene. The question of whether the present
age is so wholly different from the past as to be deemed
discontinuous with it is debated from various points of view. The
existentialist novel tries to be cheerfully godless but abounds in
a gloom which is secretly self-satisfied because, from its point of
view, man is God himself. It is this which makes that novel look
already old-fashioned. The mystical attitude is a 'second thought
about the matter and reflects the uneasy suspicion that perhaps
after all man is not God'. 'The existentialist novel shows us
freedom and virtue as the assertion of the will. The mystical novel
shows us freedom and virtue as understanding, or obedience to

the Good.' And the mystical novel (Greene, White, Bellow, Spark, Golding and by implication Murdoch herself) is the more recent development. The existentialist's is a 'natural mode of being of the capitalist era'. It is the mystic therefore who offers the deeper critique.

> As we readily recognise and sympathise with the hero of will-power, so we can also recognise and sympathise with the mystical hero. He too is a man in tension, but here the tension is not between will and nature, but between nature and good. This is the man who has given up traditional religion but is still haunted by a sense of the reality and unity of some sort of spiritual world. The imagery here is the imagery of height and distance. Much is required of us and we are far from our goal. The virtue of the mystical hero is humility. Whereas the existentialist hero is the anxious man trying to impose or assert or find himself, the mystical hero is an anxious man trying to discipline or purge or diminish himself. The chief temptation of the former is egoism, of the latter masochism. The philosophical background or protective symbolism is fairly clear in each case. The first hero is the new version of the romantic man, the man of power, abandoned by God, struggling on bravely, sincerely and alone. This image consoles by showing us man as strong, self-reliant and uncrushable. The second hero is the new version of the man of faith, believing in goodness without religious guarantees, guilty, muddled, yet not without hope. This image consoles us by showing us man as frail, godless, and yet possessed of genuine intuitions of an authoritative good. (em)

Murdoch notes that of course no pure example of either novel, or of either hero, exists. Both existentialist and mystical heroes are marked by their apparent isolation from moral norms; both are 'outsiders'. All novels must therefore be mixed. She also argues here for a new empirical and utilitarian political morality which starts at the level of food and shelter. It is worth noting that the essay argues for both empiricism and mysticism, which are not seen as in conflict. Unlike Bertrand Russell, who presented the classic, inadequate Western view in his significantly named 'Mysticism and Logic', Murdoch sees no opposition here. The mystical hero, like Tallis in *A Fairly Honourable Defeat*, can be fully engaged morally and politically: Tallis is engaged to the point of exhaustion. The mystic is rather one who has begun to grasp the absolute 'for-nothing-ness' and absolute lack of consolation involved in the Good. 'Goodness is needful, one has to be good, for nothing, for immediate and obvious reasons, because somebody is hungry or somebody is crying.' From this point of view the current demythologisation of religion is 'a great moral tonic, because it asks the ordinary believer to do what only the exceptional one could do in the past, that is live a religious life without illusions': that is, without any belief in the after-life, in rewards, or in God. In one sense a truly religious life is *uniquely* possible without belief in God.

The novel is seen in this essay as taking on an ambiguous role in purveying moral symbolism. 'The mystical novelist may or may not be a good man or a good novelist, but what he is attempting to do, perhaps unsuccessfully, is to invent new religious imagery (or twist old religious imagery) in an empty situation.' He will run the danger that he may merely 'reintroduce the old fatherly figure of God behind a facade of fantastical imagery or sentimental adventures in cosy masochism . . . . It is easy to *say* there is no God. It is not so easy to believe it and to draw the consequences.'

*

'Existentialists and Mystics' is a very important essay, which necessitates some re-reading of her work from the beginning, for *Under the Net* already has two heroes, not one – a voluntarist and a mystic, or alternatively a would-be artist and a would-be saint, one living by the will and by a hunger for aesthetic form, the other living by a constant sacrifice of the will. The essay also suggests that moral terms are a species of universal, that 'we recognise good or decent people in times and literatures remote from our own . . . . Patroclus' invariable kindness. Cordelia's truthfulness. Alyosha telling his father not to be afraid of hell.' This, too, invites us to ask new questions about her own fiction, and about what kind of man it is in it that we are being asked to admire.

Murdoch has argued for the centrality of the old naturalistic idea of character for the business of writing novels, and has also written about the ways in which too great an attention to the form of the book can damage the illusion that the characters are free. In 'Against Dryness' and 'The Sublime and the Beautiful Revisited' she argued that the task for the novelist was to recreate 'realism', which often meant avoiding the bad habits – overt design, patterning, symbol and myth – which damage it. Her fiction, however, appeared to be written by the kind of novelist she least approved of, since it was much preoccupied with pattern, utilised fantasy and myth, and had generally the character implied by the term already used – 'romance'. This gave criticism its main opportunity. She had written *of* the novel as if it were a vehicle of human differentiation and belonged to a vast campaign for the preservation of human plurality, and of the novelist as a tender detective of human souls, but herself seemed to write the novel of human resemblances and exciting symbolic conflations. The more open novels were used in England to punish the more closed and Gothic ones, and critics scrutinised the books for delinquent symmetries and wicked coincidences. Alternatively the critic, mindful that Murdoch had urged a distinction between fantasy and imagination, searched the work for 'fantasy-apprehensions' like a metaphysical park attendant, as if what was left once these were speared were some pure undiluted essence of the real. We have been given the choice between unmasking the works and denouncing their personnel.

I think criticism has been too absolutist and pious about the early theory. A writer theorises in a particular spirit. She may be trying out a variety of different positions in the effort to understand the shape and nature of her gift, rather than announcing a single unchanging campaign manifesto. The kinship between work and theory is likely to be complex in any writer worth reading. We no longer praise either Wordsworth or Ben Jonson for what, in the Preface to *Lyrical Ballads* or in *Timber*, they thought they had put into their work. A relaxed account of Murdoch's work which does not quarantine off certain works because they are generically diverse is needed. The writer has the right to as much 'organis'd innocence' as will enable her work; the critic is not obliged to follow.

I am not suggesting that those early and influential essays should be disregarded. There are arguments within them that now belong to the epoch in which they were written, and which have less relevance, and others which still stand. There is a degree of openness in them which deserves underlining. I hope for the remainder of this chapter to suggest how they can help illuminate her career.

Murdoch's theory has been too often cited as though it involved an opposition between two discrete terms, rather than a mediation between extremes. In 'Against Dryness' and 'The Sublime and the Beautiful Revisited' she does not argue for a choice between 'realism' on the one hand, and 'myth' on the other, but for a dialectic or mediation between them. She is proposing a middle way. She describes how the realism of the great nineteenth century novelists has split into two antagonistic and equally incomplete tendencies. On the one hand the 'conventional' social realism of 'journalistic' novelists produced a world of dead predictable public facts divorced from psychological inwardness. On the other hand the 'neurotic' psychological realism of 'crystalline' novelists produced a wholly spiritualised, private world of unified values divorced from facts. The split – in which she declared herself uninterested much more quickly than the critics (Bradbury, 1976) – seemed to owe something to Socrates' advice in the *Philebus* that it is bad if we arrive at the One or at the Many *too quickly*. It notably fits the literary politics of the 1920s – Woolf's differences from Arnold Bennett, say – and the division of novelists in that period into Moderns and Contemporaries. The writer Murdoch cites as an example of how to marry these two sets of warring virtue – naturalism and symbolism – is Shakespeare. 'Perhaps only Shakespeare managed to create at the highest level both images and people; and even *Hamlet* looks second rate compared with *Lear*' (ad). In 'The Sublime and the Beautiful Revisited' she argued that the greatness of Dostoevski, Melville, Emily Brontë and Hawthorne was not of the same order as that of Scott, Jane Austen, George Eliot, and especially Tolstoi. This was scarcely her last word on the matter, however. When I interviewed Miss Murdoch in 1983 she no longer recalled this distinction but said that, if obliged to 'place' these respective geniuses now, would undoubtedly consider Dostoevski a greater writer than George Eliot. She has also paid tribute to such diverse forebears as Proust, Homer, *Wuthering Heights*, Dickens and James; and to such very diverse romances as *Treasure Island*, *Peter Pan*, and *The Tempest*; and to Shakespeare generally.

A task for critics today would seem to be to understand the indebtedness of her demonic, tormented sinners and saints and of the curious coexistence in her work of malevolence and goodness, to the dark tragi-comedies of Dostoevski, and to romance; and also to focus her recoil from the rational, optimistic importunacies of George Eliot. Murdoch's assertion of the primary value of 'character' has meant that she has sometimes been placed, much too simply, in one camp. It was always her point that 'character' and 'form' must be reconcilable. Great literature would provide two satisfactions rather than one. It was never merely that 'there is a temptation for any novelist . . . to imagine that the problem of a novel is solved . . . as soon as a form in the sense of a satisfactory myth has been evolved' (sbr). The problem was also that myth is inescapable. 'The mythical is not something "extra": we live in myth and symbol all the time'(mmm). The novelist must use myth and magic to help liberate us from myth and magic, an enterprise which, since both writer and client are frail and human, can never be more than minutely successful; and the artist, in her view, had better not give himself too many airs. We are all symbol-makers, myth-makers, story-tellers, she has repeatedly asserted. Art is, as it were, the ordinary human condition, and not (or not merely) the peculiar task and property of a vain crew of specialists.

In his *Modes of Modern Writing* David Lodge usefully described the alternative virtues on the one hand of 'realism' – a writing that emphasises the uniqueness of things, persons, places – and on the other of 'modernism' – a writing which aspires to a concentrated symbolic formal unity. In the article that acts as an informal coda to this book he notably suggested that, since literary history over the last century could be seen as alternating between these two ideal types, one possible programme for a new writing might reside in the conscious attempt to combine the virtues of each in a single book.[17]

This is not unlike Murdoch's avowed aim twenty-five years before. In 1958, after publishing her first four novels, she said that

> I find myself thinking in terms of two kinds of novel which might be called 'open' and 'closed', and I cannot at the moment decide which kind I want to write: perhaps, more or less alternately, both. The open novel contains a lot of characters who rush about independently, each one eccentric and self-centred; the plot to some extent situates them in a pattern but does not integrate them into a single system. The closed novel has fewer characters and tends to draw them, as it were, toward a single point. *Under the Net* and *The Flight from the Enchanter* were, I think, ['closed'], *The Sandcastle* and *The Bell* ['open']. The advantage of the open novel is that it is bright and airy and the characters move about freely; it is more like life as it is normally lived. Its disadvantage is that it may become loose

in texture and it is more difficult to make the structure evident.
A closed novel is more intensely integrated but may be more
claustrophobic in atmosphere and the characters may lose their
sense of freedom. Ideally, and if one were a great writer, one
could, I think, combine both these things in a single work and
not have to oscillate between them.[18]

I believe that Murdoch, having oscillated between these two
kinds of work until about 1970, has since then produced a number
of superb novels that do indeed combine these two sets of virtue,
with the aesthetic interest divided equally between 'form' and
'character'. Her 'closed' novels – especially *The Unicorn* and *The
Time of the Angels* – have never been well understood in Britain.
The essay 'Existentialists and Mystics' makes clear that so far
from these religious novels being *divertissements*, or interruptions
from the business of making attempts at the 'true novel', they are
clearly, whatever their individual success, central to her purpose;
and the interview from which I have just quoted suggests that
the formal intensity of which these books are capable is one
essential ingredient in good art.

Character and image are mutually exclusive, therefore, only
in second-rate art. In good art there is a dynamic tension between
the two, and 'character' is as incalculable and private as the
symbolic whole of the art-work itself, which it resists. Just as
Murdoch has always argued for the centrifugal primary value of
'character', so she has also always argued for the centripetal value
of a strong formal unity. In a straight fight between the two,
since she is aware that she excels at the latter, she would clearly
come down on the side of 'character', and hence on the side of
the 'open' novels. What she wants is 'character' sufficiently
strongly imagined to hold its own in a living tension with the
'myth' embodied in the plot. 'I care very much about pattern,
and I want it to have a beautiful shape, an apprehensible shape.'
And she admires in Shakespeare the ways in which he has 'an
extraordinary ability to combine a marvellous pattern or myth
with the expansion of characters as absolutely free persons,
independent of each other – they have an extraordinary independence, though they're also kept in by the marvellous pattern of
the play' (Bryden, 1968). They exist freely, yet 'serve the purpose
of the tale'(Magee, 1978). Myth, she suggested to Kermode,
(1963), is not altogether the enemy – it should be present also.

Two rare book reviews might serve to drive the same point home. Writing of Brigid Brophy's *The Snow Ball* she distinguished epigrammatically 'novels one inhabits' from [crystalline] novels 'one picks up in one's hand', and added that 'perfection may belong to either'. And of De Beauvoir's *The Mandarins* she said that 'Form and economy have been sacrificed to particularity and comprehensiveness' and criticised the work for lacking that 'imaginative unity' typical of the authority of a true work of art. [19] In conversation with Magee she pertinently attacked the division between 'autonomous' and wholly 'mimetic' views of the art-work as, in its most reductive form, simply an irrelevance dreamt up by aesthetically minded critics. Good art must be both autonomous and mimetic, both unified and yet also expansive.

Murdoch's courageous exploration of Gothic romance in *The Unicorn* and *The Time of the Angels*, many years before the mode became voguish, and at the expense of the relative incomprehension of British reviewers, and her early aspiration to marry the advantages of 'realism' and 'fantasy' – 'the best novels explore and exhibit [fantasy and realism] without disjoining them'(Hobson, 1962) – are two ways in which she now seems always to have been more deeply in touch with her own time than other writers. The division between Gothic romance and realism, on the grounds that one is 'radical', the other, 'reactionary', has been exposed as facile. Gothic has for two hundred years been one element or wing within the traditional British novel and has been employed, as Marilyn Butler has shown, by writers of every political persuasion and for every possible ideological purpose. Moreover, during this century, as Gerald Graff conclusively demonstrated, if the critic were obliged to insist on one genre as the 'socially progressive' one, it would be realism. [20] Any convention, no matter how apparently austere, can cosily flatter the presuppositions of the reader, and will stay alive only so long as good writers are employing it.

What the alternation between open and closed works does, I think, evince, is a conflict between Murdoch's desire to set her characters 'free' and her belief that human beings are profoundly unfree. Her exploration of such matters is interesting, and in its very vulnerability, more compelling than the currently fashionable 'fictionalist' case, which turns on a facile self-exemption. It is not so easy, her work assures us, to become truly or honourably cultureless. As for shedding illusions, it is a curious fact about us, much displayed in all the books, that no matter how fast we think we are discarding them, there always seem to be a few more to lose. The opportunities for specious disillusion, and for seeing through everybody else's states of mind but our own, are, her work reminds us, as long as life itself. The kind of man who does earn his right to be 'outside' society turns out in her work to be the good man or 'mystical hero' unsupported by religious dogma, in the world but not of it, the man who is trying to educate his own desires.

2 *Under the Net* and the Redemption of Particulars

Iris Murdoch has called Sartre's *La Nausée* the 'instructive overture' to his work. The same description fits *Under the Net* (1954). It was at the time placed with novels such as Amis' *Lucky Jim* (which she had not read) as new 'Angry' social realism, an ascription which, despite the Dryden epigraph (''Tis well an old age is out / And time to begin a new') bears little scrutiny. It has also been related to Murdoch's interest in Sartre, to the dedicatee Raymond Queneau, and to Beckett. The hero cherishes books by Queneau and Beckett. These debts have been explored elsewhere by A. S. Byatt, Baldanza and Todd.[1] In its concern with the role of art in redeeming contingency it clearly echoes *La Nausée*; but is also a novel which differently undercuts its existentialist hero-narrator. It is in fact a novel which draws on the Romantic tradition, the first novel of a Platonist in the making, schematically enquiring into the nature of the Good man and his relations with art, with true vision, and with copying. Art as much as Jake is its hero, copying its prophetic subject-matter. It takes on anxieties about realism many decades before these became fashionable in England.

Under the Net's success has obscured the later work. It would be a very odd and unintelligent writer whose work had not developed at all over thirty years, so that her first novel remained her best; and whatever else she is as a writer, she is an exceptionally intelligent one. In comparison with *The Black Prince*, a better novel about art and the education of an artist, where the idea-play is fed by a much more interesting story and better-drawn characters, it is extraordinary but still clearly apprentice work. Apprenticeship is another of its subjects. Both Jake and Hugo end up apprenticed to their crafts, of watch-making and fiction-making respectively.

And yet if Murdoch had written nothing else she would have been remembered for *Under the Net*. It is only the stature of her late work which dwarfs it, an astonishingly assured, inventive and funny first book. She had destroyed five earlier unpublished novels on the grounds of their immaturity, and this rigour had paid dividends. It partly resembles *Pickwick Papers*: a picaresque, charming, light and innocent first novel, an episodic account of the boozy journeyings of a quixotic, illusion-ridden knight and his cannier squire. There have indeed been few critics who are not Chestertonian in their enthusiasm for the zest and buoyancy of her early novels, and because this has meant an undervaluation of the later work it seems useful to try to see the early work in a perspective which the later work makes available, and to read the early work *through* the later. I'm not – or not simply – pleading, like Edmund Wilson with the 'dark' Dickens, for a demonic and alienated later Murdoch to set off against her early optimism. One aspect of the brilliance of the later work is the critique it offers of that facile pessimism which is nowadays the insignia of the intellectual: to have a passion for imagining the worst, as John Bayley puts it in *The Characters of Love*, is the main premise for being thought serious.[2] The general movement, however, is, as Murdoch has put it, from the 'quaint, funny, absurd and touching' early work towards the 'sad and awful' later dark comedies (Bellamy, 1977). A crucial word here is 'comedy'. The later books are not only darker, much more confident and less anxious to charm us than the early ones – they are thereby also wiser and funnier. She has latterly been showing us terrible things and making us laugh, and without diminishing the awfulness one whit. The face of the mature work resembles Martin Lynch-Gibbon's in *A Severed Head*, 'the face of someone laughing at something tragic' (15). There are connexions between comedy and 'contingency' in her work which cut across all other distinctions, and where the books are less than fully successful it is often not because they are more 'symbolic', but because they are less comic.[3]

By these high standards the interest of *Under the Net* is partly in its exposition of themes which are to recur. It is the first and least disquieting of her brilliant first-person male narrations. She has called her identification with the male voice 'instinctive' (Caen, 1978); I know nothing quite like them. There are male novelists who can persuade you into the minds of young women – Tolstoi, Henry James, Angus Wilson; the reverse feat seems rarer. Virginia Woolf's pleasure in animating Orlando as a man can seem winsome and create a mild disassociation. In Murdoch what you detect is not so much the author's pleasure as her relaxed and business-like efficiency, into which she has wholly disappeared. The question of her relation with these six (to date) heroes is a legitimate one. The subversive power of these narrations comes from our intimate relation with them and hence from our identification. This is solicited through a strenuous suspension of moral judgement on the author's part, which comes to mean that judging these 'lovable monsters' resembles passing judgement on ourselves. This is one reason why reading these books can be, as well as an hilarious and spell-binding experience, also a very uncomfortable one. The prototype for this subversive relation between author-character and reader is Dostoevski's blackly comic *Underground Man*, a work to which *The Black Prince*, *A Word Child* and *The Sea, The Sea* show a debt. Dostoevski's relations with his hero, like Murdoch's, is profoundly equivocal, and depends on devious intimate play with his own potential worst self or selves. Murdoch's mastery of this equivocation is extraordinary.[4]

What might be added is that if there is a *naïveté* involved in identifying the author with these six, very different first-person narrators, as if this were a mere feat of literary transvestism, another sort of simplicity wholly detaches her from this crew as if they were moral exhibition-pieces, waxworks in some cautionary tale. Her success depends on the warmth of her identification as much as on the rigour of her simultaneous detachment. Where she gets too close (Jake in *Under the Net*), or too distant (Edmund in *The Italian Girl*) the book can be less successful. Moreover, despite conspicuous differences between these narrators, there are also evident similarities. Charles Arrowby in *The Sea, The Sea* and Jake Donaghue in *Under the Net* are both short men who blush and like swimming. All these narrators, from Jake to Charles, are within a year of their author's age at the time of writing. All are in her specially extended sense 'artists'. All are differently fastidious, are in some (not simply sexual) sense puritans, and experience that terror of multiplicity or contingency which Murdoch acknowledged in her interview with Ruth Heyd (1965). 'I hate contingency; I want everything in my life to have a sufficient reason' (24) says Jake. Such fear marks us all; what Murdoch shows in each portrait is also that relaxation of censorship at the threshold of consciousness which Schiller emphasised, in a well-known letter admired by Freud, as the peculiar, dangerous gift of the artist.[5] Her suspicion of this relaxation of censorship, and her mastery of it alike, make for a sense of drama.

*

Under the Net is told by Jake Donaghue, a Bohemian, an Irishman brought up like Murdoch in London, and a 'professional unauthorised person', a raffish outsider. Talkative yet secretive, an irresolute sentimentalist with 'shattered nerves', he announces himself as a swift intuitive type of thinker. This comes to mean as the story unfolds, that he is impulsive, restless, profoundly impressionable, romantic and somewhat lost. Jake is a charming, feckless Bohemian hack given to bouts of melancholia who earns money by translating the French novelist Breteuil whose work he despises. At the beginning he arrives back from France to find himself homeless. His squire Finn tells him that Madge, with whom they have been living rent-free in Earl's Court, is marrying and has kicked them out. The book concerns his subsequent journeyings and, as Frank Baldanza has pointed out, they represent a mixture of flight and quest.[6] Flight and quest are indeed often indistinguishable here. The mystery he is seeking seems to him partly embodied in the two Quentin sisters, Anna and Sadie, partly in his erstwhile friend Hugo Belfounder. Like Jane Austen's Emma, Jake makes mistakes about who loves whom. He thinks he loves Anna who he imagines is pursued by Hugo who he thinks must be loved by Sadie. In fact Anna pursues Hugo who loves Sadie who is keen on him, Jake. He has been told all this but has licensed his own fantasies. He similarly thinks that Breteuil will never write a good book and that Finn will never return to Ireland, though Finn often says he wishes to. Finn does return to Ireland and Breteuil wins the coveted *Prix Goncourt*. Jake is progressively disenchanted and ends the book with a newly won joy at such withering into the truth, ready to write a book of his own, and trying to eschew theory.

What distinguishes Jake's tale from that of a nineteenth century hero or heroine – Emma, or Isabel Archer, also a 'person of many theories' – is the special use of picaresque convention, which is more self-conscious than Dickens', the extraordinary relations between the two central figures and what passes between them, and finally the tale's open-enddedness. I shall discuss each of these.

A. S. Byatt notes the peculiar difficulty of discussing this 'light, amusing, rapid' book without making it sound portentous.[7] This is a problem with all of Murdoch, but especially here with her least unphilosophical novel. She has rightly resented the attempt to 'un-mask' the work, or allegorise the books as if they were merely philosophy-in-disguise, preferring to be thought a reflective, religious or speculative novelist like Dostoevski, than, like Sartre, directly a philosophical one. To use her own favourite metaphor of water, we might say that good art is philosophy swimming, or philosophy drowning. 'Ideas in art must suffer a sea-change' (Magee, 1978). There is always more event, story, incident than the idea-play can use up, here as everywhere in her work, and this surplus of sense and action over meaning helps constitute the particular mysterious and instructively frustrating atmosphere. Reviewers of the first two novels noted that there was 'too much' in them. I shall discuss this 'too much' and its function in Chapter 5.

The play with the picaresque takes two forms. Traditionally it is the quest of the knight that matters, while that of his Sancho Panza takes second place. Jake fails, however, to see that Finn too has his story. He early tells us that Finn has 'very little inner life' and that he connects this with Finn's absolute truthfulness. 'I count Finn as an inhabitant of my universe, and cannot conceive that he has one containing me; and this arrangement seems restful to both of us' (*UN* 9). Finn is the first of a series of Murdoch characters who disappear from the narrative – some commit suicide, some die by avoidable accident, others, like Luca in *The Sacred and Profane Love-Machine* are locked up in institutions – without ever having been properly apprehended. Their demise or disappearance is a direct result, we are made to feel, of the failure of the other characters to imagine their needs or see them as other than 'subsidiary' characters. This is an inability in which the author, as her virtuosity grows, is herself decreasingly complicit. When the despairing Clifford Larr dies in *A Word Child* our curiosity about him is aroused and carefully cheated. Henry James said that he felt he could pass a stiff examination on Mrs Brookenham in *The Awkward Age*. We feel that the examination Murdoch could pass on Larr would be a stiffer one than she might care to sit on Finn. This conditions our sense of her success, not in persuading us of Jake's short-sightedness, but in intimating what a longer vision might resemble. By the time she writes the later books her mastery of the confessional mode is such that you sense a greater authorial grasp of that depth of field which her narrators are busy simplifying, as well as the narrator's simplifications.

The second use of the picaresque has to do with play with a great and continuing theme in Murdoch's work, that of iconoclasm, the destruction of images, pictures and states of mind. Here the pathos and impermanence of the phenomenal world distantly mirrors, perhaps prefigures, the Socratic smashing of illusions and of all theoretical attempts to dominate reality with which the tale ends. The Hammersmith theatre where Anna conducts her mime is seen first full and then empty, and there is a film-set of ancient Rome which looks real, then rapidly collapses. The emptiness of the City of London at night, through which Jake hunts for Hugo, contrasts with the fullness of Paris on the 14th July, through which he hunts for Anna. Hugo's flat is perceived full of art-treasure (apart from his sparsely furnished bedroom) and then, soon after, in the process of being stripped. London is in this book as patiently apprehended as the characters, and this is distinctly an immediately post-war London, with bomb-sites and the coming end of Empire to link it with Catiline's Rome.

The writing which evokes all this is freshly done, the emotions are felt, the structure vivid and alive. At the same time this picaresque theme is a Platonic one. Other critics have usefully shown the book's indebtedness to Wittgenstein, from whom the title comes. The 'net' in the title alludes to *Tractatus* 6.341, the net of discourse behind which the world's particulars hide, a net which is necessary in order to elicit and describe them: language and theory alike (which constitute the net) both reveal and yet simultaneously conceal the world. I think that the use of the idea of the 'provisionality' of theory in this book is as much Platonic as Wittgensteinian. Wittgenstein, it is true, wrote of the disposability both of the 'ladder' at the end of *Tractatus* and of the various stages of his argument once understood. Murdoch's bias is Neo-platonic in the sense that it gives a primary, and highly ambiguous place to art itself in the discovery of truth, and also in that it subordinates the argument to the moral psychology of the characters. *Under the Net* enquires into the nature of the Good man *vis-à-vis* art.

Murdoch has described her novels as pilgrimages from illusion towards reality (Bradbury, 1976) and also pointed out that 'reality' as such is never arrived at in the books, any more than it is in life. The dismantling of the various scenes connects with the book's interest in the guilt and the attempted purification of art. The novel is much concerned with lies, art-as-lies, and the deceptive nature of all copying. Debates in the West about the value and the danger of art have a way of finding their way back to Plato, some version or private use of whose philosophy lies behind both most attempts to censor art by the virtuous, and also the grandest defences. Murdoch's book on this (*The Fire and the Sun: Why Plato Banished the Artists*) is notable for the sympathetic vigour of her explication of Plato's objections to art, and also for the pyrrhic victory she awards herself, and art, at the end. Her sympathy for Plato, as for all puritan thinkers about art and morals – Kant, Tolstoi, Freud, Sartre would be others – is quite clear. In a lecture at Caen (1978) she might be said to have crystallised her own objections. The magical nature of art cannot be overestimated. It is an attempt to achieve omnipotence through personal fantasy and is the abode of wish-fulfilment and power mania. It is a prime producer of illusory unities. It both pretends to be more unified than it is, and allows us in reading (or looking, listening) to conceive of ourselves as more unified than we are. Art is an egoistic substitute for and *copy* of religious discipline. To Plato, who originated a metaphysical theory about the nature of copying, art is far removed from the truth, springs from merely vicarious knowledge, is the product of the inferior part of the soul, and harms by nourishing the passions which should be educated and disciplined.

At the same time she pointed out that great art is also lofty, and expresses or explains religion to each generation. All art lies, but good art lies its way into the truth, while bad art is simply bogus. Moreover since no art is perfect, all art partakes of a degree of moral ambiguity. This theme will echo throughout the present book.

Anxieties about art have been recently much in the air again, though the most puritan reactions to it have lately come not from the censors but from formalist critics who are inclined to denounce the illusions of 'realism' as inauthentic or naïve. *Under the Net* is decades ahead of its time in its concern with these anxieties and perhaps further ahead of its time in its relaxed and cheerful mediation between two extreme positions: that truth is simply and immediately knowable, or very distantly accessible through a recession of intervening cultural conceptions. These anxieties enter into Jake's relationship with Hugo, and are thought out at the level of character. The experience of solipsistic anxiety, the apprehension of the world's inexhaustibility: Murdoch submits neither to any grand reduction, but shows them engaged in playful warfare.

Iris Murdoch has noted that Plato was one of the first to define the good man *as opposed to* the hero (*FS* 74). *Under the Net* has two heroes, not one. Jake, who is recognisably the typical jaunty anti-hero of his time, is systematically undercut by Hugo, who is presented as a truer and less visible kind of anti-hero.

Murdoch opposes to the man 'trying to impose or assert or find himself' (the existentialist hero) an alternative picture of 'the anxious man trying to discipline or purge or diminish himself (the mystical hero)' (em). In Hugo's questioning of Jake's picture of events, *Under the Net* partly mocks the voluntarist pieties of the age.

*

Jake early comments that his acquaintance with Hugo is 'the central theme of the book' (*UN* 53). At the heart of the great richness of comic incident the book affords is Jake's fascination with Hugo and the misunderstandings and relative differences between them. Jake's relation with Hugo shapes the book and helps fund its tone. Without Hugo's presence Jake has slipped into a variety of illusions. Yet just as Jake is in Anna's presence for only five minutes during the book, so he is in Hugo's for only a few moments of 'present' time at the film studio and then for half an hour at the Hospital. This half-hour constitutes the book's comic reversal and Jake's sad, partial recognition of the truth.

We early see Hugo in the Mime theatre where 'A huge and burly central figure, wearing a mask which expressed a sort of humble yearning stupidity, was being mocked by the other players' (36). The irony of the mask that Hugo wears here is that it expresses his real nature. He is the only character apart from Finn shown incapable of untruth or dissimulation. Thus towards the end Hugo speaks of Sadie to Jake with an air which Jake characterises as 'disgustingly humble' (225). In *The Sovereignty of Good* Murdoch praised humility as 'a rare virtue and an unfashionable one and one which is often hard to discern. . . . The humble man, because he sees himself as nothing, can see other things as they are. He sees the pointlessness of virtue, and its unique value, and the endless extent of its demand' (103–4).

Jake and Hugo meet in a cold-cure centre where Jake takes Hugo for a mental defective and ignores him for two days, despite the fact that they are sharing a room. Hugo puts up with this snubbing with gentle patience and self-possession. When Jake engages him in conversation he realises he is closeted with a person of great fascination – indeed 'the most purely objective and detached person' (57) Jake has ever met. Jake notes that the conversation which ensues is germane to the whole story he has to tell. For Hugo

> Each thing was absolutely unique. I had the feeling that I was meeting for the first time an almost completely truthful man; and the experience was turning out to be appropriately upsetting. I was but the more inclined to attribute a spiritual worth to Hugo in proportion as it would never have crossed his mind to think of himself in such a light.   (61)

Given the care that Murdoch has put into picturing Hugo as a man aspiring to be good, connecting this quite explicitly to his scepticism about the act of classification, there is an irony in the way critics have positively rushed to classify him. Jake early notes that to try to 'place' Hugo, as he at first attempted, was a failure of taste which showed a 'peculiar insensitivity to his unique intellectual and moral quality' (58). One critic links Hugo with pataphysics, another tells us he is an existentialist. Others have linked him with Wittgenstein,[8] with whom he certainly shares a quality of 'unnerving directness' (Mehta, 1961) in his approach to persons and problems. Like Wittgenstein Hugo is a wealthy Central European attracted to an ascetic ideal, sexually tormented, with a curious care for his *boots*, and a man who worked in his family factory, and had a capacity to renounce. But Hugo's forbears are as much literary as philosophical. In particular he seems to owe something to Dostoevski's Prince Myshkin in *The Idiot*, another holy fool, half clown, half spiritual emperor, comic-pathetic and wise. The 'sparse simplicity' of Hugo's bedroom (92), moreover, resembles not merely that of Wittgenstein but the simplified rooms of the other saintly figures in Murdoch's novels, who are extremely unlike the Austrian philosopher. It is to Hugo's renunciatory capacities, as much as his intellectual lineage, that Murdoch is drawing our attention.

It has been well observed that her novels contain only fools and holy fools.⁹ Jake is the common fool, Hugo the holy fool.

It is important to our sense of Hugo before we have met him that his flat, despite being so full of art-treasure (Renoirs, Miro, a Minton) should be left not merely unlocked but with the door ajar. His wholly austere and unornamented bedroom suggests that he is inwardly neither covetous nor attached. He has given up the armaments factory he inherited before the action commences and converted it to fireworks, and then, when these are acclaimed and pretentiously classified, lost interest in them too. At the end of the story he is giving up some remaining attachments: his passion for Sadie, whom he has persecuted, his film industry, his money, his friendship with Jake, London itself, and the role which he conceives of as false of consoling Anna. This is a different mode of detachment from Jake's, though both are 'outsider' figures, Jake an Irish expatriate, Hugo the child of German refugees. Jake spends much time wondering where he will sleep during the tale and in fact passes one night with the tramps on a bench on Charing Cross Embankment. What distinguishes these modes of detachment has everything to do with the specially enlarged sense Murdoch gives to the word 'artist'. Jake's separateness makes him extraordinary to himself; Hugo is nobly unselfconscious. If Hugo resembles anyone in the story it is the shadowy but truthful Finn who, like him, cannot imagine himself at the 'centre' of any story, or the nobly unselfconscious dog Mars whom Jake has stolen. Hugo's exit from the hospital and almost from the book is conducted on all fours, with his bottom in the air, dribbling into the boots he holds in his teeth. This noble unselfconsciousness gives him, as the would-be good man who sees objectively, an alarming ordinariness, and an odd, dogged, animal intelligence.

Jake early notes that Hugo is devoid of general theories. All his theories, if they can be called theories – for they read as exercises in patient inquisitive particular enquiry – are local. An early conversation dramatises the difference between them and concerns the problem of describing states of mind or feelings. That such description belongs to the novel as a form, as much as to moral philosophy, is important.

'There's something fishy about describing people's feelings,' said Hugo. 'All these descriptions are so dramatic.'

'What's wrong with that?' I said.

'Only,' said Hugo, 'that it means that things are falsified from the start. If I say afterwards that I felt such and such, say that I felt 'apprehensive' – well, this just isn't true.'

'What do you mean?' I asked.

'I didn't feel this,' said Hugo. 'I didn't feel anything of that kind at the time at all. This is just something I say afterwards. . . . As soon as I start to describe, I'm done for. Try describing anything, our conversation for instance, and see how absolutely instinctively you . . .'

'Touch it up?'

'It's deeper than that,' said Hugo. 'The language just won't let you present it as it really was.' (59)

'The whole language is a machine for making falsehoods' (60) Hugo adds. Jake finds Hugo's puritan suspicion of language not dessicating but life-giving because it is in the service of a love of truth and a love of the real. 'For Hugo each thing was astonishing, delightful, complicated, and mysterious. During these conversations I began to see the whole world anew' (58). For Hugo as for Plato art is a special case of copying, and he shares Plato's typically puritan suspicion of mimetic art. When Hugo creates his fireworks he 'despised the vulgarity of representational pieces' and preferred that his creations be compared, if to anything, then to music. Moreover he finds the impermanence of fireworks a positive recommendation.

> I remember his holding forth to me more than once what an *honest* thing a firework is. It was so patently an ephemeral spurt of beauty of which in a moment nothing more was left. 'That's what all art is really,' said Hugo, 'only we don't like to admit it. Leonardo understood this. He deliberately made the Last Supper perishable.' (54)

Again this echoes Plato (*Laws* 956b) who argued that 'artefacts offered to the gods should be such as can be made in a single day' (*FS* 71) – should be deliberately impermanent. It is important that when Jake and Hugo reach the conclusion that 'in that case one oughtn't to talk', they at once burst out laughing, thinking of how they had for days been doing nothing else. The puritan ideal of total silence is hedged around with irony. It is also important that, as Patrick Swinden points out, we never come into direct contact with Hugo's philosophy. Even of the 'original' conversation between Jake and Hugo we are told that it took half a dozen cold-cure sessions for them to reach this point, so that what we have been given must be an 'artistic' conflation of many weeks' talk into one discussion. This is as it were already at one remove from the truth. And given Hugo's doubts about the ways, once you tell a story, you immediately begin to 'touch it up' it is ironic that Jake immediately finds himself very guiltily working up his and Hugo's conversations into a flowery philosophical dialogue which he calls 'The Silencer'. In the excerpt that he reads, art once more plays the pivotal role. The dialogue owes something to the Romantic, and the Buddhist, quest to get beyond the duality of self and world.

> *Annandine*: . . . All theorising is flight. We must be ruled by the situation itself and this is unutterably particular. Indeed it is something to which we can never get close enough, however hard we may try as it were to crawl under the net . . . .
> *Tamarus*: So you would cut all speech, except the very simplest, out of human life altogether. To do this would be to take away our very means of understanding ourselves and making life endurable.
> *Annandine*: Why should life be made endurable? I know that nothing consoles and nothing justifies except a story – but that doesn't stop all stories from being lies. Only the greatest men can speak and still be truthful. Any artist knows this obscurely; he knows that a theory is death, and that all expression is weighted with theory. Only the strongest can rise against that weight. For most of us . . . truth can be attained, if at all, only in silence.   (81)

All speech lies, and art is only a special form of speech, yet great art can lie its way into the truth. The same idea occurs in *An Accidental Man* twenty years later, where the novelist Garth says 'you may know a truth but if it's at all complicated you have to be an artist not to utter it as a lie' (107). *Under the Net* is as full of artists as it is of philosophers – it concerns, in part, the ancient quarrel between the two, between art and truth. Jake is an artist who writes philosophy of a sort, a translator who has written and had torn up an epic poem, and who ends the book ready to write a novel. His friend Dave Gellman is a 'pure' linguistic philosopher. Mrs Tinck, whose shop Jake finds welcoming, reads 'Amazing Stories' and lives in a world 'where fact and fiction are no longer clearly distinguished' (18). Anna is a singer who, being in love with Hugo, takes over like Jake what in him is lived out (Hugo is the man trying to get beyond duality) and creates a second-hand vicarious version of it in the Mime theatre. She calls singing 'corrupt', 'exploiting one's charm to seduce people', compared to the puritan ideal of Mime which is 'very pure and very simple'.

The art-form which dominates the story and links most of its picaresque worlds – raffish-Bohemian, sporting, and high capitalist – is film. This is the world Madge is suing to enter, over which Sadie reigns as a star, and a world which rumours tell us Anna may be seduced by, though we last hear of her not in Hollywood but a singer in Paris. Murdoch has written of the necessity of thinking of reality as 'a rich receding background' (ad). This idea – which is incidentally not the assertion of a simple realist but rather one who believes that truth lies in a certain kind of directedness – gets into the text in a variety of ways. Just as we meet Hugo for most of the text only through Jake or Anna's reflections and copies of his world-view, so there is in the worldly realm of film also a recession of power figures. Hugo is involved in film-making too, which gives this recession another kind of piquancy. Jake is outwitted by Sadie and Sammy Starfield over the theft and use of a Breteuil translation he has made. They in their turn are outwitted by Madge and possibly H. K. Pringsheim, who are going to 'wipe out' Hugo's film company. Madge undergoes two changes of style during the book, and there is some 'final' paymaster behind Madge's second metamorphosis into a starlet-in-the-making, but though Jake muses about this person and imagines him in three different guises, his curiosity remains unsatisfied. Just as Hugo is the absent centre of the world of ideas, so there is some final paymaster in the world of power who also makes Jake feel peripheral.

Murdoch has drawn attention to F. M. Cornford's comparison of the cinema with Plato's Cave, a place of darkness, false glitter, specious Goods, mechanical fantasy. In *The Fire and the Sun* television figures twice as an image of Platonic *eikasia*, the lowest realm of illusion. Film's standards of truthfulness and accuracy are evoked for us in the scene at Hugo's studio in Chapter 12. Sadie is playing the part of Orestilla in a film about the Catiline conspiracy. Sallust says of Orestilla that no good man praised her save for her beauty and Cicero professed to believe her to be not only Catiline's wife but his daughter too. Despite three eminent ancient historians on the film's payroll the script presents her as 'a woman with a heart of gold and moderate reformist principles' (*UN* 140)!

Jake rejects the inglorious, tawdry consumerist fantasies of film in Paris where Madge offers him a sinecure position as script-writer, a rejection paralleled by his distancing himself from Lefty Todd's requirements also. Madge asks him to use his art, if only part-time, to prettify capitalism; Lefty wishes him to serve the revolution. Though this is to make the book sound unduly allegorical, I think the echo is there. Jake is declaring for the independence of art, which best serves society when it serves its own truth, in rejecting both Lefty and Madge.

*

The book is full of lockings-in and lockings-out, of unlocking and of theft. It is also full of jokes about copying, and Jake occupies a world perplexingly full of copies. Murdoch noted that in writing the novel she was copying Beckett and Queneau as hard as she could, but that the book resembles nothing by either of them (Caen, 1978); such an account of the book's gestation also mirrors its themes.

The theme of doubling is most apparent in Jake's feelings about the Quentin sisters who, like the painting of Gainsborough's daughters that Dora visits in the Tate gallery in *The Bell*, are 'like, yet unlike'. Jake mistakes the sisters and his feelings for them. He thinks the singer Anna 'deep' because she handles her own emotional promiscuity with an apparent slippery success, and finds the filmstar Sadie glossy and dazzling and hard. His quest is dramatised for us in the superb scene in the Tuileries where he pursues a woman he takes for Anna but who merely resembles her, and where the statuesque stone lovers mock and imitate the human ones. Moreover Paris, full on July 14th, recalls and parodies the City of London, empty at night, and the glassy Seine is explicitly compared with the tidal Thames. Notre Dame is reflected in the tideless Seine 'like a skull which appears in the glass as a reflection of a head'. There is a catalogue of churches in each. We are told that all women copy one another and approximate to a harmonious norm (*UN* 10). In another episode which has been related to G. E. Moore and David Pears,[10] Dave Gellman is writing an article for *Mind* on the incongruity of counterparts and

> he wrote sitting in front of a mirror, and alternately staring at his reflection and examining his two hands. He had several times tried to explain to me his solution but I had not yet got as far as grasping the problem.   (157)

Finally, in the last chapter, and before Jake meets Mrs Tinck and her cat, which has perplexingly but only partly copied itself, producing half Siamese and half tabby kittens, he hears in an upper room someone playing the piano. 'Someone else picked up the tune and whistled it' (224).

Thus is one of the novel's themes – plagiarism – mockingly elaborated. The sea of small, shy jokes about copying matters because copying is one of the book's great themes. Jake copies Hugo's ideas in 'The Silencer' just as Anna copies his ideas in the Mime theatre. In each case Hugo ironically turns out to be too modest to recognise the reflections. He is, as Jake comes to see, a 'man without reflections' (238). He is closest to the truth of all the characters, because he lacks much self-image. He can begin to educate Jake twice – first in showing him what the world looks like to one who lacks preconception, and then at the end by showing him the truth about his relations with the other characters. Hugo's wisdom represents the direction in which art must be pulled if it is to succeed in making a structure that illuminates what it points to without too greatly obscuring it; in a sense, without lying.

The point that Jake lies and is an unreliable narrator is made many times. He has a rule of 'never speaking frankly to women in moments of emotion' (13). He lies to the reader that he pays Madge 'little rent', and confesses that he pays none. Soon after with Anna he tells 'my first lie' (43) that he has nowhere to sleep that night. He assumes that others are lying back to him, and his habit of untruth has consequences since when Sadie – whom he has decided is a 'notorious liar' (68) – tells him plainly that Hugo is in love with her, he permits himself to believe that it is really she who loves Hugo. When questioned by Lefty he notes that under direct questioning he usually lies (96). During his crucial encounter with Hugo in the hospital his asseveration that 'I felt I had to be desperately truthful' is followed within five lines by 'uttering my first lie' (220).

Jake's habit of untruth is explicitly connected with his being an 'incorrigible artist' (25). His care for verbal shapeliness and impressiveness is evidenced when, in considering how to tell Mrs Tinck about his homelessness, he says

> But I gritted my teeth against speech. I wanted to wait until I could present my story in a more dramatic way. The thing had possibilities but as yet it lacked form. If I spoke now there was always the danger of my telling the truth: when caught unawares I usually tell the truth, and what's duller than that? (18)

We are to see a connexion between Jake's habitual carelessness with the truth and his working-up of Hugo and his talks into a stylish, shapely, pretentious dialogue. By contrast the two most truthful people in the story have problems with the very act of writing, apart from Hugo's suspicion of art. Of Finn, who 'never tells lies, he never even exaggerates', we are later told that Jake had never seen his hand-writing. 'Some of my friends had once had a theory that Finn couldn't write' (246). And of Hugo, who is 'an almost completely truthful man', we learn that, despite being so successful a businessman, he 'finds it very hard to express himself on paper at all' (67). Like Socrates, Christ and Buddha, who never wrote anything at all, the good man here is inarticulate on paper. Hugo notes that 'when I really speak the truth the words fall from my mouth completely dead' (60). He represents the charmlessness of truth itself.

In *The Philosopher's Pupil* we learn that Hugo has died and left his clocks to Jake. In that book also the philosopher Rozanov suggests that 'art is certainly the devil's work, the magic that joins good and evil together, the magic place where they joyfully *run* together. Plato was right about art' (192). Rozanov, however, dies of his perfectionism and puritanism. Against his severe judgement might be set the comment of Socrates in her unpublished Platonic dialogue 'Art and Eros'. There Plato condemns art, on similar grounds, but Socrates defends it. 'Art must *embrace* the second-best' he argues, since human beings are second-best creatures who occupy a second-best world.

Murdoch is not hostile to conceptualising, but has argued for a particular, provisional relation to it. She is scarcely an advocate of silence. In her aptly named 'A House of Theory' she blamed modern philosophy for having discouraged theorising. In her polemic 'Against Dryness' she called for a modern liberal theory of personality. 'Where we can no longer explain, we may cease to believe' (sbr). In *The Sovereignty of Good* she advocates a dialectic between theory and fact, calls for a deepening of concepts and vocabulary, and advocates a 'siege of the individual by concepts' as an access to moral growth. 'The discipline of committing oneself to clarified public form is proper and rewarding: the final and best discoveries are often made in the formulation of the statement' (*FS* 87). She has suggested that 'the paradox of our situation is that we must have theories about human nature, no theory explains everything, yet it is just the desire to explain everything which is the spur of theory' (mmm). And her Blashfield address was aptly entitled 'Salvation by Words'.

It is rather that she places no absolute trust in theory. It should be local and provisional, not general and imperial. It is a means, not an end, and she is as aware as Sartre that most cerebration tries to control experience rather than submit to it. Thought itself tries to freeze what is 'brute and nameless' behind words, to fix what is always 'more and other' than our descriptions of it.

In *Nuns and Soldiers* we are told of the Count that 'he loved Gertrude and he classified Anne' (487). The opposition between love and classification runs throughout her work. We might say, *à propos Under the Net*, that the two activities are both mutually necessary and yet permanently opposed. Classification by itself produces a world of dead facts, love a world mysteriously alive and inexhaustible. In a sense it is the capacity to love the world, as well as to be more ordinary in it, that Hugo teaches Jake; both depend on attenuating the desire for cognitive mastery, and Jake aptly at the end gives up having any 'picture' of Anna at all (238) as a premise for apprehending her aright.

*

The critic too has to struggle to crawl under the net. To study Murdoch is to become newly aware of the puritanism of critical discourse, which makes for embarrassment about the discussion of character and bewilderment about the 'centrifugal' pressures within the work: it is easy enough to speak about 'structure', but hard to find a context in which to celebrate those particulars which break away from and blur the structure, and give us the artful illusion that the work is overflowing back into life. Jake's problem is also the reader's.

In a discussion of *Under the Net* with Miss Murdoch in 1983 she pointed out that a problem with that work is how little Jake and Hugo's combat engages with the other characters, especially the women. Their relationship is, she suggested, uncompleted because they are such different kinds of being. Hugo is 'a sort of unconscious spiritual being' by whom Jake is shaken up. Jake might be a better writer later on as a result of meeting Hugo, but what Hugo is doing is not real to either of them.[11]

This seems just. In comparison with later treatments of the theme of the artist and the saint this is schematic and shadowy work, more interesting than it is good, and interesting in part because of what it foreshadows in the later work. Anna, Sadie and Madge are caught at the edge of the book's vision. It is not that we disbelieve in them, but that we never get close enough to test our unbelief.

We are nonetheless to understand that 'wisdom' is what Jake is in the process of acquiring. Hugo and Jake's whispered colloquy in the darkened hospital at night, where Jake risks and indeed loses his job, is the first of a series between artist and saint, always carried out at a pitch of difficulty in her work. Hugo, who has already divested himself of much, ends the book wishing to 'travel light. Otherwise one can never understand anything' and feels the urge to 'strip himself' (223). He advises Jake to 'clear out' as he is doing.

> 'Some situations can't be unravelled,' said Hugo, 'they just have to be dropped. The trouble with you, Jake, is that you want to understand everything sympathetically. It can't be done. One must just blunder on. Truth lies in blundering on . . . . The point is people must just do what they can do, and good luck to them.'
> 'What can you do?' I asked him.
> Hugo was silent for a long time. 'Make little intricate things with my hands,' he said (229).

What Hugo is going to do about this is become a watch-maker ('A *what*?' asks Jake) in Nottingham ('In *Where*?') and when Jake asks 'wildly' 'What about the truth? What about the search for

God?', Hugo replies 'What more do you want? . . . . God is a task. God is a detail. It all lies close to your hand' (229).

The scene is funny and touching and true. Hugo's wisdom, we might say, is centrifugal and particular. His adoption of watch-making – 'an old craft, like baking bread' – signals his calm absorption in the task of honouring the world's details. He stands for a loving empirical curiosity about particulars, for reverential 'attention', that crucial Murdochian word (ad) and proposes to Jake that he renounce the grandiloquent – the search for God – in favour of the local – seeing life as task, as blundering on, and writing, by implication, as an unpretending craft which must also negotiate the detail and contingency of the world. His face 'masked by a kind of innocence', he calls Jake a sentimentalist who is always far too impressed by people. 'Everyone must go his own way. Things don't matter as much as you think'.

Jake, who famously classifies parts of London as necessary and parts as contingent, is understandably appalled by the notion of having to live outside London, which is to say of having to give up his position at the centre. Other artist-figures share this bias. Randall in *An Unofficial Rose* declares Australia, from which the innocent Penn comes, 'a meaningless place', and Hilary in *A Word Child* can bear only London near the Park. Hugo, by contrast, is unable to conceive of himself at the centre to begin with, and, like all of Murdoch's would-be saintly characters, and in this like Cordelia too, lacks the narrative skills which would dramatise his life as Jake consistently dramatises his (speaking throughout of 'fate' and 'destiny'). Murdoch saints are always on the edge of the action, either leading happy lives or lives about whose unhappiness they have no talent for making a fuss, and which therefore lack any 'story'. They exist, as Jake sees Hugo, as an unconscious 'sign or portent' for those less luckily situated.

*

Art for Murdoch presents the problems of true vision in a special form. She has argued from first to last that particulars must be celebrated in a way that neither ties them up into some form of premature unity (symbolism) nor leaves them wholly outside the range of spirit (naturalism), condemned to banality.

In *Bruno's Dream* Bruno thinks, 'I am dying . . . but what is it *like?*' (300). It is everywhere apparent in her work that Murdoch has repeatedly asked herself 'What is it *like?*', of many disparate phenomena. In asking what the aged Bruno's experience might be like she came up with, among other things, a man who, though he would not object to being loved by someone new, has settled for the moment to looking forward to a *new kind of jam*. That touching, and, surely, *true* 'new kind of jam' might stand for an emblem of how superbly and watchfully she can inhabit other experience than her own. It is a symptom of her tender-heartedness that Bruno is rewarded by the new person too. In that novel Bruno's puritanical and self-enclosed son Miles keeps a 'Notebook of Particulars' in which he tries to overcome the problems of description. 'How hard it was to *see* things', he thinks, and chronicles some marvels, 'the ecstatic flight of a pigeon, the communion of two discarded shoes, the pattern on a piece of processed cheese' (55). Some of the most brilliant passages in *The Black Prince* appear as answers to the question 'What is it *like*?', and as her work proceeds the answers she solicits are to increasingly ordinary questions.

In her early essay 'Nostalgia for the Particular', which is ascribed as a book to the philosopher Rozanov in *The Philosopher's Pupil* thirty years later, Murdoch wrote of the 'shyness' of experience and the problems of 'cornering' it. 'It is difficult to describe the smell of the Paris Metro or what it is like to hold a mouse in one's hand.' When the oafish Otto in *The Italian Girl* asks 'Has it ever struck you that we don't eat anything *blue*?' (39), the wholly unblue food we customarily, unthinkingly eat becomes invested with a kind of strange glamour, invoked as it is from so close, yet so happily alienated a perspective. A less successful example occurs in Crystal's recounting of her seduction by the grief-stricken Gunnar in *A Word Child*, when, in the middle of a long and circumstantial narrative, she tells how Gunnar had spoken of Lappland where the reindeer 'like the smell of human water, urine' (251). Here the improbable-but-true fact is used to authenticate the improbable and not quite plausible liaison. Finally in *Nuns and Soldiers* when the recently widowed and grief-stricken Gertrude, in trouble with young Tim with whom she finds herself falling in love, thinks of her dead husband 'I shall tell Guy about it, he will help me, he will know what to do' (248) the moment is truthful as only high art can be.

Murdoch has called, citing Simone Weil, for a 'vocabulary of attention' (ad), and while it is other persons who are the worthiest objects of such skill, the natural world is always well-attended.

In *Bruno's Dream* Miles draws attention to the tiny sound of the cracking of swallows' beaks as they snap up flies; in *The Sacred and Profane Love-Machine* Luca hears the minute crepitation of wood-worm. The oddness of what we take for granted is insisted on throughout. In *The Sea, The Sea* Charles hears 'a most extraordinary rhythmical shrieking sound' (404) which it takes him a minute to recognise as his newly installed telephone. Similarly in *The Time of the Angels* Marcus, who has unknowingly fallen down a coal-hole, experiences the smell of the coal before he is able reassuringly to name it. In a variety of ways her work constantly draws attention to the holiness, or threat, of those minute particulars which dullness and self-absorption prevent us from experiencing afresh, and which language can hide or reveal.

This is to take, in a particular way, a romantic view of the function of art. I would argue that Murdoch is, in the best and most positive sense of the word, a romantic writer – the sense in which John Bayley uses the word, in *Romantic Survival*, of Yeats and of Auden.[12] Both colonise the modern urban world and in so doing give it back to us afresh. One might mention here the special poetry Murdoch gets out of London, the inclusion of the half-built motorway along which David wanders in *The Sacred and Profane Love Machine*, the disused, abandoned railway-line where Peter and Morgan embrace in *A Fairly Honourable Defeat*, and Hilda's disintegrating telephone in the same book. She has a special gift for finding, or rather 'seeing' such places and objects. In *Under the Net* the cold-cure centre in which Jake and Hugo meet, or the hairdresser's in which Jake and Sadie meet, are further instances. Hers is the gift for making the strange seem familiar (the cold-cure centre) and the familiar seem strange (the hairdresser's). Like Shakespeare, in Johnson's view of him, she 'approximates the remote, and familiarises the wonderful; the event [she] represents will not happen, but if it were possible, its effects would be as [she] has assigned'. 'Good art reveals what we are usually too selfish and too timid to recognise, the minute and absolutely random detail of the world, and reveals it together with a sense of unity and form' (*SG* 86). One might quip here that it is easy enough to understand complex things: it is what is most simple that is most unyielding and mysterious. Wittgenstein pointed out that 'the aspects of things that are most important for us are hidden because of their simplicity and familiarity. (One is unable to notice something because it is always before one's eyes)' (*Investigations* 129).

In *The Philosopher's Pupil* Rozanov describes philosophy as 'the sublime ability to say the obvious, to exhibit what is closest' (133). The same might be said, *mutatis mutandis*, about literature. The pleasure that we get from Jake's observation that if you try to direct a cat's attention it will look at your finger or elsewhere, but not at what you are pointing to (19); the pleasure that we get from his seeing Madge's defence of Sammy as 'an unhappy muddled sort of person' as 'a standard remark made by women about the men who have left them' (173) – these seem to me high pleasures exactly because they are humbly true; and, while each belongs naturally within its context, it also works outside its context. If criticism finds no way of saying so, then so much the worse for criticism. Murdoch's *aficion* about animals and persons, like the knowledge she incorporates about spiders in *Bruno's Dream*, roses in *An Unofficial Rose* or pubs and churches in *Under the Net* are proper sources of readerly pleasure.

She has described herself in different interviews as both a 'poet *manqué*' and also as an 'engineer *manqué*'.[13] My point is that these are not necessarily to be construed of as opposed interests. It is the poetry of irreducible *fact* that most interests her, a poetry excellently ascribed by Gillian Beer to Dickens, Carlyle, and Hopkins as 'romantic materialism' – a belief in the palpable and particular, not as insufficient substitutes in some platonic scheme for their own idea, but as sufficient and even ideal, in all their incompleteness and irreducibility.[14] Murdoch's Platonism is a *this*-worldly commodity, and she is concerned throughout her books to redirect the reader's attention to the sensory world in which he is immersed. 'I had forgotten about rain', says Jake at one point. The books remind us, often through that 'defamiliarisation' of the object described by the Russian formalist critic Shklovski, who argued that a leading function of art was to de-automatise perception through descriptions which made the ordinary strange and therefore fresh.[15]

Lefty tells Jake in the Skinners' Arms that 'Nothing goes on for ever' and Jake, seeing his Jewish friend Dave at the bar, says 'Except the Jews'. When Lefty concurs Jake asks him 'So you do recognise certain mysteries?' 'Yes, I'm an empiricist', he jokes (101). It is just such an empiricism, which finds miracle in what is most ordinary, that it is the book's project, through its chief agent Hugo, to instil. For Hugo each thing is 'astonishing, delightful, complicated and mysterious' (58).

Shortly after this passage in the Skinners' Arms Lefty and Jake wander through the bombed City as the twilight falls.

> The evening was by now well advanced. The darkness hung in the air but spread out in a suspended powder which only made the vanishing colours more vivid. The zenith was a strong blue, the horizon a radiant amethyst. From the darkness and shade of St Paul's Churchyard we came into Cheapside as into a bright arena and saw framed in the gap of a ruin the pale neat rectangles of St Nicholas Cole Abbey, standing alone away to the South of us on the other side of Cannon Street. In between the willow-herb waved over what remained of streets. In this desolation the coloured shells of houses still raised up filled and blank squares of wall and window. The declining sun struck on glowing bricks and warmed up the stone of an occasional fallen pillar. As we passed St Vedast the top of the sky was vibrating into a later blue . . . .   (95)

How superb that 'later' blue is! The description continues for some pages and there is in this a freshness and an intense lyricism – a quality beautifully termed by one critic 'lyrical accuracy'[16] – that brings the John Piper bombed City-scape alive. The desolation and sweet melancholy of war-torn London – the fading of Empire, perhaps – is echoed by the elegiac processes of the fading daylight, seen with a new strangeness. The light is alive in its sensuousness, a Keatsian commodity with a behaviour entirely of its own.

The search for an 'unmediated vision' beyond duality, and the failure of such search – these are great themes in high Romanticism and in contemporary deconstructionism. For the critic Geoffrey Hartman, the poet is seen trying to break through social and other determinants to some 'unmediated contact with the principle of things'. Hartman's criticism suffers from a boastful privation in that it constantly shows off about how cheated we must be of any such final contact. To require to exhibit this is, I think, naïve. In his *Logic* Hegel suggests that 'nothing is absolutely immediate in the absolute sense that it is in no way mediated; and nothing is mediated in the absolute sense that it is no way immediate'.[17] This common-sensical position is true for Murdoch too.

This is ignored by critics who insufficiently see the open-endedness even of her most apparently 'closed' novels. Rabinowitz argues that Jake at the end has now learned 'to accept contingency'. A. S. Byatt writes that Jake 'is free of his own net of fantasy' and describes his 'final enlightenment'. Malcolm Bradbury speaks of his 'learning a fresh truth' and of 'true vision'.[18] This is at odds both with every theoretical pronouncement and also with what is there in the books. On one page of *The Sovereignty of Good* (23) she speaks of the effort toward reality as 'infinitely perfectible', an 'endless task', emphasises 'inevitable imperfection' and 'necessary fallibility'. Again and again she has attacked the liberal belief in fast change as false and magical and opposed to it a truer picture of moral change as piecemeal, unending and in some sense goalless. 'It would be hard to over-estimate the amount of fantasy in any given soul'; 'even the most piercing sense of revelation accompanying greater awareness of one's moral position is likely to be partly an illusion'.[19] The fact that the action of her novels rarely takes longer than a few weeks or months might be counted here as further evidence. 'We cannot suddenly alter ourselves' (*SG* 39). Indeed the books are as least as much comedies of inveteracy as they are the Advent calendars, packed with moral surprises, that critics have made of them. 'Creative imagination and obsessive fantasy may be very close, almost indistinguishable forces in the mind of the writer' (Magee, 1978) and what works for the writer is here true of her characters too. Her famous division between self-flattering fantasy and an imagination which links us to the world needs to be read not as expressing the total discontinuity between the two, but precisely their ambiguous continuity.

Thus *Under the Net* ends with Jake's experiencing that *thauma* (wonder) that impels men to philosophise or create. 'It was the first day of the world. . . it was the morning of the first day' (251). But his sense of renewal carries with it, as it were, no guarantees. What we have is closer to the ending of *Ulysses* than *Hard Times*. Molly Bloom's decision to make her husband breakfast is a tiny token into which the reader puts as much hope as he feels the signal will bear. So with Jake's forswearing of classification. Mrs Tinck's cat, as if sharing the creativity which Jake experiences, has littered. Mrs Tinck is puzzled as to why the kittens should be half pure Siamese and half pure tabby. After some bluster Jake gives in. 'It's just one of the wonders of the world', he says, in the book's closing words.

The ending asserts that the world is most apprehensible at those moments when we are calmest about submitting to its inexhaustibility. When we give up the claim *wholly* to 'understand everything sympathetically', we may be rewarded by a vision of the world's oddness, which the urge to a completed act of comprehension will elude. Once you can admit you don't fully know, you can begin, a little, to 'see'.

3 'Against Gravity': the Early Novels and *An Accidental Man*

Under the Net presented a hero of the will at its centre and a man attempting to sacrifice his will at the edge. The pattern is common to many of the early novels and is never wholly abandoned. Malcolm Bradbury has used the word 'psychopomp' for these decentred educators or leaders-of-souls.[1] I want in this chapter to suggest that these psychopomps are of two kinds, one of them distinctly more worldly than the other, and then to look at the ambiguous idea of worldliness itself in Murdoch's work. Since a common form of illusion is to imagine that you are more virtuous than you really are, the psychopomp, who acts, however unwittingly, as a tantric master reconnecting the novice with the real, can sometimes speak with an apparent worldliness.

The Flight from the Enchanter (1956) was begun before the publication of *Under the Net*, and an early draft at Iowa makes clear that originally all the major characters were to have been refugees – not merely Mischa Fox, Nina, and the Luciewicz brothers but also Rosa Keepe and Peter Saward who, under a different name, appeared to be a Central European writing a history of the Jews. The published book distances this theme of displacement and achieves a deliberate alienation of the treatment, which is lightly comic, Lewis Carroll-like and fantastic, from the matter, which is sombre. The English too are subject to various displacements. Agnes Casement is a recruit to the bureaucracy where Rainborough works, and one who seems likely to overtake him. Rosa has made the reverse movement, declassing herself to work in a factory. Annette Cockaigne is a 'cosmopolitan ragamuffin' speaking four languages. Even the sedate and unremarkable Rainborough suffers the uprooting of an old wistaria tree with all its associations. At the centre of the book is the enchanter and refugee Mischa Fox, with one eye blue and one brown, not famous for 'anything in particular . . . just famous'(81), a figure of bad power who enslaves many of those who surround him, partly through the devices of Calvin Blick. Blick represents Fox's 'sub-conscious' dark half (Caen, 1978) and his photographic dark-room occupies the cellars of Fox's Kensington palazzo. Mischa contrives to seem innocent because the enslaved Calvin carries the full burden of consciousness and guilt. Mischa, the artist-figure, is the creator of his own myth, with which the other characters actively collude.

The magnetic difference in *Under the Net* between Hugo and Jake is echoed in the implicit opposition between Mischa and Peter Saward. Neither Mischa nor Peter are focused with the skilful energy shown in their later incarnations, Tallis and Julius, in *A Fairly Honourable Defeat*. Both are nonetheless interesting. Like Tallis, Peter has a sister who died. He has an advanced TB, lives an ascetic scholarly life trying to decipher an ancient script, and is decked out with an unclassifiable plant. Peter is other-worldly, does not read the papers, is associated – again, like Tallis – with an unconscious night wisdom, some of it nonsensical, lives with great simplicity, has long contemplative periods, and is recognised by the effete Hunter as 'almost a saint'(96). He has a personality without frontiers. 'He did not defend himself by placing others. He did not defend himself'(31), though he defends others, even the tormented and devilish Blick ('I don't know, he has a pleasant smile'). Like his anti-type Mischa he is a figure about whom the others are busy weaving fantasies. Rainborough finds himself instinctively making damaging admissions to Peter out of an instinctive if irritable trust, Rosa assumes that Peter always knows when she is lying, and he represents for her the 'sweetness of sanity and work, the gentleness of those whose ambitions are innocent, and the vulnerability of those who are incapable of contempt'(253). His virtue is necessary to the others as an object of contemplation and speculation, just as is Mischa's power. While Mischa feeds off such speculation and is fattened by it there is a simplicity in Peter which resists it. It is an acute observation that Mischa's power is invested in him by his 'creatures' and a product of their masochistic needs quite as much as it is a product of his own hard work.

Even Mischa wants to reveal himself only to Peter who, as A. S. Byatt pointed out in an excellent reading, is the only person shown to us in the role of neither victim nor predator.[2] 'Everyone has been going mad as usual', says Mischa. 'You make them mad',

Peter replies(205). Chapter 17, in which the two finally meet, resembles Jake and Hugo's meeting in the hospital in that it represents something like a still centre, sandwiched between various arbitrary violences – Annette's breaking of her leg, Miss Casement's chopping down Rainborough's wistaria. Its stillness also prefigures Julius and Tallis' meetings in the kitchen in *A Fairly Honourable Defeat* just as Mischa's more fantastic deracination ('Where was he born? What blood is in his veins? No one knows'(35)) directly prefigures the more pointed discovery of Julius' wartime internment in Belsen. In both meetings we sense a shared understanding between the two 'spiritual' characters. Peter is the only character whose pity for Mischa is shown uncorrupted by that longing to possess or destroy with which pity is here always associated. 'If the gods kill us, it is not for their sport but because we fill them with such intolerable compassion, a sort of nausea'(208) says Mischa, who is the chief repository of this nauseous compassion, a man reputed to cry when reading the newspapers and who confesses to having killed a kitten when overwhelmed by it. 'Some paradox of our natures leads us, when once we have made our fellow men the objects of our enlightened interest, to go on to make them the objects of our pity, then of our wisdom, ultimately of our coercion.'[3] Pity as an active torment, symbolised through the animal world, is a great theme in the books. There are weird communal 'damaged animal' dreams in *The Sacred and Profane Love Machine*, and Otto has a sequence of comic alarm dreams involving crushed or mutilated animals in *The Italian Girl*. In *The Philosopher's Pupil* Gabriel is tormented by the desire to rescue a fish; in *The Sandcastle* Felicity cries childishly for a lost slug and for a butterfly flown out to sea. *The Flight from the Enchanter* reads in part as a meditation on the theme of pity-and-power, and Hitler who, we are reminded, killed the pitiable and uprooted in the persons of gypsies and Jews, is, as Byatt has shown, a real presence.[4] It is a tribute to the power of the later books that they make its treatment here, for all its sharpness of outline and detail, seem abstract and whimsical in comparison. What you recall, as so often in the early books, is not so much the people as the wondrous set-pieces – Annette swinging on the chandelier, Mischa's baroque party, the Dickensian Mrs Wingfield's hilarious and uncomfortable persecution of the good Miss Foy.

Just as both Hugo and Jake are outsiders, so are Peter and Mischa. Peter's mode of dispossession again silently opposes

Mischa's exoticism. Peter is caretaker of the symbols of Mischa's own lost past, when Mischa was still rooted and still 'belonged': Peter collects photographs of Mischa's now destroyed hometown and keeps them for him.

John Bayley has acutely observed that 'the modern reflective consciousness cannot in some sense but see itself as taking part in a novel, the novel being the standard literary reflection in our age'.[5] Against this might be set Weil's dictum that 'Just as God, being outside the universe, is at the same time the centre, so each man imagines he is situated in the centre of the world. The illusion of perspective places him at the centre of space.'[6] The artists, Jake and, differently, Mischa, see themselves or are perceived as being at the centre. The saintly figures are struggling in some sense 'to give up [the] imaginary position as the centre not only intellectually but in the imaginative part of [the] soul.'[7] Decentring is the book's theme. Peter, with the strength to survive at the edge of the world, contrasts with Nina whose dispossession demoralises her, and, when no one sufficiently imagines her needs, leads to her suicide. Only for the saintly can virtue have no fixed address.

Calvin tells Rosa at the end of the book that she 'will never know the truth and you will read the signs in accordance with your deepest wishes. That is what we humans always have to do. Reality is a cipher with many solutions, all of them right ones . . . . The truth lies deeper, deeper'(278). His is a point of view Murdoch has explicitly rebutted[8], and which within the book is echoed and answered by Peter's avowal to Rosa, when his research into the script he was working on turns out to have been worthless. 'One reads the signs as best one can, and one may be totally misled. But it's never certain that the evidence will turn up that makes everything plain. It was worth trying'(287). Peter possesses that 'superior honesty required to tear up one's theory' (*SG* 96) when it is disconfirmed. His ideal of a realism of approximations and towardnesses which depends on a certain unselfish directedness is Murdoch's too. Both Peter's and Calvin's look like styles of relativism, but Calvin's depends on the notion of an absolute we are being darkly cheated and deprived of. Peter's is a more relaxed, disciplined and cheerful agnosticism.

*

The Sandcastle (1957) is a romance about the love of Mor, a prep-school master interested in politics, for the young half-French artist Rain Carter. Mor is divided between his sour and controlling wife Nan and the innocent, fey painter. Rain comes to the school to paint the retired headmaster Demoyte, a charming old despot. She loves Mor both as a man and also as a substitute for her own, now dead, jealous father. The novel treats painting as *A Severed Head* is to treat sculpture – as a paradigm case of the problems of representing the human subject in art, and an implicit analogy of the mysterious creation of the novelist. The book is consistently interesting, sensitive and moving, yet there is a slightness about its final effect which contrasts with our clear sense of the author's gravity. Nan's disappointment is never focused for us, and because it is hard to imagine the Mors' marriage when it was successful, it is also hard to imagine the book's aftermath. On the other hand Nan's rebirth of desire for Bill once she feels rejected by him is perceptively done, and the novel is full of acute touches. There is also a characteristic division in the author's sympathy which she has not yet managed fully to put to work. We experience her sympathy for Rain and the duller Mor, and therefore hope for the success of the affair. The idea-play, however, which comes from Bledyard, is on the side of respect for the proprieties of marriage. It is a less successful novel than the later study of adultery *The Sacred and Profane Love Machine* because the division in our sympathies between wife and mistress is so unequal. We begin to understand Nan's disappointment but insufficiently to want Mor to return to her. The later book is more painful and distressing because we come to know both wife and mistress.

There is also a recurrent paradox in that the central characters, who have had so much loving attention devoted to them, can be, while fully animated, less alive or less 'typical' than some of the people only half-attended to at the edge of the book. Here her successes are the silly, gauche yet innocent and unselfish headmaster Everard, who preaches unheard that '*Love knows!* There is always, if we ponder deeply enough and are ready in the end to crucify our selfish desires, some thing which we can do which is truly for the best and truly for the good of all concerned'(206); and the tender-hearted roguish tyrant Demoyte, who wishes Mor to have Rain in spite of, and because of his being in love with her himself. Lastly there is the eccentric old-Etonian art master Bledyard. Demoyte and Bledyard represent two opposite types who often compel our sympathy in the early books, one with the charm of a complete worldliness, the other intensely other-worldly. Bledyard plays the role occupied by Hugo in *Under the Net*. He is the would-be saint who represents an intolerable, charmless 'best', the puritan an-aesthetic world of silence and truth. Just as Hugo argued for the purifying effect of silence, showing Jake how to renounce and be ordinary, so Bledyard is an artist who will not or cannot paint any longer and who constantly intervenes and acts as an unsolicited voice of conscience. 'I have to bear witness . . . I think you are acting wrongly'(211). Bledyard's uninvited sermon to Mor in the squash-courts, whence he has sent Rain away from a rendezvous, argues for what Mor finds an intolerable austerity. He denounces 'happiness' as a poor and a selfish guide, and pleads in effect for Mor to crucify his desires and open himself to any hurt in concern for others. Freedom, for Bledyard, is total absence of self-concern.

Two other features of Bledyard's case deserve note. One is that he is, with his speech impediment and eccentricity, a ludicrous figure, mocked by all, including Mor and Rain. The scene in which he gives a school lecture, at which the boys have substituted a slide of the digestive tract of a frog for the enormous Socratic head of the aged Rembrandt is a triumph of controlled tone. The reader, like the audience, is convulsed with happy laughter, and yet what Bledyard is saying has always about it a disturbing impractical truthfulness. We are made to feel that Bledyard is mocked rather as Christ was mocked. The mockery is partly Murdoch's own irony and disguise, as with Socrates, for whom the ironies always were thickest when the approach to truth came nearest.

The second interesting feature of Bledyard's case is his Platonic hostility to representational art. Just as Hugo approved of Leonardo's deliberately having made the *Last Supper* perishable, and favoured the obsolescence of fireworks, so Bledyard is interested in the early debates about iconoclasm in the Eastern Church and favours Byzantine art. He feels that a loss of proper reverence occurred in the Renaissance. 'It is a fact . . . that we cannot really observe really observe our betters' [Bledyard has a speech impediment]. 'Vices and peculiarities are easy to portray. But who can look reverently enough upon another human face? The true portrait painter should be a saint – and saints have other things to do than paint portraits'(77).

Bledyard stands in relation to the rest of the book as do Hugo and Peter. Like anti-matter to matter, they are out of focus with ordinary human appetite. You can focus either the saints or their artist antitypes – which is to say, everyone else – separately, but not together. Their function in the books is to point to an (unrealisable) ideal which even they cannot wholly embody, though they are directed with a certain hope, faith, and openness towards it.

Bledyard speaks two related kinds of wisdom. One is related to moral immediacy in personal relations, the other to the interplay of truthfulness and skill necessary to the artist. In this second area Bledyard's effect is most palpable. He has a way of appearing in the book at crucial moments not just in Rain's love affair with Mor but also in her attempts to picture and 'see' Demoyte. Each time he appears Rain recognises his authority and realises that a change in her painting is necessary. Her painting comes to seem, as I think art does to Murdoch, a provisional affair, never wholly finished. Art, like morality, must be pulled at by the value of a truth or perfection which is unreachable. Rain is desolate when Bledyard criticises the painting at an early stage, yet is helped by this criticism and rethinks her task. Finally, when she renounces Mor, she sees her representation of Demoyte once more anew and remakes what she has done again. At the same time Mor is held in his marriage, not by his own sudden conversion to Bledyard's austerities, but by his wife's brave and worldly cunning in staging a public scene. This compromises him and leaves him little choice but to pursue the political career she had formerly opposed.

As the title implies, the book is much concerned with notions of form and permanence. Rain had been brought up on the tideless Mediterranean, where the sand was too dry to make a sandcastle. She finally tells Mor that since he would have had to give up his political ambitions and his children for her, their affair would have been 'all dry sand running through the fingers'(300). Characters are throughout realised by aesthetic preferences. Nan likes matching colour schemes and moves everything in the house around as an expression of her need for control and territory. Demoyte lives in the magnificence of superimposed Persian rugs, drowning in splendour. Evvy's apartments are drably unimaginative, and Bledyard characteristically lives in a stripped room, void of colour or comfort. 'The floor was scrubbed and the walls whitewashed. No picture, no coloured object adorned it. The furniture was of pale wood and even the bed had a white cover'(51). This recalls Hugo's bedroom. Goodness, for Murdoch, depends on stripping away the consolations of a private world. Most art, like most morality, is a necessary realm of compromise and second best.

*

The theme of the artist and the saint lies at the heart of *An Unofficial Rose* (1962) in the marriage of Ann and Randall Peronett, and is early dramatised in the row Randall stages to provide himself with a pretext for cutting loose and joining his mistress. A. S. Byatt has rightly drawn our attention to the book's Jamesian qualities.[9] James continues to haunt Murdoch at least until *Nuns and Soldiers*, which partly reworks the plot of *The Wings of the Dove*. Here there is 'beautiful' speech, periphrasis on the part of the narrator, and the creation of a decorous golden world. Jane Austen is another presence, and Hugh presents Miranda with her works. It is set in a *Tatler* world of two neighbouring Kentish houses and concerns the manoeuvrings which follow the death of Fanny Peronett. The title refers to the dog-rose of Rupert Brooke's 1913 poem 'The Old Vicarage, Grantchester', which, unlike the orderly flowers of Berlin in which Brooke is composing his poem, he perceives as sweetly undisciplined and 'unkempt'. The poem, itself an improvisation, hinges on the conceit that nature in Germany is punctual and formally ordered, while in England it is gloriously free.

Thus Randall, a would-be artist too rapacious to succeed, is offended by his wife's formlessness and feels stifled by her capacity for self-sacrifice. He lives for and inhabits a stylish world, farming cultivated roses, and objects to Ann in that she is as 'messy and flabby and open as a dogrose'(37). Ann is busy and unselfish and, while not odd as Bledyard is odd, has a shy awkwardness and stubborn self-withholding that offends Randall. In the slightly later *The Red and the Green* the artist Barnie is similarly hurt by his good wife Kathleen's unyielding, passive stoicism. Such virtuous characters have a special negativity which refuses the imagination of those they live with, perhaps a consequence of how hard they work at not imagining wrong. Such deliberate gracelessness offers the onlooker no imaginative foothold. This seems a just perception, and I know of no other novelist capable of making the point, or of relating it to the virtues of the art-work itself, since art depends on style and stylishness and requires and feeds off form. 'Goodness accepts the contingent. Love accepts the contingent. Nothing is more fatal to love than to want it to have form', the sententious vicar Douglas Swann says (*UR* 130). Art, in making its pact with contingency, must, however, embrace enough to test its own form without yielding to banality.

Freedom, too, is a subject in the book. Characters are frequently surprised when actions they had planned and claimed for themselves turn out to have been partly engineered by others. Randall discovers that his action in stealing Lindsay Rimmer from the aged detective-story writer Emma Sands, to whom she had been companion, was at least partly connived at by Emma. 'His action was stolen from him'(202). In direct contrast Ann finds that her inability to claim Felix Meecham for herself, despite their mutual love and despite her desertion by Randall, was worked at by her daughter Miranda, who was in love with Felix herself. 'She had been part of someone else's scheme'(325). Randall, typically, resents this threat to his supremacy. Ann, as typically, does not.

This is not to say that even the most powerful and worldly characters can ever fully 'own' their actions. All have to suffer their own unfreedom, but do so with a difference. Even the 'witch-like' Emma, despite the tough and very quick-witted front she puts on is, after all, abandoned first by Hugh, then by Lindsay, and is about to die. The prissily unappealing Miranda, who ensured her mother's disappointment, was thwarted herself; and it is not impossible that Ann will get Randall, whom she still loves, back in the end.

If there is a pecking-order in the book it has at the top not the 'freest' characters but simply those who most acutely and earthily see how things are. Lacking a taste for the fantasy of an unconditioned world, they thereby possess a power denied to those deluded by the notion of freedom. The theme recurs in *Nuns and Soldiers*. The whole complicated imbroglio of love and passion is held in being as the unstable product of a variety of different wills.

In relation to this pecking-order Ann is the most passive and acquiescent, and Emma the most cunning and authoritative of the moral agents. Murdoch's different sympathy for both seems clear. There is energy if not approval behind Emma, and like her near-homophones Honor in *A Severed Head* and Hannah in *The Unicorn* – and, though rather differently, Millie in *The Red and the Green* – she is a psychopomp, one who leads the others towards some ambiguous wisdom. That her detective stories hilariously champion a hero of the will ('Marcus Boode') suggests that we are not to take her without irony. She is, however, earthy, witty, wise, and speaks always with a humorously forthright dryness, for a practical politics of the emotions. Compared with the men who surround her, she represents the toughness of common sense itself. On her single visit to Grayhallock it takes her only a matter of minutes to intuit the various relationships.

The men in this book, as so often in Iris Murdoch, are weak and poor things who seem to be chasing phantoms. The women often provide 'all the warmth and sense of the world' (*AM* 324). The soft and romantic 'ninny' Hugh Peronett wishes to pick up with Emma after having dropped her twenty-five years earlier. His equally romantic if more caddish son Randall wants to ditch his wife for the sexy Lindsay. In wanting to reverse time (Hugh) or negate it (Randall) or simply escape (Felix's brother-in-law Humphrey) the men compare ill with the tougher-willed and more realistic women. Since the attempt to behave well can sometimes be accompanied by a new self-regard, Murdoch's respect can sometimes go to the character who, while not behaving most 'beautifully', is at least not stupefied by self-importance. Mildred, who is guileful too, reflects some of her rival Emma's practical horse sense.

There is much to hold the interest, both in the intricate story and also in the touching respect which the author never loses for the love affairs of what are sometimes elderly people. Hugh is sixty-seven. Here as in *Bruno's Dream* she paints the love affairs of the middle-aged without a trace of condescension. Few other 'liberal' novelists could have given us the sympathetic portrait of Felix Meecham the soldier, if only because his profession would at once have earned their mistrust.

If this finally is less successful than some other books it may be because its very tautness of design, with its closely interwoven destinies, is, for all its admirable economy, somewhat chill. In this it differs from the equally condensed *A Severed Head*. The rhetorical point of the plot, which is to marry the idea of unfreedom to the idea of mystery, is made better there and elsewhere. The 'love' which the characters conspire to enjoy seems, perhaps, too clearly empty.

To put these points differently: the early novels often urge on us a patience with the world's multiplicity which they cannot yet adequately enact. And this seems partly a result of the author's unrelaxed investment in mystifying us. To appreciate a mystery you renounce the patient desire to see further and understand better. The early novels sometimes buy off our curiosity with bribes to our love of surprise; and surprise can itself become a 'manner', a convention, and can exhibit the human unfreedom it ironises. The later books, which are more relaxed and assured, more often get the balance right.

*

The individual worlds of these early books are nonetheless always beautifully imagined, fully and in detail 'there'. I have been trying to suggest that there is in them some division of sympathy between two kinds of character: on the one hand the good characters who are in two senses eccentric, both decentred and also dotty or absurd – Hugo, Bledyard, Ann; and on the other hand the worldly charmers who talk a dry *realpolitik* of the emotions – Mrs Wingfield, Demoyte, Emma.

I think that in some sense she narrates, as John Bayley said of Tolstoi, by two positives[10] – Ann Peronett's positive, and Emma Sands'. I want here to develop this idea, and to do so with two readings of a mature work in which the balance is fully achieved.

Elizabeth Dipple in her book *Iris Murdoch: Work for the Spirit* argues that *An Accidental Man* represents an indictment of the 'ease of the frenetic, bitchy but comfortable bourgeois world' to which its characters are too attached. Dipple suggests that 'Only by jettisoning all the imagery of the culture and facing the ensuing blackness do characters begin to perceive reality, which is their religious duty.' It is certainly true that Murdoch has written of movement towards 'an impersonal pictureless void' as part of a complete religion (*FS* 88). Dipple apologises for Murdoch's rogues' gallery of 'hateful characters' and argues of Austin in *An Accidental Man* that he is 'an absolute triumph for Murdoch; the reader experiences a wonderfully pure hatred of him'. Twice addressing herself to Bradley Pearson's question in *The Black Prince* – 'And shall the artist have no cakes and ale?'(349) – Dipple says, 'the darkness of man's squalid limitations must give a resounding "no"'.[11] Though Dipple mentions in passing that Murdoch is not unequivocally hostile to pleasure, and appears to

give us a double frame of reference, her own refreshingly enthusiastic account of Murdoch is, I think, intensely censorious about the
characters, and gives out a missionary and humourless moral
stridency. I shall leave aside the curious assumption that Murdoch
is specially hostile to 'the bourgeois world'. Dipple's account is
remote from how the books *feel* as you read them, and remote
too, from that 'calm merciful vision . . . breath of tolerance and
generosity and intelligent kindness' as well as the capacity to
'leave the reader a space to play in' (Magee, 1978), that Murdoch
has admired in great writers of the past.

Against such severities, Lorna Sage, in the most perceptive
article on Murdoch's work that I know, also addresses herself at
one moment to *An Accidental Man* with its court of bourgeois
grandees. Sage writes compassionately of the fate of the spinster
Charlotte who 'unselfishly' looks after her mother only to find
herself disinherited when Alison dies. Sage quotes

> She owned her toothbrush but not the mug in which it
> stood . . . . Everything was entirely as usual, and yet entirely
> alienated, as if what one had taken to be someone's house had
> turned out to be an antique shop. Just for a moment all these
> things were proclaiming a secret truth . . . . Ownership was an
> illusion.   (94)

Ownership, Sage comments, is 'an illusion one can hardly live
without, however'. Dipple, who argued that morality consisted
of 'jettisoning all the imagery of the culture and facing the ensuing
blackness', fails to notice that Charlotte's disinheritance leads to
her attempted suicide, or that Austin's destruction of his brother's
priceless china is an act of spiteful and vindictive vandalism.
Dipple finds in Murdoch that radical *contemptus mundi et vitae* that
has always characterised a heretical Christian dualism. Sage, on
the other hand, finds in Murdoch a series of cautionary tales
against any such 'jettisoning' of the imagery, and aptly quotes
from Bradley Pearson's description of his deserted sister Priscilla's
abandoned Bristol flat, in *The Black Prince*:

> There was a kind of fairly solid ordinariness about that
> 'maisonette' in Bristol, with its expensive kitchen equipment
> and its horrible modern cutlery, and the imitation 'bar' in the
> corner of the drawing-room. Even the stupider vanities of the

modern world can have a kind of innocence, a sort of anchoring quality.

Priscilla dies when her marriage breaks up and she is deprived even of a few of these 'anchoring', 'steadying' possessions. Sage comments that

> In Iris Murdoch's world it is spiritual arrogance of the most dangerous kind to imagine you can become cultureless; she is not much troubled by the snobbish imperative of placing the quality of one kind of life over another, but she refuses to imagine a life that is 'free' of cultural patterns.[12]

The author that Dipple intuits behind the books is in some respects a vindictive moralist. Sage, on the other hand, finds her cheerful, complaisant and worldly. Each of these critics seems to have understood one half of Murdoch's genius, which is (roughly) to be an idealist-without-illusions. Dipple sees only the moral passion and idealism, Sage chiefly the absence of illusion and the moral scepticism. It is the combination of the two that gives Murdoch her brilliant and essentially tolerant double focus. Becoming good may very well involve a slow 'jettisoning of imagery' and a breaking of patterns. When others perform these acts of iconoclasm for us, or when we perform them ourselves too fast, the breakage can be malign. It depends on who you are; and how situated.

An Accidental Man (1971) is a marvellous book in its relaxed mediation between these stances. It resembles Henry James' *The Awkward Age* in the dryness of its irony about its strange and 'awful' crew. The only character in the book incapable of spite is the dog Pyrrhus, often-abandoned and re-named by new owners. The little scene in which Pyrrhus watches the lovers Charlotte and Mitzi row, and ponders anger as a disease of the human race is a small triumph, moving, funny and true. Dryness of course need not exclude compassion. The dreadful Austin, the accidental man of the title, is, as one of the choric party voices puts it at the end, 'like all of us, only more so'. Yet in case this makes us feel too comfortable, a second voice adds, with a double-edged complacency that cheerfully mocks our own, 'Everybody is justified somehow.' The narrator can be urbane, like her characters. Austin and his brother Matthew are dimly echoed by

Charlotte and her sister Clara. Both sets of siblings are deeply dependent on life-myths which feed and require obsessive reciprocal feelings of guilt, hostility, pity and jealous rivalry, including sexual rivalry. Austin, associated like so many men in her novels of the 1970s with Peter Pan, the 'sinister boy', on account of his immature spirituality, is a person who positively invites his own bad luck. Failure has become so much his secret consolation he resembles a vampire. Austin is a clown, a comic awful figure, and a fool. He is surrounded by a succession of demonic 'accidental' figures – Norman Monkley the incompetent blackmailer, the horrible child Henrietta Sayce who finally falls off some scaffolding and breaks her skull. There is a pervasive *Schadenfreude* in the book, a malicious delight as typical of Murdoch's world as it was of Dostoevski's. In *Crime and Punishment* Dostoevski defined this special joy in the misfortunes of others or in their deaths when he wrote after Marmeladov's accident of 'that strange inner feeling of satisfaction that may always be observed in the course of a sudden accident even in those who are closest to the victim and from which no loving man is exempt, however sincere his sympathy and compassion'.

The author cannot remain wholly outside such a system of feeling. Two characters die in circumstances that mock their and our childish desire for transcendance. The dying Alison is misheard when calling for her lawyer and has to endure a reading from the Psalms. 'The words were at home in this scene. They had been here before'(48). And the harrassed Dorina on the point of death at last realises that what she had dimly recalled as spiritual advice – '*Il faut toujours plier les genoux*' – was actually skiing instruction.

Austin is the infectious centre of this cruel pleasure, this ghoulish pity and fear. He is the most deluded and unfree, but his story is circumscribed by many others, which radiate outwards and give the illusion of a marvellous depth of field. There are chains of lovers, whose voices are overheard only through a series of letters. The letters, like the anonymous party voices, wittily punctuate the narrative. Schoolboy Patrick loves and pursues Ralph Odmore, who imagines he loves Ann Colindale, who is certain she loves Richard Pargeter, who currently dallies with Karen Arbuthnot, who loves and pursues Sebastian Odmore, who pines for Gracie Tisbourne. Gracie loves and is loved by Ludwig Leferrier, and this affair is close to the book's centre. In every other case the more dedicated lover uses the same successful gambit to attract his or her beloved – he or she feigns interest in a third party. This comedy is Bergsonian – we laugh because the characters are exhibiting, in a form carefully exaggerated for artistic purposes, their recognisable unfreedom, and obeying Proust's law that only the inaccessible love-object attracts.

The comedy of the action is at odds with the idea-play, which meditates the theme of the Good Samaritan and of not passing by on the other side. Matthew as a diplomat in Moscow witnessed a passer-by coolly joining some protesters and thus condemning himself in an instant to certain State persecution. Garth in New York stood by and watched a street murder and later tries vainly, comically to solace the dispossessed Charlotte. Ludwig, usually taken by American critics as the central character since he is American, is by-passing an issue of conscience in avoiding return to the U.S.A. to be tried for refusal to fight in Vietnam. Later, in a mood of despair over the breaking of his engagement, he passes by and thus terrifies the tormented and needy Dorina, who is reading the world entirely in terms of her own guilt-feelings and on the way to her needless 'accidental' death, just as Ludwig sees entirely in terms of his own despair. 'To walk by was the expression of his despair. His spirit was too tired, too troubled'(347). This is compassionately done. Though there is a 'tremendous moral charge' it is also morality 'at its most refined and least dogmatic', as she noted of Shakespeare (Bigsby, 1982). The parable of the Good Samaritan enjoins kindness to the unlucky. But Austin is a character who positively *wills* his own bad luck, refusing help until the end when he is seen to move his (hysterically) paralysed hand. He blames his hand, as he blames his life, on his brother. And of course his brother, like everyone else, is not blameless. Each person has his own happiness, 'however unglittering and inglorious', a succeeding book proclaims (*SPLM* 16); each person also his own guilt. Austin's bad luck, in seeming an infectious moral flaw, cheerfully shows the limitations to any Samaritan altruism, as well as its necessity.

*

Speaking at Caen in 1978 Iris Murdoch noted her father's recoil from the world of Ulster 'black Protestantism' but also recorded her own puritanism, and her attraction to Sartre as a puritan thinker of sorts. The different anti-art scepticism and puritanism of such diverse thinkers as Plato, Kant and Freud have long preoccupied her. Indeed any thinker who intelligently questions the role of art interests her. Her puritanism is not – in any obvious or simple sense – sexual. The saintliest of her characters, the Christ-like Tallis of *A Fairly Honourable Defeat*, is shown justly disappointed when Peter interrupts an 'interesting' sexual fantasy he is having; and Will's full-blooded sexuality in *Bruno's Dream* is a force making for happiness. The word 'puritan' will nonetheless echo throughout this study.

It is clearly no accident that she named that character whom she has termed the 'unconscious' of the wicked Mischa Fox, *Calvin* Blick; and she has remarked that 'Puritanism and romanticism are natural partners and we are still living with their partnership' (*SG* 81). Both puritans and romantics are marked by humourless impatience at the world's ordinary amoral diversity and wish to escape from or purge it in the direction of some simplified, purer 'Original', or some form of otherworldly release. Both puritans and romantics are other-worldly. The temptation to 'sum up a character, to round off a situation' (sbr) or to assume that 'one has got individuals and situations "taped" ' (vc), which she has stigmatised as formal temptations in art, are obviously moral temptations too. The temptations to moralise and to coerce the world are uncomfortably close, if not identical.

This may be why the villains of Murdoch's work, in so far as it admits of such, are frequently puritans or false-ascetics who, however much they be loved by the author, often take the greatest punishment from the plot, while the pagan hedonists get off most lightly. In the sheer delight it affords her work indeed asserts the pleasure principle again and again, and the novels seemed to her, in interview with Haffenden (1983), to be *'shining* with happiness . . . works of art make you happy . . . . Even *King Lear* makes you happy.' To Haffenden Murdoch concurred with a definition of art as *'pure* pleasure'.

Indeed I would suggest that, if critics have not always responded as enthusiastically to Murdoch's work as Elizabeth Dipple, this is quite as much because they are puritanically embarrassed at the feast of pleasure she affords, as that they are, as Dipple supposed, selfishly frightened at Murdoch's unremitting righteousness. What a gallery of happy and innocent sensualists there are in her novels! Danby in *Bruno's Dream* might stand in for the breed in general, a man who, if

the world were ending would at once cheer up if offered a
gin and French, and a man who even enjoyed every moment
of the *war*. Danby comes out of the book better than his
puritan foil and brother-in-law Miles, but it should also be
said that Murdoch clearly shows us the difference between
them without reaching for any crudely moralised distinctions.
Each has his own happiness, however unglittering, and however
inglorious. It is the fact of their difference that engages and
imaginatively uses her, like the factual difference in moral
temperament between the innocent, feckless worldling Dora in
The Bell, and her insensitive ascetic husband Paul; or between
Simon in *A Fairly Honourable Defeat* and his lover Axel – another
pagan innocent living with a less than fully responsive puritan.

Each of these character's natures earns its proper reproach
from the plot itself; each is cherished and chastised. In Murdoch's
own mediation between moral extremes hers might be said to be,
like Buddhism, a dynamic and cheerful philosophy of the Middle
Way. It is dynamic in that it insists on moral effort, but a
mediation in that anything but a temperate self-denial turns out
to reinforce what you already are. In her essay 'T. S. Eliot as a
Moralist', she described Eliot as an 'anti-puritan puritan', a
person who, while objecting to the vulgar Calvinism of the
Reformation, nonetheless urged some fastidious discriminations
of his own. I think the phrase 'anti-puritan puritan' admirably
fits her too. It is a symptom of the difficulty of thinking about
this area in her work that critics, who can be more royalist than
the king, have sometimes drawn a figure who, however apt the
role of scourge of egoism might be in a zealot, is insufferable as
an artist. The fact that art is a realm of moral compromise is a
matter of regret to Murdoch, as *The Fire and the Sun* shows; but
is also a fact, as well as a theme in itself.

Iris Murdoch is, I think, in some sense both the most other-
worldly *and* the most worldly of our novelists. The war between
the best and the second-best fills her characters, her idea-play,
and provides her narrative locomotion. Speaking at Caen of
women's liberation she discussed the extent to which women have
become 'more liberated . . . more *ordinary*'. That apotheosis of
ordinariness is itself typical of the emancipations her work is in
quest of. And if she could be said to urge any position in the old
quarrel between worldliness and other-worldliness it might be
Arthur Fisch's counsel to the outsider Hilary Burde in *A Word*

Child, 'the spiritual urge is mad unless it's embodied in some ordinary way of life'(88).

*

In a splendid section of *The Uses of Division* John Bayley expounds the Russian critic Shestov. Shestov thought that great writers are, however much they protest the contrary, solipsists, and that the real virtues of their work are different from what they are usually taken to be. In the nineteenth century novel this solipsism affects the way art faces its chief dilemma, that of serving the eschatological functions of which religion is no longer capable. It must 'search for and reveal salvation while showing that no such thing existed'. 'Tolstoi searched endlessly for the good and identified it with God', Bayley paraphrases Shestov, 'but what his characters want and strive for is . . . contentment and assurance, even at the cost of hypocrisy'.[13]

I shall pursue this further in discussing *The Nice and the Good* in Chapter 6. In that novel, Kate Gray has a patrician and socially useful assurance, a 'golden life-giving egoism and rich self-satisfaction'(22) which is an active force for good in the world. It might be said that in Iris Murdoch's world, just as in Shestov's, morality appears not merely as a vengeful Fury haunting the characters, though they are certainly sufficiently haunted, but as a potent ambiguity. Contentment too plays an equivocal role, since it can defend against profitless despair, but also feed a less than perfect self-delight. In *The Sea, The Sea* Charles Arrowby significantly ascribes such an ambiguous content to Shakespeare himself. 'There may be no saints, but there is at least one proof that the light of self-satisfaction can illuminate the world'(482).

The ambiguity could be examined further by comparing her fine work of moral philosophy *The Sovereignty of Good* with the novels. In that work Murdoch spoke eloquently for the unconsoled love of Good, and emerged as a puritan moralist in a tradition sanctioned by Plato, arguing for unselfing, and for the difficult task of ascesis. The austere project of the book is to rescue a religious picture of man from the collapse of dogma, to attack all forms of consolation, romanticism and self-consciousness, and to study the necessary degeneration of Good in morals.

'All is vanity' is the beginning and the end of ethics. The only genuine way is to be good 'for nothing' in the midst of a scene where every natural thing, including one's own mind, is subject to chance, that is to necessity.   (71)

She has also, however, insisted on the pursuit of happiness. In one 1982 Gifford lecture she discussed happiness as a moral duty, and she has spoken often of the ways that the desire for happiness 'keeps people sane and freshens life', and insisted that 'one should plan one's life in order to be happy, and this involves decisions about work, and marriage and where you live, and cultivating your talents and so on. I think our sort of world here provides innumerable opportunities for happiness which sometimes, it seems to me, people don't take advantage of'[14]. The villains like Austin in *An Accidental Man* and George in *The Philosopher's Pupil* are always (unlike the positive demons Mischa and Julius) *worldly* failures and incompetents.

Moreover, if there are few writers who have written as high-minded a book as *The Sovereignty of Good*, there can be few writers who have attacked or tested the high-mindedness of their own characters – their uninhabited idealism – with greater ferocity or precision. 'Wasn't it *deliciously* high-minded?' asks the Satanic Julius (*FHD* 266) of the lovers' loftily self-deluded antics, and we are chilled by his wicked irony because we are obliged to take its grim and comic point. It is Rupert, the most primly high-minded of all the characters in *A Fairly Honourable Defeat*, who is destroyed by the plot. She published this novel and the book of moral philosophy in the same year, and their ironic relation seems intentional. It is partly that 'Any man, even the greatest, can be destroyed in a moment and has no refuge; any philosophy that denies this is a lie'(*BP* 19), and that she is showing the defencelessness of all philosophy against mischance: any attempt to incarnate the Good must be vain. Nonetheless if there is something apt about the destruction of the high-minded Rupert, there is a further level of irony that Julius would surely have savoured in the swiftness with which critics have explained that Rupert really deserved to die because he was prim.

This meting out of punishment to the puritan characters is comic unless it involves disaster – as with Harriet in *The Sacred and Profane Love Machine*, who is destroyed partly because of her need 'to play a good, even an absurdly good part'(213), or Cato in *Henry and Cato*, accused by Beautiful Joe similarly of being too unworldly. Both *The Bell* and *The Unicorn* concern communities in which, as Dipple put it, the characters are attempting to jettison all the imagery of the culture and face the ensuing blackness. In each case, though the pagan innocents in the story certainly suffer, the cruellest suffering accrues to the murderously high-minded votaries of the Good itself – Hannah in *The Unicorn*, Michael in *The Bell*, who seem convicted of moral hubris or of being spiritually on the make.

The two sermons of *The Bell* debate whether it is more proper to live by James' maxim 'Be ye therefore perfect' or Michael's more tolerant 'Be ye therefore slightly improved'. The first posture is shown to be uninhabitable, and yet morality cannot survive without it: the need for the form of the Good is a moral need, not a logical need. The second posture is also inadequate. This debate, which I think funds all that she has written as an unresolvable ambiguity, is conducted in 'Art and Eros' where Plato is absolutist but Socrates argues that truth 'must include, must *embrace* the idea of the second-best'. For Socrates 'our thought will be incomplete and all our art tainted with selfishness. This doesn't mean there is no difference between good and bad in what we achieve and it doesn't mean not trying. It means trying in a humble modest and truthful spirit.' Art, for Socrates, is the realm of the second best *par excellence*. Our duty, says the Abbess in *The Bell*, is 'not necessarily to seek the highest regardless of the realities of our spiritual life'(81). In *The Sovereignty of Good* (62) Murdoch suggests that the idea of love arises necessarily in the attempt to mediate between best and second-best.

The plots have always made especially cruel fun of those puritans who wish to change themselves fast, or try in other ways to detach themselves from reality, living beyond their moral income. Three different pseudo-ascetic narrators all detach themselves from their various *milieux*, becoming self-encaged in a hermetic routine like Hilary in *A Word Child*, retreating ludicrously to 'repent of a life of egoism', like Charles in *The Sea, The Sea*, or cocooning themselves in censorious and self-serving moral rectitude, like Bradley in *The Black Prince*. The word 'puritan' is used of Bradley some dozen times. In each case a pandemonium supervenes, an irruption of the forces of low Eros out of which they had attempted a premature levitation. The idea-play of her novels urges unselfing and moral ascesis. The always rapid and compressed plots, rarely taking more than a month, constitute a set of warnings about the dangers of moral over-reaching, or of a spirituality inadequately rooted in the deep structure of the personality and in some ordinary customary way of life in the world. What John Bayley wittily termed the 'higher self-seeking' is castigated.[15]

A. S. Byatt usefully drew attention in *Degrees of Freedom* to Murdoch's debt to Simone Weil. Weil urged morality as an almost impossible counter-gravitational striving against a sinfulness so natural and irresistable it is compared to gravity itself. Weil was, in the English title of her famous book, 'Against Gravity' in the sense that she was against sin.

Weil was also, however, author of *The Need for Roots*, which Murdoch has called 'one of the very few profound and original political treatises of our time' (kv), a book which has at its heart the view that 'loss of the past, whether it be collectively or individually, is the supreme human tragedy'.[16] Weil was always aware that the attempt to change oneself too fast – or to be changed – acts as a violent deracination which could radically demoralise. She often wrote of the corruptions that can attend the act which is 'above one's natural level' – '*forçant son talent*' – and Murdoch herself paraphrased this Weilism: 'It is of no avail to act above one's natural level' – for example, 'If we give more than we find natural and easy we may hate the recipient' (kv). Drawing too on this second, sceptical aspect of Weil's genius Murdoch might be said to be 'against gravity' in a second sense, that she is antipathetic to a solemn and self-dramatising moral intensity and aware of how often sin and solemnity are secret bedfellows. The idle and selfish Gracie in *An Accidental Man* is never more sympathetic than when she finally explains to Ludwig her shy and intensely English dislike of 'moral fuss' (360); perhaps it is this quality which makes the novel so hard for American critics to write persuasively about.

This aspect of Murdoch's indebtedness to Weil and indeed to common sense has been neglected, but is just as important, or arguably more so, since it is the means by which she accommodates the individual case, escapes from allegory, and complicates any general rule. Thus in *Henry and Cato* Henry finds that his renunciation of his inheritance was not intrinsically wrong but was 'above my level. That's been my mistake all along, mistaking my moral level' (378). The moment echoes another in a novel written two decades earlier, when Michael in *The Bell*, upset that he may have distressed young Toby by kissing him, stages a scene of apology which he then comes to see has only entangled them further.

> The trouble was . . . that he had performed the action which belonged by right to a better person; and yet, too, by an austere paradox, a better person would not have been in the situation that required that action. It would have been possible to conduct the meeting with Toby in an unemotional way which left the matter completely closed; it was only not possible for Michael . . . . What he had failed to do was accurately to estimate his own resources, his own spiritual level.   (201)

The usually painful discovery of moral level is not infrequently a part of the education of the agents in her books. It is never a process that is free from paradox. As so many of her titles make clear, Murdoch's is essentially a dualistic imagination, and she repeatedly makes out of the idea of two worlds a special poetry whose resonances are complex. If many of the plots – like that of *A Word Child* or *Under the Net* – oblige the puritan dreamer to rejoin the ordinary world, the movement can be more complicated. In *An Accidental Man* the more worldly Mavis replaces her fey sister Dorina as minister to Austin and finds that this promotion or demotion is accompanied by the same supernatural manifestations that had formerly worried only Dorina. In the same book Garth and Ludwig exchange places as fiancés of Gracie, who clearly represents the pleasure-principle itself, and the half-worldly would-be contemplative Matthew makes an ambiguous escape in pursuit both of Ludwig and of moral perfection. In *Nuns and Soldiers*, whose title enacts this dualism, the acquisitive Gertrude hopes to go through life with the ex-nun Anne Cavidge, 'like Kim and the lama' (105), the very image of the mutual usefulness of a worldly cunning and an other-worldly wisdom. But these two poetries separate out.

The point that I am trying to make here is that Murdoch's moral passion, which can be felt in all that she has written, does not emerge in her fiction in a simple-minded way. She is no more simply hostile to pleasure than was Plato, who thought an enlightened hedonism might suit the majority. A final characteristic example of ambiguity might be taken from *The Philosopher's Pupil*, where the philosopher Rozanov is absolutist in ways she has disavowed (Haffenden, 1983). The war between best and second-best is present in his relations with his mad, demonic, third-rate pupil George, who finally tries to murder him to avenge a perfectionism by which he feels judged and rejected. To the question, 'What do you fear most?' Rozanov answers 'To find out that morality is unreal . . . not just an ambiguity with which one lives – but that it is nothing, a fake, absolutely unreal', a point of view that Murdoch, with provisos, has echoed (Haffenden, 1983). Of George's Alyosha-like brother Tom, the sympathetic innocent of the book, the narrator comments

> Thus Tom enlarged his ego or (according to one's point of view) broke its barriers so as to unite himself with another in joint proprietorship of the world: a movement of salvation which for him was easy, for others (George for instance) was hard.   (121)

That typical note of equivocation, which does not diminish the distance between Tom and the unspeakable George, but which certainly vexes the attempt to account for it in too simply moral a manner, is a good one on which to end the chapter.

4   Eros in *A Severed Head* and *Bruno's Dream*

One problem in discussing Murdoch's work is that the truths they meditate turn out often to be as simple as 'Nobody's perfect' and 'Handsome is as handsome does'. That such dull commonplaces can radiate as much light as apparent profundities is her point. It has proved difficult to relate her 'ordinariness' and her Platonism.

At Caen (1978) she termed her philosophy a 'moral psychology', presumably because it is a complex mass of living insight into what being human is like, rather than a simple counter-structure. The paradox for the critic is that as she moves towards a surer sense of her philosophical position, the novels become less, not more rigid in structure. Neoplatonic themes, often taken from painting, can be found in her work even at the start, and abound in the novels of the 1960s and 1970s. Lorna Sage has shown the echo of Titian's *Sacred and Profane Love* both in Rosa and Mischa's last tableau in *The Flight from the Enchanter* as well as in *The Sacred and Profane Love Machine*;[1] Apollo and Marsyas, Diana and Actaeon figure elsewhere. But the shape of her career is towards a use of myth that is consciously disposable and provisional, subordinated to the moral psychology of the characters. She becomes less absolute, more dialectical and playful, patient, comprehensive and open. After 1971 the novels do without chapters and increase, one by one, in length.

I want in this chapter to attempt a description of her philosophy as it affects her fiction. Like Hans-Georg Gadamer in his recent study of Plato, Murdoch takes the Platonic myths not as an ecstasy that transports us to another world, but as an ironic counter-image of the process by which we attain a more accurate perception of this one.[2] In a sense there is nothing new here. Since the Romantic revival, which must in part be seen as a revival of Platonic thought, two opposed strains might be elucidated, best crystallised in Pater's 1866 attack on Coleridge's 'lust for the

Absolute'. Pater chose a more relaxed, sceptical position and later argued, against the readiness of Coleridge's remorseless idealism to coerce away human difference, for the habit of 'tentative thinking and suspended judgement'.[3] For such a liberal Platonism the novel has always been an appropriate form. Julia Kristeva has noted the resemblance between Socratic dialogue and the ambivalent word of the novel, and Bakhtin too saw how the dialogues are characterised by opposition to any official monologism claiming to possess ready-made truth; and championed the traditional novel's 'polyphony'. The novel became, as D. H. Lawrence was to proclaim, mercifully incapable of the Absolute; 'a sort of Platonic ideal of the anti-Platonic Heraclitean spirit'.[4] Or as Iris Murdoch has put this, the novel is 'the most imperfect of all the great art-forms'.[5] She has always rejected the classic Neoplatonic stance of believing that art is in direct contact with the Forms. 'I cannot accept these 'Ideas' even as a metaphor of how the artist works' (Magee, 1978).

Moral terms, for her, are concrete universals, collections of their material instances. The sole exception is the Good itself, which acts both as an inexhaustible fund 'elsewhere' from which we draw energy, and also as a quality here which we dimly and always incompletely intuit in good art and good neighbours. Plato's *Timaeus* is crucial to her because its cosmogony suggests that Good participates, but inconclusively and incompletely, in reality, very much as 'order' participates incompletely in art. The possession of an intuition of the wholeness of experience, irradiating and clarifying both the perception of particulars in life and the representation of particulars in art, marks both the great artist and the good man. Until we grasp the proximate moral unity of the world, its inherent diversity escapes us too.[6]

The celebration of human and natural diversity is one aim in the novel, and the traditional novel has always been much closer to Romanticism than conventional wisdom allows. Nineteenth-century fiction, as John Bayley has shown, is a market-place in which a number of different Romanticisms bargain and quarrel, and in displaying this the novelist may 'bring the planes of reality and fantasy into one vision of life'.[7] To enter into alien life, and to unify it once you are there, are from one point of view complementary projects; but there is also a necessary tension between them. Both Murdoch and Bayley have stressed the poet's ability to understand and express all nature as it were from the inside, and argued against the devitalisation that this tradition undergoes as it develops into modernism, with its shift of emphasis onto the 'abstracting and integrative drive of the single self-conscious vision'.[8]

In this sense Murdoch is a traditional novelist, which is not of course to say that she cannot be boldly innovative whenever it suits her purpose; the innovations unassertively serve the work, rather than any prophetic impulses. Such a modesty means that her originality can escape notice, and not the least original aspect of her genius is the extraordinary marriage between Freud and Plato that she has effected, between a mechanical model of the psyche and a moral one, penetrating through her plots into the substance of the books. She has read Freud extensively and considers him a very great and an exciting thinker. A number of her plots turn on Oedipal conflict. In *The Sovereignty of Good* Freud is repeatedly invoked to underwrite the view that human beings are motored by an energy that is both highly personal and individual, and yet at the same time very powerful and not easily understood by its owner. Freud shows us that we are dark to ourselves, moved by passions and obsessions we are scarcely aware of, powered by mechanical energy of an egocentric kind. Murdoch's quarrel with Freud comes, one might say, from the fact that he has given us so authoritative an account of life in the Cave, but has little to say about life in the Sun. Murdoch identifies the fire, by whose light and heat the moral pilgrim may become mesmerised, with the ego. As a Victorian materialist Freud has an inadequate view of human perfectibility based on hostility to religion. In *The Fire and the Sun* Murdoch nonetheless also shows that Freud's tripartite division of the soul came from Plato and that, as Freud acknowledged, 'The enlarged sexuality of psychoanalysis coincides with the Eros of the divine Plato' (*FS* 37). Murdoch's attitude to Freud combines great respect with an interest in neutralising certain aspects of our inheritance from him, through imaginative appropriation.[9] One might reductively say that the 'myth' in her books often comes out of Freud, but the expansion away from it out of Plato. In both processes 'Eros' plays a major role. In her 1982 Gifford lectures 'Eros' figured as a primary moral category.

*

The single most notable feature of Murdoch plots is that they so frequently concern an action that recurs. A stylised repeating plot is the signature of the novel's structure, just as the chapter which starts with a bizarre *fait accompli* which it 'freezes' while an explanatory account of how the characters reached this new impasse typifies the local texture of her narrations. Both emphasise unfreedom, and are based on a simple observation: human beings repeat themselves irrationally. Even the supposedly 'cultivated' do. In *The Bell* Nick destroyed Michael's career fourteen years before the story begins and nearly destroys his vocation again. In *The Unicorn* the repeating plot is Gothicised into a fairy-tale cycle of suffering over seven-year epochs. In *An Accidental Man* Austin conceives that his brother Matthew was complicit in the death of his first wife, which he may ambiguously have been. The story goes on to concern Matthew's ambiguous complicity in the death of Austin's second wife. In a sense both wives are sacrificed to the rivalry between the brothers, and are victims of war, of which we are told that truth itself is always the first casualty. I shall come to some other repeating plots shortly. For Murdoch's characters, unlike Joyce's, history is a nightmare to which they are unable fully to awake, since the unenlightened personality itself is a blind realm of repetition and substitution.

Repetition and substitution are features of the machine, and the image of spirit caught within the mechanical has been resonant since the Romantic Revival. To many Romantics the mechanical is – as for Lawrence – something that culture is wickedly perpetrating on us, and associated with the higher, more cerebral reaches of the spirit. For Murdoch the truth is opposite. The machine is inside us and a feature of the least conscious part of ourselves. For her the psyche is

a historically determined individual relentlessly looking after itself. In some ways it resembles a machine; in order to operate it needs sources of energy and it is predisposed to certain patterns of activity. The area of its vaunted freedom of choice is not usually very great. One of its main pastimes is day-dreaming. It is reluctant to face unpleasant realities. Its consciousness is not normally a transparent glass through which it views the world, but a cloud of more or less fantastic reverie designed to protect the psyche from pain. It constantly seeks consolation, either through imagined inflation of self or through fictions of a theological nature. Even its loving is more often than not an assertion of self. I think we can probably recognise ourselves in this rather depressing picture. (*SG* 79)

As for Weil, the moral task is not to discern the 'facts' of the case before coming to a judgement, but to learn to perceive the situation as it is, trying to expel 'obsession, prejudice, envy, anxiety, ignorance, greed, neurosis' (*FS* 47) which obscure true vision. Virtue in the artist and the good man is the product of a selfless attention to nature, something easy to name and hard to achieve. 'The essence of both [art and morality] is love. Love is the perception of individuals. Love is the extremely difficult realisation that something other than oneself is real. Love, and so art and morals, is the discovery of reality' (sg). She has described ordinary consciousness as conceiving itself as a 'freedom caught in a trap' (*SRR* 36), oscillating between the knowledge, derived from Freud and Marx, that our consciousness is partly determined and unfree, yet simultaneously and blithely hanging on to the voluntarist piety that we can jump out of our conditioning at any moment. In a memorable phrase, 'An unexamined sense of the strength of the machine is combined with the illusion of jumping out of it' (*SG* 42). Lorna Sage has well described the Murdoch plot as a 'plot against plot', a device for humiliating those who wish to contain experience or abstract it.[10] The characters' delusion that they are autonomous is held up as a mirror to us.

> Art comes from the deep soul where a great force lives, and this force is sex and love and desire – desire for power, desire for possession, desire for knowledge, desire for God – what makes us good or bad – and without this force there is no art and no science either and no – no man – without Eros man is a ghost. But with Eros he can be – either a demon or – Socrates.

Thus Plato in 'Art and Eros' described the Eros that drives human beings.

Citing Pascal Murdoch once wrote that 'the more spirit one has the more original men one discovers. Ordinary people do not notice the differences between men'(sbr). It seems to me illuminating to subjoin this with moments from various novels. At the end of *The Italian Girl*, a novel which repeats some themes from *A Severed Head*, Edmund comes to separate out Maria, the eponymous Italian girl, from the category of 'maid' which has formerly subsumed her, and the reader feels he has made a small move in the direction of perceiving the real. Before, she had belonged to that series of 'Giulias and Gemmas and Vittorias and Carlottas [which] moved and merged dream-like in my mind'(18). Now she has begun to be an individual and mysterious in her own right. Yet his lazy conflation of Italian girls which preceded this separation was affected by his sense of absolute domination by his recently dead mother Lydia. The Oedipus conflict is a subject of this as of so many other novels. Edmund has the odd sense that he has throughout his childhood had 'as it were, *two* mothers, my mother, and the Italian girl'(18). He conflates in his mind not merely the family servants but all those women who act as mother-surrogates to him, a point underlined by the heading to Chapter 13: 'Edmund runs to Mother.' His mother is dead. It is from the Italian girl he seeks maternal comfort. And when at the end he seeks, possibly with a Platonic ring once more, to 'live in the sun, to live in the open'(171) it is with this vector, as it were, of his profound Oedipal guilt that he is to attempt belatedly to grow up. His growth, in other words, is not some impossible 'liberation' into the real but a matter of his increasing his chances of learning to perceive and love 'original men' in exactly that area of his mind where the project is most vexed. It is an ambiguous ending and a morally realistic one.

The point is made with a beautiful clarity by Bradley in *The Black Prince* when explicating *Hamlet* to Julian. 'The unconscious delights in identifying people with each other. It has only a few characters to play with'(95). Bradley's remark, as I shall show, is double-edged, referring to *The Black Prince* as well as to the Ernest Jones reading of *Hamlet*. Both are 'family romances'. The unenlightened psyche, or unenlightened level within the psyche, coerces others because it sees them playing roles within an Oedipal romance whose terms were laid down in childhood. The effort to perceive others accurately depends on 'seeing' them aright where it is impossible to separate out the literal and metaphorical constituents of the word 'sight'. All her narrators suffer into a state which may conceivably augur slightly better for their chances of deepening their sense of the otherness and separateness of other people.

This makes for a different use of myth from that of the great Moderns. In a sense it is opposed. Modernism, being marked by hostility and disdain for ordinary consciousness and for history, conceives the artist as an aristocrat doomed to exile. It 'refuses to conceive of perfection in human terms' (sbr) and uses myth and symbol to redeem the horrors of contingency. Eliot's work, for example, is marked by hatred of the present, Joyce in *Ulysses* presents his Homeric correspondences as a comically mock-epic, mock-heroic means of exalting and demeaning his characters simultaneously. Woolf holds out a promise that the flux can be redeemed through symbol, art, and love. I think that Murdoch is closer to Woolf than Eliot, but argues for, and in the later work enacts, a greater patience with the flux in which we are to be immersed. The myth for her is Freudian, and the flux is there to contest it and help emancipate us from its power. (Of course symbols such as the bell and unicorn are the writer's as much as her characters'; in the next chapter I shall suggest how in being half-achieved they become the property of the characters too.)

Myth belongs to the characters, and this can be shown in the repeating plots of *The Sea, The Sea* and *A Word Child*. Both concern pasts which Gothically repeat themselves, to which the main characters are mechanically enslaved, and deserve to be seen, like all her plots, not simply as cases of Freudian repetition-compulsion, but as studies in Buddhist *karma* – called by James in *The Sea, The Sea* 'spiritual causality', and the doctrine that we pay for all we do, say and think, but not necessarily at once. We pay later, and even if we have already decided to 'reform'. Hilary Burde tries to redeem that moment twenty years before when his adultery with his friend Gunnar's wife Anne led to her death. This attempted redemption results in his falling in love with Gunnar's lovely, very silly second wife Kitty, and in her inadvertent death too. One paradox the book shows us is that Hilary's crime in the interim was not that he exonerated himself but rather that he puritanically made himself, like Lucifer, totally responsible. In claiming Anne's death so wholly for himself he dramatised his predicament, lost his self-respect, and refused change – refused any healing surrender to history.

In the sense that the remote enclosure is always the setting for romance, it might be said that the bad man in Murdoch's work carries the box-like world of romance around in his head. Hilary expresses his misery and anger at the beginning of *A Word Child* by pulling the telephone cord out of the wall, helping to make

his psychological isolation as real and physical in the middle of
Bayswater as Hannah's in the West of Ireland in *The Unicorn.*
Similarly Carel in *The Time of the Angels* uses his maid Pattie to
refuse entry to outsiders or contact on the telephone. 'We live in
a small personal world in which we remain enclosed – great art
is liberating' (Magee, 1978), Murdoch has suggested, contrasting
the bad man who uses up all the air and diminishes those he
encounters from the rare good man who creates a sense of space
around himself and makes his interlocutors feel safe and welcome
(Haffenden, 1983).

It is characteristic of Murdoch that her use of imagery can
have a very different resonance depending upon whether it is
mostly figurative or literal. The small enclosed personal world
resembles the Platonic Cave, the world of illusion, when it is
figurative: Isabel in *The Italian Girl* recalls Saint Theresa's
description of hell as a dark cupboard, an image which recurs
throughout the work until, in *The Philosopher's Pupil*, the bad
George is perceived as a 'madman in a cupboard' (181). Yet the
good characters, or those struggling to be good, literally live in
small stripped rooms like Bledyard's, void of aesthetic imagery,
colour, and consolation. The good man earns his title to such
confinement and lack of consolation, and can continue to radiate
a good will without territory or a personal world; the bad man
even when thus supported creates a self-regarding claustrophobia.
The question as to whether Hannah in *The Unicorn* or Michael
in *The Bell* earn their right to their spiritual isolation and aesthetic
denudation is a central one in those books. Bradley in *The Black
Prince* begins like many of her heroes in a small room overlooking
a brick wall, and ends in a prison cell overlooking a different
brick wall, but now experiencing an unprecedented sense of inner
space. Thus also Charles in *The Sea, The Sea* kidnaps and
incarcerates the woman he loved as a child, and around the hurt
of whose rejection of him he has constructed a life-myth which
warrants his cruelties to the women who have had the misfortune
to love him masochistically since. The inner room, box-like and
windowless, in which he holds her, is in one sense an exteriorisation
of his own mind, from which he has never released her. It recalls
in its earliest manifestation the dark, viewless, central box-like
section of Mischa Fox's Kensington palazzo, a figure for the
unconscious, whose central job it is to resist history. 'One's deep
mind is indifferent to time' says Hilary (*WC* 267). 'The deeper

parts of the mind have so little sense of time', comments Charles. (*SS* 57)

Kierkegaard pointed out in his book *Repetition* that repetition in life always implies change and difference and forces us to understand that we do not inhabit the realm of the aesthetic.[11] This is the lesson Murdoch's characters are obliged to begin to learn. The unregenerate psyche is most brilliantly described by the Satanic Julius in *A Fairly Honourable Defeat*. Like all her demons he is given the best tunes. For humans, says Julius, 'Anyone will do to play the roles. They never really see each other at all . . . . Human beings are essentially finders of substitutes'(233). This view of the moral agent as blind puppet of his own needs is shown to be as close to the truth as the cosy pieties by which the unreconstructed liberal humanists live.

If the deep or unconscious mind, as Murdoch develops this, is mechanical, unenlightened, and the realm of myth and symbol, then it is the unconscious which reads life as romance. The unconscious aspires to a box-like 'spatial form', enclosing or stopping historical time, freezing contingency. To readers of Freud and Jung this is not news of course. But Murdoch makes her own special use of it. A myth, as Levi-Strauss noted, is a machine for the suppression of time.[12] You can service it with any amount of disparate material or information, but it is encoded only to deliver the same timeless, neurotic answer. Myth opposes particularity, history and contingency because it digests all of them, bullying the plural into the singular. It is a vehicle of monism of a premature and shallow kind. Both growing up and paying attention for Murdoch are matters of struggling to perceive the world with less preconception, and to understand the provisionality of life-myths which lead us to repeat roles in emotional systems whose patterns are laid down early.

Northrop Frye has written of the ways in which romance may receive a comic resolution when there is a transfer of energy and affection at the end from the Oedipal incestuous family situation outwards to outsiders. The close-knit family group is destroyed by its tensions and jealousies, and the group dispersed.[13] This is a familiar pattern in Murdoch. The quasi-incestuous competition of members of one family for a single beloved is ubiquitous, as is the dispersal of community. The pattern of two siblings involved with a single outsider recurs in *Under the Net, The Flight from the Enchanter, A Severed Head, Bruno's Dream, A Fairly Honourable Defeat,*

An Accidental Man, The Time of the Angels. Mother–daughter competition figures in *An Unofficial Rose, The Black Prince,* father–daughter incest, that venerable literary theme,[14] occurs in *The Time of the Angels,* brother–sister in *A Severed Head, The Bell* and *The Red and the Green.*

*

The movement towards the saving of Eros, the clarification of passion or education of desire, is one in which art itself plays an ambiguous role. Repetition must belong to the artist as well as the characters he creates. Literary realism, David Lodge has shown, is always on guard against metaphoric substitution,[15] and it is to a world free from such substitution that the characters aspire, seeing everything and everybody as does Hugo, as *sui generis.* They, like us, are simultaneously victims of an unconscious which is a secret formalist, trying to create solipsistic and self-enclosed fiction out of all it surveys. Without the artist's unconscious, as Murdoch has increasingly seen, there is however no art.

> Art is a battle with obsessive unconscious forces and in this sense Plato was right to say that the enemy was the unconscious mind, although of course the unconscious mind is also the source of art and the paradox is that if there are no unconscious forces there is no art (an).

The author, like his characters, has to learn to clarify his enslavement to the unconscious, and I think that Murdoch has increasingly seen art as exemplary because of its engagement with this ambiguous process, because of its necessary, potentially devilish pact with the low Eros it must struggle and play with. If nineteenth-century realism depended on the assumption that 'reason' was naturally supreme, then some use of 'romance' – the form closest to the unconscious and low Eros – is now likely to be sought out by writers, since such rationalist confidence is no longer available to us.

Like Socrates, who mentions in *Symposium* (178b) that love is the *only* thing he understands, Eros has always been Iris Murdoch's topic.[16] She has spoken of Eros as the 'ambiguous spiritual mediator and moving spirit of mankind'(*FS* 34) which is, in its higher manifestations – desire for knowledge, desire for God –

the force that can release the prisoners from the Cave; but in its lower – desire for power and possession – precisely the mechanical repetitive force which binds them there in the first place. It is not a matter of any refusal of the body, as I suggested in the previous chapter, but that, like Plato, Murdoch gives to sexual love and transformed sexual energy a central place in her thinking. Falling in love plays an ambiguous role in this process. I know of no other writer who has evoked its symptoms, pathology and, in a sense, its phenomenology – the changes it induces in conscious-ness – with such brilliance. 'Love has fewer preconceptions than sex, for the latter is a highly conservative instinct operating in terms of stock responses. We desire in obedience to the fixed patterns of our sexual imagination, but we fall in love when we are really seeing another person.'[17]

F. M. Cornford pointed out how diametrically opposed are the Freudian and Platonic Eroses. To Freud sublimation, whereby the love energy becomes transmuted, is dominated by the concept of evolution, so that the upward effort towards the higher manifestations of consciousness can be unmasked as a disguised version of the rude and primitive instincts of our animal ancestry. To Plato this energy has an originally 'high' source and sublima-tion is conceived of as a home-coming, rather than an aberrant form of exile.[18] Murdoch combines the different pessimism of both thinkers with a high valuation of the idea of a spiritualised sexuality, and the unconditional love which is its ultimate if unreachable goal. Her work is on increasingly good terms with religion.

The religion in question is not orthodox Christianity, and Plato is partly important here for this reason. One of the things that emerged, for this observer, from her 1982 Gifford lectures, was how *contemporary* a figure Plato is for her. Just as in *The Fire and the Sun* she moved between explication and speaking through him herself, so here she found him an acute commentator on such issues as doubt about the empirical self, and about the ontological and moral ambiguity of art. Plato's interest in the relations between iconoclasm, demythologisation and morality took on a special force since Plato, like ourselves, inhabited an epoch in which religion was being demythologised, and in which the noble lies by which man lives had become problematic. The present age returns us to a world-picture not unlike that of Plato: a world with no eschatological guarantees. Religion, in Murdoch's view, is a recent invention. Spirituality and nihilism alike are ancient. It is to something like a Buddhist world-picture – in a sense a practical application of Plato's mysticism – that we now return.

That is to say, Buddhism as it actually is, a world-transforming belief, and not as it is supposed in the West, a world-fleeing one. 'Buddhism is not at all an other-worldly religion, it's absolutely this-worldly, here and now: this is where it's all happening and there isn't anywhere else' (Haffenden, 1983). What awaits the moral pilgrim for Murdoch is not some attenuated elsewhere, but 'here' differently and freshly perceived. The paradox of her own use of Plato's 'Great Allegory' of the Cave and the Sun is that her protagonists have to give up the temptation to allegorise and must forego the pleasures of 'interpretation'. Jake knew the truth about the relations between himself, Hugo and the Quentin sisters, but had to learn to see no more than this. Charles in *The Sea, The Sea* discovers that he has been 'reading my own dream-text and not looking at reality'(499). In many of her books there is a peripheral character attempting to live by the unconditional faith and love by which such a sense of reality is vouchsafed. 'Could she live now by the ontological proof alone? Can love, in its last extremity, create its object?' Anne Cavidge asks herself in *Nuns and Soldiers*(62) once she has lost her religious belief. The question of what a wholly purified Eros might resemble travels throughout the novels, and debate about the Ontological Proof – 'Plato's main idea' (*FS* 34) – accompanies it, proclaimed by Max in *The Unicorn* as a mystery to which only the spiritual man can give himself, in secret; and mocked in *The Philosopher's Pupil* where Rozanov, who has been working on the proof, calls it 'like sending a letter to yourself'(192). One Gifford lecture was addressed to the question of whether the Ontological Proof might work, not for God, but for Good.

*

In *The Sea, The Sea* a number of characters are briefly mentioned from earlier novels, and we are told that Rosina, an actress in the present book, was 'unfortunately . . . never able to play Honor Klein'(73), a character from *A Severed Head*, which was made into a successful stage play. Murdoch is not, of course, delegating Rosina and Honor, or the books in which they figure, to different planes of reality. The small and teasing joke is not permitted the vain and gleeful expansion a more portentous or formalist writer – Nabokov or Fowles perhaps – might have given it. It is 'pure play', and local, asserting the reality of art as much as its provisionality.

From *Under the Net* onwards, with its rapidly changing and collapsing scenery, the idea of provisionality itself has had some special power for Murdoch. To purify Eros is to learn about the provisionality of myth. On the subject of provisionality Lorna Sage has written an excellent account, which connects the peculiar kind of illusion the novels are after, in which both the richness of detail and also its disposability are emphasised, to the moral quest they concern. That quest, Sage points out, involves 'in-built obsolescence, momentary illuminations (and prolific ones) which in their very nature demand to be discarded'.[19] 'About the soul we speak always in metaphors: metaphors which are best used briefly and then thrown away . . . ' is how the editor Loxias who is also Apollo discusses this in *The Black Prince*. It is precisely the hypothetical quality of fictional images, Sage argues, the fact that they are in their nature 'obsolescent, provisional, imperfect' that makes them, for a Platonist, so important. In the *Theatetus* Plato at one point dismisses an argument of his own on the grounds that what worked as an illusion of truth at a distance now that he is close makes no sense at all (208e), and at another replaces the image of the soul as a waxen block in our minds in favour of a picture of the mind as an aviary (197e). The dialogue form itself militates against false or monolithic concreteness, and in *Parmenides* and *Sophist* Plato dismantles earlier imagery to replace it with new imagery in *Timaeus* where, however, he warns the reader against looking for more than a 'likely story' (3.29). Murdoch's own work with its rapid supercession of one book by its successor, its throw-away imagery and migrating themes and motifs, feels in this sense Platonic and, since the Good itself is indefinable and cannot be inscribed, in pursuit of imperfection. In 1961 she referred to it as 'an investigation that never ends, rather than a means of resolving anything' (Barrows, 1961).

She has criticised Western or Christian art for its false concreteness since, in instinctively materialising God and the religious life, 'What should be a mediating agency becomes a non-stop barrier' (*FS* 70), an obstacle to the pursuit of the whole truth; and praised the deliberate incompleteness of Zen anti-art. 'Zen emphasises skill but favours throwaway products. Plato (*Laws* 956b) says that artefacts offered to the gods should be such as can be made in a single day' (*FS* 71).

Sage has drawn attention to the number of books or manuscripts that get torn up or remain uncompleted in her work, and related this to Murdoch's hostility to the literature of the 'metaphysical task' (*SRR* 30) – a hostility to the Moderns' scriptural pretensions to conceptual dominion. Sage relates this, too, to the fact that in any given novel 'the organising images and myths . . . are localised and acclimatised . . . , not allowed to form any grand over-arching scheme'.[20] This is partly true. What is striking, however, is that it is not simply books which get destroyed in her work. Austin disposes of his brother's china in *An Accidental Man*, and George smashes Roman glass in *The Philosopher's Pupil*. Moreover, both her saints and her demons are antipathetic to art but differently so. I have noted Hugo's antipathy to art's pretensions, and Bledyard's caveats. In *A Fairly Honourable Defeat* Julius convinces Morgan that the Turners in the Tate are amateurish and limited just after he has concluded a devilish pact with her; and in *Nuns and Soldiers* Tim's nightmare that the paintings in the National Gallery are dim and senseless comes true for him during a deep depression. These are very different cases, for all the Platonic ambivalence about art they can be induced to yield. For the bad man or the person afflicted by unhappiness, art does not matter much because nothing apart from himself matters at all; whereas Hugo devalues art because, for the good man, art is second-best and matters only to the extent that something else (religion, reality, morals, other people) matters more. The bad man evacuates meaning from art because the world is without sense, the good man because the sense of art depends upon and serves a larger sense outside it.

Such an open and sceptical stance is attractive but offers the critic special problems. Murdoch is surely right to warn that we have exaggerated the completeness even of great art – 'We don't wish to see how unfinished even great art may be' (*FS* 85) – and by implication to question the academic belief in the imperial public truth of the perfected canonical work, for ever levitating above history like an airship. On the other hand, as Sage has pointed out, this strong playfulness and incompleteness can merge into a failure to be exact or demanding, where the focus on a character is not sustained, or the sense of depth of field in a novel seems facilely achieved, and the psychological indeterminacies woolly.

*

A good author, however, might be defined by the way he earns his own good luck, and hits upon such formulae as can turn his weaknesses, as A. S. Byatt has put this, into formal strengths. I think that this happens in many of the novels of the 1970s, in which Murdoch's love of rapidly disposable pattern and of formal symmetry are tested by the outward expansion of the characters. It happens rather differently in *A Severed Head* (1961), the best of the Restoration comedies of manners that she was at that time writing. Here the mechanical substitutions of low Eros marry intimately with the idea-play, and are taken to their *reductio ad absurdum*. The familiar twentieth-century theme of the mandarin-educated-by-passion, which figures in *An Italian Girl* and (differently) *The Black Prince*, becomes high, painful comedy. Her treatment of the theme is very much her own. A Romantic like Lawrence finds in the education of the intelligence by the instincts an exciting note of authenticity, and ignores the fact that he is delivering his instinctual *frissons* in a cerebral manner. Here what we have is neither Lawrentian, nor like the high aesthetic drama Thomas Mann makes of it in *Death in Venice*, nor the nihilistic farce Nabokov might have made; Murdoch's skill is so to involve us in Martin Lynch-Gibbon's narration that his perplexities become ours. *A Severed Head* is inadvertently prophetic of what were to become the 'permissive' *moeurs* of the 1960s, and is finally interesting because of the ways *A Fairly Honourable Defeat*, one of her best books, refers to and comments on it.

Martin tells the story but alternative lines of perspective – in a sense alternative novels – are revealed by him inadvertently. They represent that larger world of other people's purposes and not of his own psyche, into which he is to be inducted, and by which immersion he is hurt and partly healed. He is an intelligent forty-one year old wine merchant with a frustrated interest in military history, which he reads and, a little, writes. He describes his state at the beginning as one of 'degenerate innocence'. The phrase is an apt one for many of her first-person narrators who are obliged, like Edmund at the end of *The Italian Girl*, to eat the apple (literally in his case) of experience to find a more durable simplicity. Martin has partly stayed in business because of his marriage. His fashionable extravagant wife Antonia is a distant relative of Virginia Woolf's, a tall actress-y beauty somewhat older than him and whom people early sometimes mistook for his mother. They occupy separate bedrooms. He also has a younger mistress, Georgie Hands, an economics lecturer at the London School of Economics, who loves him with so intelligent a restraint that he has put himself, with her, greatly at his ease. Antonia and Georgie are opposite in type and in their relations with him. Antonia, who is superbly drawn, is a bossy ageing society beauty, self-dramatising, frivolous, fascinated by powerful men (which Martin to her is not), full of a partly predatory good will and a person who uses her sexual charm, or her sexual *will* to extend her personal territory. Antonia takes Martin for granted, and Martin does the same with Georgie, who had an abortion at his request and whose desire to see New York he has out of cowardice frustrated. Antonia too is childless. He perceives Antonia as inside 'society' and Georgie as 'outside'; and, while there is some social truth here, he also keeps Georgie in a state of subservience that her own intelligence only partly serves to disguise. He plays father to Georgie, son to Antonia. The book is set in Knightsbridge, where Martin and Antonia live, Chelsea, Bloomsbury (Georgie's flat), Cambridge (Honor's house) and the Oxfordshire countryside (Martin's parents' old house where his brother Alexander now lives and sculpts). It is set therefore in the more supposedly 'civilised' *milieux* that Southern England offers. The word 'civilised' echoes through it like the Jamesian adjectives 'beautiful', 'perfect', 'splendid', 'charming'. It is partly a satire on the rationalist ethics of a Bloomsbury-descended liberalism, and is punctuated by unbearably comic *skandal* scenes, where the civilities are disrupted by the passions that underlie them – often when Antonia warm-heartedly tries to bring people closer. The book's 'expertise' on wines, incidentally, is deliberately fake. Although 'Lynch' is a Bordeaux name associated with clarets the wines themselves are named, as if to acknowledge authorial distance, after old roses.

The ancient comic device of the plot has Martin as fall-guy stumbling from one appalling revelation to another. Near the beginning Antonia, who has a sharp appetite for personal relations and a belief that all human beings 'should aspire towards and are within working distance of a perfect communion of souls', a belief which as she is beautiful tends to produce its own immediate pragmatic verification, announces to Martin that she is to leave him for her psycho-analyst Palmer Anderson. She wishes to include Martin in some way in the new relationship, a wish by which he feels neutered and deprived of power. She and the smooth Anderson are to have some 'civilised' understanding with him whereby, just as he feels he has never had to pay for Georgie's pain, so they will escape paying for their adultery. The message of the book is that there are, as Keats said, 'impossibilities in the world' – in the moral world – a message carefully angled to the theme of incest. Palmer, identified at one point with Dionysus, argues for a relaxation of the 'rules' – the social and moral conventions by which society operates – which his psychoanalytic 'religion' as Martin sees it entails. 'Only let your imagination encompass what your heart desires. Tell yourself nothing is impossible'(197) he tells Martin at one point, appearing to advocate a *ménage-à-trois*, and to suggest, like a Dostoevski villain, that 'All is permitted'. Like so many of Murdoch's devils, he is, however, given the best tunes in his description of the unenlightened psyche. 'The psyche is a strange thing . . . and it has its own mysterious methods of restoring a balance. It automatically seeks its own advantage, its consolation. It is almost entirely a matter of mechanics, and mechanical models are the best to understand it with'(31).

Thus he preaches to Martin the means by which their friendship may survive, but the homily neatly describes the rationale behind the manoeuvrings of the plot. He is a modern magician in his career of psychoanalyst just as his half-sister Honor Klein is a modern magician in her career as anthropologist. Both are experts in human similarity and difference, and in the forces that underlie ordinary 'civilised' conduct. An 'infernal pair', their forebears are the Luciewicz twins in *The Flight from the Enchanter*, the provocative Levkin brother and and sister in *The Italian Girl*, and all of these foreign siblings are finally expelled from the English Eden. Theirs is the dangerous wisdom lacking to the English innocents. Martin's surname suggests that he believes it is possible to lynch the gibbon in the human soul, to escape from the atavistic[21] and also that a Gibbonian rationalism may now be harder to sustain. As wine-merchant and military historian he is packaging or bottling the blood-lust that enables war, and the dupe of Dionysus.

In fact, though the revelation of Antonia's and Palmer's flirtation is devastating to Martin, the new relationship has partly an improvisatory quality. He lends it solidity by colluding in the masochistic role of 'virtuous' forgiving husband. Both Palmer and Antonia are struggling, as we later find out, with obsessive quasi-incestuous relationships which they have kept secret. It is one of the disadvantages of Murdoch's extraordinary skill at ambushing the reader's expectations that even most critics are too shell-shocked to go back and see how carefully she has prepared a psychological basis for her plot surprises. In this book the love-affairs between Antonia and her treacherous, charming brother-in-law Alexander on the one hand, and between Palmer and his half-sister Honor Klein on the other, have each so passionate an intensity, and are conducted with such strength of will, that they make the other relationships look unserious. On a second reading it is apparent how carefully elaborated the lines of force are throughout. Though Martin appears to us in the role of principal cuckold at the beginning, we are to infer that Antonia's pairing-off with Palmer has left two other people abandoned, jealous and suffering. Honor haunts Palmer's house white and *in extremis* with pain, and Martin is to come to see her and Palmer's love for one another as a 'dark love' of 'colossal dimensions'. Since Honor treasures a photograph of Palmer at the age of sixteen, and their mother went insane, it may have started early. Alexander and Antonia had fallen in love soon after her engagement to Martin. Of Alexander's sufferings when Antonia moves in with Palmer his, and Martin's, sister Rosemary says 'I've never seen him so shaken' and comically asks the wounded Martin to be kind and tactful to his brother. 'He suffered more than you did', Antonia finally tells Martin.

The Eros by which the characters are motivated mingles sexual passion and manoeuvring for power, and the brilliant, intricate, chilly plot bears out Palmer's assertion that the psyche is mechanical. 'Until we become good we are at the mercy of mechanical forces . . . . If we give more than we find natural we may hate the recipient. A sufferer communicates his suffering by ill-treating and distressing others. All beings tend to use all the power at their disposal'(kv): thus Murdoch, explicating Simone Weil, has glossed some of the mechanical, spiritual laws that govern the action.

Alexander, hurt by Antonia's defection, punishes her by cultivating Martin's mistress Georgie Hands. Martin has kept Georgie secret both from his wife and from Alexander: Alexander has always had a habit of stealing his girls. It is Honor who introduces them, just as it is Honor who spills the beans about Georgie to Palmer and to Antonia. Honor's motivation is obscure: she may simply have wished to provide the isolated Georgie (who has told the deaf Martin that she is in despair) with new acquaintance; or she may see in Martin's helplessness with his wife her own helplessness with Palmer, but tricked out as virtue. She certainly urges Martin, with a controlled savagery, to reclaim Antonia; and thus to free Palmer for her. Honor is inscrutable, however, and is a potent source of mystery. Of all Murdoch's 'worldly' characters it is she who appears to stand for the most savage *realpolitik* of the emotions.

There is a final regrouping. Palmer leaves for America, consoled by the newly enslaved Georgie, who became his patient after an unsuccessful suicide attempt. Antonia and Alexander, possibly given the courage or energy by Palmer that for years they had lacked, leave for Rome. Martin, who has fallen 'fatally' for the unlovely Honor Klein, is rewarded by her in an ending which, for all that he is at last with a woman whom he loves with whole-hearted (if, to the reader, mysterious) passion, is ambiguous. 'There is no resolution. Martin is just lucky – or is he lucky – in his relationship with one of his enslavers' Murdoch commented to Rose (1968).

*

A footnote in her *Sartre: Romantic Rationalist* ponders how one might decide between Freud and Sartre's interpretations of the severed Medusa's head (62). *A Severed Head* does not choose between these interpretations but contemplates them both. Frank Baldanza has usefully shown how the Sartrian theme of knowledge-as-power, and the Freudian theme of the Oedipal anxiety associated with incest, continue through all her reworkings in early drafts for the novel.[22] The theme of severed heads – Alexander's sculpted busts, Honor apparently decapitated by the car window out of which she leans to conduct Martin when he drives her in the fog – is elegantly worked out; it relates, consistently, to both knowledge and incest. The plot is thus powered by the partial revelation of secrets, and these revelations always concern incestuous or quasi-incestuous Oedipally-motivated liaisons: Martin's need to keep a child-mistress whom he can dominate; Palmer and Honor's adolescence-fixated affair; Alexander's continuing need to compete with his younger brother Martin and unman him through stealing his women. Behind all this is Martin's own profound Oedipal guilt. When he returns to Rembers after Antonia has left him for Palmer he feels

that particular painful guilty thrilling sense of being both stifled
and protected with which a return to my old home always
afflicted me; and now it was as if my pain for Antonia had
become the same pain, so close was it blended in quality,
though more intense with the obscure *malaise* of my
homecomings. (40)

In Chapter 21, immediately after his discovery of Palmer and
Antonia's incest, he has a sexual dream of his own sister, conflates
his father with Palmer to whom he is also mildly sexually
attracted, and dreams of his own castration. Freud represents as
it were the vanishing-point for the myth in this book, and Martin's
attraction to Honor, we are to infer, is obscurely connected to
the fact that she has acted out such unconscious desire.

I think that comment on Honor's famous speech about being
'a severed head such as primitive tribes used to use, anointing it
with oil to make it utter prophecies'(182) has been overdone by
critics anxious to unmask the book, for praise or blame, as fertility-
myth. Honor's awkward floweriness is a means by which her
author points to her ambiguous spiritual power, which is
connected to knowledge and to incest. What she uniquely
understands has to be told us obliquely. The problem is not that
we fail to believe in her. She is even grotesquely real as a physical
presence, with her solemn face of a Hebrew angel, down on her
upper lip, and the swordsmanship. Her darkness is partly perhaps
the product of an equivocation. To Ruth Heyd in 1965 Iris
Murdoch praised Honor as a conqueror of self-deception; speaking
to me in 1983 she emphasised rather Honor's demonic qualities.
Both are in evidence, as are the moments when she shocks us
by evidencing ordinary human weakness and kindness. She is
concerned for and kind to the stricken Georgie; her hand trembles
when Martin requests her love. Honor's spiritual rhodomontade
should not obscure for us that the subject of the book is love,
power, and the relations between them: like all the 'closed' novels
of the 1960s, it is a study of low Eros.

A Severed Head resembles Restoration comedy not merely in
being an over-plotted, dazzling, witty sexual imbroglio, but in
the ways it shows us that love *is* war and power-play; and power-
play and war are love. Antonia, for whom 'liking everyone' is a
most vital weapon, is seen hilariously trying to like even her deadly
rival Honor: 'All the same I like her'(62) before acknowledging 'I

hate that woman'(142). Palmer is seen as an old warrior, Honor as an insolent captain as well as swords-woman, and Martin reclaims Antonia for a brief spell by giving Palmer a black eye, after which the scales of power tip in his direction. This follows Palmer's Svengali-like assertion that 'Martin, you and Antonia will do as I tell you'(144), and, terrified that Martin may have exposed his incest with Honor to Antonia, he now surrenders his will. Martin begins the book with Georgie prostrating herself before him and reflecting that no one in the world could exact from him the same homage; and ends it having prostrated himself full-length on the floor before Honor.

The book's power depends on its poetry; both the poetry of its physical descriptions – fog, snow, London, Rembers, Cambridge by moonlight – which have the intense clarity and beauty of etchings; and also the poetry of its evocation of these personal relations. These too combine great clarity of outline with an earned sense of mystery. One of the book's farcically true moments occurs when Antonia attributes Palmer's coldness to her to his having found out about her and Alexander. 'Perhaps a letter or something. And he was too hurt to go on'(191). Palmer was ignorant of this liaison, just as Antonia is ignorant of Palmer's liaison with his sister. This is to remind ourselves that Antonia's 'final' version of the truth in Chapter 28 has its own self-serving moments of fantasy; no one in the book is privy to the whole truth and so nor are we. Did Georgie try to kill herself, as Martin thought, out of misery at his neglect of her? Or out of jealousy of Antonia, as Antonia of course claims, when she realised that Alexander, to whom she is nominally then engaged, 'really' loves Antonia? Or out of some fatal combination of isolation, misery and jealousy? It is in inviting us to ponder such over-determined matters that the novel's truth lies; as when Martin, observing Antonia wear a pullover and a string of pearls neither of which he has seen before, is obliged to begin to apprehend her as painfully separate from him – a recurrent *topos*, this. Murdoch's success, in other words, is to be a materialist of a delicate yet savage kind. The title may point to the *locus* of man's spiritualising and sublimating agency ('But to the *neck* do the gods inherit . . . ') but the plot enacts a sequence of comical and disturbing desublimations. There is only one happy couple in the book – the Lesbian Miss Seelhaft and Miss Hernshaw. There is much disquisition on human cruelty. Of Rosemary, for example, we are told that like most people whose marriages have failed she has a sharp appetite for news of other failed marriages. Martin fears meeting her in case she pretends 'distress such as persons feign at the death of an acquaintance and which is in fact a glow of excitement and pleasure, perceptible on waking in the morning as a not yet diagnosed sense of all being exceptionally well with the world'(35). Like Georgie, Martin experiences the instinctive masochistic desire to love those who injure him.

Yet the book's triumph is to combine such harsh assessment with a vision that is charitable. Martin finally says of the imposture practised against him by his wife and brother that he knows from his own experience 'how gentle, how far from cold-blooded, can seem to the deceiver the deliberate deception of the beloved person'(196). This does not exonerate anyone, but does suggest that Martin is less of a 'moral dreamer', as Antonia early calls him – and that he is less puritan and judgemental after the battering he has received – than he was at the start. He has not succumbed to Palmer's amoral and deterministic vision, but has accommodated from it a new realism, for which Honor stands as an ambiguous emblem.

*

The formal intensities of Murdoch's work, like those of Muriel Spark, are often in the broadest sense theological, stemming from a desire to show a pattern larger than individual purpose. It is no accident that the most closed of the novels are those with the headiest theological flavour, combining the severest view of mankind as fallen prisoners in the Cave – as slaves of their own unconscious – with the most urgent desire for redemption. A number of descriptions in *A Severed Head* linked London in that book to hell. 'Part of the drama in those closed-up, rather obsessional novels' Murdoch said in interview with Rose, 'is the struggle between love and sex', adding that sex is a great mystifier and dark force while love, which is rooted in sex, is partly able to transcend these roots.

Bruno's Dream (1968) is a closed novel and the most naked meditation on the Platonic Eros she has attempted. The paradox for the critic is that, while nothing is easier than to extract and expound the doctrine, much that makes the book alive and interesting is thereby left out. It is a Janus-faced book, and saved from abstraction by the sceptical wit and good humour it displays at the expense of its own vision, and the centrifugal energy it radiates outwards into particulars. I shall look briefly at the plot and the 'theology' before discussing this expansion.

The story, plainly told, is a pleasingly fantastic affair. Bruno Greensleave is old, sick with an illness that makes him resemble one of the spiders he loves to study (with a huge head) and feels a persistent feeble urge to put things right before his rapidly approaching death. He wishes to be reconciled to his estranged son Miles, whom he hurt and alienated on the occasion of Miles' marriage to an Indian girl Parvati, by one rash remark. Parvati was soon after killed in an aircrash. He also obscurely wishes to be reconciled to his long-dead wife Janie. His wife sickened and died soon after discovering that he had a mistress and, fearing her dying curse, he abandoned her at the moment of her death, despite her cries and entreaties. Miles and Bruno's attempted reconciliation fails disastrously and upsets them both, and Miles' second wife Diana, who married him out of a need to minister to a sad man, and her austere sister Lisa, patch things up.

Bruno's complaisant son-in-law Danby, the third bereaved male of the book, flirts with Diana, and then falls violently in love with Lisa; who reminds him (as she reminds everyone) of his morally intense and good first wife, Gwen. Witnessing this love, Miles falls for Lisa himself and finds that she has loved him since his marriage to Diana but has crucified this love. She encourages him to do the same. 'Romantic love is not an absolute'(292). Meanwhile in the sub-plot Danby has rejected his mistress and maid Adelaide who is loved by her violent cousin Will. Will, inspired by his odd and mystical twin Nigel, challenges Danby to a Thames-side duel, after which Danby swims away. The river floods and Bruno, Adelaide and Bruno's precious stamp collection are all immersed. Bruno is consoled by the self-abnegating Lisa and by Diana. Will claims Adelaide in a hilariously tearful wedding scene at which even the severe registrar is finally overcome by the epidemic of tears. Lisa, aroused by Miles into wanting happiness, claims Danby in a scene that directly recalls Honor's last passage with Martin. Miles is rewarded for his enforced renunciation of Lisa by being able at last and, after many years, to grieve properly for the death of his first wife. Then, having used poor Diana as a lavatory for this grief, he retreats and is rewarded by the appearance of his muse. Nigel leaves for India and altruism. Diana has no one left to love but Bruno. The ending sees two deaths that comment on one another. We learn that the twins' adopted aunt, always mocked for claiming to be a Czarist princess, turned out on her death to be exactly that. 'Auntie' dies in the truth; Bruno dies consoled by thinking he has completed his book on spiders, and confusing Diana with Lisa. At the moment of his death Bruno understands that his wife must have wanted to forgive and not curse him.

Edgar Wind noted that the Platonic theory of love was the key to a philosophy of dying: the perfection of love could not be arrived at without first dying to imperfect desires.[23] Love and death are the 'theological' themes and are worked with characteristic nerve and inventiveness. Each is important in so far as it can trigger changes in consciousness, and Bruno's dying is a moral summons to the others to full life and to a consciousness that at last admits the reality and claims of other people. The action takes place in Battersea, Fulham and Barons Court, bounded on the one hand by the Lots Road power station, symbol of the unmoralised energies of Eros, and on the other by the Brompton Road cemetery and by death. Bruno early has a nightmare in which he has been condemned to death, wakes relieved and then realises it is true. He tries to imagine death but fails. He knows that it is not just obelisks and angels and that it includes decay, but can come up only with consoling simulacra – his dressing-gown, symbol of his only travelling, the false sadnesses of TV, purgatory, judgement, his own disembodied voice on the telephone, on which he likes to dial wrong numbers. Death is too hard, and cannot be inscribed in his consciousness any more than it can be in the text. He knows he must cheat his mind out of a full awareness of what is to happen to it, just as his son Miles had to avoid that full recognition of Parvati's death that might have destroyed his reason. Bruno's dream is Bruno's state of illusion, and there are some dozen references to the fact that ordinary unmindful consciousness is a species of dreaming. In interview with Haffenden (1983), Murdoch suggested that death was to be considered not so much as a 'terribly special' event at the end of life, but as something that could happen all the time, in the sense of unselfing. Only the ascetic Lisa and the would-be saintly Nigel get anywhere near imagining death in this sense. Lisa nursed her father through his dying and, weeping, tells Diana that love would have to be like a huge vault opening out overhead to console a dying man. Nigel similarly teaches the aggrieved and suffering Diana that only love as self-extinction can make a 'new heaven and a new earth'.

Nigel's reference to new heaven and new earth, which recalls Blake, suggests where the energies of the book lie. Frank Kermode noted that the author expressed herself not only in terms of an ascetic vocation in this book, but also, like some of her characters, in terms of a self-interested hedonism.[24] The paradox of the book's 'Janus' face is that a civilisation like ours that is death-denying – as David Marquand has put this – is also life-denying, and a philosophy that cannot imagine a good death cannot either imagine a good life.[25] Here it is a paradox that the expansion of the specious present that all her books urge as a skill in the creation of art, and as a necessity for the moral life, is carried out by two very different kinds of people, hedonists and ascetics, both of whom are strongly motivated to attend neither to hope nor fear but to the here and now. Like Nigel, of whom the present tense is used throughout in this novel, saints and epicures inhabit the present. The transfiguration of the ordinary that Nigel calls for makes for a cleaner experience of both pleasure and pain. Kermode noted that the author's rituals are 'hazed over by pleasure, by a love which, to the best of its ability, ostracises death'.[26] The reader's pleasure coincides with the author's, and the book is saved from itself because it is full of treats.

The redemption of particulars extends to the characters, and the debate between virtue and pleasure begins here too. Danby, son of a Didcot shopkeeper, is sociable, worldly and complaisant, a shambler through pubs. He sings and jokes his way through the beginning of a number of chapters, strokes and pats those he meets, and is a man who, through liking himself, can put away self-consciousness and help others. Danby is a citizen of the present whose determined self-interest saves him from errors that a more high-minded ethic might not have done. When contemplating seducing his sister-in-law he thinks 'Naturally he'd have liked to go to bed with her. However she was married to Miles and though at first it seemed a jolly idea a more extended reflection suggested snags'(143). Danby's 'jolly' charm is invisible to puritans like Will and Miles, and, being motored by the desire for happiness, he is less remote from the real world than either.

Miles opposes him. An ascetic with a wolfish savage-sweet smile, a man who hates emotion and cares for few fellow-mortals, he would slam the door on his fellow-officers' lewd talk during the war. He is given to disgust and cold high-minded anger, seen by his father as a 'violent intense boy' and marked by the fear of being 'porlocked' – a terror not merely of the interruption of his poetic inspiration but also of the invasion of his *pudeur*. He is one type of the artist itself. Miles' romantic idea of his father is ludicrously remote from reality. This opposition between Danby and Miles recurs in many of the novels as a contrast in moral temperaments, and reaches its fruition in the quarrel between the spinsterish Bradley and the complaisant Arnold in *The Black Prince*. We are not, I think, so much invited to court-martial these characters for their evident frailties, as to marvel at the comedy of human difference.

That comedy is to be found, too, in the relations between the sisters Lisa and Diana, daughters of a Leicester chemist. Lisa is an ex-nun and ex-Communist with a first in Greats, who works in an East End School and has a penitential moral intensity that reminds everyone of Danby's dead wife Gwen – a serious girl given to making long speeches who drove herself during the war to the point of collapse. Gwen died diving off Battersea Bridge to save a young girl, who then swam safely ashore; Gwen, on the other hand, suffered a heart attack and drowned. Danby, grief-stricken at the time, comes to see the comic side of this act of futile self-sacrificing altruism. So do we, and in such touches of humour at the expense of the ruling idea of the love-that-is-the-same-as-death the book's success lies. 'Besides I love everybody' says Nigel, who is also trying to live out the philosophy of unconditional love with its attendant dangers of masochism and muddle. 'Then it can't be love' Diana ripostes tartly. 'Take your hands away please'(237). Here once more the humour is at the expense of the vision, but does not disable it. Nigel's sermon to Diana, in which he explains that human beings hardly ever think about other people but contemplate fantasms which resemble them which are decked out for the selfish purposes of the dreamer, is both wise and true.

There is a sweet sanity in the author that mocks moral excess at the same time that it invites it. Lisa, like Gwen, has driven herself to collapse through sheer moral zeal and at the end seems to suffer a change of personality. She finds herself stirred and awakened by Miles' reciprocation of her love for him and turns to the love-stricken Danby for consolation. I think that it is psychologically plausible that a self-denying person could turn into a pleasure-seeking one. 'All those self-denying years prove nothing' she tells Danby. (Anne Cavidge's story in *Nuns and Soldiers* nearly points a similar moral.) Now self-interested and unable to unlearn her new desire for happiness, Lisa leaves the story in one of those expensive cars that seem to figure for Murdoch, as they did for Virginia Woolf, as the very poetry of a shameless worldliness. She is seen smartly dressed and dining at riverside restaurants – a *venue* that, considering Gwen's death, and the role of the river throughout, constitutes a small joke in itself.

Just as Lisa becomes a beautiful *hetaera* so Diana, formerly, in a beautifully poised phrase, a 'rather severe hedonist' and the fribble of the two, takes on a more august pain than any she had felt before. Diana starts to resemble the harrowed nun-like Lisa of her self-abnegating years. It is Diana who ministers to the confused and dying Bruno, who learns to extend the specious present and understand that 'the intersection of the timeless moment with time is an occupation for the saint'. 'She tried to think about herself but there seemed to be nothing there. Things can't matter very much, she thought, because one isn't anything. Yet one loves people, this matters . . . . One isn't anything, and yet one loves people'(310). Bruno and Diana at the moving end of the book come to share the same vision, and yet to understand it apart and differently. In the book's closing words, 'She lived the reality of death and felt herself made nothing by it and denuded of desire. Yet love still existed and it was the only thing that existed.

The old spotted hand that was holding onto hers relaxed gently at last.'

Diana moves from the cave toward the sun. Lisa returns to the cave, a journey about whose necessity *The Sovereignty of Good* is eloquent. If such symmetries are one source of readerly pleasure, another comes from the very texture of the book. I noted in an earlier chapter Miles' 'Notebook of Particulars' in which he chronicles everyday marvels and apprentices himself to his art. Diana, too, at the end sees London transfigured into a new city, full of new things, perceiving perfect particulars – potted plants, green moss, dust, paper, glowing faces – anew. And Danby's Fulham and Battersea represent for him a 'mystery' on which he meditates. There are comparably pleasurable mysteries for the reader. Murdoch's rendering of Bruno's unquiet, plaintive consciousness, vexed by a circus of emotions – anxiety, guilt, self-pity, resentment – has a picturesque and imagistic density that renders its poignancies poetic and speculative. His pain is partly converted into our wonder, transmuting thinking into a weird poetry that attenuates even the most terrible things. Bruno thinking about his dead womenfolk, now preserved in his memory like his beloved spiders in formaldehyde; Bruno telling Lisa 'You see, I'd like to know what I'm *like*.' The scenes in which the wholly attentive Lisa consoles Bruno are marvellous in their combination of pathos, humour and the grotesque: for example Bruno explaining that old people still feel sex, and on being told by Lisa that he is still sexually attractive, weeping huge tears at the tender nonsense.

Bruno and Miles are both at different moments shown feeling an excited, proud, touched sense of ownership at the complexity of their emotions (a family pride); there is a delightful and playful peepshow into the future of Adelaide and twins; there are surreal descriptions – of rain, which falls sizzling, 'glittering like gramaphone needles'; of Bruno's room, recalling Magritte – 'The unlit room was a tiny grey box suspended from the window, where the racing luminous clouds were imparting a gliding motion to the black bar of the power station'(121).

'It is not easy to portray death, real death, not fake prettified death. Even Tolstoi did not really manage it in *Ivan Ilyich* [which is recalled in *Bruno's Dream* in Nigel, who, like Ilyich's groom, can soothe Bruno's suffering]. The great deaths of literature are few, but they show us with an exemplary clarity the way in which art invigorates us by a juxtaposition, almost an identification, of pointlessness and value. The death of Patroclus, the death of Cordelia, the death of Petya Rostov. All is vanity' (*SG* 87). Of course the novel cannot measure up to these fantastically high standards. Its default, however, is more interesting than many more modest successes.

Part II
'Open and Closed'

Poetic pluralism is the necessary corollary to the radical mysticism of the One.

> (Edgar Wind, *Pagan Mysteries of the Renaissance* (London, 1958) p. 176 [cited in *The Fire and the Sun*, p. 69])

5   The Sublime in *The Bell* and *The Unicorn*

In the first section I have tried to relate Iris Murdoch's 'moral psychology' to her early fiction, in which she alternates, as she has often pointed out, between 'open' and 'closed' works. In the 'closed' novels this moral psychology is employed to more didactic and poetic effect, and these works have a stronger formal intensity and more evident atmosphere. The more open novels are superficially more realistic. Before showing in the last section how in many of the novels of the 1970s she achieves a marriage of these apparently warring sets of virtue, I want now to examine the alternation of 'open' and 'closed' more closely; and to look at the variety of kinds of kinship that can exist between two very different sets of 'open' and 'closed' novel.

*

In *Nuns and Soldiers* Anne Cavidge is seen trying to like novels, and finding them 'marvellous, but too much' (53). Anne is an ex-nun who once escaped from the 'horriblenesss and dangerousness of life . . . the warmth, the mess' into the convent (242). There is a connexion between that 'too much' which characterises novels and makes them, for Murdoch, exemplary art-forms because they reflect the incompleteness and disunity of life and that 'warmth and mess' which equally alarm Anne in living. Anne's puritan horror of the contingent is experienced by many Murdoch characters, though she is an interesting example of someone whose real urge towards good is so close to, and hurt by intolerance. The same fear is for example experienced by the gentle, buffoonish and self-deceived Barney in *The Red and the Green*, distressed at the sight of the sea and rocks at Kingstown (193), and by Theo on the Dorset coast in *The Nice and the Good*.
    Such moments deliberately recall Sartre's 'nausea', or 'horror at the contingent'. Diogenes Allen has excellently shown how

Murdoch and Sartre differ in their attitude to all that the self cannot tame or make immediate sense of.[1] Roquentin's experience in *La Nausée* when looking at the roots of the chestnut tree is exemplary. He sees everything as obscene and threatening, apprehends the 'brute and nameless' character of that world which is always more and other than any description we give to it. Roquentin's moment of enlightenment is opposed to the dulled consciousness of those bourgeois fools who experience the world as solid and who are shown as thus living inauthentically. Sartre elevates such moments into a revelation of truth about the 'absurdity' of existence, and such 'absurdity' has become itself a platitude in its own right, as conventional and anodyne as any bourgeois propriety. To Sartre the defeat of reason is an affront.

Murdoch, citing Gabriel Marcel, has asked why Sartre finds the contingent over-abundance of the world nauseating rather than glorious (*SRR* 17). Sartre's horror seems to be based on a defensive egocentricity, which sees everything in the world as orbiting around us and possessing value only to the precise degree that we assign it. The super-abundance of the world can be apprehended differently, however. Its otherness and separateness can also sometimes be experienced joyously, and as an object-lesson in the insignificance of the observer. Allen points out that the scene in *The Unicorn* when Effingham Cooper nearly drowns in the bog is an anti-type to Roquentin confronting the tree roots. After his gibbering panic Cooper experiences a moment of calm in which he realises that his coming subtraction from the scene will nonetheless leave something behind.

> What was left was everything else, all that was not himself, that object which he had never before seen and upon which he now gazed with the passion of a lover. And indeed he could always have known this, for the fact of death stretches the length of life. Since he was mortal he was nothing, and since he was nothing all that was not him was filled to the brim with being, and it was from this that the light streamed. This then was love, to look and look until one exists no more, *this* was the love which was the same as death. He looked and knew, with a clarity which was one with the increasing light, that with the death of the self the world becomes quite automatically the object of a perfect love . . . .   (166)

Cooper is a conceited, immature public school ass and a suitably unlikely candidate for the central moment of enlightenment in Murdoch's *oeuvre*. Like Plato, Murdoch always veils with irony the highest truth she wishes to show us. To see reality properly, for Murdoch, is to love it, quite automatically: that one experiences love is, by a tautology, the surety that one is seeing aright. Such vision and such love occur not by any ordinary act of will but through acts of selfless attention. The practice of philosophy is a study of dying, as in the *Phaedo*, since it is in realising one's own helplessness and mortality that the alternative reality of other people can begin to be apprehended for the first time. Sartre's hero having ruled the essential self out of court can dangerously become 'an egotist without an "I"'. For Murdoch by contrast, we find ourselves not by explaining the world but by loving it. Effingham Cooper, however, loses his vision and returns to his old unregenerate self, his 'really fat and monumental egoism' (268) which in fact is what enables him to survive the rigours of the tale – he spends much of the second half of the book asleep – and returns also to the ordinary world outside the allegory at the end.

Cooper's swift loss of his vision, which significantly fades with the return of his will to live, is echoed in *The Red and the Green* when Barney in an analogous scene in a Dominican chapel experiences the almost bodily presence of perfect Goodness as a rebuke and as a loving summons, but returns almost at once to the world of temporising, half-truth, and self-deception that he had inhabited before. There is comedy in these bathetic aftermaths to moments of real and compelling vision, as well as truth. 'Even the most piercing sense of revelation accompanying a greater awareness of one's moral position is likely to be nine-tenths illusion', she argues; 'it would be hard to over-estimate the amount of illusion in any given soul'.[2]

Moreover such induction into the sublime can be two-faced. Sartre and Murdoch are not simply opposed. In Murdoch's novels as in life, characters can indeed experience the world as Roquentin, or as Kafka's K do, though such experience is no more elevated into a despotic metaphysical truth than are the positive visions. Tom in *The Philosopher's Pupil* experiences a blackening and poisoning of the imagination 'which is one of the worst as well as one of the commonest forms of human misery' (379); Miles in *Bruno's Dream* feels, after a row with his father 'utterly, utterly defiled' (118). Such states of mind are merely 'ordinary' and lack the metaphysical pretensions, and indeed the metaphysical panic, experienced by Roquentin.

Murdoch, on the other hand, in emphasising their ordinariness is also showing us, as she argues Sartre cannot, the 'power of our inherited collective view of the world' (SRR 64) which reminds us that no state of mind is permanent, and she makes of this fact as much consolation as affront. Something closer to Roquentin's *aperçu* lies at the heart of *The Time of the Angels* in which the mad and bad priest Carel shows his brother the secret of life, which is Chaos and Old Night, 'power and the marvel of power . . . chance and the marvel of chance'. Carel shows Marcus the multiplicity of the universe and tells him that such multiplicity is the triumph of evil, 'or rather of what used to be called evil and is now nameless' (164). Like Anne Cavidge, Carel's awareness is of the fact of there being 'too much'.

This negative sublime recalls Effingham's positive sublime, as A. S. Byatt points out.[3] The power of our inherited collective view of the world and our own dullness can keep out the world's beauty, and its horror, and too swift an induction into that beauty or horror can be dangerous. Whether you experience it as beautiful or horrible may depend upon your chemistry and luck at that moment. In *A Fairly Honourable Defeat* Morgan experiences both in rapid succession. The fact that it is the evil spiritual agents who like to carry out such induction (Carel in *The Time of the Angels*, Julius in *A Fairly Honourable Defeat*), as much as the saints (Hugo explaining to Jake the unutterable specificity of the world), suggests the ambiguous moral power of such denudations. The destruction of your 'mind-set' can liberate or destroy you: it can indeed be – as it is for Harriet in *The Sacred and Profane Love Machine*, or Rupert in *A Fairly Honourable Defeat* – 'too much', when they are hurt beyond help by too sudden a decentring. Not everyone will become what the Tibetan sage Milarepa termed a 'bride of desolation', living in direct contact with the world's power and beauty and horror, unmediated by the defences of the ego. To say as much, moreover, as so often with Murdoch, is to encounter her talking in the best poetry the happiest common-sense.

If the 'viscous' is the fundamental key or image by which Sartre, as Murdoch reminds us, suggests that we understand our situation, an image of consciousness, of the form of our appropriation of the world, then water and swimming and drowning are for her a counter-image. For Sartre the viscous images forth the world's messiness and the indeterminacy of consciousness. For Murdoch, who is less of an aesthetic puritan than Sartre, swimming seems to act as the unofficial counter-image of a healing surrender to the mysterious supportive properties of the world, as well as its mysterious destructive properties.

To be able to swim, for Murdoch, is almost to possess moral competence. Both depend on 'one's willingness to surrender a rigid nervous attachment to the upright position' (*UN* 107) and to feel, like Jake at the end of *Under the Net*, 'like a fish which swims calmly in deep water . . . the secure supporting pressure of my own life' (250). In *A Fairly Honourable Defeat* the devil Julius cannot swim. The sea, in which Murdoch has recounted she nearly drowned,[4] is a 'vast image of power and danger', figuring, as in *Genesis*, as an image of uncreated form itself, of 'infinite' multiplicity and contingency. As in *Our Mutual Friend* or *A Passage to India*, it may also represent 'cleansing and spiritual salvation and reconciliation'.[5] 'My people live by the river' she once said indignantly, when charged with writing 'Hampstead novels' (Bradbury, 1976) and the point seems a metaphysical more than a social one. When Dora learns to swim at the end of *The Bell* she is simultaneously trying belatedly to grow up. There are few novels in which no one swims, and drowning is the commonest death – in a swimming-pool (*A Fairly Honourable Defeat*), a bath (*An Accidental Man*), the sea (*The Sea, The Sea*), a flashflood (*The Unicorn*), the Thames (*A Word Child*), a Public Baths (*The Philosopher's Pupil*). Ordeals by water also abound. I have noted Cooper in the bog in *The Unicorn*; there are ordeals in a canal in *Nuns and Soldiers*, and in the sea in *The Nice and the Good*. This is not an exhaustive list. The descriptions of these events are superbly imagined. They also embody the wisdom, in which her books abound, that a brave immersion in the detail of the world, and of other lives, is both necessary but can carry with it no indemnity against mischance. 'I propose to give myself to the situation like a swimmer to the sea', says one character who cannot (*FHD* 211).

Such exposure to the world's particulars is discussed in the philosophy, as the 'sublime', in which the box-like enclosure of the self is attenuated and opened out. Two of Murdoch's essays incorporate the word in their titles: 'The Sublime and the Good'; 'The Sublime and the Beautiful Revisited'. Both *The Fire and the Sun* and *The Sovereignty of Good* make use of crucially placed arguments about the topic. The concept of the sublime has revived over the last two centuries as religion decayed, and gives to the failure to understand something the highest meaning, an exciting and double-edged idea, as the critic Thomas Weiskel puts it, useful to many different ideologies. It comes into play precisely in so far as man cannot attain a totality and is for this reason played down by Marxist aestheticians. Weiskel's strongly Freudian account of the sublime shows how it offers a positive resolution of the Oedipus conflict. The sublime requires and nourishes a strong super-ego, and the survival of culture depends on its interdictions.[6] In its beatification of relative weakness and humility it could be said to have one derivation in the early Socratic dialogues, which so often oblige the second speaker to admit helplessness and ignorance. Socrates, however, by including himself – 'I too am ignorant' – receives the partner into a 'community that transforms defeat into its opposite'.[7]

Samuel Monk's *The Sublime* relates the gradual domination of eighteenth-century aesthetics by the sublime to Romanticism. The sublime is both the advance-guard of a new individualism, since its affective theory of art (involving 'transport', 'rapture') moves the locus of aesthetics away from the artwork to the reader, and also an authoritarian concept putting a high value on anything that suggests man's relative weakness. The sublime has at its heart the disharmony between mind and world, and the futility on the part of the imagination of the effort to grasp and represent the formless. Kant is its major theoretician, and in Wordsworth it finds its major practical apotheoses.[8]

Murdoch has famously called for revisions of Kant's sublime. She much approves of Kant's analogy between the sublime and *Achtung*, or respect for the moral law, and calls *Achtung* one of the most beautiful and exciting things in the whole of philosophy. Both experiences mix pleasure and pain – pain at the thwarting of our sensuous nature (*Achtung*), or at reason's defeat (the sublime) – pleasure at consciousness of our rational nature (*Achtung*) or at the dignity of reason and at our spiritual nature (the sublime). She would, however, supplement Kant's natural sublime – 'Who cares what sort of emotion Kant experienced in the Alps?' – by a humanist sublime, in which the spectacle of human life itself, and the reality of persons other than ourselves, becomes the most proper trigger. It is not to her the world's formlessness, but its unreasonable particularity that offends us. She would like to reform the emotion, which is liable as Keats noticed to become an excuse for an exalted and solipsistic self-regard. The good man, her ideal candidate for the sublime, in a sense the sublime's true-born citizen, might feel 'delight, terror, but not, if he really sees what is before him, superiority' (sbr). Lastly she deplores Kant's separation of the sublime from the beautiful, which trivialises both. Kant's careful siphoning off of art into a zone of 'pure play' is a puritan response which both demoralises and presents an over-intelligible picture of the art-work. Even great art in her view is much more deliberately incomplete, more of a jumble, and on better terms with the world's multiplicity than we dare to see. The *Timaeus* is for her radiant myth because in it Good, which is present outside the world, participates in creation but only *part*-successfully. The art-work, like the cosmos in the *Timaeus*, is only partly intelligible. There is both in novels and in life 'too much', as Anne Cavidge noticed.

It is a commonplace that our consciousness in the later twentieth century is still Romantic. Murdoch argues that 'the Romantic movement shockingly cheated Kant by taking over the Sublime' (*FS* 20). In Romantic, Modernist and subsequent literature the Sublime has found its ideal habitat, first in its positive, later in its negative, Wasteland manifestation. It penetrates criticism too. We may not imagine that we resemble Sir Thomas Browne in loving to lose ourselves in a mystery or pursue our reason to an *O altitudo*! Yet the emphasis on 'profundity' as a primary critical value – since, as Weiskel points out, *altus* means either high or deep – reminds us that, in criticism too, triumph is thought to belong together with and be wrested from defeat by the super-abundance of meanings in the work. Here Socrates' perverse descendant might be said to be Derrida: Socrates' *aporias* (moments of undecidability) are dimly echoed by today's post-structuralists when they place the highest emphasis on those moments in reading when we know we are baffled. But whereas Socrates shatters false knowledge and humbles the reason of his interlocutors in the name of a Beyond whose sublimities he points to but which must remain nameless, Derrida's negative sublime of undecidability is gleefully self-sufficing.

I think that the sublime is for Murdoch a central organising metaphor, discernible in her plotting, her ethics, her aesthetics, and her use of ordeals by love and water. There is always more plot than the idea-play can use up, and this offers itself as a small hermeneutic sublime to the reader, who may feel, like one reviewer that 'there is a central, large, and simple meaning which one has somehow, just missed'.[9] Such immersion of the philosophy in the *data* of the action is paralleled by the immersion of the characters in the sublime of love. It is love, Weil reminds us, that liberates the soul from its captive state in the Cave – beauty, by means of love.[10] It is also a lower sort of love which, according to Murdoch, puts us there in the first place. So falling-in-love, besides being ordinary and interesting in itself, and a central drama in many people's lives, is a violent mock-ascesis or false loss of self, in which the contingency of all that is unself is momentarily revealed with a glorious and ambiguously sublime radiance. The centre of significance is violently ripped out of the dreamy ego and placed in another, who is suddenly perceived as shockingly separate. Then – as this is a false ascesis – the lover, if his love is not returned, can behave badly because of resentment at what appears a theft of his substance. Maturation in her books is falling out of intense 'love' ('Romantic love is not an absolute' *BD* 292) and in love with the separate world and the separate people it contains, though this love is a darker, colder, more impersonal commodity. Love, like the sublime, is a matter of unselfing. In the account of the ascent of the soul during the purification of love in the *Phaedrus* Longinus found a *locus classicus* of the sublime; the soul 'sprouts wings' and soars.

Being unselfed by the sublime, Murdoch's good characters are very different from us: they have less personality. Tallis in *A Fairly Honourable Defeat* is seen as an 'unperson' (145), Lisa during her saintly phase in *Bruno's Dream* wishes to be 'nothinged' (93). Kathleen in *The Red and the Green* has to her husband the quality of 'unlife' (189). In the Gifford lectures Murdoch proposed for the Platonic–Kantian individual who was engaged in trying to overcome egoism the pertinent term 'anti-individual', and pondered whether, when we are behaving virtuously, we could be said to have any experience at all. James in *The Sea, The Sea* could be said to take marginality and ascesis to the extremest point when he spookily renounces life itself and stops his own heart. The analogous impersonality of great art, she has suggested, helps prompt the reader's sublime (sg): it is always inferior art which seems narrowly 'individualistic'.

*

In Proust's *La Prisonnière* Marcel explains to Albertine that a great artist creates the same work over and over again and thus refracts across diverse *milieux* the unique beauty he brings into the world; a process that might be seen at work in *The Bell* (1958) and *The Unicorn* (1963). Both toy with the sublime.

In one sense the books could not be more different. *The Bell* takes place in a recognisable contemporary Gloucestershire and, though the setting is the remote enclosure of romance, its rituals are those of a lay community enclosing the Benedictine but Anglican Abbey. *The Bell* is careful about verisimilitude, and has been claimed for 'realism'. *The Unicorn* takes place in the West of Ireland in a sinister desolation deliberately recalling the Romantic sublime, with a plot borrowing from Victorian Gothic, with one mansion with seven golden-haired maids, and the other with seven black. It was mostly undervalued by reviewers, who did not always understand its Gothic convention.[11]

Yet *The Bell* is more speculative than such an opposition suggests, and *The Unicorn* interrogates the same theme, which is the value to be accorded moral self-betterment, the failure and necessity of spiritual aspiration. Each novel concerns events in two remote houses, in one of which real but invisible spiritual work is going on – the Abbey, Riders. The second more flamboyant and confused house has workings which are disclosed – Imber Court, Gaze. In both books an inmate of the more spiritual house (Max, Toby's nun) 'knows the story' of the other mansion without ever having met its inhabitants, and meditates about it. In each two innocent worldlings (Toby and Dora in *The Bell*; Marian and Effingham in *The Unicorn*), who may be less culpable than the murderously high-minded votaries of the Good, become involved in the events and attempt to rescue an agent of the numinous (the bell; Hannah). Both move from summer to intimations of winter, and end with death and the scattering of the half-contemplatives, and with the worldlings preparing to discuss the story. In both a pattern of events unconsciously repeats itself after many years. A good man (Toby, Denis) inherits a dog (Murphy, Tadg) from a spoiled man (Nick, Pip) who shoots himself. Both concern the war between the best and the second-best, and in both a peripheral character arrives unsummonsed. It says something about the very different atmosphere of the books that the unsummonsed man in *The Bell* is the gardener Patchway: the book, despite tragic events and despite being very moving, has partly the tone of a comedy in that most characters survive and renew themselves. In *The Unicorn* it is the undertaker who arrives unsummonsed because he simply 'knows'. That book is a tragedy which undercuts the notion of the tragic and ends, too, with triumphant survival as well as destruction. Finally the better of the two communities is in each book the legatee of the worse. Michael leaves the Court to the Abbey; Hannah leaves Gaze to Max. Whether or not such parallels are conscious, both novels employ a certain background Platonism and concern the ambiguities of spirit.

The central character in *The Bell* is Michael Meade, a failed priest, failed school-teacher and chaste homosexual, who left schoolmastering fourteen years earlier because of a love-affair, unconsummated, with his adolescent pupil Nick Fawley; Nick, possibly influenced by an evangelical preacher, exposed Michael to the headmaster. Michael has now given up a Palladian house he inherited, Imber Court, to become the centre for a lay religious community. Nick's sister Catherine, with whom Nick is rumoured to have had a Byronic love-affair, is shortly to enter the neighbouring Abbey as a postulant when Nick himself turns up, now a tormented drunkard and *mauvais sujet* in bad need of Michael's help. Michael's continuing inability to provide this help persists throughout the book.

Catherine and Nick, demonic siblings, contrast with the two innocents Toby Gashe, marking time while waiting to go up to Oxford, and Dora Greenfield, bullied by her pompous unhappy art historian husband Paul who is studying medieval documents at the Abbey. Dora, kind but unconfident, flighty and feckless, is the first of a series of innocent sympathetic worldlings married to insensitive ascetics. Toby and Dora recover the legendary medieval bell of the title from the lake and plan to substitute it for the new bell which is, like Catherine, about to enter the Abbey. Nick now stages a second scandal by compelling Toby to expose Michael's tenderness for him.

Catherine, who turns out to be a schizophrenic and in love with Michael too, attempts to drown herself. Nick shoots his head off. The unstable world of Imber Court dissolves, the Abbey takes over its grounds. Toby seems unscathed, Dora begins to acquire a sense of identity, to value herself, and learn to swim. Michael is broken but, romantic unfortunate that he is, has to face up to the indignities of survival.

These characters are interesting and well-imagined. They exist in a particular world of ideas and values which is interesting too. 'Those who hope, by retiring from the world, to earn a holiday from human frailty, in themselves and others, are usually disappointed' (85) comments the narrative voice, full of wise counsel, worldly yet charitable, standing for the collective wisdom of the world or the Abbey, but not of the unstable middle realm of Imber Court. All her heroes are in some sense on holiday, and rarely more so than when they ascribe some high-minded or holy purpose to their solipsism. To try to be holy may be mere play and escapism, and the Abbess, with whom Murdoch has admitted a little to identifying,[12] calls the inmates of Imber Court 'a kind of sick people' disturbed and hunted by God, unable to live either in or out of the world. Trilling once wrote of that tradition in the English novel that takes snobbery (pride of place without pride of function) as its major theme and showed how suggestive it had proved. No great novel exists, he said, which did not have 'the great joke' at its heart.[13] For Murdoch the great joke is spiritual pride, not social. 'The spiritual ruling-class', thinks Dora, with scorn, when watching Imber Court piously listening to Bach. Murdoch has recorded her own sympathy for 'the vision of an ideal community in which work would once again be creative and meaningful and human brotherhood be restored' (ht), in a contemporary essay championing the Guild Socialists and echoing the Abbess' pronouncements. It is the spiritual pretensions of Imber Court she is making gentle fun of.

The continuity between the high Eros enacted in the Abbey, and the low appetites of the outside world, is suggested in the echo between the motto *Amor Vita Mea* on the medallions of once-worldly Imber Court, and the inscription *Ego Vox Amoris Sum* on the other-worldly bell. Michael *knows* that his religion and his sexual passion 'arose deeply from the same source' (99), just as the later priest Jacoby dedicates 'his love, that is his sexuality' to God (*PP* 156). Freud always resisted pan-sexualism as a heresy threatening the entire psychoanalytic enterprise, since the explanatory value of sexuality depended on its *not* enjoying any monopoly in the realm of the instincts. Murdoch's Platonic use of Eros undercuts Freud in very much this way, and should render absurd the critical ploy of arguing that Michael's religious urge is 'just sex'. Of course it is sex. It is also religion. Murdoch's desublimations are offered to us not so much to 'unmask' the idea of virtue as bogus as to demonstrate the mysterious inaccessibility of virtue, and the dangers of too swift or un-self-sceptical an ascent. She everywhere displays the roots of virtue in sex, in the rude and primitive, out of which it can never wholly be transformed, and her books make it seem defensive to need to keep saying so.

The necessary connexions between sex and virtue form part of the back-drop to the works. The scenery here is borrowed from the *Phaedo*, with its four rivers and its insistence that the proper study of philosophy is dying, though the lake, causeway, ferry and circles may also owe something to Dante's *Inferno*[14]. An aerial map of Imber would show three sets of walls, and resemble a dart-board. The outer circle is the wall of half-stripped Imber Court, the next the wall of the wholly austere Abbey, and the last of three concentric rings, the *hortus conclusus* containing the happy cemetery with its laughing nuns. It is a Platonic map of degrees of unselfing. Only Toby penetrates by mistake to the centre, and in fact no gate is locked. That this spiritual symmetry does not obtrude may have something to do with the fact that 'the religious symbols and institutions involved are both established and discredited in our minds'.[15] The map seems a public one.

The idea-play too revolves around an issue as everyday as you could find, for all the eloquence with which it is expressed in the book. The question is: should you attempt the best act you know, or the second-best one you can be sure you will acquit yourself at? Here James and Michael's sermons in Chapters 9 and 16 provide the frame for the debate. James Tayper-Payce is a rigid moralist who is unselfconscious, perhaps unselfknowing, a character of transparent gentleness, and the younger son of an old military family. Ethics for him, as for someone in the front-line,is a matter of unthinking rules and duties. His sermon is on the theme 'Be ye therefore perfect'. The chief requirement of the good life is 'to live without any image of oneself . . . the study of personality, indeed the whole conception of personality is, as I see it, dangerous to goodness'. It seems clear that we are not to make any unconditional obeisance to James' view since we hear his sermon through Dora's musings about the way she feels judged and 'placed' by Imber. She starts to listen again when James speaks of the necessity of cherishing innocence. He uses the bell as emblem of this innocence: it has 'no hidden mechanism'. James charges Michael with having 'ideals but no principles'. He himself has both, but is obtusely lacking in any sense of human difference. He thus calls Dora a bitch, Nick a pansy, Mrs Mark – who is bossy and wrong-headed – 'such a motherly soul' and imagines that Dora likes her. Dora's growth, moreover, is the result of just such 'experience' as James decries. Yet he is an undismissable, unresentful, and authoritative figure too. His sermon is eloquent, and the action he takes of sending Toby away when the scandal breaks probably shows a surer instinct than Michael displays, since Michael's 'explanations' tend to muddle and drama.

Michael's sermon the following week focuses the conflict of sympathy on which the book depends. It follows his apologetic explanation to Toby for having kissed him, and is interrupted by his soliloquy about the deepening muddle. Having noticed that he had failed accurately to estimate his own spiritual level, his sermon urges respect for human differentiation. 'We must not arrogate to ourselves actions which belong to those whose spiritual vision is higher or other than ours' (204). Like the bell 'we too must learn to understand the mechanism of our spiritual energy, and find out where, for us, are the hiding-places of our strength' (204). His sermon is a commendation of exactly that second-best act which James had decried.

Murdoch has called the conflict here one between artist and saint. James is saintly in that he urges and seems temperamentally suited to an austere morality which is ungrateful to the imagination; Michael the artist in that he is the proponent of the second-best act and loves spiritual drama and pattern for its own sake. In *The Sovereignty of Good* Murdoch asks 'What of the command, "Be ye therefore perfect"? Would it not be more sensible to say "Be ye therefore slightly improved"?' (62) and then goes on to argue that the idea of perfection can help mediate between the two positions, because it inspires love in the worthiest part of the soul. Michael's temporisings and James' austerities are both inadequate, partial views. The Abbess, the most authoritative voice of the book, earlier suggests a proper balance of these sympathies.

Our duty . . . is not necessarily to seek the highest regardless of the realities of our spiritual life as it in fact is, but to seek

that place, that task, those people, which will make our spiritual
life most constantly grow and flourish; and in this search . . .
we must make use of a divine cunning, 'As wise as serpents, as
harmless as doves'.   (81)

*

'Not necessarily to seek the highest', while still being drawn by
the highest, is the Abbess' view: 'Remember that all our failures
are ultimately failures in love. Imperfect love must not be
condemned and rejected but made perfect. The way is always
forward, never back' (235) she finally tells Michael. It is a humane
compromise, a dynamic one, and the Abbess is shown to be as
much urbane as saintly, having practical advice for Michael
about the launching of an appeal, as well as wise counsel about
the place of the idea of perfection in the moral life. In this
interview, as in colloquies between the 'spiritual' characters in
other books, there is a minimum of aesthetic stimulus, and an
obstacle in the form of a grille. Hugo and Jake in *Under the Net*,
or Marcus and Carel in *The Time of the Angels* similarly meet in
the dark, and after some difficulty.The grille might be said to be
figuratively present in their interviews too.

The question of the war between the best and the second-best
touches on the very enterprise in which Michael and the other
'fellow travellers of holiness' are engaged. They are portrayed
with a tenderly satirical eye, alert for false notes. When Dora
politely asks Mrs Mark about her previous life she is answered
with tart condescension 'You'll think me an awful wet blanket . . .
but, do you know, we never discuss our past lives here. That's
another little rule we try to follow. No gossip. And when you
come to think of it, when people ask each other about their lives,
their motives are rarely pure, are they?' (63). This uneasy amnesia
about the past is criticised from two directions at once. Their
attempt to relinquish the past does not prevent the Marks from
continuing the quarrels they entered the community to escape.
In the Abbey, which figures as an idealised citadel of esoteric
virtue, the nuns have even changed their names, but earning
their deracination, are shown by contrast as happy and innocent
and ordinary. At the same time in 'the world' both Toby and
Dora are repeatedly shown as able to inhabit the present out of
an intelligent and spontaneous hedonism. 'That she had no
memory made [Dora] generous' (66). Toby too experiences

life as a 'series of present moments' (47) many of which are unselfconsciously happy. By comparison with the living-in-the-present either of the pleasure-seeking worldlings, or of the happily ascetic nuns, the strivings of Imber Court are made to seem parodic and *voulu*.

They are, however, always seen compassionately. What the plot might be said to distribute is a series of very different kinds of moments of sublime ascesis. It is typical of a Murdoch novel that the unselfing the characters attempt should be shown variously to be in bad faith, while the ambiguously valuable unselfing they are obliged to undergo should come to make their former stances look unserious. It is hard to draw attention to such matters without making the books seem schematic, which is not necessarily how they read. Here Toby's penetration of the Abbey's *sanctum sanctorum* – the cemetery – epicentre of the three concentric enclosing walls in Chapter 13 occurs exactly half-way through the book. It is paralleled by the destruction of Dora's mood of 'dreary trance-like solipsism' by the pictures in the National Gallery in Chapter 14: 'since something good existed, it might be that her problems would be solved after all' (191), and by the single colloquy between Michael and the Abbess that we are privy to, in Chapter 19. The self-extinction promised by the cemetery with its happy nuns, the joyous unselfing by art suffered by Dora, and the benevolent selflessness of the Abbess are related aspects of ascesis. The effect on the reader is, of course, unlike this diagrammatic account, since it is mediated through particular people. Toby feels ashamed and upset by his adventure. Michael is energised but also troubled by his consequential failure of openness about Nick, despite the Abbess' invitation to his confidence. Dora now has the energy to leave her escapade in London and face up to the real and intractable difficulties of her marriage. The message may be, as Philip Rieff described sublimation, that 'whatever is renounced is given back to us, bettered'.[16] But this message nicely subserves particular cases.

In Michael the theme finds its rich and ironic fruition. Michael has consistently solicited a 'loss of personality' (85) through religious service but comically finds that it is his force of personality that holds the community together. Michael is a romantic who constantly expects the emergence in his life of patterns and signs. He is fitted neither for the religious life nor for the world, lacking much wary or earthy understanding of either. Perhaps this is partly to say that he is singled out by the author to be an accidental man, the plot's fool, and a man who accumulates disaster.[17] Michael's false innocence contrasts with Nick's fallen knowledge. It is surely no accident that unlike the hapless Michael, of all the cast, it should be the devilish, tortured but practical Nick who best understands the working of machines ('He seemed to know a lot about engines of all kinds' (117)), whose task is to mend them, while Toby, referred to many times as Nick's 'understudy', wishes to study engineering at Oxford and shows aptitude in raising the large medieval bell of the title, against gravity, from the lake. The plot 'machinery' by which Tony replaces Nick as Michael's destroyer is lethal because of Michael's contributory but complete failure to apprehend Nick or to respond to Nick's continuing need of him. In their interviews Nick is ironic, partly because Michael is deliberately dulling himself to Nick's pain, and refusing to begin the distressing, needful task of putting the past to rest.

Against the causalities of the plot stands the bell itself, a 'thing from another world' (220). There is a useful discussion of this symbol in Byatt's *Degrees of Freedom*. What I would add is that the 'incompleteness' and, in a sense, even the clumsiness of the bell as symbolic device seem perfectly deliberate. Murdoch has consistently argued for a wariness in deploying symbol, so that the aesthetic centre it represents is resisted by a competing force within the characters. The bell seems connected to Murdoch's central idea, which is that Eros is mixed and requires patient purification. The different imaginative uses wished upon it by the characters all contribute to our sense of the bell's presence. Surviving from an age of faith but destined to finish as a museum piece, it acts as a guarantee that the rationalist explanation of events – the journalist Noel Spens' explanation – is not the final one. The bell is a numinous summoner to moral order, but one which is doomed to remain unsatisfied. It is there, in a sense, in order to be frustrated. It both asserts and ironises the moral idealism of the characters who surround it.

Michael's moment of sublime ascesis occurs, horribly and very movingly, at Nick's death. He has throughout solicited a 'loss of personality' through religion; now he is destroyed by grief instead. Michael endeavoured to jump out of the past, even in his 'pious' neglect of Nick; and the past came back and trapped him. And yet it is a symptom of Murdoch's precise moral realism that, once

again, 'Very slowly a sense of his own personality returned to
him' and beautifully, 'One day too he would experience again,
responding with his heart, that indefinitely extended requirement
that one human being makes upon another' (309). Michael
combined with his religious promptings a desire to see himself as
a dramatic hero, perhaps a tragic hero. He experiences the real
emptiness of these roles, and finds he is not built for such
austerities. So the ending of the book asserts, as do so many
Murdoch endings, the triumphant survival of the personality, the
devious tenacity and resilience of the self. It is this which makes
the book, taken together with its consistent wit and good humour,
a comedy, albeit a moving and sometimes grim one.

*

Michael wishes life to partake of the character of theological
romance. *The Unicorn* creates a world that might have satisfied
him. I have already drawn attention to common themes. Murdoch
has suggested that in good art the works are their own 'most
intimate critics' and 'provide lucid commentaries on themselves'
(sw). The point needs to be pressed home since her closed, Gothic
romances have too often been read as if they were unaware of
their own Romanticism. *The Italian Girl* sustains a debate about
exactly the problems of the 'tinification' from which it suffers.
The term is taken from Edmund's 'Gothic' [*sic*] profession as
wood-engraver but is used to promote reflection about the moral
diminishment and the formal belittlings of romance. *A Word Child*
alludes persistently to the romances of Edgar Allen Poe, to *Peter
Pan*, Flecker's *Hassan*, and implicitly to Dostoevski, Dante, Byron,
Kafka. *The Time of the Angels* has a demon who plays his way
through Tchaikovski, *The Italian Girl* a chatelaine who plays
Sibelius and Wagner, and *The Unicorn* has the poltroon Effingham
Cooper, who comes in his single moment of enlightenment to see
that 'It's not a bit like Freud and Wagner think' (172). Such
Romantic composers and thinkers are made fun of because
Romanticism, in the form of an apocalyptic yearning for redemption, is the subject-matter of these more speculative novels. They
are *about* the mythopoetic and magical powers of the imagination,
and about the limits to those powers too. They are the most
poetic of her novels: their truth is in their poetry.

The Unicorn makes striking use of the stage props and scenery
of the Romantic sublime. It is set in a prototypical 'horrid'

province of European Romanticism, a wilderness in West Ireland, where one house is crenellated and Gothic. The houses neighbour a sea which kills people, rocks with carnivorous plants, an unfeatured bog which picturesquely floods at seven-year intervals. It is a 'very ancient land' with megaliths, one of them 'seemingly pointless yet dreadfully significant'.

The governess Marian who enters the landscape in Chapter 1 is 'appalled', a primary verb in the grammar of the sublime, and experiences terror. The landscape is to prepare her for what awaits Marian in Gaze Castle. There is both more plot and more disquisition in *The Unicorn* than in *The Bell*, and the alternation between these is responsible for the book's effect of mixing sudden violence with inertia. Written in seven parts, the first two parts each have seven chapters. Like the seven-year cycle of events it recounts, it is thus in part itself a 'magical' object. About such enclosed and obsessional novels Murdoch has suggested that the characters are 'slaves' and that they concern the odd connexions which exist between spirituality and sex, and the ambiguity of the spiritual world itself (Rose, 1968). If, as a closed novel, this is the book that the more open novels are struggling to dilute or hold at bay, then it has special relevance for understanding her *oeuvre*. It is a 'mystical' novel in the sense that it addresses what lies beyond that demythologisation of Christianity she has called for;[18] and in interview with Rose it seemed a favourite book of hers.

Marian is hoping to escape from an unhappy love-affair in coming to Gaze. She finds that there are no children for her to teach. Her pupil is the fey, beautiful and imprisoned Hannah Crean-Smith, who represents the unicorn of the title, and who appears in two opposed and irreconcilable lights, half nun, half unconscious vamp and seductress. Her first name is a riddling palindrome, her second an anagram of Christ-Mean or Christ-Name, and her life can be read as an imitation of Christ.[19] She practises *contemptus mundi* in accepting her imprisonment by her absent husband Peter, for her 'crimes' of adultery and for his accident at the cliff-edge. Hannah gives away jewellery and dresses to Marian and orders new clothes for her. She has a stoical calm and a capacity to live in the moment – 'Marian had never seen anyone live so entirely in the present' (123) – which here evidence *amor fati*. The unicorn of the title is a leading symbol of Christ in medieval bestiaries, and the book abounds in other symbolic beasts, ranging from the mad hares of Chapter 10, the half-wild donkeys, and Denis' fish, all of them also symbols of Christ. Denis, clerk and keeper of the fish, brings Hannah bats, snakes, toads, hedgehogs, 'nice beasts' (39) and all symbols of the demonological.

The point about the unicorn symbol is that it is empty. No unicorn appears, Hannah fits her role imperfectly, and the title of the book invites us to ponder the role of the imagination in helping to create the world in which 'reason' sees. The imagery is disposable, and the absent centre perhaps points to Murdoch's own negative theology or secular mysticism in which the Good can be described only in terms of what it is not, and any attempt to incarnate or define it must finally be vain.

In *The Bell* the votaries of the Good occupied the servants' bedrooms at Imber. In *The Unicorn* they *are* servants. Violet Evercreech, a shabby genteel cousin of Hannah's, is housekeeper, her beautiful brother Jamesie is chauffeur, Gerald Scottow, a local youth who like Heathcliff has bettered himself, is Hannah's chief gaoler. Gerald is to the absent Peter what Calvin is to Mischa in *The Flight from the Enchanter*, the agent of his wickedest designs. He has also been Peter's lover, and is now Jamesie's.

Hannah's worshippers are also her gaolers. If she is ambiguous, so are they. She is the source and repository of the idea of the ambiguity of Eros, but in needing her to play the roles both of Christ and tainted enchantress, they collude. Spirituality, sex, and power are throughout the story richly confused. Gaze Castle might be called a brothel of mixed motives – an erotic prison masquerading as a place of religious retreat. The human being is, for Murdoch, the animal that worships – 'The impulse to worship is deep and ambiguous and old' (*SG* 100) – and such worship is rarely pure. 'Sexual feudalism' is how Peter's attitude to Gerald is described – Gerald was Peter's 'man, his serf' – but the term sexual feudalism (and not at all, as Robert Scholes has it, 'Christian feudalism'[20]) applies to most of the relationships. Jamesie, who had been Hannah's 'little page' has changed allegiance and is now, after being whipped and 'taken' by him, Scottow's slave. 'After Scottow had laid hands on him like that Jamesie worshipped Scottow and Scottow took Jamesie. That's how it was' (133). Hannah too is described as half-feudal and we are told that she regards Gerald so much as a domestic that she would have undressed in front of him. In Chapter 4 Hannah arouses Denis by putting her hand in his pocket while he cuts her hair, and later says of him 'I think he would let me kill him slowly' (43). Even Effingham, staying at nearby Riders vaguely assumes that the maid Carrie would do anything he wished and might not mind being taken into his bed 'as in some earlier and more brutish age' (157). Violet tells Marian that Jamesie would do 'anything for you, anything' (128) and importunes Marian herself.

The news from elsewhere that the story brings us is that we live in erotic servitude, powered by passions and obsessions that we only dimly understand. Murdoch's Eros is 'sex, power, desire, inspiration, *energy* for good and evil' (Art and Eros). The story creates a Manichean universe, in that it emphasises both our animality and our spirituality. Only two people are outside the chain of power. One of them is the Platonist Max, the ageing contemplative who watches events from a distance and, although he never meets Hannah, is bequeathed her house and given the most telling commentary on her drama. His house is called Riders, after the twin horses, good and bad, who drive the soul in the *Phaedrus*. The *Phaedrus* relates the attempt on truth to the purification of love. Max describes the automatic communication of power and suffering in which the denizens of Gaze are involved as *até*. Such infection, he says, is only quenched when it meets a pure being who suffers without passing the suffering on. Since he is untested himself, we never find out whether he is such a being. Hannah is not.

The gentle, virginal Denis, Christ's age at his death (thirty-three), who becomes Hannah's deputy after her death, is a second possible 'pure' being, despite Marian's seducing him. Sexual passion is one medium by which the infection of power gets transmitted. When Gerald takes Hannah this is experienced by her worshippers as a dramatic fall from grace. And after Marian sleeps with Denis she feels she has passed on to him some 'illness of the spirit, carrying it like a germ to a remote island' (206). Our sense of Marian's and Effingham's innocence, too, is tied up with their chastity.

In *The Sovereignty of Good* Murdoch has described how romanticism tended to transform the idea of death into the idea of suffering.

To do this is of course an age-old human temptation. Few ideas invented by humanity have more power to console than the idea of purgatory. To buy back evil by suffering in the embrace of the good: what could be more satisfying, or as a romantic might say, more thrilling? Indeed the central idea of Christianity lends itself to just this illegitimate transformation.   (82)

This romantic degeneration of the Good echoes an earlier analysis of sado-masochism, an enemy to clarity of vision in art or morals.

It is the peculiar subtlety of this system that, while constantly leading attention and energy back into the self, it can produce, almost all the way as it were to the summit, plausible imitations of what is good . . . . Fascinating too is the alleged relation of master to slave, of the good self to the bad self which, oddly enough, ends in such curious compromises . . . . The truly good is not a friendly tyrant to the bad, it is its deadly foe.   (68)

Purgatory, in this vision, is the realm of sado-masochistic compromise, in which the second-best masquerades as the Good. Such passages have been discussed in too simple-minded a fashion. Since no one is perfect, no endeavour is wholly free from taint. Purgatory, for Murdoch, is where we mostly live, the other name of the fallen world itself, and sado-masochism a principal form of entertainment.[21] Moreover the Platonic Good, being strictly inimitable, shares with Zeus a certain jealousy of all human striving, or of the attempt to incarnate value, which must necessarily (relatively) fail.

Nonetheless it is clear that Hannah is to embody such an impure parodic and romantic attempt on virtue. Hers is the realm of purgatory, not of true unselfing. This seems to be why so extraordinary a range of romantic truism and device is heaped on her. She is a '*princesse lointaine*' (89) in a 'castle perilous' (71), and finally 'a beautiful pale vampire . . . a *belle dame sans merci* . . . a doomed figure, a Lilith, a pale death-dealing enchantress' (268). It is the foolish Effingham who chiefly sees her so, appropriately as the man who finds it impossible to treat with woman as equals, and who from the start perceives himself as involved in the rituals of Courtly Love. 'Hannah makes romantics of us all' as he explains to Alice (78). John Bayley has described how, for Philip Larkin, romanticism is an intense effect of common reality, an elsewhere always conjured up by his sober insistence on the banality of the here and now. For Iris Murdoch 'the remote enchantment . . . the unattainable vision, the distant princess'[22] work rather differently: the here and now is dangerously and uncontrollably alive; art is on close terms with its daemonic energies, and alerts us to the deep strangeness of all we sleepily take for granted. Like Marian and Effingham, we are invited out of our ordinary world in order better to apprehend the forces which underlie it.[23] The unmasking of this strange power occurs, in the Gothic romances, through a playful *rapprochement* with the commonplaces of Romanticism, a paradox partly neutralised here by the fact that Effingham refers to the tale *as* a story – 'it had the qualities of a wonderful story' (73). 'But I'm a story for you, we remain on romantic terms' Hannah tells Effingham (91), who ponders the fact that only Gerald 'had not been paralysed by an allegory' (196).

It is easier to tease out the book's theology than it is to evoke the poetry in which the theology is dissolved, and to which it lends support. When Denis takes Marian to watch the salmon leap, 'like souls trying to reach their God' he tells her that 'suffering is no scandal. All creation suffers. It suffers from having been created if from nothing else. It suffers from being divided from God' (198); the book's Manichean theology is evident. The stylish, hectic excitements of the story and the weirdly 'beautiful' atmosphere in which it is played out matter too, however.

> How mysterious day and night are, this endless procession of dark and light. The transition always affects me. I think such sad thoughts – of people in trouble and afraid, all lonely people, all prisoners. (54)

Thus Hannah sadly and poetically rhapsodises to Marian. The rhapsody feeds the theology, of course, when Hannah adds 'Yet we all need love. Even God needs love. I suppose that why He created us.' A poignant metaphysical pathos is the book's deep element. The curious mixtures of elation and dread in which the story abounds, the 'magical' descriptions, all contribute to that atmosphere which is one of the gifts the reader takes away with him. Much poetry comes from those effects of light and dark to which Hannah referred.

> Sometimes lamps were lighted when darkness fell and sometimes not, and sometimes the ones that had been lighted

went out and one found one's way about through blackness to
intermittent glows and distant pinpoints of light,   (39)

as Marian observes of Gaze Castle. An opposition of gold and
black, light and dark, fills the story. The words 'gold' and 'golden'
occur some fifty times, and are augmented by yellow (Hannah's
dressing-gown), red, fawn, cinnamon, saffron, amethyst. Gold is
the colour of the sea in the evening-light (15), the brass bed-
knobs (18), Hannah's hair (23), Alice's hair (34), the seaweed
(31), Denis' goldfish and golden orfe (57), a necklace (51), the
silver moon which shrinks into 'a pale golden coin' (54), Pip's
troutfly (106), and the ubiquitous whisky which flows so generously.

Such effects are deliberate. They come together in their guise
as 'pure poetry' in the beautiful and moving scene in which, at
the end of the book, Marian watches the fey Denis disappear
back into his other world, and the stricken Alice sends her dog
Tadg, who loves Denis, running after him:

On the golden yellow hillside a little figure had appeared,
climbing up the path toward the bog. Marian watched it
recede. It was the last flicker, the last pinprick, that showed
the light through from that other world which she had so
briefly and uncomprehendingly inhabited . . . . Alice undid the
lead. 'Denis, Denis, Denis!' she whispered intensely to the
attentive dog, pointing her finger. Tadg hesitated: looked at
her, looked about, sniffed the ground, and then set off slowly.
He ambled, sniffing and looking back. Then he began to run
and disappeared into a dip in the ground. A little later, much
further up the hill, they saw the golden dog streaking upward
in pursuit of the man until both were lost to view in the saffron
yellow haze near the skyline.   (264)

In this small scene the imagery of light and dark, of distance as
a persistent figure for the mystery of Otherness, and of a 'pure' and
nobly unselfconscious love, all come together.Characteristically it
is through the relationship between dog and man, and not man
and man, that a reciprocated love is figured.

The imagery of light and dark develops a theological flavour
too. 'We see in the light of the Good . . . the source of light which
reveals to us all things as they really are' (*SG* 70). For Platonists

since Plotinus light has been the visible manifestation in the physical world of the life of the intelligible order,[24] and C. S. Lewis points out that the association of the radiance of the sun with that of the Good is so ancient as to appear to transcend the metaphorical.[25] The novel is full of suns setting and moons rising. The sun is the copy of the Good and the fire is, in Murdoch's Freudian reinterpretation of Plato, the ego which apes it and provides a surrogate light and heat. Hannah's room is perpetually warmed by a small turf fire, cut off from direct sunlight; it is half Platonic Cave, half ascetic's cell. Riders with its gold-haired maids is first seen in a sunny mist; Gaze with its black maids is just grey and forbidding. Such play with the idea of light, which recalls gnostic or cabbalistic light scattered through the fallen world, is not systematic; perhaps the ubiquitous emphasis on moonlight, since the moon borrows or copies the light of the sun, serves to emphasise the parodic nature of the virtue Hannah practises.

Certainly the idea of parody is itself important. The wicked Gerald is given a speech which parodies or copies Murdoch's Good when he suggests to Marian that 'life is never really happy and free in any beautiful sense. Happiness is a weak and paltry thing and perhaps "freedom" has no meaning. There are great patterns in which we are all involved.' Gerald's speech, which goes on to laud 'destinies which we love even in the moment when they destroy us' (151), is clearly a Satanic, deterministic parody of that true *amor fati* which Hannah attempts. Yet his questioning of the facility of the idea of freedom lies at the heart of the tale.

Marian and Effingham alike are the intelligent hedonists or happy egoists who believe that life should be happy and free, and their instructive disenchantment – which also reads to us as enchantment – procures the reader's pleasure. Their instruction is carried out through the story, by which both Gaze and Riders are paralysed; and by the perpetual leakage of religious terms out of their ordinary context. A landing light at Gaze shines 'as in a shrine', Marian first sees Alice comically carrying 'some sort of staff' as if she were a pilgrim. The staff turns out to be a fishing-rod, but there are mentions, of a similarly equivocal kind, of angels, rites, dark powers, sea-gods, portents, sacred objects. Effingham in the bog feels the need for a crucifix, Pip sees Hannah as a 'holy relic in a casket'. The apocalyptic vocabulary is the essence of Gothic, which has classically equivocated about the natural/supernatural status of its *data*. Murdoch, it is worth re-emphasising, is in no ordinary sense a Christian, and has no belief in God. It is morality, and love, which are to her supernatural. For her the supernatural has been internalised: we carry it, and the demonic, around inside of us, in the form of those secret imaginative lives in which we are always immersed, and which colour all we perceive.

The philosophies by which Marian and Effingham live are 'voluntaristic', which is to say philosophies of movement rather than attention, and there is an aptness in the fact that Effingham should be literally immobilised and imprisoned himself – Hannah-like, but in the bog – to be taught, momentarily, a truth. Effingham's disenchanting enlightenment – in which he learns that Freud and Wagner are disconfirmed – takes place in the featureless inhospitable wasteland of the negative sublime, a watery extension of the sea of self-extinction which abuts the houses. A single tree represents the Beckettian idea of location or place. The passage, from which I have quoted an excerpt, continues:

> He could still feel himself slowly sinking. He could not envisage what was to come. He did not want to perish whimpering. As if obeying some imperative, a larger imperative than he had ever acknowledged before, he collected himself and concentrated his attention; yet what he was concentrating on was blackness too, a very dark central blackness. He began to feel dazed and light-headed.
>
> Max had always known about death, had always sat there like a judge, in his chair facing toward death, like a judge or like a victim. Why had Effingham never realised that this was the only fact that mattered, perhaps the only fact there was? If one realised this one could have lived all one's life in the light. Yet why in the light, and why did it seem now that the dark ball at which he was staring was full of light? Something had been withdrawn, had slipped away from him in the moment of his attention and that something was simply himself. Perhaps he was dead already, the darkening image of himself forever removed. Yet what was left, for something was surely left, something existed still? It came to him with the simplicity of a simple sum. What was left was everything else, all that was not himself, that object which he had never before seen

and upon which he now gazed with the passion of a lover . . .
this was the love which was the same as death. He looked, and
knew with a clarity which was one with the increasing light,
that with the death of the self the world becomes quite
automatically the object of a perfect love . . . . (167)

The literal and figurative strikingly come together in Effingham's
beautifully described vision. The physical events provide a ritual
framework for the spiritual, but the physical and spiritual also
marry. Effingham is trapped in the bog, sinks, and is recovered
by Denis. He comes simultaneously to see that he has been
hitherto psychologically unfree. He sinks, therefore, in the phenomenal world too, to experience a sublime release from the
burden of his own selfconsciousness. His moral rescue precedes
his physical rescue. He learns that true unselfing, true love, true
perception are kin, and his brief moment of perfected love
contrasts with the imperfect loves at Gaze. Effingham, the
unremarkable fool of the sublime, briefly achieves what Hannah
has vainly striven for. 'Dawn', 'enlightenment' are used with a
brave facility that transcends the distinction between what
happens inside his head and the morning itself. The Platonic
theory of love, Wind notes, has habitually been used as a
philosophy of death,[26] and the literature of mysticism is full of
often incoherent accounts of such sublime ascesis and union with
the One. Cooper's vision is carried out with a panache which
brings together both its utter matter-of-fact-ness and its visionary
quality, and displays these as the same thing.

The beauty of the universe is revealed to him through the
momentary extinction of his own self-presence, and he is rewarded
by a further vision of the bog as newly created, in the book's
unique sunrise and only prism of primary colour, 'How beautiful
the bog looks in the sun. So many colours, reds and blues and
yellows. I never knew it had so many colours' (170). He is rescued
by Denis on a (Christ-marked) donkey. Before the after-glow has
entirely gone he tries to explain his vision to Alice, Marian and
Hannah, who appear to him as a mock-trinity or Neoplatonic
vision of the Graces. The spiritual Hannah at once understands,
Marian has no place in her jejune philosophy for such experience,
while Alice recognises it as a 'garbled version' – in fact of course
a pragmatic verification – of her father's Platonism. But his vision
wholly, and believably, fades.

A dark and perhaps over-plotted festival of substitution and repetition ensues, and Max gives the epitaph on Hannah, drowned like her returning husband. 'She could not really love the people she saw, she could not afford to, it would have made the limitations of her life too painful' (254). Hannah, like Michael in the different world of *The Bell*, was finally not made for that spiritual elsewhere which the Abbess in the earlier book, and Denis in this one, embody. Marian and Effingham return to the cave outside the story in a climate at last no longer golden, but wintry and subfusc. 'It had been a fantasy of the spiritual life, a story, a tragedy. Only the spiritual life has no story and is not tragic' the well-defended Effingham complacently but accurately reflects, on the train. Marian has been more deeply touched by the events. She arrived fighting against heartbreak over her unsuccessful love-affair with Geoffrey who has meanwhile become engaged to someone else. She goes back renewed and joyous, ready to dance at his wedding.

6 Self-sufficiency in *The Time of the Angels* and *The Nice and the Good*

Speaking on the BBC in 1968 Iris Murdoch suggested that, 'in a world such as ours, where the world of religion and God and gods has become completely problematic, there are more psychological forces working loose, as it were, as if they were demons or spirits' (Bryden, 1968). This scattering of the spiritual world forms the essential back-drop to two successive novels of the 1960s, the first 'closed' and apocalyptic, the second 'open' and benignly comic.

The Time of the Angels (1967), like *The Unicorn* (1963), is a Gothic and a religious novel, which distils a haunting atmospheric poetry. That it is also, in part, a farcical black comedy, helps make it the more successful. Carel Fisher is the mad rector of a non-existent City church of which only the Wren tower, itself shortly to be demolished, escaped wartime bombing. The isolated fog-bound Rectory in the East End exists in a perpetual wintry darkness. In the last chapter the tower is knocked down and the Rectory is to follow. The action thus takes place during a interim before the consecrated spaces of Christianity disappear, and the book is full of Nietzsche, to whom churches were now the tombs of God. Underground trains shake the Rectory, and the last Rector was pertinently an odd-looking crippled man. Murdoch again shows something like genius in her capacity to make poetry out of ordinary aspects of London life.

The title refers to the fact that the age is one of 'spirit without god', as the philosopher Rozanov, who refers to 'the time of the angels' in *The Philosopher's Pupil* (187), says. 'We must think of this time as an interregnum' (*TA* 89) suggests Carel's Bishop, and there is much pondering about what world of beliefs will follow the collapse of Christian values. The brisk ex-Fabian headmistress Norah suggests that the current amorality of the young may follow from this collapse. 'This sort of twilight-of-the-gods atmosphere will drive enough people mad before we get all that stuff out of our system', while Carel's weak brother Marcus, whom she addresses, thinks 'Could it be that the great curtain of huge and misty shapes would be rolled away at last, and if it were so, what would be revealed behind?' (18).

Within this context of demythologisation the Rectory is a claustrophobic presence. Representing an unstable half-way house between the secular and the spiritual worlds it is an analogue of Imber Court or Gaze Castle, and like them doomed to fail. But it is much more clearly demonic than either. Mircea Eliade has pointed out that 'the majority of men "without religion" still hold to pseudo-religions and degenerated mythologies'.[1] This applies as much to the rationalists outside the Rectory as to those within. Norah's brisk positivism and Marcus' Platonism are shown equally to involve faith if not superstition, while Anthea, the most shadowy of the three outsiders until the beautiful coda shows her shockingly weeping, is an ecstatic, credulous, muddled ex-Communist Buddhist, lovely, silly, with whom all three brothers, Carel, Marcus and the now dead Julian were all alike once in love. Murdoch has indeed called humanism a 'flimsy *creed*' (*SG* 47, my emphasis).

Profane life cannot do away with the religious valorisation of space, Eliade remarks. A man's birth-place, the scenes of his first love, certain places in the first foreign city he visited, all become 'holy places', spots in which he has received the revelation of a reality 'other' than that in which he participates in 'ordinary' life, and evoke in him crypto-religious behaviour.[2] Poetry has always fed on such differences. Here the black farce stems from the mutual irreconcilability of the two worlds, inside and outside the Rectory. If space can never be wholly desacralised, thresholds, both in houses and sanctuaries, take on a numinous importance, and the novel is punctuated by the attempts of the three humanist 'free-thinking' outsiders to gain entry in person or on the telephone. Carel's maid Pattie is instructed to hold them at bay. In *The Unicorn* the 'ordinary' had little tenure and had to be evoked by retrospect and letter. Here the moments of relaxation of tension outside the Rectory in Marcus' Earl's Court flat or Norah's East End house provide the make-believe of ordinary life in whose light the exotic illusions of the Rectory can be seen; and the book is a grim comedy of misproportion.

Murdoch's view is, in other words, that man is a spiritual creature willy-nilly, and her interest is in what is now to happen to such unhoused spirituality. This is the *loneliest* book in the Murdoch canon. Despite the usual diffusion of the erotic only two couplings take place, both mock-mythological: Carel makes love with black Pattie and later, as part of some blasphemous symmetry, with his blonde daughter Elizabeth. Though the ending holds out the possibility of a *rapprochement* between Marcus and Anthea, all the characters strike us, to an unusual degree, as bachelors. Solipsism is one of the book's subjects; and its obverse, self-sufficiency, another.

This is brought out in the arrangements made for meals. Muriel and Elizabeth cater for themselves, eating mainly eggs, Carel is vegetarian, Pattie cannot find the shops but lives on beans and sausages. Eugene is the only person in the Rectory to celebrate teatime. Outside, on the other hand, is the pure realm of teatime. Apart from one meal relished by the wonderfully greedy Bishop, tea is drunk or eaten on six occasions. In *The Nice and the Good* Theo is to refer to 'muffins for tea' as escapism, as part of 'the fantasy of ordinary life' (126). Here, when Norah and Marcus finally have an exchange which runs 'Muffins for tea' 'Muffins, goodie', the inanity is some sort of assurance that the ordinary cheerful selfish comforts of domesticity and appetite continue unabated, despite Carel's demonic posturings. When Dora in *The Bell* moved into the railway carriage containing the Imber pilgrims, she noticed that 'Everyone in this carriage was thinner' (17) as though a spiritual asceticism had physical signs. Here at last the language of appetite, fatness and thinness, is one by which Carel's world is judged, even as his self-mortifying diet mocks the Bishop's greed. Eugene the refugee porter is attracted to Pattie's round and comfortable shape which reminds him of Russian women. 'A thin woman is a reminder of death' (56).

The book again works through a division of sympathy. Outside the Rectory are the worthy humanist fools and moral foot-soldiers involved in those unheroic, thankless, useful tasks which keep society going. Earnest altruists all three, Marcus is a headmaster and amateur moral philosopher; Norah, a retired headmistress, full of overweight tweedy goodness, covets Marcus as a companion; Anthea is now a psychiatric social worker. All come out of a rooted and socially privileged world, and their prosy belongingness and limitations are set against the very different poetry of the

Rectory, in which values and persons alike have suffered radical displacement. Norah taught Carel's intelligent unloved daughter Muriel, who, wishing to be a poet, has dropped out. Marcus has taught the delinquent Leo, Eugene's amoral son. Eugene himself 'never made himself a place in English society'. The same could be said about everyone in the Rectory, all of whom are involved in some form of 'great refusal'. The tidy rational world which 1930s progressives like Norah hoped would come about when Christian and other superstition was at last vanquished, has wholly failed to materialise. The new world is atomised, bewildering, and demonic. Incest and theft, in this as in so many Murdoch novels, figure as paradigm forms of law-breaking. Against them Marcus' cosily optimistic values are defenceless, and he appears as a mythoclast in a world of myth, an exorcist surrounded by demons. The novel paradoxically revives that theological metaphor which Marcus, a tepid Platonist, wished to outlaw from the treatise he is writing on morality in a secular age, and such leakage penetrates the very title. Gothic has always exploited the gap between reason and imagination. Here it displays the frailties of reason, together with the potentially devilish nature of imagination.

Much of the burden of Carel Fisher's enchantment has to be carried by the imagery. It is this which creates so singular a poetry. His first name means 'cloistered enclosure'. His second makes him the impotent (fisher) king of a sterile land. It is the closed nature of his imaginings which is emphasised, from his lazily mistaking the Russian Eugene, with whom he has been living, for a Pole, to the effect he has on those who surround him. We are never shown his thoughts from the inside. The harmless, amply-made brown Pattie, bastard daughter of an Irish whore by a Jamaican client, feels taken over by Carel; she is his mistress as well as maid. When she first meets Carel she obscurely feels 'life has no outside' without understanding the phrase (31). Ten years later, when they move to London at the start of the tale, the phrase takes on flesh, since the Rectory 'seemed rather to have no exterior and, like the unimaginable circular universes which she had read about in the Sunday newspapers, to have absorbed all the other space into its substance' (21). Carel is the source of such illusions, their solipsistic centre, and hypostacised into a metaphysical region as much as a character. Neither Muriel nor Eugene can call him by name and he himself shouts ' "Come here" as if his presence were a definite locality' (34). The sun shines only twice in the book; aptly enough the second time Carel is dead, and the first time he has to wear dark-glasses because of the glare and asks for the curtains to be pulled. The reference to 'Plato's great allegory', by which Carel is seen as judged, is apparent. Muriel feels that her sister (as she in fact is) Elizabeth is the sole source of light in the 'dark unvisited cavernlike environment' (39) Carel creates around him. The fog too, like the endless dark and cold, requires to be read even more than that of *A Severed Head*, 'as if some inner darkness were being tormentingly exteriorised' (*SH* 122). Carel seems a source of the fog, as he is of the low mystification.

Cave-like environments and enclosures fill the book. Within the enclosed Rectory is Elizabeth's locked room within which Elizabeth wears a steel corset. The coal cellar into which Marcus falls, the linen-cupboard from which Muriel sees her father and Elizabeth make love, and the Russian box Muriel buys for Eugene which contains a demon of memory, are others. That Carel's is not the only mode of self-sufficiency, however, is suggested by Eugene. Appropriately for one so often displaced by war Eugene lives in a disused viewless air-raid shelter, next to the boiler, dispenser, as Eugene partly is himself, of life-giving warmth and energy. The cupboard full of dead birds which Carel summons as an image of the world's horror with which to torment Marcus is the most memorable of these enclosures.

The truthfulness of the novel, for all its air of poetic fantasy, comes from our certainty that it is not hard to find people in the world who 'are menacing, who breathe up all the air so that you can't breathe, and who diminish you' (Haffenden, 1983). Carel is a diminisher who has enlarged himself, and images of both demonic shrinkage and demonic hypertrophy, which occur in many of the novels, here help constitute the book. Since his single mind has greedily eaten up the available moral space, what is small and personal has swollen, and what should be huge and impersonal has shrunk. Muriel momentarily escapes in Chapter 13 to explain to Norah her fear of the metamorphosis of the world 'into something small and sleepy and enclosed, the interior of an egg' (131). Leo, justifying his theft of his father's icon – his sole and prized possession – says 'Supposing we're just frogspawn in somebody else's pond' (104), and Marcus, reflecting on his first visit to the Rectory, when he falls down the coal-hole, fears 'to hear Carel laugh, to see Carel move in a way that would reveal that black seething universe again. . . suddenly close at hand, like an ants' nest, like a smear of insects' eggs upon the tip of the finger' (115).

During this farcical colloquy in the dark – there has been a black-out, which figures here, as in *A Word Child*, as a failure of grace – Carel does nothing more alarming than proclaim himself the Nietzschean priest of no god, to decline any substitute form of illumination, and to proffer, in answer to Marcus' plea for physical contact, either a (priapic) carrot, or something worse.

The uncanny power of the images of demonic reduction – frogspawn, ants' eggs, perhaps too the girls' monotonous diet of eggs – is connected to the independent vitality they contain; and also, doubtless, to the fact that the novel thus provides a 'lucid commentary upon itself' and is its own 'best critic' (sw), commenting on its own status as claustrophobic romance. Reviewers who criticised the novel for being 'crystalline' failed to see that this was its point. In Carel it analyses a demonic monism which reduces the world to the single point of selfhood, and to a parody of the Good. Metaphoric reduction is its subject-matter, and it abounds in smaller instances – 'she had dried up into a little wrinkled nut' (48) – 'the mystery of Carel had shrunk to the size of a footstool' (230). Like Tennyson's vision in *In Memoriam* of men as 'the flies of latter Spring/That lay their eggs, and sting and sing,/And weave their petty cells and die', Carel's is partly a behaviorist nightmare. The motif of eggs is augmented by an associated one of bees – Muriel is haunted by a vision of stifling darkness buzzing like a tower of bees (124; 130) and has a phallic nightmare of something dark rearing up at her out of the ground. Pattie's vision of Carel shows many of the same terms, and the swarm of bees fits Carel both because of its cousinship to the flies over whom Beelzebub is lord, and because a swarm is, like Carel's people in the Rectory, homeless, clustering round an errant leader.

Burke's *Treatise on the Sublime* points out that 'the last extreme of littleness is in some measure sublime'.[3] If vastness belongs to the sublime, so littleness belongs to the little brother of the sublime, the picturesque;[4] that Murdoch rarely achieves less than such a sustained picturesqueness might be thought a measure of her success. Normally a relaxed if not a careless symbolist,

Murdoch here delegates to such local verbal effect a large
responsibility in carrying the book's truth.

*

Much is transacted through the argument and plot too. Marcus
has taken a two-term sabbatical to write a treatise on 'Morality
in a World without God', wishing to emulate Nietzsche's *Birth
of Tragedy* for its wit and energy. Like Rupert's study in *A
Fairly Honourable Defeat*, which ends disastrously, this work
resembles Murdoch's own *The Sovereignty of Good* down to its
modest final acknowledgement that he was 'after all, just a
Platonist' (68).

Nietzsche appointed Apollo and Dionysus mutually necessary
twin deities and saw the birth of tragedy as the result of the
struggle and fusion between them. The Apollonian world of
formal clarity, reason, lucidity and the *principium individuationis* is
opposed to the Dionysiac Sublime of pre-conscious formlessness.
The issue of their union is the aesthetic joy in whose light we can
apprehend the vulnerability of individual aspiration, as well as
the savage strength of the life-force itself. Carel is to show Marcus
how the Dionysiac Sublime – 'Chaos and Old Night' – now
threatens all ethical theorising, including his own, more
apocalyptically than in previous epochs.

Marcus' fears about his brother, and his fears that the truth
about human life is 'something terrible, something appalling
which one would be destroyed by contemplating' (91) are first
voiced to the worldly, greedy Bishop, a complacent demythologist
scraping Stilton from his episcopal ring, and the comically brisk
Norah ('Here, take your coffee'). Behind the Bishop's cosy
blandness 'there opened a black scene, as if the walls had rolled
away to reveal the trough of the heavens, dark, seething with
matter, riddled with void, and without any intelligible principle
of organisation' (114). This vision is actualised for Marcus by
Carel's great speech in Chapter 17, the heart of the idea-play,
and a parody, once more, of Murdoch's own views. Carel argues
that all philosophy and all interpretation of the world is childish
prattle; what lies behind these vain and talismanic attempts to
compel the world rather than submit to it, is too terrible to
contemplate. Like Hugo's disquisitions to Jake in *Under the Net*,
of which this is a direct descendant, Carel argues that in
philosophising we try to tame something which can never be

subdued. The difference is that, while for Hugo the untameable energies concealed behind language are surprising and joyous, for Carel they are (with equal validity of course) the negative sublime:

> Suppose the truth were awful, suppose it was just a black pit, or like birds huddled in the dust in a dark cupboard? Suppose only evil were real, only it was not evil since it had lost even its name? Who could face this? The philosophers never even tried. All philosophy has taught a facile optimism, even Plato did so . . . . There is only power and the marvel of power, there is only chance and the terror of chance . . . . All altruism feeds the fat ego . . . . We do not know the truth because as I told you it cannot be endured. People will endlessly conceal from themselves that good is only good if one is good for nothing . . . . One must be good for nothing, without sense or reward, in the world of Jehovah and Leviathan, and that is why goodness is impossible for us human beings. . . .   (163–5)

Citing *Romans* viii 38, as do characters in two succeeding novels (*NG* 192; *FHD* 209), Carel tells Marcus 'there are principalities and powers. Angels are the thoughts of God. Now he has been dissolved into his thoughts which are beyond our conception in their nature and their multiplicity and their power.' There is much here of Murdoch's own thought, as it were, gone wrong. She too has taught that we must be 'good for nothing', has decried the optimism of much moral thinking, and required art to exhibit 'a juxtaposition, almost an identification, of pointlessness and value' (*SG* 87); if we are to be good for nothing then the full force of that 'nothing', that pointlessness, must itself also be apprehended. And a demonic negation is paradoxically always closer to the truth than the unreconstructed liberal posture, here and elsewhere. Hence the devils have the best tunes.

In a sense she divides herself between Carel and Marcus; Marcus' thought, like hers, risks being surreptitiously dependent on the theology it claims to supplant. He is given her moral idealism; Carel her desire for a position 'beyond consolation'. Carel has been maddened by religious terrors and by his own guilt. Marcus' induction into the secret life of the Rectory is never completed. Carel's anti-sermon to him follows immediately on our shock at learning, as Marcus never does, that Carel and

Elizabeth are lovers. Marcus opens his mouth to cry 'like a banished Adam' at what Carel has to teach him, thus sharing momentarily in the condition of exile that governs Rectory life; but while he learns about Carel's negative theology, he never learns that Carel had in effect driven their younger brother Julian to suicide, impregnating his wife from motives of revenge, or that the baby born of this adventure, who is his daughter Elizabeth, is also his mistress.

These events are disclosed with a superlative energy and timing for effect. They are also placed in just such a playful fog of 'degenerate mythology' as Marcus has decried. The book abounds in parodies of the Trinity – the three Fisher brothers, the three youngsters Elizabeth, Leo, Muriel, the three liberal do-gooders, the three angels on Eugene's icon.[5] Such signs, like the blank paper darts Carel sails, are ambiguous 'empty' messages, conducing in us equally to a sense of the need, and of the impossibility, of demythologisation. Carel's complaint about 'a black thing, which kept whisking out of sight' (32) is one nicely unconfirmed diabolical manifestation, the sisters' greeting ('Hail to thee') perhaps another.

Myth combines as always with psychology. Murdoch has provided an efficient rationale for Carel's being, as Pattie accurately sees him, 'a soul in hell' (32), in his earlier, almost inadvertent destruction of his brother. He may masquerade as the Nietzschean man of will and good conscience, liberated from 'slave-morality', and decked out with a private creed of Heideggerian nullity and death. 'Possibly Heidegger is Lucifer in person', Murdoch ironically wrote (*SG* 72).[6] Other books of the 1960s share an interest in how their characters atone for past acts of violence; and in their context Carel seems a man incapable of the essential (and ambiguous) act of self-forgiveness. Like Hilary in *A Word Child* his later crimes follow from this. The many small jokes about multiplicity assist the mythological context, so that Pattie three times quotes Blake on the renewal of 'fallen, fallen light' (10, 31, 84); and the daughters play with jigsaws, which are games about multiplicity and unity, in which a world can be seen scattered or unified, or both at once. But the centre for such play is the Byronic Carel himself. He argues that Goodness is no longer there at the centre of things radiating its pattern, and that 'Multiplicity is not paganism, it is the triumph of evil, or rather of what used to be called evil and is now nameless' (164). *The*

Time of the Angels is a 'closed' novel about the dispersion of the spiritual world, its title referring to the fragmentation which follows from the perception that 'the single Good of the philosophers is a lie and a fake' (164); the succeeding novel *The Nice and the Good* is an 'open' book which points to exactly the missing value (the Good) in its title. Carel has aped and parodied the Good; his sin is spiritual pride, and that we are to take his humourless pretensions less than seriously seems clear at least from his romantic love of Tchaikovski. It seems apt that he should die to the 'Dance of the Cygnets' from Swan Lake. His death, by virtue of his punning surname, promises a restoration of fertility to the wasteland.

*

Redemption may be discussed in the novels in the high-minded language of theological romanticism. A wholly different rhetoric, however, is angled against it. According to this second-best rhetoric, Carel's mode of solipsism is only one kind of human self-sufficiency. More innocent kinds also exist. The kindly and warm-hearted Eugene, for example, has a 'really monstrous self-satisfaction' too relaxed to be called pride, an aristocratic self-possession or joy in the body paradoxically related to the moral life, and associated, throughout Murdoch's *oeuvre*, with dogs. Pattie, deprived as a child of physical love, is divided between Carel's demon self-absorption and Eugene's happier self-pride. She 'coveted [Eugene's] innocence, scarcely knowing what this meant, she rubbed herself dog-like against it. Eugene represented the good clean simple world out of which she had irrevocably slipped' (80). For Muriel too Eugene represents 'that world of thoughtless affections and free happy laughter and dogs passing by in the street from which she felt herself to be totally separated' (90). This physical force making for happinesss is weak in this novel. It lets even Eugene down in the end, and most of the cast represent, like Pattie, a 'nationality of one' – Beckettian stripped men. The discovery in the last words of the book that Eugene's first tragedy had been the death of a beloved dog suggests that his exile from the state of well-being began early; while Eugene's delinquent son Leo, who is clearly a theory-less understudy for Carel, and an accomplished exploiter of the sado-masochism that for Carel, as for Murdoch, wholly rules the fallen world, is a more comical villain than Carel. His unhesitating love of pleasure, compared to Carel's posturing asceticism, reads as a sign of grace.

Such happy animal grace plays a larger part in *The Nice and the Good* (1968), the immediately succeeding book. The succession of moods between them prefigures Morgan's two rapid visions in the railway cutting of *A Fairly Honourable Defeat*, a hellish, then a beatific vision, of the fall into multiplicity. If *The Time of the Angels* is a Song of Experience, so *The Nice and the Good* is a Song of Innocence, restoring fertility to the wasteland, and starting where the earlier book ends, with the death of a paltry Satanist. Here the wintry sunless cold, the claustrophobia and foggy obscurity of the earlier book are replaced by a perpetual Dorset sunshine in which you can 'see infinitely far'. Here it is rain, and not sun, that is awaited, and arrives in the book's last words: 'Hand in hand, the children began to run homeward through the soft warm drizzle', the culmination of a series of final images of co-operation that recalls the Peaceable Kingdom. After the winter's tale, a summer's tale.

The Nice and the Good was greeted by reviewers, mistakenly I think, as a 'true novel' after its 'fairy-tale' predecessor. In fact it is just as interested in the supernatural – in a specific 'poetic' sense – as *The Time of the Angels*, and mentions rays, *eidola*, currents, exhalations, gaseous tentacles, forces, gods, imps, graces, principalities and powers, emanations and *genii*. Its paltry Satanist Radeechy commits suicide before the action starts, rather than, like Carel, at the end; but such phenomena outlive him. Murdoch's interest in the supernatural is a problem for some readers. In *Nuns and Soldiers* Anne Cavidge has a waking vision of Christ; in *The Sea, The Sea* levitation seems to occur. 'I think paranormal things probably do happen, particularly in Tibet' (Bigsby, 1982) she has said; but this should not obscure for us that what is supernatural for Murdoch is principally the imagination itself, and love in particular, 'that old unpredictable force left out of account by natural science' (*PP* 566). The supernatural is now *inside* us, in the sense that we have fundamentally mysterious capacities to help and hurt ourselves and others, through our conduct of our own inner life.[7] The 'powers' that she mentions are naturalised: they are ways of pointing to aspects of our apprehension of other people which are not, as in a simple realism, 'inert' but full of ambiguous power. The flying saucers in this book, as in *The Philosopher's Pupil*, are thus small jokes about redemption – about the redemptive capacities of love, and its inaccessibility too.

Account of Murdoch's Shakespearian interest has tended to concentrate on the search for sources and for aesthetic excuses which I do not feel her work badly needs.[8] What is Shakespearian about this novel is its lyrical meditation, as in late romances such as *The Tempest, A Winter's Tale*, on the miraculous themes of love, forgiveness and reconciliation. An ideal world in which love could have supernatural harmonising power conflicts with intractable muddle and multiplicity; the poignant mood, like that of the mature bitter-sweet Comedies, is extraordinarily poised between joy and a sad complaisance. 'By the way, since one or two people have asked: no one in the book is good', Murdoch has pointed out;[9] but the mood is by no means severe. It is divided between a wicked court at Whitehall and its pastoral cousin, Trescombe, a Dorset Arden in a green world. Its festive ending depends on the exclusion of Casie the maid, who thinks things are managed better in Russia, and Theo, an unsententious Jaques who rails against all the other characters for not being saints (compare *As You Like It* II iv 56–7: 'I'll rail against all the first-born in Egypt'), and who, like Jaques too, prepares at the end to neglect the pompous court and leave the others to their 'Nice' (i.e. erotic) pleasures, while he goes to a Buddhist monastery. As well as exploring the Good with one half of its title the book is glazed over with the bitter-sweet pleasures of the Nice. The lack of coincidence of Nice and Good is its main – and ambiguous – moral point.

The novel is more inclusive than its predecessor, holding both fossils and flying-saucers, murder and love, Dorset and London; but it reworks similar material to a very different effect. Here the cast of displaced persons, unfortunates who have fallen out of the great social bond, is roughly held in place at the Dorset court of the philanthropic, selfish hedonists, Kate and Octavian Gray. Kate's friend Paula Biranne, who has a cold probity, concern for accuracy and for 'moral style', wrestles with a broken marriage and love affair, broken when her husband mutilated her lover. Family resemblances are beautifully observed. Her son Pierce's awkward simplicity and passion recall his mother's studious virtue. Mary Clothier, who unofficially mothers the Trescombe world, ponders the death of her husband, stupidly run over during a marital row. Her twins Henrietta and Edward are 'the only really satisfactory human beings at Trescombe' (261). Octavian's would-be saintly brother Theo had to leave the Indian Civil Service because of a scandal with a boy, and is exiled from the Buddhist community that gave him a standard to love by. Kate's daughter Barbara has a spoiled waywardness and 'missishness' which seem a wilder version of her mother's. At the farthest edge of this world is the refugee Willy Kost, in a separate cottage, only just held within the court. His demons turn out at the end to stem from his needless betrayal of two fellow-prisoners in Dachau, where he spent the war.

Paula speaks for all the characters when she thinks:

> Is it fruitless to think about the past and build up coherent pictures of what went wrong? I have never believed in remorse and repentance. But one must do something about the past. It doesn't just cease to be. It goes on existing and affecting the present, and in new and different ways, as if in some other dimension it too were growing. (122)

'What to do about the past' is one great theme of the novels of the 1960s. In *Bruno's Dream* the dying Bruno ponders whether his wife wished to curse him at the moment of her death fifty years before. She had contracted cancer soon after seeing Bruno with his mistress, and fearing her anger, he let her die alone. At the moment of his own death he realises exactly why she more probably wished to be reconciled to him. In *The Time of the Angels* Carel found no way of exorcising his past crimes; but here love and luck are given better opportunities. The same theme also links the thriller-aspect of the novel to its erotic intrigue. Octavian's colleague, and Kate's platonic lover Ducane, is given the job of investigating the satanist Radeechy's suicide, and uncovers some nasty secrets. His detective work turns out to be as much theological as civil; and it is what he uncovers about the human heart that finally matters as much as his resolution both of the scandal, and, as it happens, of the marriage between the Birannes. Can love call the world to order and heal the illness of things? Its exorcisms are shown here to be flawed and partial, but they are granted luck by the author. Luck, too is one of the novel's themes, and that luck can unfairly help neutralise the past as well as any other power is an aspect of its irony.

If love is the book's supernatural exorcising power, agnosticism is one of its guises. A certain sentimental indeterminacy rules over Trescombe. The book is full of exceptions, of special cases that transcend classification and utility. Ducane's servant Fivey becomes Scots for Ducane, West Irish for Kate and finally Welsh-Australian for Judy McGrath with whom he elopes at the end. He is there to complete the circuit of self-love of those he encounters. His mother may have been a mermaid and Ducane does not ask if she was a fake mermaid – 'he preferred not to know' (31). Agnosticism about the marvellous fills the book. Indeed, the relinquishing of the attempt to exercise a dessicating reason is a *source* here of the marvellous. Theo charges Willy in his editing of the great Latin poet of love and elegy Propertius, of serving not some high-minded ideal (the Good) but merely his own sublime egotism (the Nice). Willy returns – and it is a crucial agnosticism to the book – 'That is possible . . . . But I don't see why one should necessarily know. You are a great one for not knowing things. Let's not know that, shall we?' (127).

Willy may come from Prague, as Ducane maintains, or Vienna, as Octavian insists, while Mary 'had no theory, coming at last to accept Willy's sad European mysteriousness as a sort of physical quality and one which racked her tenderness more than any positive knowledge could have done' (91). The connexions between tenderness and seeing everything, as did Hugo in *Under the Net*, as *sui generis*, whimsically outside classification, are made many times. Mary, unable to determine the colour of Theo's eyes, finds that in his passport he has charmingly described them as 'mud'. The beloved dog Mingo, a somewhat poodle-like animal, is more like a sheep than a dog owing to sheep ancestry. The cat Montrose is a tabby animal with a talent for looking like a bird. There are discussions about the nature of miracles, and about why Shakespeare never wrote a play about Merlin. Mary suggests that the world of magical relationships, not quite in the real world, was insufficiently *large* for his purposes (103). The novel is as clearly self-conscious about its own status as a romance here as when the 'great-souled' twins (185) are rewarded by their final glimpse of the flying saucer. The mood, in all these instances, is that of Jakes's final discovery that the world is mysteriously larger than our descriptions of it. The same discovery helped to madden Carel. Here it is a source of joy.

The novel does not urge the eschewing of curiosity – quite the contrary – but merely the postponing of curiosity's final 'satisfaction'. Thus the great-souled twins also show a persistent factual curiosity about such question as how the Greeks cooked eggs, why animals do not blow their noses, how large a breast-bone a human being would need to fly, and the symbiotic relationship between bears and honey-guiding birds in the Amazonian jungle. Kate at once thinks of applying to them when wondering if there is a dew in Africa, and they are shown trying to find out how the tendons work inside a chicken-leg. It is imagination which is the supernatural faculty, and the twins, by being attentive in this best sense, also know that Pierce means exactly what he says when he threatens to enter the cave (292); and that their father would return to them (352).

The twins also confuse human classification, as well as clarifying it, and are constantly undoing, for example, the boundary between the house and the shore, putting seaweed in the bath (a cure for rheumatism). 'The sea shore invaded the house. The children's rooms were gritty with sand and stones and crushed sea shells and dried up marine entities of animal and vegetable origin' (12). The sea, which contains all things, is the very image of the contingent, the dangerously changeable – a neat phrase speaks of the 'ocean of accident' (309) – and it is *poetically* apt that Trescombe, in having a lucky relationship with the forces that make for multiplicity, should be on such good terms with it. This is a book full of odd serendipitous poetic lists, which dramatise the brute randomness of nature and the limits to the power of spirit over it. Searching for chicken-legs the twins pull out 'screwed-up paper, coffee beans, old lettuce leaves, and human hair'. Ducane's jealous ex-mistress Jessica catalogues the contents of his wastepaper basket and his pockets. In all these lists the anonymous word 'entities' recurs, and, as an artist Jessica also collects 'entities' which are neither ornaments nor works of art – 'She wandered the rubbish tips at night, bringing back bricks, tiles, pieces of wood, tangles of wire. Sometimes she made these things into other things. Sometimes they were allowed to remain themselves' (25).

The problems of how far you can tolerate the world's random-ness is dramatised at various points. Octavian is benignly tolerant of his wife's random collecting of people, while, for his brother Theo, multiplicity, despite the fungoid litter of underwear and newspapers with which he is surrounded, is a problem. I mentioned in the last chapter the recurrent topos in Murdoch's work of someone reacting to the randomness of the stones on a seashore, taking force from that moment in *Nausea* when Roquentin is impressed by their brutal solidity. Here the goodish twins collect stones, seeing them as a 'treasury of lovable individuals' and wish they could distinguish every stone with their attentions, while the tormented, lazy Theo finds them a nightmare. 'Their multiplicity and randomness appalled him. The intention of God could reach only a little way through the opacity of matter, and where it failed there was just jumble and desolation . . . . Does nature suffer here, in her extremities, Theo wondered, or is all dead here? Jumble and desolation, was it not all an expanse of senseless random nature, and he himself as meaningless as these stones, since in real truth there was no God?' (153–4).

Such incommensurabilities between mind and world in this novel are held in place. The human world is neither shrunken nor swollen as it was in *The Time of the Angels*. The ruling harmony or proportion is referred to when Ducane notices, in the novel's only italicised phrase, that

> Everything in Dorset is round . . . . The little hills are round, these bricks are round, the yew . . . the veronica bushes, the catalpa tree, the crowns of the acacia, the pebbles on the beach, the clump of small bamboos beside the arch. He thought, everything in Dorset is *just the right size*. This thought gave him immense satisfaction and sent out through the other layers and compartments of his mind a stream of warm and soothing particles. Thus he walked on with Kate at his side, conveying along with him his jumbled cloud of thoughts whose self-protective and self-adjusting chemistry is known as mental health.   (47)

The tolerant, mocking precision which gives us that last donnish phrase marks a new phase of ironic benevolence about the urgencies of the ego. The requirements of the self are, of course, connected to mental health and ordinary unambitious moral orientation, which have in Ducane's case to withstand his desperate girlfriend Jessica whom he fears as 'an entangling power that was *growing*' (133). They have also themselves finally to acknowledge a limit: 'The puffed up and affronted self must cease its importunities at last' (79), Ducane thinks. Murdoch seems to associate a traditional pictorial realism with moral proportion, and in Chapter 13, describing the London as opposed to the Dorset summer, in which Radeechy has been practising his paltry demonism,

> The whole district vibrated, jerked and shifted slightly, as if something else and very nasty were trying, through faults and knots and little crazy corners where lines just failed to meet, to make its way into the ordinary world.   (112)

The lines which fail to meet recall the corner of the linen-cupboard through which Muriel witnesses her father's incest with her sister. But the point about the resurrection of the image here as a metaphor is to equate deformed perspective with moral enormity. When Ducane during his disorientating ordeal in the cave at last finds Pierce, this evidence that he is not alone provokes in him the sensation that 'all round him he could feel things resume their natural sizes' (297). Natural size here goes with natural shape; and natural shape, by the elaboration of an authorial joke which in its context has a pleasing poetry about it is throughout, *round*. Roundness in this book seems to figure for a benevolent solipsism, and is ubiquitous. The twins give Theo a spherical long-tailed tit's nest, Willy gives Mary an almost perfect glass sphere, worked by the sea and semi-transparent. I noted how in *The Time of the Angels* Carel's thinness became something like a moral attribute, connected to demonic shrinking and hypertrophy. Solipsism made of the tiny self a cosmos, and of the cosmos a puny egg. Here Mary experiences the Grays' virtues as 'somehow expressed in their roundness' (19), Octavian is described as a 'perfect sphere' (7) by his wife, and as 'that perfect O' by his brother. Such a rhetoric is connected to the attempt, clearer in this than any preceding book, to locate all experience in the body. Mary realises at the end that she loves Ducane, as she never loved Willy, 'with her whole thought-body'. 'We think with our body, with its yearnings and its shrinkings and its ghostly walkings' (334), comments the narrative voice.

*

John Bayley's *Tolstoi and the Novel* throws light on this. Bayley writes of Platon Karataev's '*roundness* (the roundness of the single unit shows its separation from other units)'. Bayley criticises Platon on the ground that Tolstoi writes best only when he feels his characters from the inside as if wearing them on his body. The simplest of Tolstoi's characters when they come off, are not nobly unconscious of themselves but full of a sense, on the contrary,of what it means to be them. All Tolstoi's characters begin with a body, and everywhere in his work we can find reference to characters being pleased with themselves. Like Chaucer, Tolstoi is, in a marvellous phrase, 'a profound and delighted connoisseur of self-satisfaction', and

> this confidence is deeply aristocratic, not so much in the class sense – though that of course comes into it – but in the sense in which complete self-sufficiency is the most aristocratic of feelings, the feeling which may unite king and beggar; and which does in fact unite Pierre . . . with the simple Karataev.

While this calm invincible aristocratic conceit may offend us, Bayley shows the connexions between such joyous profitable solipsism and virtue. Bravery, for example, may imply 'the ability to create, as Petya does before his death, a complete world of our own in the midst of alien circumstances', and that man who is most securely himself can be, on occasion, the most instinctively unselfish. Noting that Tolstoi tends to take physical contentment as a sign of spiritual advancement – 'and perhaps it is such a sign?' – Bayley writes about the tutelary genius of this *samodovolnost* (self-sufficiency or self-esteem), Stiva Oblonsky in *Anna Karenina*. Stiva is the centre of worldliness and the Nice in that book, a squalid philanderer who hurts his wife and yet a curiously innocent altruist too:

> Stiva can do, and does, a great deal of good in his own world. He can make others happy, and everyone is glad to see him. In acknowledging his gifts and his graces Tolstoi puts aside the innocence of analysis and the innocence of uncompromising severity. In an imperfect world the imperfect Stiva can be an agent of light and in recognising this Tolstoi recognises on a typically though equivocally heroic scale the necessary imperfection of things. Such an admission is the essence of worldliness.[10]

If Stiva has soul-fellows in *The Nice and the Good* these are the Grays, who represent the ('Nice') virtue of *samodovolnost* in the purest form it takes in Murdoch's work. Enjoying the 'deep superiority of the socially secure' (19), they are happily married and 'spontaneous in their efforts to cause happiness in others' (20). Kate's capacity to live in the present makes her 'eternally and unreflectively happy' (210) 'always happy' (97). Such happiness reads as a real and resilient simulacrum of virtue. When Kate meditates on her sentimental friendship with Ducane she believes she can square everyone concerned. '[Ducane's] still worried about Octavian but he'll soon see that all is perfectly well, and then he'll settle down to being happy too' (124).

This parody suggests that Dame Julian's millennium – invoked in almost every Murdoch novel by at least one character – could be brought about by an extension of low Eros, by everyone 'loving' everyone else in no matter how covetous or promiscuous a fashion. And Kate's friendship with Ducane is as unstable as any such *amitié amoureuse* in Murdoch's novels. From another point of view this doesn't matter. After the disasters that separate her and John at the end she laments 'All our house seems broken apart', to which Octavian ripostes 'Darling, you'll soon get other ones' (342). Octavian's remark is funny because, though unkind, it is also true. Kate had acquisitively wished she could 'have' Ducane's servant Fivey. She inhabits the fallen world of substitution and repetition, but does so in a manner that is by no means witless. In an imperfect world the imperfect Kate is – like Stiva – unequivocally an agent of light. For example with Mary, whom she has 'collected' and who is useful to her:

> Kate, who was not even conscious of Mary as a disappointed person, half cured her. Kate, eternally and unreflectingly happy herself, made Mary want happiness, and startled her, by a sort of electrical contact, into the hope of it . . . . *The golden and life-giving egoism and rich self-satisfaction of Kate and her husband* inspired in Mary a certain hedonism which, puny as it was by comparision, was for her a saving grace. (22) [my emphasis]

Kate is not simply inattentive – she notices Paula's depression for example (62). It is rather, and it is a point worth emphasising, since such absolutist readings of Murdoch's novels are sometimes to be found, that 'golden egoism' can, with luck, figure as a potentially life-giving force. Ducane similarly prays for a 'saving egoism' in Jessica (271). Here Octavian's adultery, of which we learn late, might be compared with Paula's. Octavian occasionally stays late at the office with his secretary, but 'easily forgave himself, so completely forgetting the matter as to feel blameless, and as he frequently decided that each occasion was the last he did not view himself as a deceiver of his wife. His knowledge that there was indeed nothing which she concealed from him was a profound source of happiness and satisfaction' (343). Octavian's genial moral torpor and self-deception here are very funny, because very recognisable. By contrast the Trescombe women, Paula and Mary, who are by normal standards more moral – certainly, in their different ways, more studious and less able to live in the present, tormented as they are by different memories – appear culpably intense. Indeed Mary charges herself, in a chapter in which her compulsive worries explicitly contrast with Kate's voluptuous pleasures ('Oh, how utterly marvellous it is to be me!', thinks Kate), with being 'stupidly, *wickedly* anxious' (123). This does not diminish the distance between virtue and pleasure; it beautifully suggests that matters are not as simple in life as they are in a Neoplatonic allegory about virtue and pleasure, such as the Bronzino *Venus, Cupid, Folly and Time*, which provides one aesthetic centre, and around which the Birannes comically and movingly remeet. This painting depicts the pleasures of love as futile, fallacious, and its dangers and tortures as great and real evils.[11] *The Nice and the Good* is embattled too, but more ambiguously than this, and Biranne's passion and sensual expertise is not under-rated as a force for happiness.

The outwardly placid Theo movingly defines the gap enshrined in the title towards the end of the novel

> Theo had begun to glimpse the distance which separates the nice from the good and the vision of this gap had terrified his soul. He had seen, far off, what is perhaps the most dreadful thing in the world, the other face of love, its blank face. Everything that he was, even the best that he was, was connected with possessive self-filling human love.   (350)

This ending, in which the broken Theo consoles Casie, whom he both affectionately insults, but also feels kin to, is full of ironies.

Casie is crying at the television; Theo at the shabbiness of his life. Murdoch has compared television with Platonic *eikasia*, the lowest, most irrational kind of awareness, equivalent to a vague image-ridden illusion (*FS* 65). There is no guarantee that Theo's grief, which is consoling too in its own way, represents a 'higher' state of illusion than Casie's. And it is the worldly Octavian who is seen at one point as a 'fat golden Buddha' (270); his spiritual brother Theo with his 'considerable gift for being physically relaxed' has an 'animal placidity' that, Bayley reminds us, may or may not be a sign of spiritual advancement. Stylistic symmetries and repetitions are used throughout to suggest that, *contra* Tolstoi, it is in unhappiness that we most resemble one another; and only the happy are fully differentiated.

*

In fact all the characters are seen in terms of their kinship with the animal world. The novel reads as if partly *about* the problems of incarnation, and the characters apprehend one another as animals as well as spirits. In *An Accidental Man* Garth is to tell Gracie authoritatively, 'Intellect is sexless, but spirit is almost all sex. In fact it is all sex, only it sounds misleading to say so . . . . Consider Shakespeare. All sex, all spirit' (*AM* 395). It is not simply a matter of Murdoch seeking a balance between the claims of sex (body) and spirit, though that comes into it, but of her constantly showing us the artificiality of considering them as discontinuous. When Mary recognises that what is wrong with her relationship with Willy is its 'want of animal cheerfulness' and invokes a bouncy physical well-being that seems to help (123), this indivisibility is truthfully displayed. Theo resembles a dog and constitutes, with Mingo, a dog–man pair. Paula has a keen smiling dog face, Pierce a nose which his acquaintances seek to stroke 'like a pony' (22), Fivey (spaniel) and McGrath (kitten) meet 'like two dogs' (174). Judy as Circe has the knack of turning all mankind into animals.

The games the twins play comment obliquely on all this. Rodents are associated throughout with cunning self-seeking ('the rat-runs of fantasy' is a potent phrase from *The Sovereignty of Good*, 86). Paula feels she has played a 'mean scurrying part' (40) with her husband. Judy tells Ducane not to let the rats in and explains that she means cats. Radeechy habitually saw rats and used mice in his Satanic ceremonies (68). And both Ducane and Theo see themselves unflatteringly as rodents. 'I live in myself like a mouse in a ruin. I am huge, sprawling, corrupt, and empty. The mouse moves, the ruin moulders. That is all' (350), thinks Theo. Ducane's recognition comes in the cave where he nearly drowns with Pierce and Mingo:

> He saw himself now as a little rat, a busy little scurrying rat seeking out its own little advantages and comforts. To live easily, to have cosy familiar pleasures, to be well thought of . . . . Nothing is worth doing except to kill the little rat . . . .   (307)

I think that the twins' game called, no one discovers why, 'Noble Mice' (22) may jokingly refer to the second-best principled egoism – that intelligent hedonism thought by Plato to be the best moral guide for the majority[12] – which the book with due irony discusses and criticises; 'Feathers', another game, recalls the dead birds in Radeechy's cellar, symbolising, like the dead birds in the cupboard Carel summons as an image with which to horrify Marcus, the impossibility of transcendence. In this book these dead birds are actualised for us in Radeechy's paltry rites. What is physical for Murdoch is always containable in its mystery and horror. It is the metaphoric which (as in the next book, where these enclosed dead birds partly become, once more, an image) is the source of creative instability.

Smell, the most instinctive, least educable of the senses, is repeatedly used to suggest both the animal nature of our apprehensions of one another and also the unselfconscious connexions between such responses and the moral faculty. The most spiritual people (always) stink. Radeechy stank (215) and Theo, who has the saintly gift of making himself almost invisible, has also the odour of his (apprentice) sanctity. And luck too has bodily signs. Kate's health and temperamental good luck contrasts with Paula's ex-lover Eric, who approaches by sea from Australia, and with the hapless Willy. Willy's first tragedy, exactly like Eugene's in *The Time of the Angels*, involved the death, when he was a small boy, of a beloved dog. The peevish Eric sounds from his letters a moral incompetent. Both he and Willy are stigmatised by the fact that they *limp*, as if bad luck, too, had its physical symptoms or were a form of contagion. Luck enters, in this novel as in life, into how easily one is let off – or lets oneself off – and Kate, who tries dutifully to think about the Indian peasantry, is conspicuously unsuccessful (97). This is wryly funny and wholly persuasive. *The Nice and the Good* reads at times as a meditation on the motto 'to him that hath'. Though Kate doesn't get the 'all fun and no pain' (320) with Ducane she hoped for, she does not strike us as likely to make her pain into a feast, as the more puritan characters do. To say this is not merely to typify her as frivolous. 'Being good', thinks Kate, 'is a matter of temperament in the end.' The story shows her to be *half* right.

Ducane's is the story's central consciousness and central exorcist also. A. S. Byatt pointed out that he is more real to us as a moral consciousness than as a sensual presence.[13] This might suggest that Murdoch's success here is more atmospheric than particular. We remember the generous spirit of the book, and the rueful happiness of its ending, as much as its characters. There are marvellous set-pieces – the eighteenth century churchyard, the three women's visits to London and to scenes of past disaster in Chapter 17; Theo and Willy's mournful, chorus-like disquisitions; the scene in the cave where Ducane and Pierce nearly drown is superb. While the characters at the edge of the action – the twins, Kate, Theo – (none of the characters is wholly central) – are excellently done – Ducane remains somewhat shadowy. His predicament as a puritan whose 'lively self-aware altruism' (181) comes under strain because he needs to think well of himself, but feels a loss of moral power, moves us but not, in the book's own terms, bodily. Our sympathy is not, as it is for Kate, Pierce and Theo, physical. The same is true of Jessica, who loves Ducane fruitlessly, and who experiences the pain of his withdrawal from her until Willy, in a fantastic, funny, touching scene redirects her energies. Jessica has pretended to be an interior decorator to have an excuse to search Ducane's flat. Willy makes love to her, and gives her a wise sermon about jealousy to boot. Jessica's pain is oddly more real to us than she is.

Jessica, Theo, Willy and Pierce are all shown differently suffering fruitless, unreturned love and desire. The question as to how an unreciprocated love is to be borne – Theo's 'other face of love, its blank face' which invokes the self-sufficiency of the Good itself – is central. The novel turns on the same ambiguity about a moral or cultural stripping that vivifies all Murdoch's fiction. Jessica, a not so young Bohemian, 'had never developed the faculty of colouring and structuring her surroundings into a moral habitation, the faculty which is sometimes called moral sense' (82). This denudation is above her moral level. She suffers in the void she has made for herself, and, at the end, 'is drawn into the imaginable world', as Sage nicely puts it.[14] Yet the opposite movement is constantly debated by Willy and Theo, in envisaging an ultimate, and therefore coldly impersonal love – that 'other side of love' by which Theo feels rebuked, since it is without supports, reciprocity, guarantee or, in the ordinary sense, 'purpose'. This love which is 'good for nothing' is invoked by them but, like Godbole's Sri Krishna, declines to come. Theo expresses his defeated moral passion in a comic Jaques-like railing against the muddled egoism and erotic greed of all the other characters. To Willy he says

'You and I are the only people here who know [that *all* is vanity] but we also know that we not know. Our hearts are too corrupt to know such a thing as truth, we know it only as illusion.'
'Is there no way out?'
'There are a million ways out on *this* side, back into the fantasy of ordinary life. Muffins for tea is a way out. Propertius is a way out. But these are just boltholes. One ought to be able to get . . . through . . . to the other side.'   (126)

A later reference to *katabasis* recalls this conversation. Willy tells Mary (Chapter 32) about *Aeneid* Book vi, and Mary asks him whether he thinks everyone should descend to the Underworld. Willy suggests that they should not, since to be in hell is to lack any energy for good change. As he spent the war in Dachau, where he 'got through to the other side' in a way that has left him derelict, his answer has authority. Both conversations are echoed when Ducane suffers his own two *katabases*, going down into Radeechy's cellar, and later into Gunnar's cave, both stripped and empty places beyond colour, consolation, ordinary support.

To love and to reconcile and to forgive, only this matters. All power is sin and all law is frailty. Love is the only justice. Forgiveness, reconciliation, not law   (307)

he discovers; but is glad to return to 'the fantasy of ordinary life' that he can bear. He dispenses such loving justice to the Birannes, and then renounces earthly power, tendering his resignation from the Civil Service and leaving the story in another of those expensive cars that figure for Murdoch as the very poetry of worldly pleasure; with Mary, who, like him, represents the highest practical, as opposed to contemplative moral achievement, in the book. The ending is a good deal more ironic than commentators noticed. So far from being, as the *Times Literary Supplement* reviewer suggested, 'not far from soppy', it in fact sustains the ambiguities of the tale to the end.[15]

Jessica pursues Willy to the graveyard, but without evidence that either of them is yet capable of a happy relationship. Kate and Octavian prepare to make love with their usual perfunctory, comic enquiry – 'Ready, darling?' 'Ready, sweetheart' (343). Casie and Theo, their affinity early established, are left uncoupled and separately weeping. Theo, like Jaques, now that Trescombe has become a centre, like Arden, of worldly pleasure, plans to move on to a new position as outsider and court-fool, this time in India. Pierce, who has finally deflowered Barbara in a touching and funny scene, prepares to abandon her for the Pember-Smith's yacht. 'I do love you darling Barb. But yachts are important too' (340). The carnival of reconciliations extends as far as the dog and cat, unable equably to share a basket until then. But this is, like the other reconciliations, as much a truce as a promise. The mood here resembles Shakespearian romantic comedy. The heart is permitted to embrace what the head has been taught to recognise as false. The earthly rewards that are apportioned are shown as both real and illusory. As with Bayley's Tolstoi, the physical side is often superb, the spiritual claim undemonstrable. And for those who lack the strength that will enable them to profit from a spiritual demoralisation, such physical pleasures, however unvirtuous, are the next available thing.

Part III
'The Closest Compression of Form with the Widest Expansion of Meaning. . . '

John Bayley, *The Characters of Love* (London, 1965), p.47

7 A Fairly Honourable Defeat

I have argued that both Murdoch's 'closed' novels – like *The Unicorn* and *The Time of the Angels* – and also her 'open' novels – like *The Bell* and *The Nice and the Good* – offer truth and pleasure. With *A Fairly Honourable Defeat* (1970) a new phase in her career has begun, in which she has often combined the satisfactions of each genre in a single book. In these last chapters I want to examine works which are I think products of a new artistic maturity, and in which the structure of the work and the characters at last carry equal aesthetic weight. Each brilliantly combines 'myth' with psychology, often through exploring Shakespearian convention, and is deeply, darkly comic.

The subject of *A Fairly Honourable Defeat* is pointed to when the Satanic Julius says 'Human beings are essentially finders of substitutes'(233). This has always been a great Murdochian theme. We might take *A Severed Head* as exemplifying the *reductio ad absurdum* of its claim: in that work almost every coupling you might have thought of occurs, as well as (as Bradbury pointed out[1]) some you didn't. The hurt produced by the removal of one relationship is compensated for by the substitution of a new one. Latterly, in *Nuns and Soldiers* the theme is still there, but treated at its most leisurely and patiently with, in place of the multiple substitutions and repetitions of the novels of the 1960s, a *single* substitution at the heart of the book. There Gertrude Openshaw loses her authoritative husband Guy and falls in love with the young, feckless, innocent, Tim Reede. 'She married her father, now she's married her son' is how one choric character describes this process (307). The success of that novel depends on our learning to understand what happens both from inside, as painful 'free' drama, as it might seem if it happened to us, and then later from the outside, as a much more conditioned Oedipal transaction.

Ann Wordsworth has pointed out that the Freudian description of mourning is very different from the 'flattering' humanist description. Freud, in *Mourning and Melancholia*, gives a harsh assessment of our psychic life, where 'the work of mourning is to force the ego into a testing of reality which will prove that the beloved no longer exists and that therefore all libido must be withdrawn from the dead and reinvested . . . . Narcissism and aggressivity mark both the work of mourning and the writing of poems.'[2] But no amount of reading of Freud makes us *experience* mourning quite like this, just as no amount of reading of 'flattering' humanists makes us able to experience the pain of someone else's bereavement as if it were ours. On such dissonances great fiction has always fed; and Gertrude appears in the end like Petronius' widow of Ephesus in *The Satyricon*, right to covet a happy substitution, rather than the unhappy void for which she is not built.

The harsh assessment has its own truth too, of course. Murdoch's closed novels, where the characters are 'slaves', are its kingdom. Humanists who admire Murdoch's work do not, it seems to me, always appreciate how much steel there is in her vision, coexisting, not always comfortably, with warmer and more romantic elements. In *A Fairly Honourable Defeat* the elements come together and produce a brilliant and decisive master-piece. *A Fairly Honourable Defeat* is an elegant open novel which tests out the premises on which the closed novels are based. In *A Severed Head* two brothers compete for women; in *Bruno's Dream* two sisters love the same man but the unmarried sister renounces her claim. In *A Fairly Honourable Defeat*, Julius tries to manipulate two sisters into such competition, and (partly) fails. The sequence is one of a gradual opening out of the incestuous plot. Perhaps the mechanical plot of *A Severed Head* insisted too much on a 'harsh assessment'. In *A Fairly Honourable Defeat* Murdoch tests out this harsh assessment through Julius King, who is Satan in person:

> Human beings are roughly constructed entities full of indeterminacies and vaguenesses and empty spaces. Driven along by their private needs they latch blindly onto each other, then pull away, then clutch again. Their little sadisms and their little masochisms are surface phenomena. *Anyone will do to play the roles.* They never really see each other at all. There is no relationship . . . which cannot easily be broken and there is none the breaking of which is a matter of any genuine seriousness. *Human beings are essentially finders of substitutes.* (233) [my emphases]

This is Julius preaching to Morgan in the Tate gallery, and his view becomes the subject of a wager between them which makes the tragicomic plot of the book. It is also the heart of Murdoch's grimly comic aesthetic, the law which governs the rapid erotic substitutions of the early work. Criticism of Murdoch has not always taken account of it. In both *The Fire and the Sun* (13) and *Henry and Cato* (397), she writes that 'human affairs are not serious, though they have to be taken seriously', ascribing this view to Plato's *Laws*. Clearly Murdoch does not endorse Julius' frivolity, which depends on his ignoring the second part of the maxim. She shows that the breaking of a relationship can yield a very powerful anguish, and that the cultivation of customary relationships combines pleasure and virtue. But the disturbing brilliance of the novel comes, once again, from the way that the devil is given the best tunes.

Julius' diabolism is contested by the novel's own peculiar achievement. 'What novelist ever succeeded in making a good man interesting?' Julius asks provocatively (223). Tallis, the book's Christ-figure, is both good and interesting. Rupert, whom Julius addresses here, and who gets destroyed, is both less good and less interesting. The book to that degree disconfirms what Julius knows. The characters are wholly persuasive and sympathetic creations, with a being which extends generously beyond the immediate requirements of the plot and idea-play. The depiction of a happy homosexual relationship between Simon and Axel is itself a small triumph. To the degree that any are dull, to that degree they are evidence for Julius' prosecution, since Julius sees human beings as profoundly conventionalised and tending to stock type. If the book fails for Murdoch it succeeds for Julius. The title, which refers to the defeat of good by evil, here enters oddly into the book's substance. The novel is a research into the substantiality of the self.

And these are not 'stock' characters. They are interesting, believable, even memorable. The hugely sympathetic Simon, 'sensitive and child-like and pleasure-loving' (18); Hilda the wife who put husband before career, intelligent without pretension, strong and comfortable; Rupert her pompous well-meaning husband, the stiff Axel, the disturbed Morgan and Peter, the good Tallis: the characters are alive, and alive through the relationships which define them, and by virtue of which they exist. Hilda and Morgan's closeness and dependency which excluded and hurt their mother while she lived; Morgan and Simon's affectionate and flirtatious friendship; Hilda and Peter's mother–son love, frustrated and gone 'underground' now that he is adolescent. Perhaps more than in any other novel these characters give us that illusion of independent existence which their author so values. The network feels fully imagined wherever we test it, fully '*there*', and because it is real for us as a small society, the novel has the 'feel' of its time and place in a way that is the opposite of limiting. From *Under the Net* on, Murdoch has always had an extraordinary gift for evoking time and place. Here this gift approaches some high point.

The structure of the book comes from religious allegory, but it is an enabling, not a determining structure. Julius King is Satan, Tallis a Christ figure, and Tallis' father God the Father who finds that it's all gone wrong. A draft for the novel makes clear that Chapter 6's discussions of birth-signs was to have included the information that Tallis was born, Christ-like, on December 25th. This is omitted in the published version, presumably because the story is, once you grant its marvellously artificial premise, realistic too. It is the expansion outward from the *psychomachia* that she wished to emphasise. The allegorical elements are partly disguised, where Tallis is concerned, by being ascribed to the quixotic Morgan, who represents the human soul for which the two spiritual magnates are battling.[3] It is for her that Tallis represents 'holy poverty or some such stuff' (221). 'Living in Malory', Morgan envisages Tallis as 'an Arthurian knight' (249).

*

The novel's opening words are 'Julius King'. Its closing words 'Life was good' apply, with considerable dryness, to Julius' Paris excursion through a series of small, real pleasures. Julius, who thus frames the book, is the Lord of this world. But the novel has two books, and the division between them is important. The first 'open' book involves a patient and wonderfully assured depiction of the small Murdochian court, precisely locating the characters in a believable South Kensington world. Hilda and Rupert Foster are rich, successful, happily married Old Guard Socialists who judiciously combine pleasure and virtue. Rupert, a Senior Civil Servant, has denied himself a knighthood but not a swimming-pool, makes payment to many charities, including Oxfam, which read both as genuine benefactions and also as talismans against loss of their superabundant good luck. By any normal standards the Fosters are good people, socially concerned, conscientious paragons of the virtuous intellectual bourgeoisie. They are, as Hilda puts it, the 'decent self-centred habit-ridden hedonists who keep society going' (131) and occupy that world where, in normal circumstances, 'money and good breeding precluded screams and blows' (112). The high social and moral tone of the book are necessary, as in Dorothea Krook's view of Henry James, to its comic enquiry: the fall from grace from within a high-toned world can be especially dramatic.

Rupert who is emotionally unstable and untested, as Axel suggests, calls himself a Sunday metaphysician and like Marcus is writing a treatise on morality in a secular age. He is twice referred to as a Platonist. He represents a cosy and uninhabited version of Murdoch's own philosophy, and Julius' is the wisdom his morality needs to accommodate if it is not to be vulnerable through its silly optimism. From another, equally valid, point of view it is the *point* about Murdoch's philosophy that no one can adequately inhabit it. 'Any man, even the greatest, can be broken in a moment and has no refuge. Any theory which denies this is a lie' a later narrator puts this (*BP* 19), and from this point of view the woolly Rupert is simply very unlucky. Being tested by Satan in South Kensington must count as bad luck.

The breakage of a series of social rituals provides the momentum: wedding anniversary, dinner party, birthday party, and party to celebrate the completion of Rupert's book. Two expository chapters, which introduce the cast with a great relaxed *bravura* reminiscent of the high confidence of a Victorian novelist, are followed by the Fosters' celebrating their twenty-year marriage. Hilda's sister Morgan, acting like a woman possessed, disturbs the idyll by arriving unheralded from America fresh from a failed love affair with Julius. A dinner party of Rupert's younger brother Simon, and Axel his homosexual lover, to celebrate Julius' subsequent return is then disrupted by the arrival, unannounced, of Morgan's estranged husband Tallis, trying to discover his wife's whereabouts. It is disturbed therefore by the inadvertent meeting of the rivals in love, both earthly and transcendental. 'What a very strange little person', Julius comments. 'He ought to be sitting on a toadstool' (85). It is disturbed, too, by Julius' bizarre, clandestine invitation to Simon to visit him in his Brook Street flat. A festive afternoon by the Fosters' new swimming-pool in Chapter 11 is disrupted by the arrival, again unsummoned, of the Fosters' only and disturbed child Peter, who has dropped out of Cambridge. After a series of mock-coronations with a rose-crown Peter offers a denunciation of the 'civilised' values by which his parents live. This denunciation is a dress-rehearsal for Julius' and Rupert's confrontation. For this first book ends with two disputations, one on the nature of morality between the devil Julius and the bland Rupert, a discourse on the speciousness of all human goods and the frailty of all human nature. This is followed by a more particular wager between Julius and Morgan about the giddiness of the human heart. Morgan bets Julius ten guineas that he cannot break off the relationship between Simon and Axel. He decides to make things more interesting by breaking off Rupert and Hilda's marriage as well, through engineering a love affair between Morgan and Rupert. A practical demonstration of morals in a Chinese restaurant ensues, where Tallis defeats a group of louts terrorising a Jamaican, while Axel blusters, Simon intervenes to little effect, and Julius watches with thrilled fascinated interest, his eyes gleaming with pleasure. This first part thus ends with evil suffering a dishonourable defeat at the hands of good.

The wager which is the plot's central device has a long pedigree in literature. It borrows from Shakespeare, Mozart, and the book of *Job*. Patrick Swinden has pointed out that the plot's detail comes from Shakespeare's comedies, but that the shape of the whole is tragic.[4] The book is a distressingly funny tragi-comedy or problem comedy. The masque in the Prince Regent Museum recalls the pleached bower in *Much Ado About Nothing*, Julius refers to midsummer enchantments, and Hilda, like the lovers in *A Midsummer Night's Dream*, wanders all night over the Pembrokeshire moors. The piquant humour and insouciant, puzzling ironies complicate this effect. The vision that the novel tests may be that of Benedick's final speech 'Man is a giddy thing and this is my conclusion'; but the gamble is unlike the good-humoured wager in *Much Ado About Nothing*. Julius does try, like Don Pedro, to join one couple and, like Don John, to separate another. But the mood is closer to the wagers in *Cymbeline*, *Job*, or even *Cosi Fan Tutte*: what is contested is a harshly cynical and sour view of the inconstancy of the human heart. Julius, as prime mover of strategems which depend on jealousy, gullibility, and on physical concealment, is as close to Iachimo as to Iago. Like

Iachimo too, he goes scot-free, and truth is arrived at through a fantastic plot.

This is also to admit that the comic elements succeed better than the tragic. Leonard's speech in Chapter 9 derives in its detail from *Job*, another nearly tragic story of Satan making a wager about the destruction of a good man. Though distressed by Rupert's destruction we are not, I think however, deeply moved. Rupert has been too much an ironic butt.

Northrop Frye has pointed out that the true descendant of Shakespearian romantic comedy with its twins, disguises, and concealments is Romantic opera, and this brings me to the third wager. References to opera abound in this book and are carefully chosen.[5] There is an early reference to *Don Giovanni*, another story about the rewards of promiscuity. *Fidelio*, which deals with slavery and emancipation of the enslaved into the sunlight, figures in Chapter 6. There is a discussion of Mozart and *Die Entfuehrung aus dem Serail*, which again concerns erotic slavery and emancipation, and Julius is last and pointedly shown, as I shall explain, looking forward to Monteverdi. At one level the book is close to *Cosi Fan Tutte*, with its disturbingly frivolous and stylised morality, its concealed ironic depths, and its own bet about human inconstancy; (the women in *Cosi Fan Tutte* discuss male inconstancy too).

Book Two sees the acting out of the wager, isolating the romance elements implicit in the more realistic first part, and employing a Mozartian plot – The Purloined Letters, as it might be – to try out the values contested in the first, enquiring into the problematics of 'civilised' lying and intelligent hypocrisy, power, repression, love, sex. It is both a stylishly 'light' and a grimly dark comedy of manners, moving again from an integrated to a scattered court, and ending with the 'fairly honourable defeat' of good by evil, with Rupert dead of hubris; but, before that, the breaking of two feasts occurs in scenes which are more comic as they are also more distressing. Julius deliberately arrives late at Axel's birthday party, spoiling Simon's carefully prepared meal, ingeniously arousing Axel's jealousy, and crowning the event by presenting the fastidious, humourless Axel with a vast pink teddy-bear. The last of these disastrous parties is staged to celebrate Rupert's completion of his book on ethics, completed at exactly the moment when he has been apparently exposed to his wife and himself as bankrupt of precisely those values he has celebrated so fulsomely in print. Hilda, distraught at what she believes to be her betrayal by both her husband and her beloved sister, has decided that she cannot cancel the occasion 'without letting them know that you know' (351). Like Maggie in *The Golden Bowl* she hopes to save face, if not redeem everyone concerned, by sustaining her social role at a pitch of extreme suffering. The result is ludicrous, distressing, and wildly, painfully funny. Here relations between Simon and Axel have also broken down and are kept up in public as pure, agonising charade. Simon, tormented beyond endurance by Julius, pitches him into the swimming-pool though he cannot swim. Hilda rejects Rupert, while Simon and Axel learn to trust one another again. Julius, assisted by Peter, has meanwhile torn up Rupert's magniloquent moralisings into confetti.

This is the culmination of a series of decreations. Hilda twice upsets or breaks bottles of lotion. Morgan tears up at different points a photograph of Tallis, Simon's trousers, a letter from Tallis unread, a letter from Hilda, and breaks Tallis' amber necklace. Morgan at her most destructive acts always as the lieutenant or agent of Julius; his mode of breaking off his relationship with her seems calculated to derive the maximum of frenzy and restlessness in her. ('Tie me down' she asks Rupert when she first sees Julius.) Julius has seduced her by cutting up a newspaper, and in one of the novel's great *scènes-à-faire* enthrals her by cutting up her dress, brassiere, pants and stockings. Morgan then destroys a T'ang horse, the Brook Street curtains and some of the plaster, in the effort to stay warm.

Such deconstruction reads as both real and metaphoric. Morgan early asserts when reunited with Hilda and Rupert that they make her feel continuous. 'One ought to feel continuous, oughtn't one?' (91). A persistent and reticent rhetoric endorses the sentiment. 'Human beings cannot live without custom' (441) reflects the quietly authoritative Tallis, though the book attempts a discrimination between good custom and bad. Thus when Morgan first visits Tallis and seeks a source of energy with which to fight her own love for him, she draws upon her own capacity to live 'existentially' (i.e. amorally), as though butchering her own moral consciousness:

> So long as I can keep it all dismembered, she thought. Keep everything small and separate and manageable . . . . Detail, detail, detail, keep everything small and separate.   (120)

The breakage and disembowelling of the Pembrokeshire telephone at a critical juncture and perhaps also the subsequent failure of Hilda's car, evoked with the usual panache and vividness, belong too to this chain of *dégringolades*. Dismemberment has long been a commonplace Neoplatonic symbol of the fall into multiplicity.[6]

There is, similarly, a chain of immersions and near-drownings. At the start of the book Hilda instructs Rupert to rescue a bumble-bee from the pool. 'I do wish insects had more sense of self-preservation. I do hope our hedgehog won't fall in' (16). Later the hedgehog does indeed fall in and drown (353) and later still, lacking both common-sense and the instinct for self-preservation, so does Rupert, dead, as Julius cruelly puts it, of vanity as much as drowning. Tallis' rescue of a fly early in the book (180) from drowning in a glass of sherry evidences his own contrasting care for all of creaturekind.

*

In *A Fairly Honourable Defeat* the scattering of the court is paralleled by the destruction of specious goods incarnated in Rupert. It is a comedy because the ego is again seen not merely as the source of depravity but also, for all but saints, as the locus of stability, *amour propre*, and that 'self-preservation' whose absence destroys the hedgehog and Rupert as much as does his vanity. In a real sense Rupert's hedgehog-like lack of 'self-preservation' *constitutes* his moral vanity. He dangerously thinks himself tougher than he is.

The role of Julius is thus equivocal, and it is worth considering his literary pedigree in more detail. Murdoch has suggested that 'If Iago were just an embodiment of evil I think we wouldn't be so interested' (Bigsby, 1982). The same is true of Julius. He is a brilliant success within the book – a disturbing, uncanny creation, with his colourless hair and violet-brown eyes – exactly because his 'myth', to employ the term persistently used of him, is combined with just enough 'psychology' to tease curiosity. We early learn of him that he possesses the kind of style that would enable him to get away with wearing a monocle. And he in fact appears equipped with a silver-handled cane, and umbrella with an ivory handle and lotus design, and in an evening dress with an opera cape. He is given to such old-world gallantry as hand-kissing. He dresses *clerically* (a word twice used of him) and accompanies his sartorial dandyism with a verbal dandyism, a mock-sententiousness designed to generate unease:

> Hilda, what perfectly delicious fresh lemonade. What are the
> more vaunted pleasures of the flesh compared with the wild
> joy of quenching one's thirst on a hot day? (283)

He is a persistently witty and indeed funny demon. The fact that
his manipulations cause real hurt and damage to those for whom
we have been taught to feel is a part of his sinister and very
uncomfortable appeal. When he replies to Rupert's remark: 'At
my age, Julius, I don't worry too much about my motives. It's
enough for me if I can see the right thing to do and do it.' 'That's
beautiful. I hope it comes into your book' (221); or when he
ripostes to Morgan's 'I'm beginning to see myself clearly at last'.
'A remarkable feat, if true' (229), the humour of the situation in
each case depends on the ways in which Julius' viewpoint is close
to that of the author, though not his mordant and Nietzschean
cynicism. Murdoch makes quite clear how fruitless she considers
the examination of one's motives to be, and also how undesirable
and how little possible it is to'see oneself clearly': the effort siphons
off energy properly used for seeing all that is 'unself', and the
attempt usually degenerates into prevarication and untruth.
    But his challenge is deeper than this. In appearance he recalls
the shabby genteel devil of Book II of *Karamazov*, flashy, be-
ringed, be-lorgnetted, and also Dickens' dandy-gentleman Rigaud
in *Little Dorrit*. His scepticism about moral substantiality is tied
to a desire to transmute *all* substance into style, to aestheticise
what he sees. In this he parodies the intelligent hypocrisy of those
high bourgeois manners he observes and exemplifies. He is both
a very rich *rentier* who could afford to occupy a symbolic apex of
this world when he considers buying a house in the Boltons, and
also a Jewish outsider, belonging and yet homeless. Julius' function
in the book, apart from manipulator of the action, is also close
to Dostoevski's Grand Inquisitor so far as the idea-play is
concerned: it is his role to speak for a *realpolitik* of the emotions,
for a devastating cynicism about the human heart and the fragility
of its moral attainments and attachments. Of the Grand Inquisitor
D. H. Lawrence wrote that his was 'the final and unanswerable
criticism of Christ'. Christianity – or, in Rupert's case, a
Christianised Platonism – is the ideal, but it is impossible: 'Man
can but be true to his own nature. No inspiration whatsoever will
ever get him permanently beyond his limits.' The legend of the
Grand Inquisitor implies a rediscovery of the fallen nature of

man, an item of knowledge, as Lawrence saw it, excluded by the facile perfectibilitarian optimism of the Enlightenment. The Grand Inquisitor accuses Christ of 'tragically over-estimating the stature of man or his ability to bear the agonies of free will'.[7] Just as the Grand Inquisitor's legend forms the crisis and resolution of the running debate between Ivan and Alyosha over the roles of spiritual nihilism and idealism, so Julius' nihilism is opposed to Rupert's idealism.

Julius' psychology is revealed to us piecemeal. We learn at the start that he has been experimenting with germ-warfare, and has given this up not because he views it as immoral but because he is easily bored. Later we find that he spent the war in Belsen, at the same time that we find that Tallis' sister died; not, as Tallis claimed, from polio, but after being raped and killed by a sex maniac. These two facts provide a context for one another. Simone Weil believed that extreme affliction is passed on by all but the saintly. Murdoch is philosemitic, and meant no more by making Julius a Jew than that Satan had been a Jewish invention (Caen, 1978). These sensational disclosures provide, as it were, a partial rationale for Julius' destructiveness: he is a restless, deracinate spiritual force actively involved in the business of transmitting suffering; Tallis, on the other hand, absorbs it.

Julius also shows a yearning for justice in its way as remarkable, and arguably more 'profound', than Rupert's. To Rupert he suggests that the sense of being justly judged would console 'most of all, most of all, most of all', and adds 'If there were a perfectly just judge I would kiss his feet and accept his punishments upon my knees' (226). He likes Simon for saying that Tallis should not have taken Julius' hand when they first met, and later congratulates Simon, glittering-eyed, for having revenged his humiliations by pushing Julius into the swimming-pool. When he watches Tallis' defeat of the louts in the Chinese restaurant he is full of thrilled fascinated interest, radiant with delight, feeding pathologically on the spectacle of violence and cruelty. This *Schadenfreude* he shares with Morgan: 'I adore violence! . . . her eyes bright with interest' (138).

Above all, however, Julius is, as he twice remarks of himself, an artist. 'After all I am an artist' (431) he says, when helping Tallis at last to clear up the appalling mess in his flat. Julius, by contrast, is a fanatically neat man; his exposure of Rupert to

Peter can be put down by him to 'just my instinct as an artist, it was entirely impromptu' (408).

*

The gap which lies at the heart of this tragi-comedy is that between the wisdom which is professed and the wisdom which is lived from the heart. It is a gap which Julius as artist is uniquely equipped to unmask, and one which only Tallis – significantly a man who does not rate himself as an intellectual – is able to overcome. Rupert's exposure is the book's largest tribute to the theme but it radiates everywhere. The historical setting helps it. The challenge to bourgeois proprieties offered by the dionysiac ferment of the 1960s prefigures and enables Julius' attack. In the first chapter Rupert suggests of the younger generation that they are really 'consumed by a sort of incoherent love' and that such love must rightfully be used to oppose cynicism. 'Rot', Hilda replies to this. The book explores what the right kind of love to oppose to cynicism might look like, and it is Tallis', if anyone's, not Peter's. Tallis' attempts to expunge fantasy and live in the present are not, unlike Peter's, irresponsible or self-serving.

Given the importance of this quarrel between love and cynicism, it is worth noticing the comic circumspection of the narrative voice. A Sikh tenant in Tallis' house is early mentioned as in dispute at the bus depot over the wearing of his turban. In the penultimate chapter the dispute is over: 'The men had got used to their fellow worker. The Sikh was now happily united with his fellow males in an attempt to sabotage a campaign for women drivers.' A dry impassivity here marks the recognition of the imperfection of earthly things. This can be read either as a systematic small improvement, so that Sikhs, like the homosexual Axel and Simon, will be treated less inequitably; or the emphasis can be placed on the pyrrhic nature of the victory – the defeat of one species of bigotry at the expense of strengthening another. This comic moral realism is echoed in the exchange between Tallis and Julius over Tallis' relations with his father. Julius is learning to love Tallis as the nearest to the 'perfectly just judge' he is likely to find, and asks concernedly: 'Are you on good terms with him?' 'Yes. We shout at one another' (337).

Tallis plays saint or holy fool to Julius' artist. He is shown to us in a double focus, both admirable and absurd. Where the other characters articulate various 'philosophies' of love, it is

Tallis who is shown to be, however incompetently, trying to put the thing into practice. 'Love' and 'value' are related securely in him, and arbitrated variously by the others. The characters who know themselves to be but slight creations, who have a humble self-contempt, come off best; the intellectuals worst. Simon considers himself 'flimsy' (434) compared to Axel, but it is Simon's life which is 'filled by love' (40), Axel's by caution. Hilda likewise considers herself to have been 'a very dull wife for such a brilliant man' (321) but, like the feminine Simon, is a practitioner, not a murderously high-minded theoretician.'What is the purpose of life, Hilda?' asks Morgan and her sister answers 'I think loving people' (56). The depiction of her relationship with her teenage son Peter is superb. She puts up 'humbly and uncomplainingly with any degree of casualness and neglect. Peter knew that it was a metaphysical impossibility that her love for him should diminish by one iota whatever he might or might not do, and this precisely enabled him to dismiss her altogether from his mind' (291); and criticism is not currently well equipped with terms to praise its truthfulness. Even the dry Axel when challenged to produce a philosophy replies that he wishes 'to do my work and have innocent friendships with gentle intelligent people' (82). 'I have to follow the kind of love that I am capable of' (214) the hopelessly self-deceived Morgan asseverates. This turns out often to mean a self-serving, careless and witless romanticism.

The point is nicely made in her exchange with Simon in Chapter 16. Morgan speaks first: 'I've made a discovery.' 'Tell me! Or is it a secret?' 'It is possible to love people.' 'Oh. I knew that already actually' (197). The ironies here are multiple. Simon loves Axel and puts up with Axel's unacknowledged jealousy, withdrawals, depressions and bullyings, while Morgan behaves like a malevolent spirit or light-weight adventuress undergoing a nervous breakdown, pursuing a callow and destructive ideal of freedom, and within minutes of her protestation that she is 'learning to love people' betrays Simon casually to Axel as she is later to betray both Rupert and Hilda's confidences to Julius. Julius significantly suggests that Morgan's new creed is roughly 'a broken down version of Rupert's stuff' (404). Both are theoreticians of love, which the book makes clear is the only kind of romanticism worth advancing, but neither can put it fully to work. This is not merely because of their inadequacies; loving is hard to do. 'I think young people *really* don't know how wretched and vulnerable every human heart really is', Morgan, at her sympathetically perceptive best observes of Peter's attack on his parents' *moeurs* (138). The real cost is discussed in Chapter 2 when Simon declares the planet void of any redeeming grace, for which the agony of Marsyas being flayed by Apollo – blood, pain, no love – is the apt emblem. Simon, though an art historian, is first ignorant of and then denies to the flaying of Marsyas its customary Neoplatonic value as an image of divinely inspired ascesis. Axel knows such recondite matters, but it is the ignorant Simon who can practise them, living in a constant condition of 'ecstatic pain' (39) while the puritan and expert Axel is shown to be the more self-regarding. As with Dora and Paul in *The Bell*, an innocent worldling is coupled with an insensitive ascetic, and it is not the ascetic who comes off best.

Rupert, however, presents the most fulsome and mellifluous version of the love-philosophy when he early tells Hilda that:

> . . . love is what tells in the end, Hilda. There are times when one's just got to go on loving somebody helplessly, with blank hope and blank faith. When love just *is* hope and faith in their most denuded form. Then love becomes almost impersonal and loses its attractiveness and its ability to console. But it is just then that it may exert its greatest power. It is just then that it may be able to redeem. Love has its own cunning beyond our conscious wiles. (26)

This is very much the voice of *The Sovereignty of Good*, and a voice heard at some point in most of the novels. What Rupert is criticised for is not the philosophy but his consistently clumsy inability to live by it. He is persistently shown to us as shy and wooden, in a recognisably English way and, despite warm intentions, he bungles his encounters.

It is not only Julius who repeatedly points this out. Axel teases Rupert when he maliciously says he is most impatient to see his book. 'I expect to be told how to live, my dear fellow. I shall take it as my guide to good behaviour and follow it slavishly' (46). Peter asks whether his father intends to read aloud from his book at the dinner table; Julius satirically pretends to hope that the cast will all have to make 'philosophical speeches just like in the *Symposium*, I should like that' (221). When Rupert says to

Morgan: 'Love is the last and secret name of all the virtues' she innocently replies: 'That's pretty. Do you say that in your book?' (94). And such satire has, as it were, a purgative function: wisdom in this book, as in *Phaedrus* and the *Seventh Letter* is ultra-verbal, and simulacra or copies may degenerate in the client's mind once committed to print. Rupert's philosophy is in fact a doctrine of love, as he comes to ponder when under extreme pressure from Julius' manipulations and his own frailty:

> The top of the moral structure was no dream, and he had proved this by exercises in loving attention: loving people, loving art, loving work, loving paving stones and leaves on trees. This had been his happiness . . . . He had written about it in a formal half disguised way, as if it were a secret, in his philosophy book. (359)

Rupert tries to restore Morgan to wholeness through such an exercise in high Eros, supported by his 'deep age-old confidence in the power of goodness' (359) and the philosophy of loving he has not been able properly to communicate even to Hilda. Julius was right to invoke the *Symposium*: as in that dialogue each character here praises and lives by a different view of love, which is to say, by a different personal history and character.

The gap between love and its working materials is occupied in part by lying, a theme about which the book has much to say. The breakage of the celebration by the swimming-pool occurs when Peter denounces the hypocrisy behind his parents' 'good manners'. He accurately says that his parents' coterie hide the reservations they have about one another in public and betray one another in private. To this Axel ripostes that civilisation is based on *not* saying what you think (135), and when charged with cowardice about concealing his homosexuality accuses Peter in return with concealing behind his rejection of bourgeois values an equally cowardly fear of his own mediocrity. The sheer force of the scene comes in part from Murdoch's success in identifying with every participant in it, and, behind that, her identification both with the case that love is, as Rupert argues, the primary obligation, is what is compulsory, and her countervailing sense of what and how much it is that resists love, of how intractable the materials are on which the force of love is to work or play.

Axel is puritanically truthful, Simon tells instinctive small lies about which he has a bad conscience that Julius can easily exploit. Julius' actions always widen the 'gap'. He exploits Hilda's secret subsidy of Peter, and Rupert's of Morgan, and involves all the major characters in an imbroglio of lying until they are envenomed by it. Even Hilda, inexperienced in inventing plausible falsehoods, has by the end to solicit Julius' help in fabricating untruth.

Not all lying is presented thus. Tallis agonises over whether or not to tell his father the truth about his illness, and lies about his sister's death, just as Julius, aside from his more ambitious fraudulences, fails to disclose where he spent the war. It is Tallis who lives but cannot articulate the philosophy of love. He is early referred to by Julius as an 'unperson', and his lack of egoism makes him both a saviour and a constant mild irritant to the others. A Christ-figure, he provides himself with a latter-day stigma when wounding his palm with a screw-driver, parodies the Passion in walking through London with a hand-cart piled high with Morgan's possessions, which he is renouncing though they are precious to him as mementoes of her, instead of a cross. Morgan, in a clear reference to Original Sin, feels that she offended Tallis 'years before she knew him, years before either of them were born' (152). Like Julius, who smells of perfume, and Murdoch's daemonic characters in general, Tallis *smells*. He suffers visitations from his dead sister and others, and what may be epileptically induced hallucinations about flying. He may have doubles, one of whom Morgan sights (329).

Though he is comically bewildered by Rupert's disquisition on why stealing is wrong – the arguments of a linguistic philosopher – and by Julius' – the sophistry of a utilitarian – he is never shown to be in much doubt about the ethics. He is tolerant and loving to Peter, though contemptuous of his stealing, and correctly predicts that Peter's problems will require a psychiatrist. He is interestingly a Fabian or liberal Christ, working that is to say within the system, assisting the police in general except when on instinct he suddenly decides not to, a perpetrator of multifarious and unending good works, many of them uncompleted. It has been argued that Tallis is, unlike Julius, a saintly apostle of contingency – the disorder into which his house sinks once more in the penultimate chapter[8] despite Julius' ministrations, being taken as conclusive evidence. That opposition is too schematic. Hilda gives the book's authoritative verdict on the matter when she thinks: 'Wherever Tallis is there's always muddle! Then she thought, this is unjust. Wherever there is muddle, there Tallis is' (178). Both Julius and Tallis seek order, it should be said, but of different kinds, at different speeds, and for wholly different ends.

Tallis' inner life is distinguished from that of all the other characters. Simon, for example, while drawn with great sympathy, and shown as quixotically loving, is given to 'immense flights of fantasy' involving his possessive jealousy and fear of losing Axel. It is on such fantasies that Julius is able to practise. Hilda, like Tallis, has little self-image, and when manipulated by Julius answers 'I don't want to imagine anything' – so that Julius has to conspire with more than usual devilishness to coerce her into a *detailed* imagining of the putative adultery. ('How quickly one can lose one's faith and abandon one's standards' thinks Hilda (345) once the idea of searching Rupert's desk has been planted.) Peter is an easier victim: 'I told him, in fact, in a curtailed version, the truth, and his imagination did the rest' (408). Rupert and Morgan are easily gulled by pity, vanity, novelty and fundamental humourlessness into imagining that the other has indeed fallen in love, and take the first stages themselves of falling in love in return as a result. Axel likewise 'imagines it all into existence' (396), imagines that Simon has started an erotic adventure with Julius and 'all the details and everything seemed to fit'.

Tallis is different. Imagination for him, too, is a source of temptation – his Greenford W. E. A. class seem hostilely to enjoy catching him out 'but perhaps it was all imagination' (442). Half-way through the book, when Morgan has rejected him and is behaving with more than usual destructiveness, he tells Julius that correspondence with Morgan helps ease his hurt. 'If one writes letters one can go on hoping.'

> 'Your particular kind of tenacity amazes me,' said Julius. 'I could understand your going round and making a scene and I could understand your switching off altogether and looking for someone else. *This dull holding on and hoping* I find incomprehensible .... Perhaps it's a virtue. I suppose there are such things.' (401) [my emphasis]

In the penultimate chapter Tallis is still and movingly holding on and refusing to imagine less than charitably, or in detail. Morgan never writes to him. 'He did not even wonder if he would

see her again. He simply let her continue to occupy his heart.'
He struggles much harder than the others to imagine neither less
nor more than the truth; and when told by Julius of Rupert and
Morgan's suppositious liaison is the only person to say 'That
simply cannot be true' (339); and to add, appropriately enough
(as Julius is his interlocutor) 'Oh go to hell.' His is in fact that
'blank hope and blank faith' early and vainly invoked (26) by
Rupert. It is he that leads Julius to the telephone to instigate his
confession.

*

'The incomplete pseudo-object, the work of art, is a lucid
commentary upon itself' Murdoch has suggested (sw). I should
like to suggest further in what ways this is true here. The burden
of what Julius argues to Morgan in the Tate Gallery is that the
unconscious has few types to play with. A saint might perceive
the world as full of 'absolute individuals', but, as he has asserted
already to Rupert, modern psychology makes the claims of
saintliness look dubious, and 'Most so-called saints really interest
us because they are artists or because they have been portrayed
by artists, or else because they are men of power' (224).

Julius' pessimism about the individual potential for good is
partly Murdoch's. A saint might be endowed with the capacity
for seeing the world as full of absolute individuals, but an artist
is no saint, must in some sense be anti-type to the saint. The
defeat of Rupert, of good by evil at the book's close, is only an
ambiguous victory for the comic realm of mechanical substitution
and repetition. It is partly redeemed by Axel and Simon having
the wit to break down and trust one another, though not to warn
Rupert and Hilda of Julius' machinations. Murdoch's triumph is
to give the harsh, behaviouristic assessment its full rein, and yet
to persuade us that these are 'real people' who are simultaneously
inward and free, and about whom we care. The conflict is formal
as well as moral. The triumph of Julius' view would tend to
produce the claustrophobic, centripetal world of Murdoch's closed
romances.

Rupert twice uses art as *exemplum* of the reality of value-
judgements (130, 222). But intuitions of the negative sublime,
in which the experience of value is wholly withheld, abound
throughout. The distribution of these moments is interesting.
Simon early proclaims the planet as lacking in any redeeming

grace except sexual love, but is shown to us as a virtuous pagan who can find innocent sensual pleasure (almost) everywhere. Leonard, a Beckettian God the Father who finds that it has all gone wrong, sees the world as a 'stinking dung-heap' (64) which went wrong from the start. He is given a series of Swiftian jeremiads about the horror, for example, of sex, eating, the coming end of the world, which do much to establish the prevailing tone of *comédie noire*.

Julius is appropriately the dean or impresario of such moments of negative sublime. When Morgan recalls the feeling of revelation which accompanied part of the experience of falling in love with Julius, she speaks of a sense of 'deep truth' revealed:

> It had been like a mystical vision into the heart of reality, as if one were to be promised the secret of the universe and then, with all the sense of significance and finality fully preserved, to be shown a few mouldering chicken bones lying in a dark corner covered with dust and filth. (149)

This 'lesson' is of course couched in exactly the terms of Carel's anti-sermon to Marcus, and what Radeechy's black magic turned out partly to consist in. Just as the metaphor comes weirdly to life between the two earlier books, so this vision of trapped avian, and hence spiritual life, is also, later in this book, to come to life.

Before that Morgan and Peter dispute the essential beauty or wickedness of the universe, after Morgan has experienced each in succession. She has a marvellously evoked experience of 'dionysiac biolatry', an experience of idyll, which immediately follows an experience of the most negative asceticism and horror.[9] This contest between two visions of the world immediately precedes Morgan and Peter's 'quarrel': 'Everything is contaminated and muddled and nasty and slimed over and cracked', says Peter, and Morgan opposes to this view first of all the splendour of nature, symbolised by a vetch flower, and then, when Peter protests that he has in mind *human* things, she opposes culture, and sings or recites 'Full Fathom Five' from *The Tempest*.

The love which Peter and Morgan discover for one another and decide to express chastely here is, Morgan suggests, 'outside the machine. This is felicity, blessing, luck, sheer wonderful undeserved luck.' The 'machine' in this book is the name of the world seen deterministically, void of spirit, repetitive, outside hope of real change. 'Human beings are so mechanical, certain relations, certain situations, inevitably make one behave rottenly. This one can do the opposite' (193). Morgan's protestation that a grace wholly outside the machine is possible is one that the plot painfully ironises. By placing her own need for admiration above Peter's more urgent requirements Morgan betrays this moment of affection. The desire to step outside the mechanism, however, runs through the novel. Hilda and Rupert agree that they are both rather 'mechanised' about Peter; both long to 'break down the mechanism' (26). Leonard in the first of his mock-Swiftian disquisitions on the absurdity and horror of humanity discourses on sex as 'the invention of a mere mechanic': low Eros is again the realm of mechanical substitution and repetition itself. The Notting Hill house is also closer to the sources of suffering and evil than Priory Grove. Tallis hopes this will educate Peter:

> Here the causes of human misery, though they were infinitely complex, were shadowily visible and one could see the machine. Tallis had trusted that a glimpse of the machine might make Peter understand something, might make him see that revolt may be itself mechanical, and that human ills need thought and work which are disciplines of the imagination.   (112)

Imagination, too, therefore, is the vehicle of the mechanical, is its vehicle in a sense *par excellence*, and it is in disciplining the imagination that the machine may be altered. Morgan is peculiarly liable to perceiving the world in mechanical terms. 'I must see him as a puppet. I must go through this like a machine' (119), she thinks in an early interview with Tallis; and, in a much later one tells him: 'It's no good, Tallis. You keep talking but I can't hear you. I'm mechanical. I'm just a machine. I look like a human being but I'm really a robot' (284).

The crux of the argument about the mechanical nature of human imagining comes in the disputation between Rupert and Julius:

> 'You make human beings sound like puppets.'
> 'But they *are* puppets, Rupert. And we didn't need modern psychology to tell us that. Your friend Plato knew all about it, when he wrote *The Laws*, after he had given up those dreams of high places which so captivate you.'   (225)

When Rupert receives what purports to be Morgan's ecstatic love letter to him he seeks 'to latch himself onto the machinery of virtue and decent decision' (254). Shortly after this Julius 'produces', as if in a masque, the preliminary love-dance of Rupert and Morgan, after promising Simon, appropriately enough, a 'puppet show' (268). When it is finished he says to Simon 'let them work the machinery themselves' (268).

This is indeed what they do. It is not merely Morgan who declares herself a robot. By the time of the last broken feast Hilda and Rupert's marriage seems on the point of break-down, but Rupert ponders

> There must be some way to halt the destruction, to switch off the machine.
> 'Hilda, I will not let you destroy our marriage.'
> 'I am not destroying it. Rupert, don't you see that these things are completely automatic?' (378)

This rhetoric helps to give special force to the virtuoso Kafkaesque writing of Book Two's Chapter 10, where Morgan repeatedly experiences 'the horror, the horror of the world' (331) in a quasi-'objective' form. Morgan struggles to liberate a pigeon trapped within the Underground at Piccadilly Circus, associated early with Simon's promiscuous adventures. The bird, though it is nowhere clearly stated, becomes, like the chicken in the unwholesome vision somehow conveyed to her by Julius, a figure for spirit itself, trapped within the machine. We experience Morgan's distress and the bird's confusion together as though in each case spirit were subordinated to matter, 'freedom' to determinism. The Underground, as in *A Word Child*, stands aptly enough for the Underworld; and it is at the point at which Morgan is most restlessly destructive, when the fate of her soul might be said to hang in the balance, that this episode occurs.

Finally, when Julius makes his Iachimo-like voluntary confession to Tallis he says:

> I must say, they have behaved predictably to an extent which is quite staggering. Indeed if any of them had been less than predictable the whole enterprise would have collapsed at an early stage. They really are puppets, *puppets*. (408)

Julius explains how he 'set the machine going' by sending off the purloined letters ('letters are such powerful tools': 402), and describes women in particular in behaviouristic terms:

> You know, any woman can be flattered into doing anything. You just can't lay it on too thick. Just flatter them outrageously, it simply doesn't matter how outrageously, and they will lose their minds, like some birds and animals when they're tickled in a certain kind of way.   (406)

Morgan too muses, 'How very peculiar one's mind is. There's no foothold in it, no leverage, no way of changing oneself into a responsible just being. One's lost in one's psyche' (96). The unenlightened mind behaves like a machine, and machines work through a repeating action with component parts which are replaceable. There is much play about the idea of substitution, as there is about the mechanical.

Julius may be the impresario of such substitutions, as of the negative sublime, but Morgan is his deputy. When Morgan and Peter have their odd, convincing love-passage Peter comments: 'You're my mother's sister, but that's what's so marvellous. You're like my mother and yet you're quite different. That makes you perfect' (191). With Morgan he hopes to experience the perfect gratification of his incestuous love of his mother, dulling the Oedipal pain through taking Morgan as mother-substitute. This substitute-incest, like that also implicit but not consummated between Morgan and Rupert, figures, as in *The Time of the Angels*, together with theft as a paradigm form of law-breaking. High Eros might mean perceiving the unutterable particularity of each love-object; the confusions and substitutions of low Eros give us here two proximate incests, between Morgan and her nephew, and Morgan and her brother-in-law. Substitution also has laws which operate within the social group. Julius is able to carry out his imposture with letters since:

> The style of letters in a certain class of society is remarkably similar. This is particularly true of women's letters, even of intellectual women's letters. I've had hundreds of them. That sort of ecstatic self-indulgent running on has an almost impersonal quality.   (405)

Against all this, however, Simon has moved from promiscuous erotic substitution to the attempt to love someone in particular. In the magnificent, surreal scene in his Brook Street flat in which Julius cuts up Morgan's clothes, Morgan turns out to fit Simon's clothes exactly, and afterwards Simon has a nightmare in which his mother appears wearing Morgan's steel-rimmed spectacles, leading him to what appears to be the corpse of his father but is actually Rupert's (167). At one level this predicts Morgan's complicity in Rupert's death. At another it places Julius' claim that 'human beings are essentially finders of substitutes' in the unconscious, from which Simon's dream comes. Simon, who forever sees himself as a small boy, perceives the world as full of parents and parent-surrogates. The ending of the book, in which Axel can divest himself of some mock-paternal authority and distance, is thus also a hopeful one. All the characters, it is worth repeating, are felt from the inside with a sympathy so vivid and precise that the harsh 'outside' and 'mechanical' view has to exist in a balance, or contest. We experience this contest, as readers, in our involvement with the characters' fates. It is as if in this book Murdoch had solved both her formal problem (how to create a realism which does not underestimate the world's darkness and unintelligibility) and her moral problem (how to show human beings as possessing real, limited subjective freedom as well as appearing, as we do to others, predictable) together. For want of any better term, the achievement of such balance might still be praised as 'realism'. It is a superlative achievement.

*

It is a realism perfectly consonant with, and feeding off, the highest artifice. Much of the dialogue between Tallis and Julius acknowledges their awareness of one another as supernatural beings. Julius twice declines to explain the motivation of some particular piece of wickedness since 'You know why' (402, 408). He speaks of 'another big assignment' (431), leaving open whether a job like his research into germ warfare, or a job like his research into Rupert's moral frailty, is intended. 'In the nature of things we'll meet again' he salutes Tallis finally (430), in reference to the spiritual zone they share. This last colloquy is interesting not least because of the apologetics Julius stages. Axel had early referred to Julius as 'a man of principle' (34). The ironies of the phrase reverberate, firstly because the description seems testimony to Axel's obtuseness, and then, much later, because there is a curious sense in which it is half-true. Julius conducts an insolent running monologue of self-justification with agnostic replies from Tallis: 'Possibly', 'Mmm', 'Maybe'.

Tallis leaves two remarks of Julius' entirely unanswered. When Julius asserts that Rupert died not of drowning but of vanity Tallis is silent. And Julius' last remark in the book is 'You concede that I am an instrument of justice?' (431). To this Tallis merely smiles. Tallis concurs in part with Julius' diagnosis of human ills but not with the pleasure Julius derives from showing that it is so. His own authoritative judgement is given, when, two chapters on, 'He grieved blankly over something which seemed, in its disastrous compound of human failure, muddle and sheer chance, so like what it was all like' (443).

Julius, like the artist he professes himself, or like the novelist in particular, has the uncomfortable role of showing how things are, and at the same time of being guiltily complicit in their being so. Murdoch's plots have always tended to test their characters to breaking-point; here the guilt is Julius'. Tallis' calm grieving contrasts with Julius' provocative and guilty *Schadenfreude*, but Julius is a 'man of principle' and an 'instrument of justice' because he attacks spurious *simulacra* of the true unity to whose existence Tallis is ambiguous testimony. It is Julius who tells Morgan that he is 'allergic to reproductions' (236) and given the novel's wit on the subject of copying the joke is a metaphysical as well as a snobbish one. Thus in Chapter 2 of the second book, he also attacks Morgan's 'glossematics' in terms which recall his attack on Rupert's facile High Church Platonism. But the destruction of 'copies' – Rupert's creed (literally torn up, just as Rupert is destroyed), Morgan's fashionable investigations – does not necessarily disconfirm the existence of an 'original' Good. It throws the question, especially as it is Julius who is the mischief-making antagonist, once more open.

The end sees an ironic distribution of appropriate destinies, in the mode of a pastiche Victorian novel. Rupert may or may not be dead of vanity, but Morgan, Peter and Hilda are rewarded or punished by a Californian house with Spanish tiles, carport, and ocean view, and a psychiatrist for Peter. The court is scattered and only Tallis continues as and where he began, in a life of charmless holiness and endless good works. Axel and Simon are rewarded by provincial France on their way to Italy, by a renewal and strengthening of their love for one another, and ironically blessed by 'a very battered Christ who opened long arms and huge hands, receiving, judging' (436). Axel will in future open and give himself more.

Julius, like a Victorian villain, ends in pagan and libertine Paris, looking forward to *L'Incoronazione di Poppea*, an opera that dignifies and prettifies another diabolical anarch – Nero – and which also concerns the pain and the politics of an earlier erotic substitution. Nero capriciously replaces his old wife (Ottavia) with a new one (Poppea), after banishing both her erstwhile husband and his own former wife. Its sweet final duet celebrates, too, the relative triumph of evil.

8   *The Black Prince*

The Black Prince (1973) is an extraordinary achievement. The writing throughout is electric with energy and power. The characterisation is assured; its people, in all their awfulness, frailty, sadness, and ordinary human incompleteness, are real to the reader. It is both a very funny and an acutely distressing book, and a book which does many different things. Dostoevski the 'inquisitive writer' who sought to understand human pain is referred to once (351). He is as real a 'presence' behind the book as Shakespeare. John Bayley has suggested that the true legacy of the great fiction of the last century, which showed us that the social contract was both 'insufferable but invaluable' and gave us 'characters', may come to us through Dostoevski's subversive Underground Man, 'a man who is offered to us by his author in a spirit of complete intimacy, but also of complete equivocation'.[1] *The Black Prince* partly resembles a *Death. in Venice* written by Dostoevski's Underground Man: it is a poetic novel about the ways in which 'The creator of form must suffer formlessness' (44), told from the point of view of a narrator whose testimony about the existence of the 'highest and best' (as the Underground Man puts it) is equivocal.

Dostoevski, as well as being master of a particular blend of comedy and horror, is also surely the great poet of *embarrassment* among novelists, who both suffers and enjoys the assault on his own and our fastidiousness. Fastidiousness is one of *The Black Prince*'s topics. The settings of the book – Bradley's 'precious', pretty flat in the 'perpetual seedy *brouhaha*' of Fitzrovia, the Baffins' cheerfully vulgar Ealing house, Christian's 'Hollywood 1950s' Notting Hill flat, Bristol – are all most vividly realised. The brilliant 'set-pieces' – Bradley and Julian's colloquy in the Post Office Tower restaurant, Bradley vomiting over the Covent Garden peaches in the middle of *Rosenkavalier*, the visit to the assaulted Rachel, and later to the murdered Arnold – are no longer recalled, as are so many superlatively imagined episodes from earlier books, as detachable. They belong wholly in the novel. The book's 'meanings' are digested into its substance, and flow outward from that security. It is a superb thriller, a black book about marriage, a dark book about authorial rivalry. It is also a reflective book about love and it is this aspect which I shall emphasise.

It is the story, in three parts, of Bradley Pearson's love affair with Julian Baffin, the daughter of his friend, enemy and fellow-writer Arnold Baffin. The first part ends at the point at which Bradley realises that he has fallen in love with Julian. The second part deals with his declaration of this love and with the response of the small court of characters. The third part concerns elopement, consummation and almost immediate discovery of the lovers by Julian's father. The book's subtitle 'A Celebration of Love' suggests that it is a novel about Platonic *Eros* (referred to in *Symposium* as a sophist) and its relationship with true artistic and moral vision.

The book is framed by a Foreword and Afterword by a suprositious 'Editor', one Loxias by name, a soubriquet of Apollo. There is also a Foreword and a Postscript by Pearson, and there are four Postscripts by *Dramatis Personae* who cast doubt on Pearson's version of events and speculate as to the identity of Loxias.

The Black Prince is, as Pearson argues of *Hamlet*, the author's most inventive and involuted literary exercise. It keeps up a running commentary about *Hamlet* and is also full of writers and readers. The two major characters are writers. Arnold's young and unformed daughter Julian is to become a writer. His embittered powerful wife Rachel conceives herself a frustrated artist. Bradley's neglected office friends Hartbourne and Grey-Pelham are Civil Servants but also 'literary and journalistic persons'. Julian's friend Septimus Leech recurs in *The Sacred and Profane Love-Machine* as a blocked writer being treated by Blaise. The novel also contains peripheral jokes about its own status as an invention. The four postscripts are by characters who have read Bradley's novel and are critics and interpreters. The narrator, as well as telling his story, keeps up a series of Hamlet-like soliloquies about the relations between life, art, sex, suffering, truth.

At the end of the book Bradley receives a letter from Julian painfully ending their love affair, saying that she is going to stay

with some friends of her father's who 'live in a quiet remote
village, a little place in the mountains amid the "snow and ice" '
(371). Bradley interprets this as follows:

> The letter's in code. 'Snow and ice', to which she had drawn
> attention, patently meant Venice. The Italian for 'snow' is
> 'neve', and together with the reference to 'Italian words', the
> anagram was obvious.   (372)

This little cameo – like Julian's schoolgirl annotation to 'Oh what
a Noble Mind is Here O'erthrown' ('Feeble') – is a joke about
the connexions between all interpretation and that egoism which,
at its darkly comic extreme, is paranoia itself. Bradley hears even
music as 'a sinister gabbling which is, one suspects, *about oneself*'
(257).

The book has received diverse readings. A. S. Byatt has
commented unfavourably on its deliberate indeterminism.
Richard Todd argues that there is nothing to stop us reading it
as the story of a foot-fetichist. Lorna Sage argues, by contrast,
that it 'could have been told in the omniscient third person –
there would have been much lost in the way of local effect, but
nothing of consequence in "placing" the story as a whole'.[2]
Murdoch calls it 'an authoritarian work', dismisses the postscripts
as 'just play' and says that, for the attentive reader, it is made
clear 'how you should interpret the wanderings and maunderings
of a narrator and where you should believe him and where you
should not believe him' (Bigsby, 1982).

In fact realism or illusionism cohabit in this novel perfectly
comfortably with much that questions their premises. This is
Elizabeth Dipple's argument in a partly persuasive discussion.
Dipple convincingly argues that *The Black Prince* is the story of
Bradley's ascesis through love. She unfortunately neglects the
question of sex in relation to this ascesis, and is thus unwittingly
pushed into appearing to argue that Bradley's trial and imprisonment for a murder he did not commit is an apt comeuppance for
a writer who, Dipple surmises, secretly wished to be lionised. This
is to force the book unduly towards 'poetic justice'; Bradley's
death from cancer alone makes this look too neat.

Speaking of the ways in which ideas in art must suffer a sea-
change Murdoch has argued that 'There is always something
moral which goes down further than the ideas, the structures of

good literary works are to do with erotic mysteries and also deep dark struggles between good and evil' (Magee, 1978). 'Erotic' in this quotation has as much a Platonic as a Freudian resonance and the competition between these readings of Eros has much to do with the novel's apparent *aporia*. *The Black Prince* is about the direction in which the acquisition of a true unmediated vision might lie. The paradox of the *trompe l'oeil* organisation of the novel is that a tricksterish frame should be required to propose this direction. 'Mystagogues must speak in riddles', Pico della Mirandola argued.[3] 'The virtues have secret names; they are, so difficult of access, secret things' (11) argues Bradley, an apprentice mystic. The ambiguities of Eros are crucial to the idea-play.

Bradley's account of events is finally ratified by the fact that all four of the postscripts are in precisely the self-centred characters that Bradley has throughout ascribed to their writers.[4] They thus service our sense of the plot more than they destabilise our grasp of it. While puritan Bradley inculpates himself throughout the story, presenting himself as a guilty man seeking redemption, the others all exculpate themselves. The covetous Christian has married Hartbourne, whom there is no evidence that she knew before, and might thus be thought of as as fast and acquisitive in these matters as Bradley has judged her. Francis confirms Bradley's predictions, sustained throughout, that he will Freudianise the entire story; he advertises a Freudian pamphlet on Bradley's 'case'. Both Christian and the murderous, vengeful Rachel maintain that Bradley was in love with them and not the other way about, thus extending that style of egoism which his account of them – and of the position and predicament of women generally – seems to predict. Loxias' verdict – that the postscripts are small-minded self-advertisements – is right. Gabriel Pearson has aptly termed *The Black Prince* an 'anti-anti-novel', built to explore but withstand 'the sporadic sense of its own self-invention'.[5]

Loxias' circumstantial account of his possession of the manuscript belongs to a tradition of realism going back as far as Defoe, while his *persona* as Apollo is understated.[6] He is the recipient, goad and urger of that high Eros to which Bradley's pilgrimage – he calls his life at the end a 'quest and an ascesis' (391) – is to lead him. Loxias' postscript includes jokes about his status as *deus ex machina*. He denies that he is an invention of Bradley's and endorses Rachel's version of his identity which was 'a notorious rapist and murderer, a well-known musical virtuoso, whose murder by a peculiarly horrible method of a successful fellow-musician made the head-lines some considerable time ago' (407). This nicely provides a darkly comic echo of the main plot, since Bradley is a writer condemned for murdering by a peculiarly horrible method a successful fellow-writer, a murder also exploited by the newspapers. It is also the novel's one clear reference to the myth of Apollo and Marsyas, around which, though she does not mention this reference, Dipple correctly builds her reading. Apollo flayed his rival musician Marsyas alive, and such an ironic allusion to the myth must serve to warn us against any reading of the novel as simple poetic justice. The myth of Apollo and Marsyas is in part a cautionary tale about competing with the divine, as well as a tale of divinely inspired ascesis.

About this customary Neoplatonic theme Edgar Wind wrote:

The musical contest between Apollo and Marsyas was . . . concerned with the relative powers of Dionysian darkness and Apollonian clarity; and if the contest ended with the flaying of Marsyas, it was because flaying was itself a Dionysian rite, a tragic ordeal of purification by which the ugliness of the outward man was thrown off and the beauty of his inward self revealed.[7]

Murdoch has identified Apollo, hymned by so many poets, both as the god of art, and also with the black Eros itself 'destructive and violent' (Caen, 1978). In conversation with me she made clear her view that Dionysus is for her a minor god, and one aspect of Apollo himself. What happens to Bradley, from one point of view, is that he is saved as an artist, taught 'the pain and final joy gained from loss of self and loving attention to the world'.[8] From another point of view the 'flaying' he undergoes in the book destroys him, and at Caen she reminded her audience that Apollo, as a rapist and violent murderer, is by no means simply to be regarded as a 'good' figure. He is a figure of ambiguous power. In conversation with me Miss Murdoch added that Bradley at the end can be seen as a minor artist whom the god rewards and comforts for his patient zeal and longing.

Loxias' foreword proposes for the story the largest resonance and dignity. The novel is subtitled 'A Celebration of Love' and 'Every artist is an unhappy lover. And unhappy lovers want to tell their story' (10). Loxias extends what we normally understand by 'love' and points towards Bradley's Neoplatonism when he adds that 'Man's creative struggle, his search for wisdom and truth, is a love story' (9). This is a novel about the whole of Eros. Bradley's foreword amounts to a Neoplatonic manifesto. He begins a discourse on the secret nature of the virtues, explaining that his narrative technique will be that of a retrospective diary. He identifies a 'wise' later narrator and a foolish narrator contemporary with the events narrated, and adds that this later wisdom must necessarily irradiate the tale. He notes that he will be the inglorious 'hero' and describes himself as a 'seeker' (12), providing homilies on the relation of virtue to the experience of time, in and out of art. He describes himself as a retired Tax Collector. In *Sartre* Murdoch asked the question, derived from Kierkegaard, whether 'the Knight of Faith can really go on looking like a Tax Collector' (67). Like Kierkegaard's Knight, Bradley is a pilgrim in quest of Virtue.[9] He describes his sense of himself at the time of the story as awaiting an ordeal, and describes himself as 'conventional, nervous, puritanical, the slave of habit' (18). 'Though I am a creative person, I am a puritan rather than an aesthete. I know that human life is horrible. I know that it is utterly unlike art' (18). Bradley's puritanism and his aestheticism are less far apart than this disclaimer suggests; and the novel is in part designed to remind us of the gap between horror in life and the prettifying attentions it earns in art: its narrative 'jokes', which make it look formalist, in fact are partly anti-formalist. They are not intended as boasts about the artwork's narcissistic self-sufficiency, but as reminders that it is there for our consumption, and our use.

*

The Black Prince, like *An Accidental Man* and all the novels which follow, without chapter divisions, seems designed to accommodate a larger illusion of formlessness.

It might be most dramatically effective to begin the tale at the moment when Arnold Baffin rang me up and said, 'Bradley, could you come round here please, I think I may have just killed my wife'. A deeper pattern however suggests Francis Marloe as the first speaker, the page or house-boy (these images would appeal to him) who, some half hour before Arnold's momentous telephone call, initiates the action. For the news that Francis brought me forms the frame, or counter point, or outward packaging of what happened then and later in the drama of Arnold Baffin. There are indeed many places where I could start. I might start with Rachel's tears, or Priscilla's. There is much shedding of tears in this story. (21)

The opening displays an artfully distracted narrative technique. The deft hesitations make clear the book's project both to tell an exciting story ('Stories are art too' (240)) and also to slacken its terrible Dostoevskian speed (two weeks) which recalls the hectic opening section of *The Idiot*. It also refers to the distress of other centres of significance than Bradley alone. Baffin's telephone call suggests the sensational thriller the book partly is ('Art is adventure stories' (414), and Bradley is to die wishing he had written *Treasure Island*[10]). The symmetry here depends upon Rachel's call at the end, announcing, in effect, her murder of Arnold. The distress of the women proposes the recurrent theme of the horrors of married life, and the decision to use Francis points to his double function in the book, as Freudian booby, quintessentially reductive reader, and as debased saintly buffoon, a Dostoevskian figure of nearly invisible degraded sanctity.

Bradley early speaks of his novel as 'the story of my relations with Arnold and the astounding climax to which these relations led' (29), which recalls Jake's statement that 'my acquaintance with Hugo is the central theme of this book' (*UN* 53). Gabriel Pearson nicely wrote that

> The cat and mouse relationship between Bradley and Arnold . . . struck me as the equivalent of an overdue debate between that aspect of Iris Murdoch's activity that has poured out fifteen novels with fatal fluency and the chaste and strict mind that wrote the book on Sartre and *The Sovereignty of Good*. It is a debate that need have no outcome to be illuminating.[11]

About this debate A. S. Byatt suggests that it is also a contest between the 'crystalline' and 'journalistic'.[12] It is a conflict between, on the one hand, Bradley's ferocious and censorious puritanism, and, on the other, Baffin's tolerant, inquisitive and inclusive complaisance: it continues the great quarrel between the best and second-best. The conflict between artist and saint occurs inside each as much as between them. Both are artists, both would-be moral beings far from sanctity.

It is in fact very hard to focus Bradley adequately; and the difficulty of doing so is a triumph of art. He is dark and opaque to himself as we are to ourselves. This central darkness fills the book, and renders his view of Arnold, for example, equivocal too. Here, as Paul Ricoeur noted in a different context, the aporias of interpretation seem to be those of reflection itself.[13]

The word most often used of him is 'puritan'. He describes himself as a perfectionist, a worldly failure, ineffective both as a sensualist and as a monk, a seeker, a devotee of silence, 'gentle to timidity', a fastidious, easily disgusted self-absorbed person who detests the *ad hoc* and spontaneous. He likes to fix his appointments with his sister weeks in advance and by letter. 'What does he fear? is usually the key to the artist's mind' (82), he notes. Pearson fears predatory women, or women *tout court* (109), betrayal, tears, trains as 'object lessons in the foul contingency of life' (66), his friends becoming mutually acquainted. He fears missing trains. He also comically fears arriving so early that he has only a few minutes to spare to catch the predecessor of the train he feared missing . . . . Bradley is a puritan ruled by *pudeur* who fears contingency, a Platonist and monist. The novel shows Bradley's comically, grotesquely undergoing much that terrifies him.

At one point Bradley notes that the gap between 'the self-knowledge which we gain by observing ourselves objectively and the self-awareness which we have by ourselves subjectively' (189) probably prevents our ever arriving at the truth. The verdicts of our friends contribute to both. Bradley's circle is no exception. Christian twice compares him with Don Quixote and sees him as a potentially spiritual man, a refuge from the world of Chicago sexual and monetary acquisitiveness with which she has become embroiled; her study of Zen has made her a far more deadly flirt and entrepreneur than she had been before beginning such religious practice. Rachel too sees him as ascetic but also as a masochist who enjoys Arnold's attacks on him and, at a moment of tension, speaks of him as 'a deeply censorious and self-righteous person' who means well, 'a nice chap' (181). Arnold, admittedly intent on flattering him in order to pre-empt his love affair with Julian, calls him 'a decent rational man and a moral being' (281).

What distinguishes Bradley from anybody else in the tale is guilt and spinsterishness. He is the most censorious and repressed of the books' many egoists. He calls himself to Rachel 'pre-permissive' (156) and adds that 'one *doesn't*, with one's best friend's wife' (my emphasis) and indeed he doesn't. He tells Rachel priggishly that 'morals is simple' and is shown as trying – and failing – to live by these simplicities. When Rachel agonises over her subjection to her husband he calls her thoughts 'very base'. You can be a puritan without, however, as Rachel in the Postscript points out, being good. Bradley is cocooned in self-righteousness. So, when Priscilla is suicidally depressed in his flat he has a 'long and reassuring conversation' with his doctor – about himself, prefiguring his critical neglect of her when he elopes, and her suicide. Though married to Christian he was never sufficiently curious to discover that she is of Jewish background, a fact that Arnold elicits at once. He consistently neglects his old office-friend Hartbourne, and implicitly therefore also that wider more open world for which Hartbourne seems intended to stand.

Arnold, by contrast, is both intensely curious, a quality about which they quarrel, and complaisant. Just as Jake's block as a writer was somehow healed by the attrition he underwent at the unwitting hands of Hugo's capacity to honour the particular, so Bradley's block is cured by surrender to that open and contingent world with which Arnold lives on easier terms. This is surely why Bradley's book itself is, as Byatt says, very Baffinesque.[14] Both Jake and Bradley see the world as it suits them and have to begin to learn a difficult relaxation of the moral will. Arnold is of course very different from Hugo, the holy fool who saw everything *sui generis*. He is an apostle of that lazy substitute second-best virtue that haunts Murdoch's work as *samodovolnost*. As his wife puts it 'Arnold is so self-satisfied that he's really generous, it's real virtue' (181). 'He liked and accepted everything' (187). Arnold does not, unlike Bradley, 'try to be perfect', as Julian complains (58). He is a meddler who, for example, takes Bradley's unpleasant letter to Christian unasked. The descriptions of his work are (apart from the fact that he does not describe love) clearly designed to parody unflattering descriptions of Murdoch's own. Thus Bradley's account of the plot of Arnold's latest book is a sensational parody of a Murdochian novel, comprising two worlds, one religious and one profane, conversion and apostasy, a near-drowning in an overflowing reservoir, and a sensational death from a falling crucifix (146). Arnold's books comprise 'inquisitive chatter and cataloguing of things one's spotted' (49), are 'chat plus fantasy' (50). Julian sees her father living 'in a sort of rosy haze with Jesus and Mary and Buddha and Shiva and the Fisher King all chasing round and round dressed up as people in Chelsea' (37). To Bradley, 'the cause of his failure was, in part at least, a kind of enthusiastic garrulous religiosity' (187) and Arnold is a *gabbler*.

> But the gabble was not just casual and slipshod, it was an aspect of what one might call his 'metaphysic'. Arnold was always trying, as it were, to take over the world by emptying himself over it like scented bathwater. (187)

So Arnold's work, by all accounts, lacks that tense self-contained form, that internally related necessity, which, as much as an (apodeictic) openness to the world, marks, for Murdoch, great art. Arnold lacks the restraint and silence necessary for such performance but has an openness to his material. Bradley has the former and lacks the latter. To Bradley art is connected to the priestly quest for the good life. To Arnold it is fun. To Murdoch it should, ideally, be both. And both Arnold and Bradley equally undergo the ministrations of the black Eros. Arnold writes to Bradley as if his love for Christian might become for him the saving ordeal that Bradley's love for Julian is for Bradley.

Partly for this reason Shakespeare, who is the novel's tutelary deity after Loxias, offers an ambiguous moral example. Bradley early soliloquises that virtue, when closely examined, often turns out to be

> no glorious thing, not the turning back by reason or godhead of the flood of natural evil, but simply a special operation of self-love, devised perhaps by Nature herself who has, or she could not survive in her polycephalic creation, many different and even incompatible moods. (109)

Here Good appears to unify the awful contingency of the cosmos, but turns out to be second-best, *samodovolnost*, on closer scrutiny. Shakespeare is seen as greatest of all artists, as 'the king of

masochists, his writing thrills with that secret' (200) and also as
high-priest of *samodovolnost*. There may be no saints but 'there is
at least one proof that the light of self-satisfaction can illuminate
the world' Charles Arrowby is to announce (*SS* 482). Bradley too
sees Shakespeare as quintessentially *worldly*: 'Can there be a
natural, as it were Shakespearian felicity in the moral life? Or are
the Eastern sages right to set as task to their disciples the gradual
total destruction of the dreaming ego?' (190). It is true that in
his disquisition on *Hamlet* he will compare Shakespeare persuasively with Marsyas. Yet even there his last word assimilates
Shakespeare to the *mondain*.

> 'Bradley, I wish I'd understood that stuff you spouted about
> *Hamlet*.'
> 'Forget it. No high theory about Shakespeare is any good, not
> because he's so divine but because he's so human. Even great
> art is jumble in the end'.   (240)

Murdoch's ideal artist, induced by his Eros to experience his
own and others' pain and delight with greater (Marsyas-like)
nakedness is more, not less human. If he is god-like at all, it is
this exceptional ordinariness that makes him so.

*

The Black Prince invents imaginary readers as well as imaginary
writers. In his Foreword Bradley says 'My mother filled me with
exasperation and shame but I loved her. (Be quiet Francis
Marloe)' (15). Bradley explains that Francis belongs to a sad
crew of semi-educated theorisers who prefer any general blunted
'symbolic' explanation to the horror of confronting a unique
human history. Such 'interpreters' recur throughout the book,
ranking as a secondary chorus. The Freudians who rival the
Platonic Good as listeners are described as 'diminishers'. They
exist both as agents *within* the text – Christian like Francis is a
'diminisher' (92), Bradley himself fears that his account diminishes
Arnold (186) – and also outside it, in the book's real readership.
One of the book's disquisitions addresses the problem of the
current unthinking apotheosis of the sexual urges: ' . . . there's
nothing sex cannot be said to explain, by cynics and pseudo-
scientists such as Francis Marloe . . . I am myself no sort of
Freudian . . .' (143). Bradley goes on to reprimand an 'obtuse

person' who might wish to diminish his story according to such principles. Christian's notion that he might consider being analysed is greeted, with the book's sole such rash of exclamation marks, 'Analysed!! Certainly not!!' (168).

There is a connexion between Bradley's ceaseless anathematising of these Freudian 'cynics', 'diminishers', 'obtuse persons', and 'pseudo-scientists' – more are invoked early in Part Two – and the theme of *Hamlet* and how we are to read it. The most striking thing about trying to relate *Hamlet* to *The Black Prince* is how hard it is. Todd notes that we are never sure whether to identify Hamlet with Bradley who delays writing his book and consummating his affair as Hamlet delays revenge, and suffers from 'a thing about smells' reminiscent of Hamlet's disgust; or with Julian, who once dresses as Hamlet.[15]

In interview Murdoch has said that 'The black prince is not Hamlet of course, but that's by the way' (Bellamy, 1977). While the novel is full of felicitous quotation from *Hamlet*, and contains two discussions of how we are to read and understand the play, only one *situation* reflects, both in its language and its formal properties, Bradley's view of the original play.

When Baffin violently interrupts Bradley and Julian's erotic idyll by the sea he agrees to Julian's staying the night with Bradley on one condition which he is too emotional to do more than hint at: 'And don't – any more tonight – oh hell – you can't think or imagine what you've done to me' (338). The echo is clear:

> Goodnight, but go not to my uncle's bed,
> Assume a virtue if you have it not . . .
> . . . Refrain tonight
> And that shall lend a kind of easiness
> To the next abstinence, the next more easy. (III iv, 159–67)

If we are now to add Arnold to the list of people who act out Hamlet then the allusion is a good deal more complex than Todd suggests. Identification *between* these two texts is not exactly what is at issue, but identification *within* each text is. Arnold's *veto* on Bradley and Julian's sexual expression of their love is the culmination of series of clues as to the intensity of his and Julian's mutual feelings. When the Baffin parents first find out that

Bradley loves Julian, Rachel asks if they have been to bed together: ' "Oh Christ, *Christ*", said Arnold, "of course he hasn't, he's not a criminal" ' (282). Since Julian is twenty the act he fears can in no ordinary sense be thought of as criminal. Later when Arnold finds that they have indeed become lovers he exclaims ' "I regard this relationship as a defilement" ' (337). When Julian writes to Bradley ending her relationship with him she guilelessly includes the lines:

> Father is quite relaxed now about it all and sends you his best wishes by the way. (*Everyone at the hotel thinks we are lovers!*) . . . I think I never made it clear enough to you how much I love my father. (Perhaps he is *the* man in my life!)   (370) [first emphasis mine]

The analogy which *The Black Prince* proposes between itself and *Hamlet* – made explicit in Bradley's seminar to Julian – is that both texts invite and require a Freudian reading, and neither can be satisfied or exhausted by it. Like the Post Office Tower, which so dominates this novel, both *Hamlet* and *The Black Prince* exemplify an Eros both Freudian and also Platonic. 'And every man in London is obsessed with the Post Office Tower' (153) argues Bradley, demythologising the merely Freudian content of the symbol.

Thus we come to Bradley's seminar on *Hamlet* with Julian. I have noted Murdoch's interest in the Oedipus conflict in many of the novels. What is striking about Bradley's discussion is that, first of all, he begins with a brilliant and succinct précis of Ernest Jones' Freudian reading of the play,[16] and then suggests the qualified relevance of such a reading to the sophisticated reader.

To reduce an already reductive reading yet more: Hamlet delays because he identifies Claudius with his father, and is cruel to Ophelia because he identifies her with Gertrude. 'The unconscious mind delights in identifying people with each other. It has only a few characters to play with' (195). Hamlet feels guilty in condemning Claudius to death for adultery because he unconsciously wishes to sleep with his mother, and feels guilty in condemning him to death for murder because he unconsciously wished to kill his father. The conversation proceeds:

> 'Shut up. That dreary stuff about Hamlet and his ma and pa you can get out of a book. I'll tell you which one.'

'So it's not true?'

'It is true but it doesn't matter. A sophisticated reader takes such things in his stride. You are a sophisticated reader *in ovo*.' (197)

'Ma and pa' nicely domesticates *Hamlet* and brings it closer to Ealing, but 'it is true but it doesn't matter' is, in a sense, precisely what the novel invites us to feel about its own Oedipal or family romance.[17] Arnold clearly loves his daughter to a degree that Bradley's love affair with her strikes him as 'criminal', 'a defilement', since it is an acting-out of his own unconscious wishes. There is similarly an element within Julian's love for Bradley which is a deferment of her love for her father, an expression through a (just) permissible surrogate of what would otherwise be taboo.[18] During the Baffin family row which precedes Arnold's actually locking up his daughter, Julian moreover recounts that 'he shouted that she [Rachel] was jealous of me, and she shouted that he was in love with me' (294). From Julian's, Rachel's, and Loxias' Postscripts we learn that Julian and her mother have not met, after the events of the novel, for some years. Their estrangement is symptomatic of this double rivalry, both for Arnold's love, then later for Bradley's.

*

Such identifications do not matter because the book's true topic is the subsuming of such low Freudian Eros within a higher Eros where the substitutions and repetitions of the Oedipal family romance might have less coercive imaginative power; and individual essence might be honoured and dignified as if it were, at least partly, autonomous product. Thus the identifications between the plot of *Hamlet* and *The Black Prince* are multifarious. When Julian asks why Ophelia could not save Hamlet, Bradley – prophetically identifying Julian with Ophelia – answers 'Because, my dear Julian, pure ignorant young girls cannot save complicated neurotic over-educated old men from disaster . . .' (196). And in a former colloquy about *Hamlet* Bradley had farcically suggested that '[the king and Claudius] were in love. Gertrude killed her husband because he was having a love affair with Claudius. Hamlet knew of course. No wonder he was neurotic' (160). This joke points to a further identification between the personnel of each work since, on the independent testimony of both Rachel and Francis, there is an intensity of emotion between Bradley and Arnold which can best be understood if we see it as a sublimated 'sexual' attraction and rivalry. The point is not to establish that *Hamlet* haunts *The Black Prince* in such a manner that it can be *reduced* to it, but that the psyche is haunted by the constant possibility of such reductions in its day-to-day commerce with the world, that the unconscious 'has only a few characters to play with'.

So the dance of attachments in the first part of the story reflects the power struggle between Arnold and Bradley and is its inescapable product. Rachel tries to get closer to Bradley to compensate for the pain and frustration in her marriage. But she early tells Bradley that 'you can't *separate* me, you'd have to focus your attention on me very hard to do that, and you won't'. Two pages later Bradley's vision endorses the truth of this: 'Then I saw her again, and again and again. Oxford Street was full of tired ageing women with dazed faces, pushing blindly against each other like a herd of animals' (183). Rachel comes to symbolise the horror of predatory unloved middle-aged women for him. She is, of course, more than such a personification in an allegory, but insufficiently more for *him* for his love for her to be so purified that she can be perceived as separate and unique. Against so generalised a vision he discusses in a tone of wonder the way in which his love for Julian partakes of that absolute character which is 'indifferent to substitutes' (316).

Thus, from the Freudian reading of *Hamlet* Bradley moves to a Neoplatonic one, which he is to term 'esoteric lore', and which also has consequences for the way that we are invited to read *The Black Prince*.

Hamlet is nearer to the wind than Shakespeare ever sailed, even in the *Sonnets*. Did Shakespeare hate his father? Of course. Was he in love with his mother? Of course. But that is only the beginning of what he is telling us about himself. . . . He has performed a supreme creative feat, a work endlessly reflecting upon itself, not discursively but in its very substance, a Chinese box of words as high as the tower of Babel, a meditation upon the bottomless trickery of consciousness and the redemptive role of words in the lives of those without identity, that is, human beings. *Hamlet* is words and so is Hamlet. He is as witty as Jesus Christ, but whereas Jesus Christ speaks, Hamlet is speech. He is the empty tormented sinful consciousness of man seared by the bright light of art, the god's flayed victim dancing the dance of creation. The cry of anguish is obscure because it is overheard. It is the eloquence of direct speech, it is *oratio recta* not *oratio obliqua*. But it is not addressed to us. Shakespeare is passionately exposing himself to the ground and author of his being. He is speaking as few artists can speak, in the first person yet at the pinnacle of artifice. (199)

Northrop Frye once wrote of 'the unmistakable roar of Shakespeare's mighty rhetorical engines'.[19] It makes sense to speak here of Murdoch's mighty rhetorical engines. The passage from which this fragment is quoted continues at the same pitch of excitement and intensity, and with the same degree of difficult lucidity, for a further page. These punnings about the self-referring quality of *Hamlet* are partly to be applied to *The Black Prince* as well. In this novel, as she tacitly concurred in interview with Bellamy, we also feel the authorial presence to be closer to Bradley than it is to other of her narrators. Here, too, Murdoch is writing in the first person but at the pinnacle of artifice. The sheer quantity of discursive first-person meditation in this novel demands, in homage to *Hamlet*, to be thought of as 'soliloquy'. Bradley's soliloquies, like Hamlet's, are often metaphysical complaints which meditate on life's horrors.

*

Murdoch has spoken of her career as a move from the quaint, absurd, touching and funny in *Under the Net*, to the 'sad and awful' later dark comedies (Bellamy, 1977). 'In real life, that which is horrible lacks the significance of art. The novel is intensely aware of this fact' (132). This is a movement away from charm, and towards horror, and these two words recur rather as 'love' and 'cynicism' polarise *A Fairly Honourable Defeat*.

What causes Bradley's 'reform' is the irruption of contingency and the consequent attenuation of his ego. Horror breaks in. This horror is chiefly that of bad marriage, unhappy love, and the 'betrayal' of friends, but is repeatedly and explicitly linked to other forms of horror for which these are a shorthand (184: 'war, concentration camps, the awful privacy of family life and marriage'; see also the soliloquy on page 348 on the world defined as a place of suffering).

Moreover *The Black Prince* reads at times as though written as
a meditation on *Hamlet* III i 156: 'I say, let there be no more
marriages'. The Baffin marriage with its emotional and physical
violence figures at the beginning. The Saxe marriage repeats it
in yet more grotesque form. Priscilla, a pathetic defeated snob
like her mother, appears, we gather, to have inveigled Roger into
marriage by pretending to be pregnant. Among the torments
Roger has devised for her has been an episode in which he
pretended to poison her. Francis recounts a third terrible marriage
where his father, a violent man, possibly killed his and Christian's
mother. Bradley and Priscilla's parents 'could not see each other
at all'. And Christian spent much of her second marriage waiting
for her husband to die. Moreover these 'little pictures out of hell'
recur in the world at large: the London of this book is repeatedly
full of defeated and despairing people.

The book abounds in extraordinary and apt images of the
horror of human pair-bonding. Francis loved one boy who
committed suicide. Bradley refers to his horrible sense of connexion
with Christian as being 'Siamese-twinned to her mind. We reeled
about, joined at the head' (92). Rachel speaks of her subjection
to Arnold thus: '[A married woman] is a subdivision of her
husband's mind, and he can release misery into her consciousness
whenever he pleases, like ink spreading into water' (176). Women
in this novel arguably suffer more than men. Priscilla, abandoned,
pleads pathetically for Bradley to fetch 'a few things of her own'
to help provide her with a sense of her own continuity: 'And the
little ornaments, that stripey vase' (88). Rachel unconsciously
echoes Priscilla's complaint when she pleads for 'a little privacy,
a little secrecy, a few things of my own that aren't absolutely
dyed and saturated with Arnold. But it seems to be impossible'
(179). Women suffer the larger dispossession, either literal, or
figurative as in Rachel's case.

> I know that human life is horrible. I know that it is utterly
> unlike art. I have no religion except my own task of being.
> Conventional religions are dream stuff. Always a world of fear
> and horror lies but a millimetre away. Any man, even the
> greatest, can be broken in a moment and has no refuge. Any
> theory which denies that is a lie.   (19)

Horror cannot be charmed by theory, and Freudianism is early
cited as a means of eschewing 'the horror of confronting a unique

human existence' (15). Priscilla's weeping suggests to Bradley 'The horror of the world glimpsed without charm' (85).

Priscilla early suggests to Bradley that he is blocked as a writer because 'You understand nothing of the horror . . . you don't see the horror' (224). The theme is not new. It is related, once more, to the Dionysiac and sublime chaos Carel shows to Marcus and acts out himself, and to the emotional anarchy Julius engineers among the sophisticates of *A Fairly Honourable Defeat*. *The Black Prince* represents Murdoch's most *detailed* attempt at picturing such a negative sublime in human terms, and the unloved, unlovely women of the first Part are its emissaries, marriage its *mise-en-scène*. Rachel and Priscilla are shown four times climbing fully dressed into bed in despair, and the last time Priscilla prophetically resembles 'a corpse climbing into its coffin'. Rachel is reported to us repeating the same sentences over and over. Priscilla is shown doing this. The word 'hell' recurs in context after context. 'Priscilla is in hell. Well we all are. Life is torture, consciousness is torture. All our little devices are just morphia to stop us from screaming' (152), Francis philosophises. Bradley repeatedly soliloquises that no quantity of moral discipline will suffice 'when horror breaks in' (184). ' . . . Life is horrible, without metaphysical sense, wrecked by chance, pain and the close prospect of death' (81).

In one of the last of his soliloquies Bradley argues that

> The world is perhaps ultimately to be defined as a place of suffering. Man is a suffering animal, subject to ceaseless anxiety and pain and fear, subject to the rule of what the Buddhists call *dukha*, the endless unsatisfied anguish of a being who passionately desires only illusory goods . . . . That this world is a place of *horror* must affect every serious artist and thinker, darkening his reflection, ruining his system, sometimes actually driving him mad. (348)

Neither Bradley's ascesis nor Arnold's complaisance help them much. Both end the book dead. Meanwhile Bradley seeks whether there can be an honourable specific against horror: 'And shall the artist have no cakes and ale? Must he who makes happy be a liar, and can the spirit that sees the truth also speak it? What is, and what can be, the range of the sufficiently serious heart?' (349).

Falling in love is oddly angled to horror; within it the negative sublime is partly transposed into the sublime. When at the start of Book Two Bradley gives the first of many soliloquies about the experience of falling in love, he describes it in a highly pertinent opposition as 'more astonishing because more counter-natural, than life's horrors'. He then points out that love 'generates, or rather reveals something which may be called *absolute charm*. In the beloved nothing is gauche.' When, previously, Bradley had been engaged in the act of falling in love with Julian, she asked him whether or not her feet smelt, and he replied, 'Yes, but it's charming' (200). This is, as it were, an anterior demonstration of the truth of the absolute charm revealed by love, and not, as the most curious and Freudian of articles on this novel has it, a clue to Bradley's secret foot fetichism.[20] (When at the beginning Julian's mother, whom Bradley found not wholly unattractive, took off *her* shoes, he commented merely 'A pungent sour odour joined the vapid smell of the room' (39).)

This point seems worth labouring because commentators have widely, and above all puritanically, failed to see the role of Eros in Murdoch's *oeuvre*. It is of course the very centre of her thought. She is far away from the puritan moralism of this same critic who describes Marloe as 'degenerate' and who feels it necessary to defend Murdoch's tolerance of homosexuality on the grounds that 'no-one is too depraved to write about'.[21]

The paradox of Bradley's case is that, before his seizure by Dionysus–Apollo, his personality is an apparent parody of the Apollonian – obsessive, spinsterish, purportedly rational. And the parallels which spring to mind for Bradley's morganatic alliance are von Ashenbach's for Tadzio in *Death in Venice* or the Professor's for Lola in *The Blue Angel*. Like them, Bradley is a mandarin destroyed, or educated, by passion. This is the anti-moral implicit in Bradley's censoriousness about his brother-in-law's relationship with Marigold; like Julian, Marigold is many years the younger. The action of the novel teaches him a loving tolerance learnt only through Bradley's seizure by Eros and concomitant access to a greater openness.

The point is made at the moment of his falling in love. Both he and Julian have been sweating in his hot, needlessly stuffy flat, when he opens the window, and lets in, as it were, contingency: 'a massed-up buzz of various noise filled the room, cars, voices, the endless hum of London's being' (201). The novel makes no sense unless we grant that this love is, like all great love, totally compelling and real to its protagonists, *as well as*, like all but the 'highest' states of consciousness, illusory. The 'illusions' of love are by no means valueless. Its reality might be said to lie in the fact that it involves an apparent loss of self in the lover and a concentration on the reality of someone other than oneself. Its unreality follows, in that such keen insight should be democratised, spread more evenly. Erotic love provokes tunnel vision and makes the rest of the world invisible. Priscilla is the casualty of this love as much as she is of that of Roger and Marigold. Rachel, to a lesser degree perhaps, suffers both from Bradley's affair with Julian and from Arnold's with Christian.

Eros is thus a sophist, teaching a vital truth but a partial one. Eros transfigures the world and the passages evoking its sensations are unsurpassed even in Murdoch, which is to say a great deal. Such evocations are both particular and general. The book abounds in virtuoso passages seemingly designed to answer the question: 'What is it like?'

Passages evoke the nature of women's apparent characterlessness (34), how discovering that someone is Jewish makes them look at once a lot cleverer (148), the dependence of wrong-doing on anaesthetising the imagination (170), the way the mind is engaged in filing damage done to its vanity (191). Mimesis reaches a high point, for example, in the phrase 'a prowling desire to vomit' (78). The mind is often here conceived of as a passive theatre of sensations. Inspiration – 'those dark globules in the head, those tinglings in the fingers' (212); giddiness – 'locates itself in the genitals' (239); vomiting (261); consciousness (205); fainting – 'that odd, absolutely unique sensation of a black *baldacchino* being lowered like an extinguisher over one's head' (226); jealousy – 'the sense that a part of oneself has been irrevocably alienated and stolen' (247); hysterics (225); sleep (231), imagining minds other than one's own (289), listening to music (257), *angst* (145), erection (163).

This last case might be taken as an example of how language in this novel is insistently Platonised: 'physical desire with its absurd, alarming, unmistakable symptoms, the anti-gravitational *aspiration* of the male organ, one of the oddest and most unnerving things in nature' (163–4) [my emphasis]. Physical desire itself is thus quietly assimilated to the language of moral ascent and spiritual ambition. Desire is later brilliantly evoked as 'the great *scar* of desire' (257), a phrase both accurately redolent of the pain involved, but also reminiscent of Aristophanes' account of the bisection of primal beings in the *Symposium* (109B) and their consequent painful yearning and questing. Aristophanes' account precedes Socrates/Diotima's, it will be recalled, and belongs to that 'matter' or mystery which only Diotima can properly explain. Passage after passage in the novel asserts a comparable continuity between high and low Eros, between sex and true moral vison.

> Sex is our great connection with the world, and at its most felicitous and spiritual it is no servitude since it informs everything and enables us to inhabit and enjoy all that we touch and look upon. (245)

> How right Plato was to think that, embracing a lovely boy, he was on the road to the Good . . . . Why cannot this release from self provide a foothold in a new place which we can then colonise and enlarge until at last we will *all* that is not ourselves. That was Plato's dream. It is not impossible. (210)

> When sexual desire is also love it connects us with the whole world and becomes a new mode of experience. Sex then reveals itself as the great connective principle whereby we overcome duality, the force which made separateness as an aspect of oneness at some moment of bliss in the mind of God. (211)

> Human love is the gateway to all knowledge, as Plato saw. (390)

Even Julian, who threatens in her Postscript to turn into a greater puritan, if that were possible, than Bradley, argues that 'Soul energy may be *called* sex down to the bottom. (Or up to the top)' (410).

*

Bradley, we recall, criticised Arnold's work for its 'garrulous religiosity'. The redemption by Eros he recounts can only be figured in religious terms. He early sees Francis' and Arnold's faces when he visits the battered Rachel as 'faces in a crucifixion crowd' (33). When he sees Julian scattering love letter fragments he mistakes her for a 'hieratic boy' and the scattering for a religious ritual (56). The novel is marked by invocations to gods and to the divine. The shoeshop where Bradley buys Julian her boots is 'the temple of some old unpassionate rather ascetic cult' (163) and he later describes the purchase as having been 'rather like a mystical experience' (205). In Bristol collecting Priscilla's belongings he meditates as follows:

> Kites have always meant a lot to me. What an image of our condition, the distant high thing, the sensitive pull, the feel of the cord, its invisibility, its length, the fear of loss . . .
> They were shooting pigeons. What an image of our condition, the loud report, the poor flapping bundle on the ground, trying helplessly, desperately, vainly to rise again.   (107)

The images of flight and of fall here work quite apparently to propose for 'our condition' a vertical hierarchy, a ladder of ascent and descent, as aspiration and subjection to chance and mortality.

He describes the experience of falling in love in religious terms. Bradley's love for Julian makes 'the whole of life into a sacrament' (212). He returns to his flat soon after his *coup de foudre* merely to think about Julian: 'So holy men return to temples and crusading knights feed upon the blessed sacrament' (219). Christian describes his appearance at this time as if he had suffered transfiguration and had become a saint. London becomes for him Jerusalem. He regards himself as a god sustaining Julian in being. His book is to be Julian's 'deification' and 'immortality' (389). At the same time we observe him behaving with a manic generosity, even to Roger and Marigold, which is ludicrous, touching, and wholly believable.

On three occasions he compares the experience of falling in love with that of the Platonic pilgrim emerging from his enslavement to mere appearance in the Cave, into the Sun. He has early established this analogy between mind and Cave:

> These images which float in the mind's cave (and whatever the philosophers may say the mind *is* a dark cave full of drifting beings) are of course not neutral apparitions but are already saturated with judgement, lurid with it.   (192)

Immediately after recognising his love for Julian he describes his 'joy in my marvellous achievement of absolute love. In this blaze of light of course a few more mundane thoughts flitted to and fro like little birds, scarcely descried by one who was dazzled by emergence from the cave' (208). 'This morning I had felt like a cave-dweller emerging into the sun. She was the truth of my life' (285). He is convinced of inhabiting and at last envisioning a real world. 'There was an overwhelming sense of reality, of being at last the real and seeing the real. The tables, the chairs, the sherry glasses, the curls on the rug, the dust: real' (209).

This loss of self or ascesis is, as he will come to see, partly false, partly true. He lacks any sense of either Priscilla's or Francis' reality. Julian has drawn all the available reality into her – or he has invested it there, so that, when they dine at the Post Office Tower he echoes that most Platonist part of *Corinthians*: 'We conversed as angels might converse, not through a glass darkly but face to face' (240). Though Francis keeps trying to suggest how much attention Priscilla needs, he casually tells her about Roger's adultery, and, brutalised by euphoria, adds unnecessary details about the mistress in the case and her pregnancy. He takes Francis wholly for granted. Bradley and Julian have a need of one another to whose ferocious urgency all other requirements have to be sacrificed. Priscilla dies of this inequitable distribution of love energy, a point rubbed home by the fact that she takes her overdose at the only time in the book that the lonely Francis is shown seeking erotic consolation, with the louche Rigby upstairs.

'So we must go beyond love or utterly change it' (350), Bradley later writes in one of those parenthetic asides through which Murdoch herself manages to suggest *oratio recta*. The false loss of self of the second part is followed in the third part by a deeper ascesis. Again, he feels 'in a real place and in the presence of a real person' (365) after having lost Julian, and this time his employment of the term 'real' is at least ratified by the fact that he is shown for the first time in the book showing ordinary human curiosity about Francis, and Francis' own unhappy love-life.

Without the black and partly destructive Eros, however, Bradley would never have arrived at this point. Eros is necessary to Bradley's quest. In such ways the novel refuses to be a simple and hygienic *conte morale* or tract. It is too *profoundly* moral to be content as a simple moral fable. The conceptual chain which surrounds the idea of individual discontinuity within the book might help to make this ambiguity clearer. 'We often make important moves in our life in a de-individualised condition. We feel suddenly that we are typifying something. This can be a source of inspiration and also a way of excusing ourselves' (184), Bradley early homilises, and the connexion between a discontinuous sense of time or the self, and moral defection of one sort or another, is asserted throughout. The artist, like the saint, is characterised by his skill in opening up the specious present so that old patterns are not endlessly repeated.

> In art, as in morality, great things go by the board because at the crucial moment we blink our eyes. When is the crucial moment? Greatness is to recognise it and be able to hold it and extend it. (13)

> There are no spare unrecorded moments in which we can behave 'anyhow' and then expect to resume life where we left off. The wicked regard time as discontinuous, the wicked dull their natural sense of causality. (125)

> I daresay wickedness is sometimes the product of a sort of conscious leeringly evil intent . . . . But more usually it is the product of a semi-deliberate inattention, a sort of swooning relationship to time. (189)

The ambiguous language of unselfing also surrounds the experience of love. After their successful love-making both Julian and Bradley feel 'quite impersonal' through the 'power of love . . . the god, the black Eros' (331). (Arnold echoes this when he writes to Bradley that his love for Christian has made him live 'in a sort of myth, I've been depersonalised and made into somebody else' (253).) When Francis Marloe tells Bradley on the telephone about Priscilla's death he tries to 'obliterate it from history' (326). 'Only the insane think that there are planes which are quite different from other planes' Rachel tells Bradley, once the affair is over, reminding him that only two weeks ago she and he had lain in one another's arms. 'Love is an illusion, all that certainty is an illusion' (359), she tells him.

We thus experience Julian and Bradley's love both as they do from the inside as if it had an intensely moving logic which resisted time, and also from the outside as if the past from which it tried to amputate itself were still connected to it.

In his great speech about *Hamlet*, Bradley refers to human beings as 'those without identity'. 'We are tissues and tissues of different *personae* and yet we are nothing at all. What redeems us is that speech is ultimately divine' (200). The destruction of identity in love and in morals is the theme of *The Black Prince* and, perhaps, the redemption of identity in art and morals. It is the grand paradox of the novel that Bradley has to undergo an erotic *katabasis*, descent or desublimation, before achieving his ambiguous apotheosis – ambiguous both because it is untested and untestable in the real world, a serenity cloistered and then cut short by death, and also because the moral thrust of the book is, of course, towards sublimation. The way down has to be the way up. This seems to me the significance of the third reference hidden within the 'black prince': 'The black prince, sir, alias the prince of darkness, alias the devil' (*All's Well*: IV v 39). *All's Well That Ends Well* is a fiction, like *Rosenkavalier*, of *mésalliance* and erotic quest. As a catch-phrase 'all's well that ends well' occurs twice within the novel (42, 353). The black prince is Apollo-Dionysus and the devil.

If Bradley is marked by a single characteristic, it is what Nietzsche termed 'bad conscience'. He comments of his trial that he was 'almost mad with guilt, with a sort of general guilt about my whole life' (383). 'In a purely technical sense I was condemned for having murdered Arnold . . . . In a more extended sense, and this too provided fruit for meditation, I was condemned for being a certain sort of awful person' (387).

At this point the ironies of the ending are most inscrutable. While Bradley was jealous of Arnold, and committed symbolic acts of violence on him in his mean-minded review, and then in tearing up all his work, both his guilt and its 'final exorcism' (388) in the trial seem excessive. Rachel has murdered her husband; Bradley takes her guilt upon himself and sacrifices himself, Christ-like. Partly because of this, despite much disquisition about the comic, and despite a prevailing tone best described as tragi-comic, the end approaches the tragic.

Of Aschenbach's death Lionel Trilling wrote:

> If [he] dies at the height of his intellectual and artistic powers, overcome by passion which his reason condemns, we do not take this to be a defeat, rather a kind of terrible rebirth: at his

latter end the artist knows a reality that he had until now refused to admit to consciousness.

We feel something like this about Bradley's poignant death. *Death in Venice*, as Trilling pointed out, seems to endorse the Nietzschean moral that 'tragedy denies ethics'.[22] *The Black Prince* points from beginning to end to the ways in which the formal properties of art fake aesthetic unity. It does not, of course, 'deny ethics', though it shows their for-nothing-ness, enacting the juxtaposition, 'almost an identification, of pointlessness and value' (*SG* 87). 'Any man, even the greatest, can be broken in a moment and has no refuge. Any theory which denies this is a lie' (17), he says at the beginning, and Loxias finally comments 'The creator of form must suffer formlessness. Even risk dying of it' (414). The disruptions built into the novel are not simply self-regarding but point to the charmless and dangerous world that lies, undomesticated, outside. About such pointing Bradley says to Loxias–Apollo:

You have taught me to live in the present and to foreswear the fruitless pain which binds to past and future our miserable local arc of the great wheel of desire. Art is a vain and hollow show, a toy of gross illusion, unless it points beyond itself and moves ever whither it points. (392)

9   The Sacred and Profane Love Machine and Henry and Cato

The 1970s seems to me the time of Murdoch's great flowering. I want in this chapter to look at two lesser but still undismissible works which take the idea of doubleness, the double life or twin heroes, as their theme. Her imagination has always worked by such embattled pairings and through dialectic – 'The Sublime and the Good', *The Nice and the Good*, existentialist and mystic, neurotic and conventional, *The Fire and the Sun*, *Nuns and Soldiers*: many of the novels turn on the paradox of two worlds, one ordinary, one spiritual, and two heroes, one contemplative, one active. In *The Italian Girl* one chapter is entitled 'Two kinds of Jew'; in *Nuns and Soldiers* there are two kinds of Irish face (78). Monty Small refers to philosophy as the 'doubling of an already doubled world' (*SPLM* 123); so, of course, is art, and art can ape and mock the troubled love affairs of binaries as well as of its characters.[1] Both *The Sacred and Profane Love Machine* (1974) and *Henry and Cato* (1976) have two heroes and two worlds. Both are black comedies about male vanity and female power. Both so play on the idea of doubleness as to create out of their small casts the illusion of a whole society.

Blaise Gavender and Monty Small are neighbours in a commuter Buckinghamshire itself stranded between two worlds, neither fully countrified nor citified and with a new motorway about to be opened on its flank. At the end of the book the motorway opens and the first hare is squashed on it, 'a monogram of fur and blood'(316). Blaise the psychiatrist, Harriet his good matronly wife and David their fastidious nineteen-year-old son live in Hood House, which is distinguished and early Victorian, resembling a sea-side house with its wrought-iron balconies. It once had a large garden but lost it to its more recent *art nouveau* neighbour Locketts. Sitting at one end of this L-shaped garden Locketts possesses an orchard that Blaise covets.

Monty lives in Locketts and is a short, dandyish, detective story writer in early middle age. His intense, pretty, difficult vamp-like Swiss wife Sophie, with whom he was much in love but of whom he was also tormentingly jealous, has recently died of cancer. Monty does not know how to begin to recover from his loss and from the rows that preceded and accompanied it, and ruined his married life. He lives joylessly, unable to grieve and giving away knick-knacks in the attempt to strip his house, meditating fruitlessly on his life and its 'failure'. He is a half ascetic, half Nietzschean dandy, and the dupe of an heroic self-image created in adolescence which was partly the monstrous progeny of a continuing love-contest between himself and his mother, and later exteriorised as the thin, sardonic, remorseless detective-hero Milo Fane, a hero of the will. An early provisional title for the book was 'A monster and its mother'. Monty thinks about giving up writing these successful detective stories and becoming a schoolmaster. Letters from his absent mother, Leonie, punctuate the book and provide a comic refrain. She is pretentious, managing, bossy, hungry and hard-headed, the sort of woman who, as her final appearance shows, expects others to be of service to her. His mother repeatedly advises him to sell nothing. He sees himself as a failed artist.

Blaise on the other hand sees himself as a failed psychiatrist. He can take away his patients' pain but has lost faith in any 'deep' theories of the mind. Like the earlier psycho-analyst Palmer in *A Severed Head*, whose time-serving blandness hid a multitude of sins, Blaise is a temporiser and cheat, a weak and second-rate man who constantly seeks incompatible goods. He wants to become a doctor but lacks the money. Harriet is early shown pleading on his behalf both for a loan from Monty to finance these medical studies and also for Monty to sell him the orchard. Such a hunger for irreconcilable goods also characterises his love-life. As a psychiatrist we learn from Monty's experience as his patient that he is a poor listener who reduces experience to formula. We see him depending on 'sex', 'castration', 'masturbation' as explanatory devices.

Blaise has kept a mistress for nine years in Putney, Emily MacHugh, whose stepfather beat up her mother. She recently lost her job as a school-teacher, being in command neither of her subject nor of her class, and now lives in relative poverty and in angry distress with her ex-char Pinn, who is as Blaise observes 'socially speaking, in fairly rapid motion'. In other senses 'command' is Emily's *métier*. Blaise fell for her because of sexual peculiarities they share and which make them uniquely fitted to one another. The sub-text of dream and conversation suggests that Emily humiliates Blaise in a way that gratifies them both and perhaps both excites and relieves his self-contempt. Both women are his victims. Emily abandoned her thesis on starting her affair with him. Harriet abandoned her art, since Blaise made it clear he had no belief in her talent. The danger of his and Emily's situation first added piquancy but now conduces to a sense of moral squalor. His son by Emily, Luca, whom at one stage Emily hit out of frustration, has withdrawn from them both.

Blaise takes Monty's advice in inventing a pretext for seeing Emily; and Monty has come up with one Magnus Bowles, a nocturnal patient who sleeps during the day and so has to be visited at night. Monty weekly invents new symptoms for Magnus. Magnus is homosexual, surrounded by ghosts, asserts against all evidence that he has cut off his little finger, dreams he is being followed by a Bishop with a wooden leg. Finally, a compulsive eater, he fears his limbs are withdrawing inside his body, his face flattening out and his features disappearing: he is turning into a huge white egg floating in a sea of turquoise blue and has swallowed the universe. Milo Fane is only one of Monty's demonic *alter egos*. Milo, who is so thin he needs a diet of cream, Guinness and chocolate biscuits not to waste away, represents Monty's puritan and Nietzschean persona; Magnus, in his neurotic solipsism, his haunted masochistic persona.

Blaise's good wife Harriet takes particular pleasure in hearing about Magnus. She is anti-type to Emily, Blaise's sacred rather than profane wife, the Pandemian Venus, as Pausanias terms it in *Symposium*, for whom he feels a different reverence, and who represents respectable family life. The daughter and sister of soldiers, neither of whom rose above the rank of major (all the men in this book are characterised by failure) she is typified by love and by the desire to mother. She loves Blaise, her house, her old-fashioned kitchen, her son David who is withdrawing from her rather as Luca has withdrawn from Emily. She loves the 'slow parade of the English year' with its sad 'increasing store of memories'. She mothers awkward and unwanted domestic oddments and equally homeless neurotic dogs that she saves from the dogs' home and names after mythical heroes.She tries to think loving thoughts even about the dead. She would like to mother Blaise's patients, to mend their clothes. She suffers an excess of love, 'like having too much milk in the breasts'. Harriet is like a less sophisticated, more domestic version of Hilda in *A Fairly Honourable Defeat*; though in what happens to test her, she resembles as much Hilda's husband Rupert.

The domestic calm of Hood House is broken by Luca, who makes a habit of stowing away in Blaise's car and appearing there, joining the two worlds, like the tree in Giorgione's demon-infested picture of St Antony and St George (which Harriet contemplates) and like the Cupid in Titian's *Sacred and Profane Love*. Luca makes the double world single. Blaise sees he must tell Harriet the truth and rely on her goodness to save the situation. Harriet finds herself able to move from the role of loving and successful wife to that of confidant and forgiving wronged wife. At first energised by her pain, and by the certainty that she can direct, encircle and 'own' what is happening, she remains in control, creating a 'sisterly' complicity with Emily, who finds she cannot hate this old-fashioned, calm, decent person. Harriet also half-wittingly allots Emily and Blaise the role of wrong-doers.

Two things end this phase. Harriet overplays her hand, partly from sheer nerves, and finds it psychologically necessary to play (like Rupert) 'a good, even an absurdly good part'(213). She holds and presides over a fateful tea-party. Into this party Monty's fat, boyish, neuter old college friend Edgar Demarney irrupts and breaks the idyll. If you include Luca and David, Edgar is the fifth mother-dominated man in the story; we learn that he has never ceased mourning his mother's death. His attitude to women resembles Effingham Cooper's – it is one of courtly worship. Despite being head of an Oxford college, Fellow of the Royal Academy, and a world-famous classicist, he is given to pronouncements such as 'God I'm such a wet, such a failure.' 'Who is this comical man please?' asks Pinn when he shows up drunk at Harriet's tea-party; 'He's rather fun, isn't he', answers Emily (210). Edgar has a Myshkin-like innocence, a boyish incapacity to grow up, and takes a certain masochistic pleasure in loving fruitlessly. He adores Monty and has enjoyed and suffered Monty's humiliation of him for years, and also was one of Sophie's admirers. Harriet becomes a new object of this doggy devotion and his hurt on her behalf over Blaise's infidelity is partly real empathy, partly anger at Harriet's humiliation because he needs a goddess to worship. He breaks up the tea-party, denounces Blaise and gives him a black eye.

Emily then runs from the party and forces Blaise to choose between his women. Given the role of violence and of masochism in their relationship the savage blow she gives his already wounded face with her hand-bag when he pursues her may be regarded as setting the seal on her new possession of him. The 'picture' has now wholly reversed. Instead of being Harriet's husband and making clandestine visits to the suffering Emily, he sets up a ménage with Emily and is to reward the suffering Harriet with the occasional visit. The Titian painting to which the title refers is a puzzle picture. The same model was used to portray both kinds of love, and it equivocates our ordinary notions of sacred and profane. Instead of being based on a medieval moralism that would wholly separate the good from the wicked mistress, it presents them as cases of a single principle of Eros in two different modes of existence and in two grades of perfection.[2] Readers who criticise Murdoch for being apolitical do not see how deep and savage an awareness she shows of the respective 'value' of being, as Martin puts this of his two women in *A Severed Head*, 'inside' and 'outside' society. The uncomfortable truth that we are here shown is that Emily, formerly shrill and bitter, in beginning at last to be happy and fulfilled, actually improves; and that poor Harriet, in being gradually stripped of all that has made her life what it was, comes to offend in various ways the aesthetic sense of those who have cared for her. This is the kind of truth Simone Weil so brilliantly wrote about – that there are forms of suffering so intense that they are aesthetically displeasing and which repel the sympathy of the onlooker; few novelists can show us such truth without either gloating or special pleading. The distressing pleasure the work evokes comes from the fact that the poetic justice we childishly yearn for forms so little part of life, though it abounds in bad art.

The stripping of Harriet approaches the tragic, moving pity and fear, though it is also carefully kept away from tragedy too. 'When comedy fails what we have is misery, not tragedy'(130), says Monty. Harriet at the opening of the book ponders David's withdrawal from her and wonders 'Would one be condemned to break the links one by one?'(16). This is indeed what she has to do and her stripping is terrible. She had been married young and, having in a sense stayed innocent, now comes to doubt her own goodness. Like Rupert she needs to think well of herself; she realises she cannot now play the part of second-best wife. At first she is fierce and decisive and announces the end of her vigil at Hood House. She moves into Locketts. In a sense what also helps to kill her is her own love-energy which no longer has any adequate object. She starts to redirect this to Luca, with whom she has an instinctive rapport, and also to Monty, towards whom she has felt anxious and protective. Monty, however, is ready for no new claim on his affection and is ill-equipped to fend off with any grace the advances that his very coolness seems to invite. He has already been harsh to Edgar, who quite likes it. He is now brutally honest to Harriet at a moment when she is acutely vulnerable. Harriet now turns to Edgar, who had offered her asylum at Mockingham, his country house. Since Monty has finally broken down, expressed and explained his grief, and promised to come to Mockingham himself, where Harriet can now no longer be pleased to see him (and where Edgar in any case wants Monty to himself) Edgar too now rejects her.

Harriet has two further rejections to undergo. The first is so comically grotesque that it is hard to imagine another writer pulling it off. She announces to Monty that she will seek out Magnus Bowles. 'I've got to talk to Magnus Bowles, I've *got* to, I feel certain he could help me. Blaise said I was the only woman who really existed for Magnus. He must need me. And if he needs me I need him. And he's the last one –' (307). Monty at once invents and announces Magnus' suicide. Harriet now leaves for her brother Adrian at Hohne in Germany, accompanied by Luca but not by David who, full of adolescent misery and also hurt by loss of his status as only son, runs off and rejects her too. At Hanover airport Harriet is killed by a terrorist, while shielding Luca's body from the bullets.

'An author's irony often conceals his glee'(37) Monty early saw. The ending sees a triumph for the second-best, with Luca in a home where the psychiatrist 'did not regard his case as hopeless', and consolation prizes for the others. David's acute distress is assuaged when he loses his virginity to the unconvincing character Pinn, and is finally consoled by Edgar at an expensive luncheon, a beautiful small scene at which the secret worldliness of the authorial wit seems to tell us that the wisdom Edgar administers is not merely high-mindedness, though he certainly has wise things to say. The food helps too, just a little, or could. Blaise and Emily make a huge bonfire of Harriet's possessions, destroy her sweetly old-fashioned kitchen, and promise to become an ordinary unambitious comfortable, selfish suburban couple. Blaise, despite his medical ambitions, acquires new patients. Monty resents Edgar's having witnessed his breaking down and again rejects him in a cutting letter. But three women – Pinn, Leonie (Monty's mother) and Kiki – arrive in the book's closing pages and promise to visit him in Oxford or at Mockingham. 'Three good-looking women, he thought, and all of them after *me*! And he could not help being a little bit cheered up and consoled as he got into the Bentley and set off alone for Oxford.' These are the final words and the tone is one of a comic sadness, with Edgar unshaken, despite Monty's cynicism, in his belief that 'Every little thing matters.'

Readers have found Harriet's death shocking and arbitrary. While I agree that it is shocking, its apparent arbitrariness is clearly very carefully planned for, whether or not this makes it 'earned'. It can be considered in many different lights. Blaise has early wished her dead, as he has also wished Emily dead on occasion, and Emily prays for Harriet's death, feels a secret sense of accomplishment in her elimination, and further proclaims early on that she often feels like 'people who go to an airport with a gun and just shoot everyone on sight. You simply have no idea how I suffer'(94). That thoughts are both dangerous and consequential is one of the messages shared by all the books. Of Sophie's death we are authoritatively told that Monty's mother, who detested her, 'had doubtless willed her death, who knows how ineffectually'(33), as if to establish a quasi-magical context in which bad thoughts cause accidents. But here Monty's own case is the one that best illuminates Blaise's. Monty recovers at the end because he is cheered up by the never wholly believable Kiki's gift to him of her virginity, and also because he has confessed to Monty, and been purged by the confession, that when Sophie was dying she so tormented him and forced him to share her pain that he killed her. He killed her out of anger, spite, jealousy, and 'wild awful pity'. She would have died hereafter, of course, but he 'as good as' murdered her.

The book invites us to ponder two questions here. One is to interrogate our own desire for poetic justice, that is, to see Harriet rewarded and Blaise and Emily punished. In the Gifford lectures

Murdoch approvingly cited Schopenhauer's scorn for those neoclassical critics who found the absence of poetic justice – for example in *King Lear* – too distressing to bear. The novel makes a small joke at the expense of 'poetic justice' around the myth of Diana and Actaeon. Actaeon was punished for spying on the bathing Diana and her nymphs by being torn apart by hounds. Here David is the voyeur who watches the girls bathing, aided by Pinn in a baroquely fantastic scene; but Blaise is the man punished and nearly savaged to death by his starving dogs. The second question connects with the whole idea of 'doubleness'. Blaise has two wives and two sons, the book has two anti-heroes one of whom has two *alter egos*. It abounds both in dream animals and in real ones. The question here might be said to be: if Monty 'as good as' murdered Sophie, to what extent did Blaise 'as good as' murder Harriet, both through having two families and through his rejection of her?

There can be no tidy answer, of course. What seems clear is that when Sophie dies Monty cannot let go of her memory, while when Harriet dies she is disposed of too brusquely for our comfort. 'It is so important to think quiet loving thoughts about people in idle moments, especially about the dead who being substanceless so desperately need our thoughts'(15) Harriet early thinks. 'Perhaps our thoughts hold the dead captive as they do the living; and perhaps their thoughts can touch us too' thinks the tormented Monty. The novel nicely equivocates in this area. There is much play about the idea of haunting. Monty perceives Edgar at his first appearance as a 'mucky revenant'(45); Blaise perceives his wife's neurotic dogs as 'little black ghosts' as well as symbols of his own sexual shame, with their genitals shamelessly exposed. Emily's destructive cats – one of them satirically named 'Little Bilham', the character advised in Henry James' *The Ambassadors* to 'live all you can' – which is precisely what Emily's situation prevents her from doing – read as do Harriet's dogs both as real and indeed minutely and beautifully particularised, and also as emanations from her psychological predicament. Even the children can seem part of such a system of feeling. Panofsky tells us that each Venus (in the myth behind Titian) has an appropriate son;[3] and Luca's near-autism, David's squeamish unease, serve to comment on their respective psychological *milieux*. David moreover sees Hood House as 'haunted, infested' (317) by Luca. And in one of those demonic *coups* that can make Murdoch's plots as unnerving for the reader as for her characters, Monty keeps a tape of Sophie and himself arguing, just before the end of her life, which is overheard by Edgar, and later by Harriet, and terrifies them both. On this second occasion, when Harriet overhears it, Monty also suffers his catharsis and, to the unseen Harriet, it was 'as if a wind blew through the house, as if an airy shape passed through, passed by, and Harriet felt cold, cold' (302). Like Patroclus in the passage from the *Iliad* that moves David to public grief, Sophie's spirit here suffers an ambiguous release. 'The spirit like a vapour fled away beneath the earth, gibbering faintly'(201).

Moreover twenty or so dreams help prepare us for Harriet's death. These – with their phallic dogs and fishes – are both jokes at the expense of Blaise's reductive misuse of Freud – like Monty's description of his deflowering of Kiki as 'forced entry'(326) and also premonitory. David dreams of mermaids, girl-fish chimeras, in dreams which combine horror, religion, sex, and, at one point, his mother. Harriet has night fears and dreams of a child's face in a tree. Monty dreams of a baby monster bewailing its decapitated mother, of nuns (one of them Sophie), of an ordeal by water, of himself as a blinded chained animal and of his sacrifice by a woman. Blaise dreams of playing the woman to a winged snake, of fish-humans drowning a cat, and of hanged dogs metamorphosed into garden implements. Emily dreams of skinning a live cat, of a cat with a deformed head disintegrating into blobs in a drain. The emotions evoked by these dreams always combine some mixture of horror or terror, grief and fascinated pity. Pity and horror stalk one another throughout the tale – as when Harriet and Luca make their affecting visit to the dogs' home to choose 'Lucky', whom they feel sorry for, and thereby possibly condemn the dogs that they *cannot* choose. All this foreshadows the mixture of pity and horror that assails us and the characters both about Sophie's death – her consciousness filling Monty with 'pain and so much wild awful pity' that he stopped her life (325); and Harriet's. Harriet appears to Blaise to be stretching up 'little hands or tentacles of dreadful pity from the grave', which he has to cut off.

This is the novel's heart, its driving momentum. We can partly feel that Murdoch's relation to the distressed Harriet resembles Monty's to the distressed and dying Sophie, where Monty is so appalled and filled with nauseous pity (like Mischa Fox who drowned a kitten when so afflicted), that he can bear it no longer. The book, however, is a comedy too, and does not invite us to build any metaphysic out of such black matters. Its truth lies at its edge as well as at its centre. Blaise is a shadowy creation, about whose family we learn little. He has only a snobbish mother who unexpectedly approved of Harriet, to complement Monty's snobbish mother who could never approve or even forgive Sophie for marrying Monty. The possible title 'A monster and its mother' suggests that a number of the men in the book can be read as victims in one way or another of mother–son love, a theme further explored in Gerda and Henry's relation in *Henry and Cato*. Here what we recall are the marvellous scenes of Luca's early materialisations at Hood House; Emily and Harriet's early *rapprochement*; Luca inviting David to see a toad, and later choosing a dog; indeed all of Harriet's marvellously individualised dogs are memorable, but perhaps especially the collie Lawrence, who is certain he is a human being '[leaning] familiarly against Luca's shoulder and [looking] with superior indulgence upon the canine congregation'(161); Monty consoling David and laughing at the boy's question as to whether he 'still' has sexual fantasies at his age; the never wholly solid Pinn arriving uninvited in Monty's bedroom to tell him 'I'm yours I tell you. God, you're lucky'(257).

*

In her 1982 Gifford lectures 'Metaphysics as a Guide to Morals' Iris Murdoch pointed out that Plato's great allegory of the Cave and the Sun may be conceived of as a series of iconoclasms and demythologisations. The soul, journeying through its four stages of enlightenment, progressively discovers that 'what it was treating as realities were only shadows or images of something else' (*SG* 94). Since the borderline between literal and metaphorical in the case of vision is unclear, moral change may be figured, in a strikingly eclectic list, as a 'progressive discarding of relative false goods, of hypotheses, images and shadows, eventually seen as such' (*FS* 65). Plato's philosophy, like Murdoch's novel-writing, enacts the iconoclasm it enjoins, being both fertile in the production of new imagery, and also carelessly destructive of it. On the one hand 'we are all image-makers' (*PP* 189); on the other 'great art destroys the cloud of comfortable images with which each one of us surrounds himself in his daily living'.[4] I earlier tried to show

how the picaresque of *Under the Net* already explored such matters, since the rapid dismantling of scenes prefigured Hugo's unwitting but Socratic smashing of Jake's illusions at the end. In *Henry and Cato* the idea of moral change – of escape from and return to the Cave, which Ficino, citing *Republic* Book VII, pointed out had best be done slowly, lest the moral agent become dazzled[5] – is central; and so is the theme of iconoclasm.

Henry and Cato takes the chiasmus that marks the end of *Bruno's Dream* – Lisa and Diana exchanging roles of nun and hetaera – and also marks the last part of *The Sacred and Profane Love Machine*, with Emily and Harriet exchanging roles inside and outside society – and makes it into the central device of the plot.

There are two stories that increasingly intersect. Cato Forbes sees himself as a failed priest and tries to laicise himself. His faith is disturbed during work in the East End, and then, in a Paddington mission, he loses it. He simultaneously falls disastrously in love with a seventeen-year-old Irish 'baby crook' called Beautiful Joe. At the same time his friend Henry Marshalson, who by contrast perceives himself as a failed demon and failed artist, wishes to renounce his inheritance of the vainglorious old beautiful house Laxlinden and all its appurtenances. Cato gives up religion and tries to return to the cave; Henry aspires to give up the world and live in the sun. The book is an extraordinary, accomplished mixture of farcical comedy and melodrama. Henry's story is a comedy at which we laugh when violence fails, Cato's a 'tragedy' at which we grieve when violence succeeds.[6] Like Auden's 'Musée des Beaux Arts' the book concerns the coexistence of different worlds of suffering and happiness.

Henry has escaped from his mother and brother to teach 'fifty great pictures' in a vacuous mid-Western liberal arts college, living *à trois* with a surrogate family in Russ and Bella Fischer. He plans to write a book on the German expressionist painter Max Beckmann, a 'spawner of obese and dotty symbolism', and identifies with an 'upside-down' man in a Beckmann painting. He resents the pomposity of European art and sees himself as an iconoclast. To the reader he is a Beckmann clown. He is described as 'refugee Henry', 'inferior Henry', 'dark manic Henry' and these running comic epithets in the early part of the book, or failed kennings, establish both that Henry perceives himself as a mythic hero and that we see him differently. When his hated, envied brother Sandy dies in a car crash he returns delightedly to England to destroy his mother Gerda's 'feudal dream world' and sees himself, we infer, as Orestes committing symbolic matricide by dispossessing her. To Cato's father John Forbes he is, rather, 'that young squirt'. He plans to dismantle and sell Laxlinden and use the money for various good causes. If there is an Aegistheus in the case the part is played, or rather guyed, by the ageing white-haired failed Bloomsbury poet Lucius Lamb. Lucius gives Gerda a dog-like devotion, affects a dark cloak, and plans to write his spiritual autobiography in rhyming hexameters.

Henry writes to his American friend Bella that his inheritance is 'not just a spiritual burden, it's a bloody material practical one: walls, roofs, trees, servants, drainage, taxes'(234). But it is the spiritual aspects of this renunciation that appeal to his imagination. 'You gave up the world, why can't I?' he asks the poverty-stricken Cato, who possesses only a kettle, itself in danger of being stolen. Henry has always wanted to 'travel light and live a stripped life' (199). 'I could have been a holy person after my fashion' he is finally to soliloquise (383). The novel shows how far away he is from any such ascesis. The real motives behind his socially levelling iconoclasm are, as the equally troubled Cato sees, spiteful Oedipal revenge against his family for his having been the less loved younger son.

Cato is described by his good mentor Brendan Craddock as 'rushing about' and having 'antics' (193), but this aptly describes the sulky Henry too and rubs home their kinship. After pulling down a tapestry of Athena seizing Achilles by the hair, Henry says 'Mother, it's all going to disappear like Aladdin's palace' (237); hating social pretension he wants to 'drop it all, to smash it to pieces' (258). His egalitarian act is not implicitly wrong, as he finally comes to see, but merely 'above my moral level. That's been my mistake all along, mistaking my moral level'(378). Despite his pose of being unattached, for example, he resents Lucius' presence in the house as a scrounger, and also because he is unconsciously jealous of anyone with whom he has to share his mother.

When Henry left America Bella predicted that he would fall for 'some ravaged tart' and he has indeed fallen for Stephanie Whitehouse, whom he supposes an ex-prostitute and a mistress of Sandy's. The bad faith behind his act of renunciation is clear when he refers to Stephanie as his 'property' and then later when Cato has been kidnapped, and Henry now thinks despairingly of having to give up 'all he possesses' to pay the ransom, but without getting any moral credit for doing so. At one point he looks out at the beautifully detailed, decorous English landscape and 'it was like looking at his own mind, his own being, perhaps his only reality. So much the worse for reality then, he thought . . . . It must all be destroyed, all rolled up like a tapestry'(334).

Stephanie pretends to be an ex-whore but is in fact a failed typist and char-woman who has suffered a breakdown and has a fantasy-life as picturesque as Henry's. His image-breaking leads him to bring Stephanie home to meet his mother, in the hope once more of shocking her pieties. In fact Gerda attends to Stephanie much better than Henry, who neither 'sees' her nor attends to her needs. Gerda gets to know Stephanie, disarms her and draws her into complicity – 'I don't think [politics] suits a woman, do you?'(213). Henry is ambushed by the combined good offices of his mother, through Stephanie's withdrawal, and through Cato's sister, the virginal Colette. Like Achilles seized by the hair by Athena, he is claimed by Colette, and, having begun malevolent, Henry is subverted by happiness, frustrated by good luck. Through possessing Stephanie he draws the sting of his envy of Sandy; through Colette he can undo his deep childish hurts – 'That's what a wife is for. You tell her awful things and she tells you they're not really awful at all and you cheer up'(381). He is doomed to turn into a contented man. At the end he has compromised by selling off only a small part of the estate and some pictures, and plans a model housing estate, while Colette plans black swans and peacocks to decorate what remains of the view. He tells her 'Our beautiful housing estate is a snare and a delusion', to which Colette returns 'Tell that to the people who are going to live there! A house is about the most real of all material things'(379).

In the hierarchy of the real and the illusory, houses and rooms figure importantly. A description of the 'encampment of easy chairs'(72) in the drawing-room nicely brings together the way that the material world here behaves as if it were wholly solid and yet also dangerously temporary. The rituals of Laxlinden – the two kinds of tea, the small ceremonies – are beautifully caught.

Where Henry starts spiteful but is cheered up, Cato begins in what he takes for unhappiness but is made so derelict as to come to see how comparatively equable he was before. By the end he is showing signs of the malice Henry has abjured. Henry tries to jettison material paraphernalia and the divisive social rituals they stood for; Cato renounces or feels abandoned by the things of the spirit. Cato's domineering father John is an ex-Quaker and a vehement austere rationalist who hates the 'sickly picturesque paraphernalia' of Catholicism. As a rationalist he is equally affronted that Colette wants, not higher education, but love and six children. The opposition between his iconoclastic puritanism and the aesthetic imagery of Cato's Catholicism suggests a position beyond either. John's rationalism is clearly shown to be inadequate.

Cato experiences his conversion to Catholicism 'as if he had not only emerged from the cave, but was looking at the Sun'(38). Athena seizing Achilles by the hair is here echoed when he watches the Christ-like kestrel stoop for a mouse. He becomes a monkish, other-worldly priest and then loses his faith and finds the return to the cave problematic. Both Henry and Cato are romantics and puritans who dramatise their predicaments in such a way as to narrow their vision. 'You're too unworldly, Father. What do you want really? Do you want us to become lovers?' asks Joe (208); but Cato cannot make his love for Joe sufficiently ordinary. Brendan politely asks to meet Joe but the request is ignored; and Cato later treats a lunch invitation that might bring Colette and Joe together as an impossibility. Just as Henry's silly romanticism leads him to force his mother and Stephanie to meet, which leads to his comic undoing, so Cato makes an opposite error in siphoning off the problem of Joe so that their love has no possible social context. The ambiguous chaste romance he seeks with Joe is as much above his moral level as Henry's more obviously pretentious renunciations. Colette pertinently remarks to her father that Cato is not an officer. Neither is Henry. And neither Joe nor Stephanie, despite their ingenious fantasies, is as void of moral resilience or animal cunning as Henry or Cato wish to conceive them.

Against both Henry and Cato's exaltations, the two characters who are shown, very differently, as able to attend to the particular are the realists Gerda, and Brendan Craddock. Gerda's wisdom is of course practical and worldly. She may at the end be rewarded by John Forbes' courtship of her. Brendan, on the other hand, is presented as virtuous and intelligent, a Platonist who believes that 'Aristotle was the beginning of the end'(172), and it is he who tries to tutor Cato into a new and propaedeutic way of conceiving of images and that truth they may point to but can never enshrine or possess. Brendan's is a Platonic negative theology, touched by the pseudo-Dionysius,[7] which argues that 'Being a Christian is a long, long task of unselfing', a 'death-sentence' on the ego. Addressing Cato's loss of faith in a personal God he says

> Ordinary consciousness is a tissue of illusion. Our chief illusion is our conception of ourselves, of our importance which must not be violated, our dignity which must not be mocked. All our resentment flows from this illusion, all our desire to do violence, to avenge insults, to assert ourselves . . . . But in reality there are no insults because there is nobody there to be insulted. And when you say 'there is no one there' perhaps you are on the brink of an important truth.   (174)

Brendan's insistence on the fictionality of the self, and the novel's interest in the idea of experience as illusion, owes much to Buddhism, to which the maverick priest Reggie Poole is converted in Japan. In this book Murdoch's stance as a Christian–Buddhist without belief in a personal God, but with Christ as the Western saint of this Buddhism, is consequential. A cheerful iconoclasm, as well as an ambiguous love, surrounds the idea of the incarnation. About the crucifixion Joe comments 'If a gang done that they'd get ten years even if the bugger survived'(88).

The novel shows that it is harder to renounce the fictions of the ego than it is to give up either possessions or religious dogmata. Like a house the ego is both intractably there and transient. Brendan himself lives in a long, thin cell-like room with a single window overlooking a brick wall. His life-style is early described in a beautifully poised phrase as 'meticulously spartan luxury'(80). At the end it is pertinently *his* flat and not Henry's Laxlinden, which is being quietly, unobtrusively dismembered. Unlike either Henry or Cato, he has earned the right to renounce in good faith. The contents of drawers and bookshelves lie about on the floor and Brendan is leaving for India. It is in exactly this *half*-stripped cell that the novel's debate about the right uses of disillusion culminates at the end. The book once more accords a primacy to the imagination (as both Protestantism and Buddhism differently do) as a premise for its purification. The imagination too has, as it were, its own sumptuary laws, and while the novel urges renunciation it also shows the importance, by an old paradox, of the imagination keeping up with this ascesis, so that the stripping of images is prevented from becoming, perversely, a conceited form of accumulation. The ego has to give up some of the density of *its* illusion too.

Thus Cato has stripped himself of more illusion than he is ready to do without, and lives in a squalid room that is the antithesis of Laxlinden, and which prompts Henry to envy. This cell or cave is nastily parodied in the yet further stripped underground room in which Joe locks him up, deluding him, Henry, and finally Colette, into thinking he is part of a gang. A violent person has immense psychological power, the story shows, and the fact that the fear experienced by Joe's victims is 'purely imaginary' does not make it less real or calamitous. Here the plot links Joe with Henry, who is at last seen by his wife as having formerly been 'just a terrorist, not pure in heart'(377).

Cato's unselfing takes place in the cruellest way. Terrified and reduced by Joe into doing what he asks it is only finally when 'all was destroyed and surrendered and there was an emptiness that was not even space'(325) that he hears his sister scream and kills Joe. He explains to Henry that he has now lost the 'selfish complacent illusions and vanities' of the moral life, that once self-esteem is gone 'there's nothing left but fury, fury of unbridled egoism'(349). Self-esteem is a great defence against temptation, for all but saints, and he adds that 'Once that spiritual decor is stripped away there's nothing but a demon left'(393).

The word 'decor', like the earlier 'paraphernalia', explicitly invites a comparison with Henry's mock-ascesis. 'I think one should go easy smashing other people's lies. Better to concentrate on one's own'(153) Cato had early advised Henry, and it is a moral behind which we hear the author's ambiguous assent, since Henry, as it ironically turns out, is fortunate in being left with some of his illusions about himself intact; it is Cato who has his forcibly smashed. The ideal limit at which unselfing and truth might coexist is suggested in the book's fine and moving last scene when Brendan expounds that Platonic *via negativa* in which *all* knowledge is partial knowledge and all virtue a cognitive and loving task. Brendan is discussing Cato's love for Christ, his high Eros, but in terms that work equally well for his low Eros, his love of Joe.

You fell in love. That's a start, but it's only a start. Falling in love is egoism, it's being obsessed by images and being consoled by them, images of the beloved, images of oneself. It's the greatest pain and the greatest paradox of all that personal love has to break at some point, the ego has to break, something absolutely natural and seemingly good, seemingly perhaps the only good, has to be given up. After that there's darkness and silence and space. And God is there. Where the images end you fall into the abyss, but it is the abyss of faith . . . . Those who can live with death can live in the truth, only this is almost unendurable . . . . Death is the great destroyer of all images and all stories, and human beings will do anything rather than envisage it . . . .

. . . The point is one will never get to the bottom of it, never, never, never. And that never, never, never is what you must take for your hope and your shield and your most glorious promise. Everything that we concoct about God is an illusion.   (394–8)

The book might be said to offer, like Shakespearian drama, something for everyone. It is a great deal funnier and more exciting than this brief and 'dry' account can suggest. And it warns us, within the same compass, about the dangers involved both in the facile destruction of images, and also in the unexamined dependence on them. The moral of the second part, which is entitled 'The Great Teacher' from the *haiku* Lucius Lamb scribbles on his death-bed:

> So many dawns I was blind to.
> Now the illumination of night
> Comes to me too late, O great teacher

is the message the novel comically and movingly points to; but shows at the same time to be too hard for everyone involved, with the possible exception of Brendan. What is urged is selfless attention here and now, and Lucius' predicament, since he is the minor character whom no one will attend to or cease taking for granted, is well equipped to urge it. Like both Henry and Cato, Lucius is a superfluous man, but unlike them a comically innocent one. It is only when he is dying that he finds, with an easy symbolism, that he can at last understand Rhoda the maid, otherwise comprehensible only to Gerda. Gerda, who appears tough but suffers stoically throughout both her loss of her beloved Sandy and also her failures with Henry, has her own superbly crafted moment of self-exposure; as does the callow-seeming Clara in *An Accidental Man*. Gerda explains her apparent neglect of Henry as a child. Her husband demanded everything, Henry had competed and then sulked, and 'a child's hostility can hurt too'(356); and there is great art in the way that relations between Henry and Gerda are shown after this single moment of intimacy and exposure to be both changed and improved and yet still imperfect. Beyond Gerda and Rhoda, at the book's far edge, is Dame Pat Raven who, like Lucius and Rhoda, is made invisible by service: she has been acting as John Forbes' mistress out of love for John's dead wife Ruth and, since she probably prefers to love her own sex, has thus also been commanding that Kantian 'pathological' love that Murdoch has suggested (sg) might be enjoined. Her moral charity places John's crude and harshly puritanical judgementalism very clearly for us.

The problem within each imagination of the relation between moral effort and imaginative purification extends also to the minor characters. Lucius clearly flatters himself both when he imagines he has seen through all the philosophies – 'Is that all? he had felt as he mastered them'(26) – and when he chooses to see his long sojourn at Laxlinden in thrall to Gerda as comparable to that of Odysseus detained by Calypso; or later as Tiresias. When Gertrude asks him to destroy his poems and the less than flattering images of her she conceives them to contain, he at once complies in the tiny iconoclasm, but comically knows them by heart anyway. Lucius puts his inability to gain Gerda, whom he worships in a courtly manner, down to his other-worldiness, but it is timidity too. 'Moral incompetence' is a phrase he at one stage uses, which nicely captures the particular ambiguous marriage of spirit and pragmatism that he lacks. When he suggests to Gerda that 'if we lived in the East we would be thinking of entering a monastery. Perhaps we ought really to give up the world', she rightly and comically replies 'You aren't fit to give up the world' (239).

Murdoch's own use of imagery is carelessly brilliant and profligate as ever. To take two examples: when Lucius contemplates writing poetry he conceives that 'All you have to do is just record your thoughts one by one, like bats emerging from a hole'(79); the sheer macabre and incongruous beauty of the simile momentarily obscures the fact so lazy a way of conceiving of his task may connect with Lucius' relative unsuccess as a poet. The image also platonises the imagination and observes it as moving, once more, from a cave into the daylight. Later Henry looks at the log fire in the library at Laxlinden which had 'subsided into a mobile mound of twinkling glowing embers, resembling a hill city at night'(352). The simile here is, like the first, intensely visual but less insubordinate to its context. Its felicity is also to wed the circumstantial to the marvellous, in a way characteristic of surrealism.

Two further similes might help suggest how Murdoch works to save her own writing from the false concreteness its very vividness seems to invite. 'He went on celebrating mass each day, but the mass was dead to him, seemed literally dead, as if each morning he were handling some dead creature'(49). Cato's inner experience is evoked for us through a trope that purports to make its privacy public. As the mass was never 'literally' alive to him its current morbidity must be comparably provisional. The publicising of the experience of spiritual loss in this way works to distance Cato's negative sublime, as well as focus it, since it is reported to us through a literal-mindedness more extreme than his own. Cato's unbelief, in other words, begins to seem as superstitious as his belief, and thus his anguished disillusion has no conceivable end. Shortly before he kills Joe he experiences the absence of God with a force that makes even this disillusion seem unserious.

> There is no god, he thought, and he felt that it was the first time that he had ever really experienced the positive truth of this; and with the experience came an extraordinary breaking as if all the strings and tendons of his body had been cut, and he lay there limp as one to whom death has come unexpectedly.   (319)

This time godlessness is something he is not so much handling as having incarnated within him: he 'becomes' the dead creature who is beyond redemption. Yet this, too, is illusion. The worst is not, so long as we can say, 'This is the worst': the scene is followed,

almost at once, by his murder of Joe, his discovery, despite the
protective secrecy of the others, that Joe was alone and without
accomplices, and that he is thus a gull as well as an assassin, and
subsequently by the marriage of his sister to the friend he thinks
unworthy of her, and the defection of his one saintly friend to
India. The 'romantic' unselfing he unwittingly sought is a fragile
commodity, and the truer ascesis now thrust upon him makes
him a man in hell. His story is a story of the demythologisation
and iconoclasm that Henry sought, and its ending is wholly
ambiguous, echoing as it does, the beginning:

> The revolver in its case, heavy and awkward inside his
> mackintosh pocket, banged irregularly against his thigh at
> every step. (9)

> The crucifix, in its case, heavy and awkward inside his
> mackintosh pocket, banged heavily against his thigh at every
> step. (400)

This seems to point to the possibility that, as Sage points out,[8]
Cato may in future learn to see illusion as Brendan sees it, as
both precarious and intractable, and disillusion as a progressive
process, to be tackled more gently than either hero has, and a
process without any end except death. The icon he carries at the
end, like the icon he carried at the beginning, is dangerous and
possibly necessary. Only for the very saintly – like Brendan
Craddock – in Murdoch's fiction, can virtue and Eros have no
fixed address, no culture, no icons and no imagery.

10 *The Sea, The Sea*

The three first-person narratives of the 1970s – *The Black Prince*, *A Word Child* and *The Sea, The Sea* – share some common terms. Each has an 'artist' as narrator. Hilary in *A Word Child* disclaims being a practising artist, but, in creating a small enclosed world whose meanings he tries wholly to legislate, he is nonetheless in this broad sense one too. Each is about the education of its narrator, each compared with the 'sinister boy' Peter Pan,[1] and is a dark comedy of justified paranoia: the narrators haunt themselves through the intensity of their fantasies of power, possession and betrayal; all are partly about the power of (and limits to) fantasy as self-validating prediction. The power of the past is a continuing topic.

I believe *The Sea, The Sea* (1978) to be the greatest of these, possibly the finest of all the books to date. *The Black Prince* took magnificent and fully conscious risks in marrying its thriller and love-plot to such superb rhetoric and reflection. It faces the danger that the reader will latch on to the philosophy at the expense of the ingenious plot which prompts it, as I have partly done, or neglect the idea-play altogether. It is something like an artistic manifesto on its author's part.[2] *A Word Child* is a Gothic tale whose atmosphere partly recalls that of *The Time of the Angels* or *The Unicorn*: it concerns fall and redemption, and is full of a weird suffocating eschatological intensity, speaking constantly of heaven, hell, death, damnation. It is stylish, gripping and memorable, with an atmosphere that haunts and stays with you. For all its neatness and brilliance of conception, it is a smaller book than *The Sea, The Sea*. This is also a tale of obsession, and in it many of its author's own writerly obsessions – the sea, the box-like enclosure, the persecuted maiden, the interaction of magic, religion, guilt and the quest for virtue – all reach some culmination. Here a Gothic claustrophobia combines with – gives way to – a magnificent openness. *The Sea, The Sea* is built to last, and has an exemplary universality. The house by the sea, the life of the theatre, erotic obsession, the contrast of simple and sophisticate, the artist and the ascetic soldier, the different women, its 'types' have the durability and strength of great art. To possess a personality is by definition to be built from such apparently 'time-less' moments of pain and pleasure as Charles has to learn to distance himself from. Charles' story is in this sense everyman's. Malcolm Bradbury saw it as a merciless and painful book, Gabriele Annan finally as a 'comedy with portholes for looking out at the cosmos'.[3] The mixture of pain and comedy here reaches some high point. It deserved the great acclaim and Booker Prize which it won.

The novel has six parts in its central section, which is named 'History'. It has also an introductory section named 'Pre-history' and a reflective Postscript 'Life goes on'. Its title comes from Valéry's great poem 'The Graveyard by the Sea'. The narrator Charles Arrowby early refers to 'a most attractive *cimetière marin*' in the village of Narrowdean to which he has come to retire. In *The Unicorn* Marian taught Hannah the poem. In *The Time of the Angels* Muriel wrote a pastiche of it. In *The Nice and the Good* a marine cemetery was actualised in Dorset just as it is here on a Northern coast, where it provides the title – 'La mer, la mer, toujours recommencée.' I shall return later to the sea as subject. The poem concerns escape from and return to the world and is about the inevitable artifice of poetry.[4]

In the first deliberately slow section we are introduced to the narrator, his friends, his tastes and prejudices. Charles Arrowby, a famous theatre director, and also an occasional actor and playwright, has retired to the sea. 'To repent of a life of egoism? Not exactly, yet something of the sort' (1). He is writing something between a memoir and a diary, and the book has a different kind of immediacy from that of *The Black Prince*. There we accept the convention of a foolish Bradley contemporary with the events he described, and a wiser Bradley who was impersonating his earlier immature self but interrupted himself from time to time to administer some stern or dispassionate reflection. If there was obfuscation in that book, there was also much simple painful truth. Here Charles' self-deceptions have to speak through his confessional, which they amply do, and the author until the end denies him and us the privileges of hindsight. The risks are opposite in kind but pay greater dividends.

The sea which lies before me as I write glows rather than
sparkles in the bland May sunshine. With the tide turning, it
leans quietly against the land, almost unflecked by ripples or
by foam. Near to the horizon it is a luxurious purple, spotted
with regular lines of emerald green . . . .   (1)

Charles interrupts his beautiful 'word-picture': 'I had written the
above, destined to be the opening paragraph of my memoirs,
when something happened which was so extraordinary and so
horrible that I cannot bring myself to describe it.' Leaving us in
suspense, he proceeds to explain his uncertainty as to whether
the 'chronicle' he is writing will be more a diary or a memoir.
The narrative works locally by that series of small shocks and
jumps which, from *Under the Net* on, Murdoch has made her own.
A new section lands the reader in a new dramatic situation, *fait
accompli*, which the narrator then back-tracks in order to explain.
The drama acts as a bribe to take us through the rationalisation
of its history. But the technique here is differently sophisticated.
Here there is less of Bradley's pretence of former ignorance, or of
the quotation marks by which he distances himself from his own
perceptions. Suspense is manipulated with a masterful control –
and with the special relaxation which is the gift of the fully
confident artist. Despite its theme of enclosure, this is simultaneously a relaxed and open novel.

If *The Black Prince* meditated *Hamlet*, *The Sea, The Sea* meditates
The Tempest, which Murdoch in 1969 had called 'perhaps my
favourite of all plays. It is to do with reconciliation and virtue
and the triumph of virtue.'[5] Charles has come to 'abjure magic'
(2): both the magic of the theatre, about whose trickery he speaks,
and also personal power. That it is hard to give up power
or significantly change is one of the book's messages. The
'extraordinary and horrible' event which disrupted his narrative
turns out to be one of a series. His house, Shruff End, appears to
be haunted. It is an ugly red brick isolated house without
electricity but with running water and mains drainage. It would
look at home in a Birmingham suburb. From its upper windows
the view is 'total sea' and it has various peculiarities. On each of
its two floors there is an empty, dark inner enclosed room without
any outward-facing windows. There is a bead curtain upstairs
which rattles, across a spooky landing that seems to have the
expectant air of a stage set. At first Charles thinks that the house

possesses a memory. Later it comes to seem that it has the capacity
to register the future as well.

A horrible vase shatters. An 1890s mirror dislodges from the wall.
A sea-monster is sighted with green eyes. A face appears at a
window, too high for there to be a body supporting it. Most of these
early occurrences are naturalised and explained. A monstrous
fleshy spider turns out at once to be a toad. Rosina Vamburgh, a
jealous, predatory, piratical ex-lover is shown to have been haunting Charles in revenge for his having made overtures to another
ex-lover, the gentle Lizzie Scherer, and has been smashing his
belongings. 'Jealousy is born with love, but does not always die
with it.' The French proverb is more than once invoked. The law
governing the book is *karma*, called by James 'spiritual causality',
by which we pay inexorably for every thought as well as every
action. Charles imagines that he can now step outside experience
to contemplate it calmly; in fact he is only now about to start paying
for being what he is. The sea-monster may be the post-eidetic image
of a lugworm, at which Charles was staring, or the recurrence of a
bad trip he once made on LSD.

Charles explains himself to us. In the press he was spoken of
as a 'tyrant, a tartar, a power-crazed monster' (3). He disavows
this description. We learn that he was in the habit of quoting the
young Hal in the last act of *Henry IV Part II*, 'This is the English,
not the Turkish court', to his actors. Hal sought by it to reassure
his court that he would be merciful and temperate. The fact that
Charles required the phrase points to his real power over his
'court' and to their fear of him. It is a power exercised most
clearly in his love affairs. He feels an 'old familiar possessive
feeling, the desire to grab and hold' (94). He is not 'over-sexed'
as most contemporary heroes make a point of claiming to be; but
he enjoys power, and power and sex here as in life cannot be
wholly separated. He has carelessly smashed Rosina's marriage
with Peregrine Arbelow, many years before, and then, once he
had enjoyed Rosina's subjection to him, purged her of friends
and apparently prevented her having children, he has just as
carelessly, discarded her. Now he hears that Lizzie, whose mode
of loving and suffering for him he found least threatening, has a
happy, sexless but loving ménage with the old trouper Gilbert
Opian. Parallels with *The Tempest* are playfully used throughout.
Lizzie figures in part as Ariel and is often so named. Charles,
Prospero-like, refuses to release her from her love and need of

him. He simultaneously tries to break up her new relationship. It is a feature of Murdoch's monsters that everyone loves them despite, or rather masochistically *for* their monstrous egoism. Gilbert Opian though now elderly wears make-up and hunts for boys, and is a Caliban-figure who chops wood for Charles and serves him. Gilbert loves Charles too, calls him 'Darling', and wears 'that faint air of quizzical cynicism which clever elderly people often instinctively put on, and which may be quite new to them, a last defence' (92).

The early narrative is interspersed with wondrous sea-scapes and with disquisitions on food and how to eat it, a 'subject about which no writer lies' (8). Murdoch has admitted to culinary views 'not absolutely unlike' Charles'.[6] These recipes (denounced by reviewers as 'horrible'!) are entertainments which have a more than culinary interest. They establish Charles as partly a puritan, who 'hates mess' (38), a squeamish soul, who intelligently makes a ceremony out of small pleasures. He is much more confident and aggressive than Bradley, but also concerned with control – and he calls his views on food, with irony, 'absolute truths'. Like Hugo's fireworks in *Under the Net*, cooking is the most temporary and disposable of art-forms, in a novel concerned with the impermanence and improvisatory nature of all human endeavour. His culinary obsessions lastly establish Charles, for all his fastidiousness, as a person expert in the detail of our most ordinary appropriation of the world's bounty. He is emotionally greedy, 'eating up' not merely the women he covets, but other items too. We learn that he stole a photograph as a boy; he refers more than once to his cousin James' jade objects as 'have-worthy' and worth 'pocketing'.

Appetite and possessive hunger partly characterise him. His life has been spent acquiring fame, women, worldly success. Though he is sixty he has never grown up. His youthful appearance is insisted on by everyone. Peregrine suggests that he only needs to shave once a month, and in this as in other matters he contrasts with his envied, disturbing cousin James, who shaves twice a day. He is a Peter Pan figure, and he loved to direct that play. What has helped keep him young and innocent, so that he has never had to pay for his misdemeanours, is a love-affair with Mary Hartley Smith, conducted when they were both children, and then cut off by Mary – or Hartley, as he calls her – in mid-adolescence. He loved Hartley with a 'pure' child-like ardour, and, in this a male Miss Havisham, never recovered from her rejection of him. It is 'the most important thing in my life' (77). He has never passed a day without thinking of her, or pondering this hurt. Like the Irish in (Irish) Peregrine's diatribe against them Charles is hooked on a fixed view of history. He fears the possibility of any new source of pain in his life, and has been unable to commit himself emotionally to anybody, with the possible exception of Clement Makin, the successful actress who, though twenty years his senior, was his first mistress. Clement helped make him successful and died while still with him. Careful indirections help us believe that Clement is to be the book's main topic, rather than Hartley.

The more detached he is, the more his women adore him. Here is a large part of the book's truth. It is not quite, or merely, 'Those that have power to hurt and will do none', because Charles does punish his women by a deep cold uninvolvement which is nonetheless possessive, partly in revenge for his own rejection by Hartley. It is rather that people who feel 'trapped . . . elect other people to play roles in their lives, to be gods or destroyers' (Bellamy, 1977). The others partly choose the role of victim, partly want to be manipulated. This has been a theme since her second novel *The Flight from the Enchanter*. *The Sea, The Sea* makes that book look shadowy, thin and quite excessively *polite*. There is no reason why Mischa Fox should exert the power he does, indeed no reason why he should not, so hazy a commodity is he. Charles' power, on the other hand, is palpable and detailed, as well as a matter in his circle of imitative fashion. There are as always some Freudian hints as to what makes Charles what he is, in the depiction of his relationship with his mother. Charles rarely wants to spend the night with a woman he has made love to. 'In the morning she looks to me like a whore' (52). He is aware of feeling a connexion with Clement kin to what he feels for his mother; and experiences 'something strange and awful' when watching people, especially women, sing – 'the wet white teeth, the moist red interior' (60). Such Oedipal stuff, however, is not there either to exonerate or 'explain' him.

The evocation of his and Hartley's love-affair is superbly done, as are the portraits of his friends. 'Oh Hartley, Hartley, how timeless, how absolute love is. My love for you is unaware that I am old and you perhaps are dead' (86). But he is shown to us being greatly moved and excited by his own descriptions, and this warns us against swallowing what he has to tell us whole. To put this another way, we are given, in as perfect an equipoise as I think she has managed, both an 'inside' and an 'outside' view of Charles, so that we are moved and uneasy at once.

The 'explanation' of the unearthly occurrences early in the story has two functions. It relaxes us to find that we are in a world in which the uncanny can be explained, and prepares us for the much more uncanny events that are to follow. Like *The Tempest*, this is a book about magic, and is not in the narrowest of senses 'naturalistic'. It is not a likely tale, though it is a true one. The sheer narrative intensity takes us over the implausibilities. It turns out that the fey Hartley is living in the village, apparently a sad other-worldly drab, married to an ex-soldier and retired fire-extinguisher salesman named Ben Fitch, who bullies her jealously, and to whom she submits. During the early description of his family life and of relations between his father Adam Arrowby's household, and his younger brother Abel's richer, more envied and glamorous set-up (their Christian names emphasise the fall-myth Charles has made of his life), he comments that his aunt and uncle may have thought his upbringing too strict. 'Outsiders who see rules and not the love that runs through them are often too ready to label other people as "prisoners" ' (61). This turns out a prophetic observation. Charles ascertains what he thinks to be the 'truth' of Hartley's marriage, through an awkward scene of eavesdropping, and sees only the sado-masochistic structure of Hartley's marriage, not the deep habit and secret needs it has come to fulfil. His love for her has stayed still.

The Fitch's bungalow, 'Nibletts', is as real a presence as Shruff End. One of the pleasures of reading the book comes not just from the difference between these two worlds, one worldly and sophisticated, the other unpretending and suburban, but from the absolute lack of condescension Murdoch shows, through Charles, to either. The pert knowing women and vain egotistical men of Charles' world, and the quiet dullness and mysteriously ordinary 'bad taste' of Hartley's, are even-handedly portrayed. The mystery of each, we feel tempted to say, is respected and explored. Charles misreads the conventions of Hartley's world, arriving to interrupt their evening meal, which is tea, at the time he expects to be offered drinks.

Her husband Ben has always called Hartley by her first name, 'Mary'; and it is typical of the comedy of the book that Charles is amazed that Ben, who has been married to Mary for forty years, does not know her 'real', i.e. middle, name; just as he calls Peregrine 'Perry' despite early noting that Peregrine detests this abbreviation. To name the world is to try to compel it. He notes after these early passages a conversation with Peregrine that is 'relevant to my situation. Indeed, now I come to think of it, nearly everything in the world is relevant to my situation' (159). Since human beings are necessarily egoists, the relevance he notes is there, though not as he imagines it.

The appearance of the Fitches' adopted son Titus, missing for two years, gives Charles his opportunity. Ben is as obsessively jealous a man as is Charles, and when, after some years of married life, Mary/Hartley told him of her childish love of Charles, Ben suffered retrospective jealousy, partly displaced onto Titus, who was adopted after a longish separation between the Fitches, when Mary was away nursing her dying father. By the deep unconscious logic of his jealousy – which is the ruling emotion, with guilt, of the tale – he accused Mary of still seeing Charles, and Titus of being her son by him. Titus escaped two years before, out of the bad relationship with Ben, to study 'electricity' at a Polytechnic, and to find his real father. The story of Charles having sired him has preoccupied him too. He arrives at Charles' to find out if it is true. Charles, who likes him, also uses him as a decoy or bribe to attract Hartley to Shruff End, where he puts her in the upstairs 'inner room', locking the door when she admits to feeling despairing and suicidal. Titus' arrival complicates the web of jealousy that already exists between Charles and the various witnesses to this incarceration. These are at various moments Lizzie, Rosina, Peregrine, Gilbert, and finally his cousin, the ex-General James. At first his half-willing accomplices, they become increasingly appalled. Rosina confides to Charles that, when he left her, he also left the problem of an unwanted pregnancy that she had to deal with on her own; ingenious in hurting him she leaves to console Ben, another of those attractive, violent men of power with whom she loves to fight. James rallies the others to help Charles return Hartley to Ben which, after a nearly public screaming fit on her part, he unwillingly but at last agrees to do.

At the moment of Hartley's return, James recognises Ben as hero of a bloody revolt in an Ardennes prisoner-of-war camp in 1945. (Ben's heroism may have been partly revenge, another theme in the book.) His recognition pleases and also steadies Ben.

Rosina's attentions may also have helped heal his pride. The scene is set for Charles' 'recovery' which is assisted by two disasters. First of all someone pushes him into Minn's Cauldron, a lethally enclosed deep whirlpool with twenty-foot steep and polished sides, from which James mysteriously rescues him. Then Titus drowns.

Charles blames Ben for both events. James once more sorts this out. Peregrine admits to having pushed Charles, when drunk, and out of an unappeased miserable anger at Charles' theft, many years before, of Rosina, and at his wanton breakage of their marriage. The anger had been awoken by sight of Rosina hurling stones at his car. Out of vicarious proprietorial vanity about Titus' youth and a related unwillingness to admit that he is himself old, Charles omitted ever to warn Titus either how dangerous the sea was, or how difficult it was to get out of. The sea always undid the ropes he tried to attach to the rock. Titus died accidentally, needlessly.

These two disasters help to provoke the ending of the tale, which is, for most of the survivors, a comic one. Rosina is so touched by Peregrine's having tried to murder Charles – it was 'so sort of sporting and splendid of Peregrine' – that she and he get together again. Rosina's finding Peregrine newly attractive after he tries to kill Charles recalls Antonia's return to Martin after he knocks Palmer out in *A Severed Head*. Both women long to submit to men of power. There are signs amid the plentiful gossip with which the story ends that this rekindling may not, either, have been permanent. Charles learns to play the role of uncle or celibate priest to them, as James is to predict. They go off to Londonderry to a 'darling little theatre, that's only a bit bombed' (435). Here Peregrine's attempt to bring theatre to the people, we later learn, is rewarded by his murder by terrorists.

Charles' admission that 'I do admire Peregrine for trying to kill me' recalls Julius' admiration for the push Simon gives him into the swimming-pool. One lesson throughout is that demons and monsters do not exist without our own deep complicity and cannot play their roles unaided. The 'monster' may with half his mind wish for our help in finding a new role, and find that help unforthcoming.

Through Titus' death, and his own near-murder, he begins to come to understand his own guilt, but not to overplay this, as he did his obsession. Lizzie and Gilbert get together again, despite a jealous scene in which James explains that Lizzie and he have met from time to time while Charles was away, either abroad, or with other women. James has given Lizzie reassurance. So intense is Charles' jealousy of his cousin that for a while he will not forgive him. This directly echoes Hartley's more serious failure to tell Ben of her relationship with Charles. Both Ben and Charles are violently jealous men – each differently associated with jealous spite. Charles sees Ben as 'a foul insanely jealous bullying maniac' (303) but is seen by James, who is just and authoritative, as having 'an insanely jealous disposition' himself (406). He begins to learn to forgive and bless Lizzie and Gilbert as he did Rosina and Peregrine.

He came to the sea wishing to play-act at renunciation, but the plot has forced him through a series of savagely painful renunciations that make his early desire for repentance look a posturing nonsense. Meanwhile Hartley and Ben disappear to Australia, and James leaves him too, dying in mysterious circumstances as if he had renounced life voluntarily. Charles forswears an easy ending to his tale, after the second of the two nights that he spends out of doors, with magnificently pictured star-scapes, followed by the appearance of four benign seals. Instead of this orthodox ending with everything picked up in 'radiant bland ambiguous higher significance, in calm of mind, all passion spent', he returns to the flat James has left him, with all its oriental junk, and ends the book in sporadic gossip and reflection about the events of the tale.

*

Early in the book Charles speaks of his relations with his cousin James. 'When I was young I could never decide whether James was real and I was unreal, or vice versa. Somehow it was clear we could not both be real; one of us must inhabit the world of shadows' (57). The relation between Charles and James is, like that of Tallis and Julius, Hugo and Jake, another reworking of the theme of the saint and artist. It is not construed by Charles like this until the end. Since childhood he has been full of both jealousy and envy of James' money, education, assurance. '*Cousinage, dangereux voisinage*', he more than once quotes. Charles has pursued success out of rivalry with James and a desire to be 'one up' on him.

James went to Winchester, pursued an army career, became a Buddhist and spiritual seeker after a stay in Tibet, and has now left the army under some unspecified cloud. James' importance, Charles finally realises, has always lain entirely in Charles' own mind. But then, as the story again and again shows, that is the place in which all such considerations are transacted.

As a small child James was an uncanny path-finder and once seriously attempted to learn to fly. He is more than a catalogue of eccentricities but is certainly equipped with various small signs, or stigmata, of his spiritual status. James offers us, as well as his creator, a certain quizzical, humorous pleasure. On two occasions his appearance is preceded by a sound resembling the wooden clappers (*hyoshigi*) used on the Japanese stage to increase suspense or announce doom. The first time this is 'naturalised' by the fact that workmen are hammering (171); the second time by the noises from Minn's Cauldron (440). He has an unearthly detachment and is repeatedly shown just faintly – and comically – out of focus with ordinary life and ordinary appetites. He has prehensile toes and a somehow beautifully, exactly right 'inane grin'. He writes to Charles on the occasion of Charles' retirement to the sea a spectacularly unremarkable letter until the bizarre remark, 'It is good to see the horizon as a clean line' (56). After his materialisation in the Wallace Collection, Charles goes to his Pimlico flat where a fly lands on James' finger. 'James and the fly looked at each other' (179). Charles feels cheated by James, who always seems to be withholding himself. James' Pimlico flat resembles an oriental emporium, full of fetiches and statues. He treasures the poems of Milarepa, great sinner turned great saint. James remembers everything he is, however idly, told, and in this contrasts with Charles, who lives and talks with some casualness. For James every moment tells.

The rivalry between Charles and James is entirely inside Charles' head. In this it is the direct descendant of Jake and Hugo's relationship. Jake also imagined various resentful feelings onto Hugo, and they also turned out at the end to be exclusively a projection of his own guilt. So, too, James feels nothing for Charles but, we are to intuit, a baffled love. And just as Hugo, properly apprehended, is a source of wisdom and light in Jake's life, so once more James' mode of being, as much as what he has to tell Charles, is at least in part a rebuke and a lesson to Charles.

One clue as to James' real feelings for Charles occurs early in Part 5. They are discussing Charles' feelings for Hartley, whose return to Ben James has successfully negotiated. Charles is still full of illusion about her.

> 'I've got to wait. She'll come to me here. She's part of me, it's not a caprice or a dream. When you've known someone from childhood, when you can't remember when they weren't there, that's not an illusion. She's woven into me. Don't you understand how one can be absolutely connected with somebody like that?'
> 'Yes', said James. 'Well, I must go . . . .'   (355)

The irony of this conversation is that James, whose deepest affections seem to be for his own sex, clearly feels connected to Charles in something approximating to the way that Charles feels connected to Hartley. He makes Charles his sole heir. Just as Charles recalls every detail of his relations with Hartley – or is haunted by those details he can recall – so James is repeatedly shown recalling Charles as a child. He remembers throwing stones with Charles, remembers that Charles liked black beetles, demonstrates the sense of connexion he feels for Charles in a variety of ways. He pockets the hammer Charles is mending, intuiting that he means no good by it. In a sense he nurses him.[7]

James significantly returns again and again to see Charles, who is never wholly at ease with him, and on the occasion of his revealing his acquaintanceship with Lizzie, is murderously abusive. James' return to Charles parallels Charles' return to Hartley, but is an opposite case. Where Charles has been unable to let go of his memories of Hartley and the pained and pity-filled love he bears her, James returns to Charles both to release himself from his own attachment to Charles, and also to assist Charles in releasing him and weaning him off his obsession with Hartley. Charles returns to the past to grab and freeze it. James returns to it gently to cut it loose. This is partly related to James' Buddhism, partly to common sense: obsessive attachment is a dangerous force whatever your religious belief or lack of it.

There is an implicit parallel between James and Charles' modes of detachment which runs through the novel. Charles' is an immature inability to commit himself emotionally which maddens and compels those who love him. James' is an achieved state of near-ascesis which calms and cheers those he comes in contact with. Gilbert, Titus and Peregrine each come separately to tell Charles how much they like James, who is 'a centre of magnetic attraction to the other three' (328), and in this he is an unconscious foil to Charles' attractiveness. Just as Ben mirrors Charles' violence and jealous spite, so James mirrors Charles' power and magic. What is shadowy and mostly unachieved in the relations between the two outsiders Jake and Hugo in *Under the Net* here takes on a detailed realisation between the two outsiders James and Charles, more consonant with the patience that both books urge. James stands for this more open perception. He is comically shocked at different times that Charles has never heard of gannets, cannot distinguish shag from cormorant, and has failed to notice a guillemot-covered rock. He shows throughout a talent for sharp perception, memory, and discrimination, for which this ornithology has to stand as simple emblem. Obsession narrows Charles' focus; virtue widens James'.

Charles comes in the last pages to see that he and James had the same problem. 'When I went to the sea I imagined that I was giving up the world. But one surrenders power in one form, and grasps it in another' (500). This reflects an earlier pronouncement of James' to the same effect. Charles sought to give up the magic of the theatre, itself an image here for the magic of personal power. James sought to give up that spiritual magic which, as he and various books on his Tibetan Buddhism witness, is a degenerate by-product of the quest for virtue and wisdom.[8] 'The last achievement is the absolute surrender of magic itself, what you call superstition. Yet how does it happen? Goodness is giving up power and acting on the world negatively. The good are unimaginable.' He is shown capable of 'tricks' which echo the magical tricks of the theatre: he can raise his body-temperature, and once failed by this means to save the life of a young sherpa in a snow-pass. He raised Charles from Minn's Cauldron after Peregrine had thrown him in, using either his prehensile toes, or levitation. This is later echoed, though not explained, by a photo of his father dancing with his mother and appearing to lift her off the ground 'simply by the force of his love' (488). Finally he selects the moment of his death, and dies smiling, as the 'Indian' doctor Tsang testifies. There is much in James' part in all this of Kipling's *Kim*, a favourite book of Murdoch's, a splendid imperial adventure tale with espionage, a military and spiritual penumbra, and a Tibetan lama to boot. *Kim* was written for children but is appreciated increasingly by adults too.[9] There is a level at which our enjoyment of James is like our innocent pleasure in *Kim*, though James' 'tricks' are designed too to recall Prospero's magic; as well as Charles' theatrical trickery, and personal charisma.[10]

While being playful, James' is also a serious portrait. There is, however, something 'unimaginable' at this deeper level about him. Is this a failure of art, and if so is it a necessary failure? The mutual irreconcilability of 'good' and art is, after all, an obsessive theme and at the very centre of this novel. I think that her other good characters – Bledyard, Ann Peronett, Tallis Browne, and Anne Cavidge in *Nuns and Soldiers* – come off better. The 'emptiness' of James is an interesting emptiness, and he is shown in the process of trying to make himself yet emptier. Partly because of Charles' obtuseness, it is never quite clear what a young 'full' James resembled. What is evident is that he is too partial to the magical side of religion, and also that, as Murdoch has said in interview, we are to imagine him at the end neither as having gone underground as a spy, as Charles crazily speculates, nor in Bardo, but dead and at peace (Bigsby, 1982). Bardo is to Tibetans a realm not unlike the Homeric Hades where the soul wanders after death, meeting demons of its own manufacture, and awaiting rebirth. Charles finally and authoritatively says 'there are spiritual beings in the world, perhaps James was one, but there are no saints' (482).

*

Bardo, however, is in some sense the realm of the whole novel. It is certainly Charles' realm. Coleridge once complained that 'A hunger-bitten and idea-less philosophy naturally produces a starveling and comfortless religion. It is among the miseries of the present age that it recognises no medium between *Literal* and *Metaphorical*.'[11] Bardo might be said to figure in the book as an in-between world, not merely because it separates death and rebirth, but also because it is the realm in which one's own projections are seen to be real. It is an image for the ways in which the mind persistently haunts itself. Bardo names a tormented version of Coleridge's happy break-down between literal and figurative. In this sense it is prefigured when Charles, in speaking of his failure as a playwright, argues that 'Unless one is very talented indeed there is no resting-place between the naive and the ironic' (35). Part of the sense we have of the sheer *size* of this novel comes from the poise with which it negotiates the gap between the naive and the ironic, the literal and the figurative. What could be simpler, more naive, more true or human than the book's premise of a man unable to grow up and fixated on an adolescent romance? What could be more sophisticated and ironic than the treatment it receives, of which this account will necessarily leave areas untouched. Here one might compare Iris Murdoch both with Shakespeare's last romances, also half naive, half ironic, and with her near-contemporary John Fowles, a man who has made much of the theme of the enclosed or persecuted maiden. In *The Collector* the girl is locked in a cellar, and in *The French Lieutenant's Woman* she is trying to get out of a somewhat vulgarised picture of the nineteenth century. From Rainborough's brief immolation of Annette in his cupboard in *The Flight from the Enchanter*, through *The Unicorn* and *The Time of the Angels*, where it is the heart of the plot, to Rozanov's sequestration of Hattie in the slipper house in *The Philosopher's Pupil*, the theme of the enclosed or persecuted maiden resonates through Murdoch's fiction too. In the difference between *The Collector* and *The Sea, The Sea* one might study the contrast between an author gratifying a private fantasy and one transmuting fantasy into life-giving imagination.[12]

A persistent strain of equivocation runs through the book about credulity. Charles early jokes about his own audience who 'yearn to believe and they believe, because believing is easier than disbelieving, and because anything which is written down is likely to be "true in a way"' (76). Such careful disingenuous play is not simply a mannerist intensification of the illusions of the story. It is also there to draw attention to the magical and mythopoetic qualities of imagination itself. 'I must try to describe Hartley. Oh, my darling, how clearly I can see you now. Surely this is perception, not imagination' (79). *The Sea, The Sea* is a novel about how 'seeing with the mind's eye' is more than a dead metaphor.

This is clearest in the play about the sea-serpent by which Charles is twice terrified. Charles is to speak finally of the ways in which he lets loose his own demons, 'not least the sea-serpent of jealousy' (492) and describes sexual jealousy as 'closely, blackly, coiled together' (152) with anger, when he realises Hartley and

Ben still sleep together; these coils recalling those of the sea-serpent. At one point when Rosina is jealously tormenting him he momentarily sees on her 'the snake-like head and teeth and pink opening mouth of my sea monster . . . not really a vision but just a thought' (105). The second time he sees the monster, in Minn's Cauldron after Peregrine has thrown him in, the water is bottle-green. So are the sea-serpent's eyes. Murdoch makes the question as to whether the green-eyed monster is 'real' or not seem literal-minded. One might say that the question of the reality of the sea-serpent (and the reality of sexual jealousy) is a kind of satire on those behaviourist philosophers and literary critics who relegate all inner experience to the realm of a ghostly and unimportant shadow of the public and measurable act. *Introspectabilia*, despite being continually legislated out of existence, continue to haunt us as they do Charles. Jealousy, like guilt, is a major theme of the book, and that the monster appears on the first page is some sort of warning that Charles' desire to leap out of his former way of life is dangerous when the inner world, the world of fantasies and projections, remains unweeded and undisciplined. Charles produces the green-eyed monster of jealousy just as he produces a phantasmagoric picture of Hartley. Both take their revenge on him.

Something similar might be written of the other two master images of the book, the 'box' and the 'sea'. I discussed their general relevance earlier. These have so huge a force – both 'literal' and 'metaphoric' – that to call them symbols is to demean them. They seem more like concrete metaphors. Both Charles and James speak, in the tone of Murdoch's own Freudianised Platonism, of the mind as a cavern with variously available light-sources. In a sense what Charles has done, in self-defence against the pain of losing her, is to mistake Hartley for 'the one great light', the Good itself (77). All forms of 'absolute' metaphysic in Murdoch's work are vulnerable, as in life. Charles' has the special defensive poignancy of 'young love' fetishised. The contrast between the force of this love and its object, the frail over-imaginative old moustachio'd woman that Hartley now is, is awesome. It is not impossible that Hartley might still love him. It is more simply that we gradually but clearly see that she does not – though she feels guilt, pity and other emotions. She found him too 'sort of bossy' and the reader sees what she means. She did not want him to become an actor but to go to University instead. He failed to arouse her physically perhaps – certainly Charles' dim, final realisation that Ben may have awakened Hartley sexually, helped on by Rosina's finding Ben attractive, has a terrible pathos and an evident truth. But memory is fallible, and even Hartley can no longer be sure why she rejected him. Her guilt about having left him renders her powerless. Peregrine early states that all marriage is ruled over by the law that 'the spouse who feels guilty, even irrationally, is endlessly the victim of the whims of the other, and can take no moral stance' (162). One reading of the novel might devote itself solely to exploring how this ruling truth operates. Much of Charles' power over his women (unlike James' power) has to do with his rendering them frightened and guilty.

What does seem clear is that the 'truth' if any behind Hartley's rejection of him is not now to be ascertained, and indeed that no human love ever admits of any clean or simple history. The novel's scepticism about this is acute and convincing, so elaborately imagined and felt are the particulars of this relationship. But Charles, at least until the end, refuses to see it. The power of the image of the 'box' – which is both the extremely dark, entirely empty enclosed inner room without outside windows, and also the cavern of his own mind – is that he has locked up a simulacrum of her within his mind, and is to act out this incarceration in reality. He is given to seeing Hartley as imprisoned within the 'cage' of her marriage. On one page (201) the word 'cage' is repeated three times. Seeing her thus, he encages her himself. The only time he spoke of this love to the worldly and apparently wise Clement, she listened and then advised him 'Put her away in your old toy cupboard now, dear boy' (428), which suggests once more the most accurate picture we finally gain of his psychological treatment of her memory as well as his physical treatment of her person. During the terrible days he holds her captive he 'felt like a child who rushes to the cage of its new pet fearing to find a lifeless body' (282).

The box is also the unconscious parts of the mind in particular. 'The deeper parts of the mind have so little sense of time' (57). Charles writes many times of the ways that certain intentions are located in time and space. He callously dismisses Lizzie's claims on him since the letter that he wrote her, which was designed to provoke her love and raise her expectations, 'said nothing of time and space' (48). The way that Lizzie and Rosina's love for

Charles is re-ignited after many years clearly echoes Charles'
renewed feelings about Hartley. But whereas Hartley clearly and
specifically rejected him forty-five years before, Charles has been
careful to leave his women in sufficient uncertainty for him to
make continuing demands on them in future. Here the failure of
all these renewed loves, including Rosina and Peregrine's, if we
are to believe the rumours about their second marriage, seems to
point the same moral.

All attachments are vulnerable and finally impermanent, and
the best love would be unpossessive. Seeing Hartley again gives
Charles a shock that 'annihilates space and time' (111). But such
annihilation must be illusory. James gives the authoritative
verdict, when in his last interview, still weaning Charles off his
obsession, he predicts his recovery:

> You've built a cage of needs and installed her in an empty
> space in the middle. The strong feelings are all round her –
> vanity, revenge, your love for your youth – they aren't focused
> on her, they don't touch her. She seems to be their prisoner,
> but you don't harm her at all. You are using her image, a doll,
> a simulacrum, it's an exorcism. Soon you will start to see her
> as a wicked enchantress. Then you will have nothing to do
> except forgive her and that will be within your capacity.   (442)

Once more the language asserts the absolute importance of the
inner world, as well as the fantastic nature of much human action.
James twice reminds Charles that according to Stesichorus the
heroes of the Trojan war fought for a phantom Helen, and speaks
of the ontological proof. 'If even a dog's tooth is truly worshipped
it glows with light' (175), and 'the worshipper endows the
worshipped object with power, real power not imaginary power,
that is the sense of the ontological proof, one of the most
ambiguous ideas clever men ever thought of. But this power is
dreadful stuff. Our lusts and our attachments compose our god'
(445).[13] For such reasons damage is done to the integrity of her
work when critics treat her division between 'fantasy' and
'imagination' as if it could be absolute. What Murdoch continually
asserts is not the discontinuity, but the continuity between the
two. The man who might have the power to perceive – or
imagine – the true as opposed to the phantom Helen is the man
who has purified these 'lusts and attachments', which include

guilt, revenge and jealousy. Such a man could worship purely, but unless he were a great artist would be unable to tell us what he could see, since it lies beyond the realm of images.

*

The world which lies beyond the realm of images, from which all form comes and returns, is partly figured by the sea. One of the sad aspects of writing about this book is how much of its glorious physical description must be left aside. Like Charles' picnic meals, these have the cunning grace of happy improvisations, as-if-casually thrown off, but to be savoured slowly. 'Towards evening, the usual cloud-show. Great cliffs and headlands of light golden-brown cloud build up to majestic heights, with a froth of pure gold clinging to their huge sides' (31). 'I could no longer concentrate upon those brilliant lucid little civilisations, although in the strong light the coloured pebbles and the miniature seaweed trees looked like jewels by Fabergé. I watched a dance of prawns and the progress of a green transparent sea-slug, and saw again the long coiling red worm which had somehow reminded me of my sea serpent' (140). 'There were a few clouds, big lazy chryselephantine clouds that loafed round over the water exuding light. I gazed at them and wondered at myself for being too obsessed to be able to share the marvels that surrounded me' (426). That consort of rare word (chryselephantine) and colloquial (loafing about) startles us into vision, makes the ordinary magical. Charles early remarks that he could fill a book with these word-pictures, and Murdoch has had a problem in putting her own naked wonder and delight in seeing and describing such phenomena into Charles' supposed obsessive blindness to all but himself and Hartley.

'It's sublime, yes, in the strict sense, sublime' says James (330) of the sea. Given the variety and fertility of description of the sea's many states, moods, and colours, it seems tactless to colonise it as a 'literary device'. Its point, in fact, is its resistance to human devices, its miscellaneous nature, its hugeness and unpredictability. The starry firmament above, which Charles most memorably watches on two occasions, and which reminds him of the Odeons of his youth, reminded Kant of the moral law within: two wonders. Both sea-scape and star-scape are conventional triggers of the sublime, and the sublime here might be defined by its opposition to the box of obsession; dwarfing both Charles' one-pointed maundering pain about Hartley, and his pain about his life, are the multiplicity and disorder of the natural world. Charles has given Hartley the status of absolute in his life. Sea and stars decree that such incarnate absolutes must be delusive. Charles has been a philosophical 'Monist' with Hartley as the point of total connexion in his private religion; the sea, in changing from second to second while he watches it, mocks such transcendence, declares it premature. Like so many other Murdoch heroes Charles fights off but eventually learns to begin to embrace a healing surrender to the particulars of the world he inhabits. The first chronicler of the sublime, Longinus, spoke of the experience as like being 'scorched, pierced, *inundated*, blown down and generally knocked about'.[14] Charles' inundation is again both real and figurative.

I feel that the uses to which the sea is put succeed better here than in any other novel. In *The Philosopher's Pupil* water is explored with great ingenuity as an explicitly public symbol in an imaginary spa town. It becomes something like a figure for Eros itself, the 'natural' spring of desire, and an object of ambiguous worship. The very publicity of the theme in that book can produce a certain knowing effect wholly lacking here. Murdoch has referred to her interest in water by saying 'all human beings are symbolic animals – one's always got certain obsessive symbols which seem to represent deep metaphysical ideas or moral ideas'.[15]

It is its very freedom which, in *The Sea, The Sea*, holds the gaze. This freedom could be glossed in different ways. Nearly one half of the Judaic creation is concerned with God's struggle, as Auden pointed out, with undifferentiated flux in which water plays a major role, and Greek cosmology reflects similar ideas. The sea contains and represents 'everything', is a symbol for the uncoerced unconscious, source of all symbols, from which identity comes and to which it returns. As in *Death in Venice*, a work referred to in *The Fire and the Sun*, it is the mother of forms: it is the ideal concrete metaphor for Murdoch's own *Ozeanisches Gefuehl*, the zone of contingency. 'My imagination lives near the sea and under the sea' she said in 1978.[16] To Magee she suggested that 'ideas in art must suffer a sea-change' (277), a way of putting her hostility to ideological art that proposes for the sea the power of transmutation, indeterminacy and flux: everything, in fact, that Charles' obsession is opposed to.

Here the sea early undoes the knots in the various ropes Charles tries to attach to his rocks to ease his bathing and can thus be felicitously used, much later, as a figure for impermanence: 'Time, like the sea, unties all knots. Judgements on people are never final, they emerge from summings up which at once suggest the need of a reconsideration. Human arrangements are nothing but loose ends and hazy reckoning, whatever art may otherwise pretend in order to console us' (477). And there is something apt in the fact that when he finally retires back to London it is not to his unhappy Shepherd's Bush flat but to James' Pimlico, 'with the wind beating down the Thames at the end of the street' (477). He is to live on marginally better terms with the contingent from now on. Poseidon, James avers, was an ancestor of Plato's.

There is something awkward about the critical exercise of trying to 'totalise' Murdoch's image of the untotalisable, the uncontainable. A case could be made for *The Sea, The Sea* as a great classic of anti-Modernism, at least as Modernism was twenty years ago described. I mean that its use of myth and metaphor is deliberately incomplete, throw-away, and provisional. Like her other books, this one seems to possess no unconscious, no latency. Charles has an unconscious, yet his book does not. Analogy is restlessly sought, patiently used, then cast away. Myth is seen always as a part of Charles' defeated attempts to colonise and contain experience. Here psychology precedes myth, flirts with it, but is abandoned by it. Charles visits Titian's *Perseus and Andromeda* in the Wallace Collection. The dragon partly resembles his sea-monster, just as he also conceives himself as Perseus rescuing Hartley from the monster Ben. The myth is false, as is the dream he has of Hartley as a ballerina – mocked by a walk with Lizzie which passes 'the ruin of a big house, with the box hedges of the formal garden grown into a forest and covered with rambler roses' (401). Charles is more like Peter Pan than Perseus: Hartley is not the Sleeping Beauty. Nor is she Cinderella or Galatea, both alluded to. Murdoch's own extra-psychological small and deliberate symmetries – the 'Shruff' of Shruff End purportedly means 'black', and the house is finally bought by some people called 'Schwarzkopf' – have more the feeling of delighted play or joke than of any palpable symbolic design on the reader. Charles' quest is to begin to understand the fictional quality of his own projections, which is to say also their *reality* and consequentiality. If the book has a project it is to distance and ironise the notion of aesthetic unity in life.

In this process the image of the theatre, the most provisional of all great art-forms, can make a convenient back-drop. Few other novelists would have resisted the temptation to use the theatre to flatten the book's own illusionism. 'I am in favour of illusion, not alienation' (35), says Charles, and we feel his creator's concurrence. Charles spurns the banal, dramaturgical analogy by virtue of which anyone '*might* do anything' (em) and can play any role at all in life. 'And we are masked figures, ideally the masks barely touch us. (Such is my view, with which some fools will differ)' (37). The true and equivocal nature of these masks becomes a subject-matter.[17] I have discussed in another chapter the small joke about Rosina who 'unfortunately . . . was never able to play Honor Klein' (73). Such play is as disposable as the use of the myth of Perseus; it holds the author's and our attention for a moment, and is then discarded. The theatre is useful to the plot since we are less bothered by the spectacle of theatre people over-acting. It is useful to the idea-play, since it is connected with the themes of magic, directorial power, obsession, and impermanence. In the introductory Pre-History Charles memorably describes the theatre as an attack on mankind carried out by magic (33), and points out that in it works concerning authorial obsession are acted out in an atmosphere owing much to the obsessions of directors and actors.

Drama is described as the genre which must *stoop* to catch its audience's attention, partly preparing the way for the shameless manipulations of the plot itself. It is associated with impermanence – 'perpetual construction followed by perpetual destruction . . . endings . . . partings . . . packings up and dismantlings' (36) – and thus introduces the theme of the necessary surrender to time. When the action of the novel is imaged forth for us in theatrical terms, it is this aspect which is often called upon. For example when Charles learns that Hartley is married and living with her husband 'a whole world of possibilities gradually folded themselves up, like some trick of stagecraft, quietly collapsing, folding, merging, becoming very small and vanishing' (115).

The theatre is finally important since 'the most essentially frivolous and rootless of all the serious arts has produced the greatest of all writers' (36). Shakespeare, once more, is the novel's

tutelary deity. *The Sea, The Sea* has the bland unconcern with
probability of the late romances. It combines strict formal and
dramatic compression with an outward flow of meaning. Like
The Tempest it combines humour and pathos in a structure which
struggles with and never quite embraces 'allegory'. Both take
place in a zone pitched weirdly between what Charles calls the
naive and ironic. Both concern power, fraternal rivalry and
reconciliation. The openness is helped by the fact that Murdoch
had defeated her temptation to make the plot incestuous. Rosina's
relations with Ben, and Titus' possible relations with James, for
which a novel like *A Word Child* contains explicit analogues,
remain here nicely shadowy. The vicious circuit of love, which
acts in Murdoch's books as a paranoia-provoking parody of
virtuous connexion, is uncompleted.

I want now to move toward the ending, in which Charles
remarks 'What an egoist I must seem in the preceding pages. But
am I so exceptional?' (482). To what extent does he succeed in
being, for all his rapacious egoism, merely *averagely* wicked? He
is clearly so by the standards of the book. Just as Hartley lives in
his mind, so Lizzie, Rosina and Peregrine all permit themselves
to be destructively haunted by Charles. 'You live in my mind',
writes Lizzie (43), and both Arbelows testify to the ways he has
been a demon or devil in their imagination. Such haunting is
discussed in *The Nice and the Good* as the responsibility of the
emanator as much as the haunted mind, where we are told that
'maybe a saint would be known by the utter absence of such
gaseous tentacles' (146). Here the guilt of having so unhygienic
an inner life seems divided more equitably between the dreamer
and the dreamt-of. Charles soliloquises that fantasies, such as his
murderous hatred of Ben, 'can cause accidents' (490), and we
notice that Titus' death by drowning occurred soon after Charles
had begun to mix his real affection for the boy with resentment
of his claims on him, as though thoughts could literally kill. That
would be a magical conclusion, and the story is circumspect about
magic, and provides naturalistic explanations too. Charles had
imagined that his one-time chauffeur Freddie Arkwright regarded
him 'with rancorous hatred' (30), but when he meets him near
the end finds that, on the contrary, Freddie sees him as a
beneficent deity. Not all projections are punished. The truth
about Charles seems to include the role of rapacious egoist he
acts out, and Freddie's more flattering view.

There are far more felicities of observation of human behaviour, as of the natural scene, than the critic can do justice to. Few other novelists could use the characters' part-singing to such odd and happy effect. Its many internal echoes and ambiguities seem closer to those of ordinary reflection than to interpretation as a specialised subject. There is at least one awkward moment in the plotting, when Titus is cremated in a distant town. It is hard to believe that 'Shruff End' would not have met 'Nibletts' at the service.

The reflective Postscript 'Life goes on' is beautifully handled. Charles returns to London and notes with an hilariously unaware pomposity that 'people have got over the excitement of my return' (485). He learns to blaspheme against his memory of Hartley, as James predicted he would, and begins also to see her, as Hannah was finally seen in *The Unicorn*, as a harpy and sorceress. His recovery has started. Having resented paying money throughout the tale – 'at my expense' becomes a jokey refrain – he is generous, financially and in terms of his concern, to his secretary, and starts to give his money away. In one of those shifts of perspective that in the early work can electrify without wholly persuading, he comes to speak not of Hartley but of Clement Makin, who was originally to have played a large role in his reminiscence, and acts throughout as an absent centre, as the reason he never married. This shift reads as wholly earned, and has the natural effect of great art. He has started to neutralise Hartley as a pain-source in his life. The life-long habit of *needing* such consoling explanatory figures, centres of blame and of shriving, dies harder. What the book calls an 'intention-trace' survives for a time the impulse to change.

He has a chest pain and begins to envisage his mortality. On a BBC quiz someone fails to recognise his name. It is moving towards Christmas, nearly always a time of promise for Murdoch characters, as it is for Hilary at the end of *A Word Child*, if not for Guy who dies on Christmas Eve in *Nuns and Soldiers*. Charles agrees to see Peregrine's provocative step-daughter, Angie, who has been pestering him to give her a child, and who is incidentally about Hartley's age at the time of the breakage of their relationship.

Charles contemplates, with an effect beautifully poised between pathos and ripe humour:

Can one change oneself? I doubt it. Or if there is any change it must be measured as the millionth part of a millimetre.

When the poor ghosts have gone, what remains are ordinary obligations and ordinary interests. One can live quietly and try to do tiny good things and harm no one. I cannot think of any tiny good thing to do at the moment, but perhaps I shall think of one tomorrow.   (501)

Finally James' casket, which may contain a demon, drops off the wall. 'Upon the demon-ridden pilgrimage of human life, what next I wonder?' It is a perfectly judged ending, pointing to the inability of art to compel life, of consciousness to contain experience, mocking the idea of endings themselves.

11 Conclusion: *Nuns and Soldiers* and *The Philosopher's Pupil*

> The great artist, like the great saint, calms us by a kind
> of simple unassuming lucidity. He speaks with the voice
> we hear in Homer and Shakespeare and the Gospels.
>
> ('Salvation by Words')

My aim here is to open areas of enquiry, not close them. An inquisitive and speculative close seems aptest for a writer who has so fought for open-endedness. Iris Murdoch's work has had some dull and tired objections brought to it. I have tried to show that it is solid enough to deserve some interesting new ones. There are faults enough, of course, as there are faults in Dickens and other major artists. The work seems big enough to withstand them. (To her admirers even the faults have a quality of reassurance.)

I would plead for a gentle detachment of the work from the theory, so that the reader can surrender to the experience of the work – its detail and authority – without rushing back panic-stricken to the full safety of the ideas. Where the ideas have been given priority the work is either derogated into being a sorry 'illustration' of them, or is safely collapsed back into its supposed 'source'. I am aware of not always having avoided these dangers and am pleading not for the neglect of the theory but for its distancing. The ideas are interesting of course, and formidably well-expressed. There is a heroic innocence and strength about them, however, that does damage to the intelligence of otherwise sane men. One critic conclusively dismisses her characters (Mischa, Honor, Hannah) on the grounds that they could not exist in George Eliot's work or Tolstoi's.[1] Faced with this level of debate one is reduced to truism: nor could George Eliot's characters exist in Tolstoi's work or vice versa or the characters from *Anna Karenina* survive in *The Death of Ivan Illych*. Another critic, an American Ph.D., came to the conclusion that Murdoch's theories about negative capability cannot be true because 'if self-abnegation were sufficient for art, Shakespeare's plays would have existed before he wrote them'.[2] And a British critic seriously suggested to me that Murdoch's ambition has been to recreate characters like those of *The Mill on the Floss* but could not since she belonged to the twentieth century. Leaving aside that George Eliot is as I have shown in no sense a model for her, it often seems that what she is being secretly chastised for is for failing to bring us back to the nineteenth century itself. This is indeed to credit her with large powers, and must account for much disappointment.

She has argued, not for a return to the values of the last century, but for an art that is still nourished by the continuing *fact*, and the continuing mystery, of human difference. We have not ceased to differ from one another, a perception recently given force for literary critics – whose sense of reality so often needs to be accredited by reference to approved sources – by the rediscovery of Bakhtin's work and his championing of the polyphony that feeds the 'traditional' novel.[3] She has combined this sense of human difference, at her best, with a fully contemporary sense of the ways in which – as for Sartre – individual essence is not simply 'given' but can appear to be in crisis. Yet there are people even today for whom 'personal identity' is not the most compelling issue; and in showing us this too she is simultaneously pointing to a truth just as interesting, and more mysterious.

In admiring what Bradley Pearson terms 'our strong and sentimental forbears' her aim is not to recreate Dickens' characters but to make up her own in a living process that can be inspired by the art of the past. And she is utterly of her time. Most considerable artists feed off one another: art nourishes art and so does life. The paradox exists only for hygienically-minded critics, never for artists themselves, who mainly continue untroubled by the necessary ambiguities of their trade. Of course there can be no 'return'. Or, to put the same point another way, the *desire* for return has always been a revolutionary one and has provoked the most interesting new syntheses. It is the desire to leave the past wholly behind that can create the stalest repetitions.

At the other extreme the theories can be used to underwrite the books absolutely, as if a writer who had managed to get the 'Good' on her side could do little wrong. In Dipple's *Work for the*

Spirit **this** enlistment occurs around 1970, a time when I agree that her work came of age. It must be confessed that Murdoch's admirers have not always escaped a certain priggishness. Recognising that hers is an art preoccupied by the moral, the critic can behave like a species of moral terrorist, conducting a series of ethical unmaskings and denunciations of the characters. Dipple shows a Calvinism wholly at odds with Murdoch's own generosity when she tells us that it is 'proven' [*sic*] by certain signs that David in *The Sacred and Profane Love Machine* – who is nineteen years old – will come to resemble his father; or that Miles in *Bruno's Dream* could never produce great art. Since the gap between the moral and aesthetic – as well as their putative but distant identity – has been Murdoch's laborious point from the start, this is, for all Dipple's generosity elsewhere, seriously wrong-headed. 'Good artists can be bad men; the virtue may . . . reside entirely in the work, the just vision be attainable only there' (*FS* 84).

As well as the theory being used to justify or question the work, the work must also question the theory. This is normal in any critical discussion. Murdoch must be unique among artists in the way that critics have begun, as it were, at the wrong end. The necessary job of discriminating between her works must wait on the task of describing the pleasures of each. Here the work is not an illustration of theory; though it may well comment on it.

*

It is generally a sign of health and stature when a writer is attacked simultaneously for wholly opposite reasons. It suggests that there is something of real substance there. Murdoch has been attacked for being too romantic and too realistic, too comfortable in her assertion of novelistic continuities and too unconsoling in her creation of characters, who are described as 'awful' and 'hateful'. The reader will have his own opinion here. My sense is that there is much quiet truth in her depiction of human awfulness, and that her triumph has often been to show precisely how innocent and unconscious it can be: literally 'thoughtless'. Chapter 2 of *Sense and Sensibility* is so profound an analysis of human nastiness because it shows it as deeply ordinary, a slow and gradual self-deception on the part of Mr and Mrs John Dashwood who persuade themselves that their heroic mean-mindedness is really a strict *duty*. It is in this sense that Austin in *An Accidental*

Man is 'like all of us only more so' (428) and that Henry in *Henry and Cato* can be seen by the authoritative Pat Raven both as a 'poppet' (390) and yet also as self-deluded. Even Christian critics seem oddly squeamish about drawing any full-blooded conclusions from a doctrine of original sin. As for rationalistic liberals, much of the criticism of her work has come from exactly the unreconstructed liberal posture she has questioned. It is hard for critics with no belief in human privacy, difference or change to come to grips with her work, but it has also proved hard for those with too facile a belief in these to do so. Of Brian in *The Philosopher's Pupil* we learn that he was nicer than his awful brother George but he was not all *that* nice. The simple but deep reason was 'he was selfish'. Her characters seem to me recognisable, despite or because of such epic simplicities. The work is so intricate and yet the message so simple: this makes it hard to describe.

*

Are the 'levels' in her work coherently articulated? Is the work unified? Sufficiently so, I believe. An extra problem here is that the criticism of the mid-century so exaggerated the unity and perfection of great art. 'All this is not quite true' is what Barney in *The Red and the Green* considers writing on his comically self-serving memoirs. This might be the epitaph on the New Criticism, which so ignored the untidy centrifugal powers of art. We are paying now for the pretension of Neosymbolist claims in the anarchy of deconstruction, which takes the opposing view that the work is made from fissile material always about to go off. It is an apt come-uppance but the truth lies in between. A task for criticism now seems to be to go back and rediscover the relative disunity of all good art. Terry Eagleton has written of Hardy's mingling of orthodox verisimilitude, realist narration, classical tragedy, folk-fable, melodrama, 'philosophical' discourse, social commentary, to 'betray' the laborious constructedness of literary production. Eagleton makes a revolutionary tableau out of this impurity and delightedly calls it 'scandalous'.[4] Yet does not a comparable impurity and contradiction mark *all* considerable art – certainly all so-called realist art? Barthes showed this apocalyptically, of course, but it seems literal-minded to make so big a fuss about it. There need be no great epistemological drama here. Realism was always contentedly impure, which was exactly

Henry James' quarrel with Thackeray and Trollope's art: it was the Moderns who were puritanically obsessed with art's 'laborious constructedness' and who were literal-minded about illusion and story. As Murdoch suggested in the Gifford lectures, we do not normally look for a *single* criterion of truthfulness in good art, but for a variety of different criteria, and the ordinary reader needs little tuition in how to apply these. The quasi-allegorical characters of Julius and Tallis coexist comfortably with the more realistic characters and it seems literal-minded to object. They 'come off' in different ways. Loxias tells Julian in *The Black Prince* that one day she may be privileged to understand even Shakespeare's vulgarity: it's only art, after all.

*

In retreating from the vanity and inflated claims of the Moderns does she risk becoming middle-brow? Yes. But the word obscures as much as it illuminates. Dickens and Dostoevski were accessible to non-specialist audiences and have remained so.

*

In middle-brow work we can feel that the author expresses a deep and humane concern for cardboard characters. There can be a dissonance between the achievement of 'character' and the light in which it is seen in her work too; but her least satisfactory characters usually have something interesting about them. They may, though, be uninhabited or alternatively ventriloquised for purposes of moral design. Arthur Fisch in *A Word Child* is uncharacteristically eloquent to Hilary about Hilary's problems and personifies 'meekness of heart' and 'wise counsel'; Ducane in *The Nice and the Good* seems less than fully inhabited. The characters who work best engage not merely her moral intelligence but also – as in John Bayley's view of Tolstoi – her physical sympathy; and these two may be opposed. The presence or absence of such an opposition is as important as the existence of a 'pattern' to which their autonomy may or may not be sacrificed, in creating successful character. Contrary to the doctrine that autonomy of form means a loss of autonomy of character, the inhabitants of her Gothic romances are often both alive and interesting. All the characters of *A Severed Head* are successful, and part of the pleasure of the book comes from watching wholly believable characters in a series of bizarre fixes. Many of the characters in *The Unicorn* (Effingham, Marian, Hannah, Violet, Jamesie) in the first part of the book, in *The Time of the Angels* (Carel, Muriel, Elizabeth and the do-gooders Norah, Anthea, Marcus), and in *A Word Child* (Hilary, Lady Kitty, Gunnar, Christopher) are memorable too. There is always physical sympathy at work in the Gothic romances, and in a sense these books are *about*, as I have tried to suggest, the darkness and blindness of the least conscious, most 'physical' and determined needs of the imagination, in full conflict with the most spiritual and conscious needs. Such books are full of a diffused eroticism without quite being in the ordinary sense sexy.

Where the characters are vague, in all the books, it is often for the odd reason that the relationships they are engaged in are more real than they are. Character in her work may be sometimes half-imagined; but relationship is nearly always fully imagined. The characters in being victims of their own needs repeat certain relationships, whose casualties they then become. Here one might see a concession to a structuralist climate of thought: the unenlightened psyche in her work is typically a set of ancient emotions on the loose, seeking some essentially anonymous pretext for expressing itself. Identity may be resolved with little remainder into these repeating patterns and needs, for all but the good man, or the good parts of the psyche, which escape from the world of pure relationship through a process of unselfing. For structuralism the ordinary man is 'spoken by' language while only the intellectual, who is a kind of poet out on the borders of language manufacturing new concepts, is free.[5] For Murdoch what the ordinary man is 'spoken by', is blind need and desire, and it is the good man, not necessarily an intellectual, who is freed through education of desire, and other-centredness. There are characters of power both good and bad – Emma, Anne, Honor, Hannah, Tallis, Julius, and many of the first-person narrators – where we feel the authorial presence to be close. They are often hard to 'place' and this difficulty may become a theme in the book. But they too work best when there is a division of sympathy behind them. Even Julius is made admirably and accurately witty, for all his deviltry, and is for this reason more alive.

In the early essays Murdoch criticises the work in which the author simply divides himself into the contradictory cast of characters inside his own head and sets this small society to work, at odds with itself, for his own salvation. In the later work there seems to be a deeper understanding of how 'the family', with its Freudian tensions, can itself act as just such a Hegelian monster. Even when we sense in her an authorial *psychomachia* of the kind she deplored, she shows a curiosity about the characters that makes for openness, and a willingness to set them free from this patterning. The book, as well as trying to collapse inwards, also radiates its meanings away from this centre in a thousand felicitous details. In the best work (*A Fairly Honourable Defeat, The Black Prince, The Sea, The Sea, An Accidental Man, A Severed Head*) the two pressures approach being equal and opposite.

*

She seems both traditional in her use of story and 'voice' and, in the cant phrase, 'post-modern' in her exploration of the comic, the playful, the open-ended and the idea of reality as an infinite regress. Her triumph has been to reconstitute the direct address (in all its ambiguity) of traditional fiction, and it is clear that many of her readers feel as 'spoken to' as did Dickens' audience. Although she has pleaded, following T. S. Eliot, for a certain impersonality in good art (sbr), this need not mean that the work lacks a distinctive voice. In her work the voice is used both to disappear into the consciousnesses it depicts and sometimes – as with Ducane and Jessica's relationship in *The Nice and the Good* – to offer wise counsel.

For some critics this use of voice can lead – as Christopher Ricks has unkindly noted – to a kind of chatter. She can pile up adjectives and over-use 'a sort of' and 'a kind of'. Ricks calls this a formula for lying, mystery, pseudo-exactness.[6] The criticism could be inverted. She uses approximations because of a certainty that the truth about her characters – like the truth about us – cannot be wholly possessed and because what chiefly characterises mental states is indeterminacy.[7] Her style mixes a tactful restraint about any such possession with an insistence (with exceptions) on its own referentiality. The style deliberately defaults on the demand that it be narcissistically 'perfect' and austere, in the interests of the human truths to which it points. The books are wounded so that their meanings can, as it were, leak back into life rather than create a hermetically sealed world. She refuses to be more than human, and my case is that she is big enough to withstand the carelessness and repetition that is an integral part of such a posture. Moreover, as Alasdair MacIntyre has pointed out, Ricks' strictures are less damaging about the story-telling voice, concerned as it is with events in time and with the creation of stories.[8] 'Stories are art too, you know' (*BP* 240).

I suggested that her interest in the idea of an infinite regress is of its time. In *The Red and the Green* Barney finally feels that he is in the presence of his niece Frances for the first time 'as if the real Frances had just broken through a screen upon which a picture of her had been painted'. Connoisseurs of her work will know that Barney's moment of enlightenment here can no more be final than was his moment of revelation in the chapel, which seemed at the time to be equally absolute but whose truths he gradually dissipated over the succeeding weeks. A new image of Frances will always be waiting to break through any 'final' version of her reality *ad infinitum* – or until such time as, like Jake with Anna at the end of *Under the Net*, he gives up having any picture of her at all. Murdoch is wholly of our time in her insistence that 'truth' cannot be secured. There are short glimpses of clarity and insight but the single Big Truth is always illusory. Conceptual mastery falsifies and all strategies of possession are mocked by time. Her genius has been to marry such a sense of truth-as-infinite-regress with a notion of 'towardness' whereby it is, incidentally, containable within the traditional novel. The recession of views is related to the moral life, and does not burst the work's bounds (as in Fowles' *The Magus*). Fowles' fiction, for example, is in search of the absolute of self-realisation. Murdoch's is suspicious of all absolutes, especially those of 'self-realisation', and despite showing that moral change is in some sense goalless she does not evacuate it of meaning: on the contrary, she reconstitutes it. As for Yeats, a man may not know a truth; but he may embody one.

Her books are open-ended for similar reasons. An ending is always the most conventional moment in a literary work, but, since life has no conclusions apart from death, art must mock its own. Her books, which grow longer one-by-one, have been said not so much to end as simply to stop.[9] In *The Sea, The Sea* the coda solves her problems very neatly. It satisfies our demand for totality and also mocks it. Elsewhere the lack of resolution is handed playfully on to us for our participation. Schiller made of the instinct towards play a characteristic of the highest creativity, and in 'post-modern' art the ludic finds its natural habitat.

Murdoch is a playful writer, playing with pattern, playing with the reader, yet the play is somehow serious as well as playful.

My sense is that we need more discussion of the poetry and comedy of the work and less of their 'contingency'. Lorna Sage has, surely rightly, called the debates about contingency 'literal-minded, doomed researches'[10] and shows how Murdoch's main achievement is not to offer 'brief peeps at unadulterated Contingency' but to awaken and feed in the reader a 'moral greed' that flows outwards into life.[11] Comedy creates the space in which the different levels of the work can comfortably coexist. Murdoch has repeatedly asserted that the novel is a comic form, that tragedy belongs only in art. What we have in life when comedy fails is misery, not tragedy. A newly vitalised sense of the comic also marks much contemporary writing. Even when they are most grim, Murdoch's novels are funny.

*

Terry Eagleton has suggested, *à propos* discussion of Harold Bloom, that no humanism that overlooked Freud, Marx and Derrida could offer itself as reputedly modern; but that having taken the theories of these three on board, its own capacity to affirm must become 'almost maniacally wilful'.[12] Murdoch has addressed all three thinkers. Does her capacity to affirm look 'almost maniacally wilful'? I don't think that in that sense affirmation is her business, exciting as it would doubtless be. She is too busy simply looking at the way things are. She is fond of quoting Rilke who said of Cézanne that he did not paint 'I like it' but 'It is there.' This marks the realism she is in quest of, and in this she resembles many ordinary people in being too busily engaged with the detail of the world to be much concerned with 'affirmation', whether maniacally wilful or other; and also unconcerned with any grand metaphysical reduction.

At another level this is disingenuous. 'In a way nothing matters very much, though in a way everything matters absolutely' (*AM* 109) is how Garth expressed it to Ludwig, and such a serene and beatific and yet also paradoxically affirmative nihilism – in which 'every little thing matters' (*SPLM* 366) – marks both novels and theory alike. Schopenhauer or Buddhism might be enlisted to underwrite such a stance, but it also, incidentally, is very English. In *The Sovereignty of Good* 'affirmation' is groundless and only has value when accompanied by an understanding of its own pointlessness. 'The great deaths of literature are few, but they show us with an exemplary clarity the way in which art invigorates us by a juxtaposition, almost an identification, of pointlessness and value' (*SG* 87).

One philosopher commented on her ethic of 'cold impersonal love' that good old warm personal love was quite good enough for him, thank you very much, and this is a joke that she would, one feels, appreciate.[13] The ethic in other words stands in the same relation to the work as the other theorising – as an ideal limit in the direction of which the artist or moral agent is to be pulled, though neither can reach it. It is because she is generously unattached, even to her own dearest positions within the work, that the reader experiences so much freedom.

'We should always beware of doctrines of necessity that show us (with professions of regret) the eminently desirable, the good, as being, alas, the impossible'(sbr). The reader of the moral philosophy may at times feel that she has not escaped this danger herself; the reader of the novels feels it more rarely because even in her most misanthropic work she can call on her own acceptant, even-handed realism and simple sense of the fun to divert attention from any such profundities.

*

John Bayley has shown how much the 'realistic' novel owes to the Romantic Revival, in its desire to marry competing views of reality into a single vision of life.[14] In this century the urge to marry a materialistic view of life to a sense of value, to knit up fact and value, culture and spirit came under strain and Bloomsbury, as whose 'best heir' she has been (too limitingly, I think) seen,[15] chronicled the resulting tensions. Woolf criticised Forster for trying unsuccessfully to marry two kinds of writing where 'the conjunction of those two realities (poetic and material-ist) casts doubt on both';[16] and Forster in return wrote of Woolf as 'belonging to the world of poetry but fascinated by another world, she is always stretching out from her enchanted tree and snatching bits from the flux of daily life'.[17] Murdoch certainly shares with both an interest in the ways that love makes for wholeness of perception, wholeness of being, and in the failures of that love; and this too is of course a theme of Romantic humanism. I think she is a better novelist than either Forster or Woolf. She has a firmer grasp of human difference than Woolf, as well as a much fiercer sense of the dangers and urgencies of the moral life; and hers is, at its best, a larger, airier world than Forster's. She is also more interested in her subjects than either, and has a greater intellectual power and a greater scepticism about the aesthetic morality all three can seem at moments to share.[18] Nonetheless the problem for her too has presented itself, as 'Against Dryness' recorded, in similar terms: how to marry the inner and outer worlds, how to create fictions that honour both a strict causality and a strict sense of the privacy and 'freedom' that the moral agent may experience himself as endowed with.

*

Her two most recent novels make some play with this inheritance from earlier writers. *Nuns and Soldiers* is fed by Henry James' *The Wings of the Dove*, whose story of two impoverished outsiders plotting an opportunistic marriage it plays with and substantially alters, and whose famous final line ('We shall never be again as we were') it twice echoes. 'Stale sandwiches are delicious fried', the author parenthetically notes, as if jesting about such matters. It is a novel about a happy resolution of the Oedipus conflict, and mixes comedy and pain in a story that also recalls Petronius' widow of Ephesus, who fell in love by her first husband's tomb, and whose love and initiative saved her second husband's life. A single substitution here follows the multiple substitutions of *A Severed Head*, and the repercussions of this on a court of characters is explored in depth. There is a recession of worlds of will and of power that recalls the equally Jamesian *An Unofficial Rose*. A late chapter decentres the main characters and marvellously shows how, where they thought themselves freest, others too were, as James puts it, 'working' the situation. The perspective alters, as it can in life, and the sad and innocent Count, loud, good-hearted Daisy, virtuous yet censorious Anne, emotionally covetous Gertrude, change with it. There is a Homeric innocence about this Anglo-Jewish world and its hangers-on – there are allusions to the *Odyssey* too – that puzzles and pleases simultaneously.

I want to emphasise one Jamesian aspect. Murdoch has always shared with James an interest in the respective 'poetry' as well as the respective pain, of feeling yourself to be inside or outside society. The orphan Tim feels himself an outsider at the affluent flat of Guy and Gertrude Openshaw and when hungry has been known to raid the fridge. At the end he has married Gertrude and it will be the turn of others to raid the fridge. The dying Guy is one of those characters in Murdoch's world who act as guarantors of meaning, continuity and stability to those who surround him. He represses his own cruelty, and is generous financially, morally, emotionally, expecting a calm dignity in those to whose problems he patiently listens. In Murdoch's godless world such people shine out with something of the force that once accrued to the Church. For Tim, Guy's Ebury Street flat is an 'abode of value', and gives him a sense of family. Tim is calmer and more rational in his life, simply because of Guy's patient affection; for the Count too, Guy's existence guarantees stability and proof of meaning, and he finds a 'home' in the big flat.

To what degree are these values a function of money, as Tim at the end of the third section, when he hopes to enter a new life of virtue himself in Ebury Street, is to ponder? It is because of a candour about such things that her readers trust her. Iris Murdoch has noted the difficulty, when we admire Knightley in Jane Austen's *Emma*, of knowing whether we are not merely admiring the excellence – 'such as they are' – of the social arrangements he represents,[19] and has admitted the possibility that in the long run 'the virtues as we have known them will turn out to be something local, supported by temporary phenomena such as organised religions and hierarchical societies'(em). This is not a possibility that she welcomes, but in 'placing' her good characters as she does socially she seems to be making an ironic bow in the direction of this half-truth. The eccentric Bledyard went to Eton and is only once shown at ease, when he meets the School governors; James Arrowby went to Winchester, the patrician Brendan Craddock to Downside; only Tallis Browne of her saintly characters has a lowly background as child of a porter in an abattoir, and he seems unavailable as evidence through being 'the only real saint as it were, or symbolic good religious figure in the books' (Bigsby, 1982); we seem invited to put as much emphasis on the word 'symbolic' as on the word 'good'.

Does realism go with good birth, as Chips Lovell puts this in Anthony Powell's *At Lady Molly's*? It is not an unreasonable question, nor need it be a disequipping one. C. L. Barber has beautifully shown how in *Twelfth Night* Shakespeare celebrates the idea of heritage and creates in Sir Toby a character who has faith – 'the faith that goes with belonging'.[20] Murdoch has consistently taught us to ask both of moral philosophy and of literature the subversively simple Platonic question: what kind of good man are we here being asked to admire? In such characters as the Grays in *The Nice and the Good* who enjoy the 'deep superiority of the socially secure' and who use that confidence to make their courtiers happy and good, she seems to be having things – as great art can – both ways. The Grays are echoed in the many patrician couples in her books who reign with a sometimes predatory good will – the Tisbournes in *An Accidental Man*, Fosters in *A Fairly Honourable Defeat*, Impiatts in *A Word Child*. All are mildly progressive altruists; Hilda Foster is typical of the breed when she approves her husband's high-mindedly turning down his knighthood but has a sneaking regret since ' "Lady Foster" would have sounded rather well. I could have had some pink postcards printed with *From Lady Foster* on them' (*FHD* 27); Freddie Impiatt, half of another 'childless couple full of good works and enterprises' (*WC* 5) went to Eton where patriotism was regarded 'as bad form'. 'Eton is so bolshie', his wife jests, and Freddie, for all the Impiatt altruism, is soon heard comically declaiming 'I'm fed up with hearing the proles binding on about the price of meat' (*WC* 10). *A Word Child* is a book that uses the social hierarchy to act as a figure for metaphysical and even moral distance, but there is no sense here, any more than there was in *A Severed Head*, that the governing classes represent any spiritualised essence or special Platonic achievement. They just happen to be where they are, and make the best of it. Her Platonism is not merely an idealisation of class privilege. In the play *The Servants and the Snow* she accommodates political power to Eros and enslavement too; like personal power it is a trick by which both practitioner and victim are duped. Guy and Gertrude Openshaw are the most recent and worthiest in this series, yet, as the new light we gain on Gertrude at the end makes clear, her imperfections are seen justly and tolerantly by her author. Murdoch rarely idealises her characters, and the virtues they have, like the virtues of Jane Austen's characters, are shown to be continuous with their social context. She is not directly concerned to judge the system any more than was Austen; and yet there are judgements in both.[21]

The question might then be rephrased thus: given that a nobly unselfconscious virtue is hard to attain, is not a *secure* self-love, of all the possible styles of self-love, the ironic second-best in her world? If we cannot be saints, are we invited to become gentlemen?

Her work tells us quite as much about self-satisfaction as it does about virtue, and the man whose self-esteem has been destroyed is, again and again, shown – unless he be saintly – to have nothing to keep him from hell. Cato in *Henry and Cato*, Rupert in *A Fairly Honourable Defeat*, Harriet in *The Sacred and Profane Love Machine*: all of these lose their self-respect and are destroyed in the process. On the one hand, she points towards a 'higher' and more sublimated consciousness, associated with virtue. On the other, her plots are chronicles of desublimation and of the punishment and annihilation of puritans. The idea-play promotes a slow unselfing; the action warns against fast unselfing. She is merciless in exposing specious goods and specious virtues; and all virtue, in being compounded deeply of frailty, is partly specious. Though she draws very different conclusions from his, her world-view can look as bleak as Nietzsche's, once you probe beneath the comedy.

But it can also look very comic, despite the grimness, as I have emphasised throughout. One might see in her work some distant echo of Ford's and Waugh's saintly squires and T. S. Eliot's and Henry James's self-abnegating gentlefolk – British literature in this century has not lacked tributes to the character who must, as Edgar Wind noted, combine as a Platonic saint in one person the types of mystic and trimmer; and if self-effacement has always been the religion of the ruling-classes, it is not her chief purpose to remind us of the connexion.[22] Her moral heroes show a dislike of emotional intensity as English as the so-English lemony furniture polish they also employ; and we sense her ironic endorsement of this 'Englishness'.

*

The Philosopher's Pupil is not one of her more successful romances, but to the serious student of her work it is not the least interesting, and we may in any case be too close to judge it with any fairness. In *Henry and Cato* the dying Lucius ponders the gap between the joy of youth, of 'unsullied unpuzzled nature', and the joy sought by 'dirty old men in caves' (*HC* 386). *The Philosopher's Pupil* might be discussed as an extended debate about such romantic matters as this search for innocence, the nature of religion, morality, redemption, damnation. It feeds off Dostoevski's *The Brothers Karamazov*, with three brothers, one of whom – George – carries out a symbolic act of parricide in attacking his teacher Rozanov, the philosopher of the title. George is also compared with Hitler and is another example of a man whose loss of self-respect has accompanied his moral decline.

One reviewer noted that this is 'not a novel that values the experience it is made up of' and that the 'affection, happiness and wisdom' finally predicted for the characters Emma and Pearl are words that have been emptied of much meaning in the preceding 600 pages.[23] The older characters seem more awful than any she has created before, and the younger innocents – the foolish Tom, Hattie, Emma – by contrast, sentimentally drawn. Perhaps there is too much in this book; or perhaps – as with late work by, say, Titian or Verdi – this is simply a new kind of art. The delight of inventing a whole world has never been more palpable since *The Bell*; the water of the imaginary spa town in which it is set acts as a figure for unpurified Eros perhaps, and it is a much elaborated motif.

At the heart of the book the ageing philosopher who finds his task too hard, and the unbelieving priest with his 'paltry mind' discuss with an intense and purging scepticism some of the primary categories of Murdoch's belief. The priest Jacoby speaks first:

> 'I believe in a spiritual world as if it were very close to this one, as if it were . . . exactly the same and yet absolutely different.'
> 'You have an experience?'
> 'Not like a vision. More like a vibration.'
> 'Isn't that sex?'
> 'Well, isn't sex everywhere? Is it not an image of spirit, is it not spirit itself? Can spirit, our spirit and there is no other, ever rise so high that it leaves sex behind?'
> 'Death excludes sex. Its proximity kills desire. Wisdom is the practice of dying.'
> 'Surely sex as spirit embraces death too.'
> 'That old romantic stuff! I am surprised at you. Your spiritual sex is about suffering . . . .' (188)

Perhaps no recent novel has so demonstrated the continuity of romantic concerns into the present day as this one; or raised so insistently the ambiguity in the heart of our Romantic inheritance that if, twenty years ago, we tended to see Romanticism as a disease, we now increasingly realise that there may also be another Romanticism that needs the name of cure.²⁴

*

The Philosopher's Pupil may well be the untidiest book she has yet written. 'Art may glory in a lot of random, unintelligible stuff' Murdoch suggested to Magee, and in her vocabulary 'muddle' and 'jumble' are not necessarily pejorative terms. 'Even great art is jumble in the end'(*BP* 240). Only Lorna Sage among her critics has noted the fruitful central confusion this aesthetic of imperfection creates in her work. It makes, Sage argues, for fictions that console us by their 'energy and curiosity and continuance' rather than their 'shapeliness or writtenness or perfection';²⁵ It countenances 'casual signs of haste and writing by formula' and can have the effect of producing an 'emblematic blur in the middle distance' where the sense of depth of field is not destroyed but comes to seem 'too facilely achieved'.²⁶

It would be hard not to agree that such dangers attend her work, but the best work, I have argued, contrives to be both shapely *and* inquisitive, nonetheless, and to tread a cunning path between strict shapeliness and 'jumble'.

The critic Margaret Scanlan finds in Murdoch's work 'as radical a statement of original sin as can be found today';²⁷ while the *Times Literary Supplement* reviewer of *The Bell* wrote that, more than any other writer of her generation, 'Iris Murdoch presents life as worth living'.²⁸ These are not necessarily incompatible judgements: she has shown us that we are almost wholly dark to ourselves; but also that this truth can be invigorating. The conflict, if there is one, matters in the moral philosophy, but, so far as art is concerned, 'at an austere philosophy it can only mock'(*BP* 414). In her art these poles define between them an enabling environment in which her world can be peopled – and it is a densely populated world, full of memorable people and memorable *tableaux*. There is a Shakespearian generosity in her best work that opens a space for the reader to feel and reflect in, and turns him, while he is reading, into a poet and philosopher. At the end of *The Characters of Love* John Bayley speaks of the essential lightness and joy that attend the great and unself-important art of the past. 'The joy in Nature is a logical consequence of love, the logical consequence of the artist's feeling for the freedom of his creation: and joy is the follower and companion of freedom.' Iris Murdoch's novels abound in this unillusioned joy.

Appendix: 'Romanticism'

Hostile critics have sometimes used Murdoch's attacks on Romanticism in the early essays against her; and she has noted that 'philosophers attack their own faults' (*FS* 14). She is clearly indebted to the great tradition of Romantic humanism to which she is simultaneously so fierce a goad and sceptical a purifier. A division of her work into 'romantic' and 'unromantic' novels seems to me a futile proceeding; if Romanticism, with its wistfulness about instant redemptions, has in some sense never stopped, then the attempt to levitate out of it on the instant – as with Sartre's 'romantic rationalism' – is a foolish secondary symptom of the illness itself. Murdoch might be conceived as trying to rescue the objective idealism of the early Romantics from the subjective absolutism that can appear to characterise our legacy from later Romantics and Moderns; and in this sense we need an account of Romanticism that makes it seem, like Derrida's *pharmakon*, a cure as well as disease.

Using 'romantic' as a strictly neutral or exploratory term there are various distinctions in her work that are part of our general Romantic heritage. Her distinctions between a visionary imagination and a self-blinded fantasy recalls Coleridge's attack on the mechanical associationisms of fancy. The insistence that a knowledge of particularity must precede apprehension of the whole, that individuation must precede integration, the value placed on minute particulars, and the moral psychology that posits energy, vision, imagination, love and negative capability at its heart, recall the best of the Romantic Revival; the opposition between mechanical and vital, the nostalgia for a pure vision unmediated by theory, the view of man as moral pilgrim, the emphasis on the sublime, the dream of a trans-dualistic merging of mind and mind, or mind and world, and the metaphysical pathos or dark comedy that surrounds the failure of the attempt, the view of art as an impossible high calling involving repeated quest and failure, the fear of a 'dry' view of man bequeathed us by science, and the desire to make such a view subserve a humanist vocabulary – 'There are not two cultures. There is only one and words are its basis' (sw) – all this too is in the best sense part of our Romantic inheritance.

So, moreover, is the Romantic remedy of drawing the antidote to self-consciousness from consciousness itself. 'To explore the transition from self-consciousness to imagination, and achieve the transition while exploring it is the most crucial Romantic concern', argues Geoffrey Hartman. For Murdoch outward attention extinguishes self-consciousness and reveals the world, a process in which art can assist; for the Romantics the intelligence was a perverse if necessary specialisation of the soul and art was a means to resist the intelligence intelligently. The Romantic triad of Eden, Fall and Redemption is here echoed in the triad Nature, Self-consciousness and Imagination. Murdoch's work often militates against 'high-mindedness' in the name of a radical innocence, often figured by the animal or dog-world. 'To suffer like an animal. That would be god-like' (*IG* 77). Lovejoy has shown that the renascence of the sense of sin is one of the most evident of the 'Romanticisms' and Abrams pointed out how the resulting yearning for a renewed innocence puts faith in history under enormous strain. The continued trust in human aspirations to which no worldly object is adequate, together with a disbelief in the reality of any objects of human aspiration beyond those which fail to satisfy them, for Abrams, typifies Romantic *Sehnsucht*.

In drawing these lines of filiation I am not trying to collapse Iris Murdoch's achievement back into any suppositious source. Malcolm Bradbury has pointed out that hers is a modified Romanticism whose end is human renewal itself, a rebirth of a sense of the world's wonder, and a reawakening of the possibility of change; and this artist's job of 'making people pay attention' (Rose, 1982) is, surely, a perennial one; and also one shared by many of her contemporaries. It is also an aim of the Buddhism she admires. See: Peter Kemp, 'The fight against fantasy', *Modern Fiction Studies*, xv, no. 3 (Aug. 1969) 403–15; Gabriel Pearson, 'Iris Murdoch and the Romantic Novel', *New Left Review*, xiii–xiv (Jan–April 1962), 137–45; John Bayley, *Romantic Survival* (London, 1957); J. Derrida, 'Plato's pharmacy' in B. Johnson, (trans), *Dissemination* (London and Chicago, 1981) (referred to in *FS* 31); Malcolm Bradbury, 'The Romantic Miss Murdoch', *Spectator*, 3 Sep. 1965, 293; David Newsome, *Two Classes of Men:*

'*Platonism and English Romantic Thought* (London, 1972); Geoffrey Hartman, 'Romanticism and "Anti-Self-Consciousness" ', *Centennial Review*, VI (1962), 553–65; M. H. Abrams, *Natural Supernaturalism* (Toronto, 1971); T. E. Hulme, in H. Read (ed.), 'Romanticism and Classicism' in *Speculations* (London, 1936); D. T. Suzuki, *Studies in Zen* (1955); John Blofield, *The Way of Power* (London, 1970); and D. Majdiak, 'Romanticism in the Aesthetics of Iris Murdoch', *Texas Studies in Literature and Language*, XIV, no. 2 (1972) 359–75.

Notes

CHAPTER 1: INTRODUCTION: 'EXISTENTIALIST AND MYSTIC'

1. The phrase is Lorna Sage's in 'No Trespassers' (review of *FS*) in *New Review*, Sep. 1977, 49–50.
2. In a letter to me Miss Murdoch has indicated that she finds the description of her work as 'romance' perfectly acceptable. So far as the related concept of 'romanticism' is concerned, she would prefer that the idea be explored as it is in relation to Shakespeare's 'romantic' comedies. Speaking to Bryden (*Listener*, 4 Apr. 1968, 432–6) she acknowledged that the patterns holding up the structure of her work were 'sexual, mythological, psychological and not the great hub of society which a 19th-century writer relied on'.
3. See Northrop Frye, *The Secular Scripture: A Study of the Structure of Romance* (Cambridge, Mass., and London, 1976) and Gillian Beer, *Romance* (London, 1970) for useful discussions of Romance.
4. Her characters are not infrequently opera-goers and the operas are often chosen to comment wryly and momentarily on their predicament. Martin in *A Severed Head* finds that his wife and her lover have gone to *Götterdämmerung* at a point when he too, like mankind in that opera, might reasonably hope for some apocalyptic liberation from the realm of the mythic; Bradley Pearson in *The Black Prince* declares his love by rushing out of *Rosenkavalier* and vomiting over some peaches outside. As he dies at the end he asks his mentor what happened to the Marschallin and finds that she, too, was rejected by her younger lover. 'Well that was right wasn't it.' And in *Nuns and Soldiers* the opera tickets that change hands so freely among the subsidiary characters – the chorus – are both a caste-mark and also point to the operatic realism that Murdoch has so singularly made her own. Other operatic (or romance-like) features would include the eavesdroppings, physical concealments and voyeurisms, discovered and stolen letters, incest, the supernatural, the instantaneous loves, sense of spectacle, precipitate reversals, and the persecuted maidens in their remote enclosures.

5. Nicholas Mosley, 'The Philosopher Fails – The Artist Succeeds' in the *Listener*, 28 Apr. 1983, 19–20.

6. As Lorna Sage put this in 'Female Fictions', in M. Bradbury and D. Palmer (eds), *The Contemporary English Novel* (London, 1979) pp. 67–87.

7. H. A. Taine, 'Charles Dickens, son talent es ses oeuvres', *Revue des Deux mondes*, February 1856, later incorporated into his *History of English Literature*, bk 5, ch. 1, and collected in Stephen Wall (ed.), *Charles Dickens* (Penguin Critical Anthologies) (London. 1970) p. 103.

8. John Bayley discusses how the message gets dissolved in its 'purr of beatitude' in 'Under Cover of Decadence', in P. Quennell (ed.), *Nabokov, A Tribute* (London, 1979) pp. 42–58.

9. In a review of De Beauvoir's *Ethics of Ambiguity*, in *Mind*, LIX (1950) 127–8. For a different view of her relations with Sartre from mine, see B. Obumselu, 'Iris Murdoch and Sartre', *ELH*, XLII (Summer 1975) 296–317.

10. 'Existentialist Bite', in *Spectator*, 12 July 1957, 68–9.

11. See Marilyn Butler, *Jane Austen and the War of Ideas* (London, 1975) and Angus Wilson, 'Evil in the English Novel', *Kenyon Review*, 29 (Mar. 1967), 167–93, and *Listener*, 27 Dec. 1962–17 Jan. 1963, collected in K. McSweeney (ed.), *Diversity and Depth in Fiction* (London, 1983) pp. 3–24, for general discussion of this theme.

12. 'Full Circle' (letter), *New Statesman*, 3 May 1941.

13. 'Midnight Hour', *Adelphi*, Jan.–Mar. 1943, 60–1; 'Rebirth of Christianity', *Adelphi*, July–Sep. 1943, 125–6; 'Worship and Common Life', *Adelphi*, July–Sep. 1944, 134–5.

14. 'Iris Murdoch', entry in Jay L. Halio (ed.), *Dictionary of Literary Biography*, vol. 14 (*British Novelists since 1960*), pt 2 (Gale Research, Detroit, 1983) pp. 546–61.

15. This account is conflated from three interviews she gave: with Ruth Heyd, *University of Windsor Review*, XXX (1965) 61–82; with M. Bellamy, *Contemporary Literature*, XVIII (1977) 129–40; and M. Bradbury, 27 Feb. 1976, British Council tape no. RS 2001.

16. See, for example, 'The Moral Decision about Homosexuality', *Man and Society*, 7 (1964) 3–7; 'Political Morality', *Listener*, 21 Sep. 1967, 353–4; Contribution to C. Woolf and J. Bagguley (eds), *Authors Take Sides on Vietnam* (London, 1967) p. 40; and 'Socialism and Selection', in C. B. Cox and R. Boyson (eds), *Black Paper 3* (London, 1975) 7–9. Speaking to Bradbury (see n. 15) she said that leaving aside an openly political novel like *The Red and the Green*, most of the novels 'contain quite a lot of criticism of society. Things about work . . . about the struggle between different age groups, things about class, things about money and work . . . I think there is a lot of social comment in my own work.'

17. D. Lodge, *The Modes of Modern Writing: Metaphor, Metonymy, and the Typology of Modern Literature* (London, 1977); and 'Historicism and Literary History', *New Literary History*, x (Spring 1979) 3, 547–55.
18. Anon, *Bookman*, Nov. 1958, 26. The terms 'open' and 'closed' were reversed in the interview; this appears to have been an error.
19. 'A Jewelled Occasion', *The Sunday Times*, 19 Jan. 1964, and 'Important Things', *The Sunday Times*, 17 Feb. 1957, reprinted in *Encore* (London, 1963) pp. 299–301.
20. See Butler, *Jane Austen and the War of Ideas*, and also in *Romantics, Rebels and Reactionaries* (Oxford, 1981); and Gerald Graff, 'The Pseudo-Politics of Interpretation', *Critical Inquiry*, ix, no. 3 (Mar. 1983) 597–610.

CHAPTER 2: *Under the Net* AND THE REDEMPTION OF PARTICULARS

1. See A. S. Byatt, *Degrees of Freedom* (London, 1965) ch.2; Frank Baldanza, *Iris Murdoch* (New York, 1974) ch.2; and R. Todd, *Iris Murdoch* (London, 1984) ch.2.
2. John Bayley, *The Characters of Love* (London, 1960) p. 290.
3. As William Hall has excellently shown in ' "The Third Way": The Novels of Iris Murdoch' in *Dalhousie Review*, 46 (Aut. 1966) 306–18: Hall points out that accounts of her work that do not give a prime place to the comedy risk some grotesque distortions.
4. See John Bayley's, 'Character and Consciousness', in *New Literary History*, v(Winter/2, 1975) 225–35 for a discussion of this legacy.
5. In a letter to Körner of 1 Dec. 1788; see F. Schiller's *On the Aesthetic Education of Man* (trans. and eds E. Wilkinson and L. Willoughby) (Oxford, 1967) pp. 292–3.
6. F. Baldanza, *Iris Murdoch* (New York, 1974) p. 37.
7. A. S. Byatt, *Degrees of Freedom: The Novels of Iris Murdoch* (London, 1965) p. 39.
8. P. Swinden, *Unofficial Selves* (London, 1973) p. 238, links him with pataphysics; Baldanza, *Iris Murdoch*, p. 36 with existentialism; the Wittgenstein comparison is ubiquitous.
9. David Holloway, review of *PP* in *Daily Telegraph*, 28 Apr. 1983, 14.
10. See Rubin Rabinowitz, *Iris Murdoch* (New York, 1968), repr. in G. Stade (ed.), *Six Contemporary British Novelists* (New York, 1976) p. 279.
11. Unpublished interview with Miss Murdoch by the author, Nov. 1983.
12. Bayley, *Romantic Survival* (London, 1957), *passim*. Northrop Frye has defined the romantic picturesque as the alienated seen as happy, and the cult of the exotic as the unfamiliar seen as pleasurable – *A*

Study of English Romanticism (1983) p.29; this is strikingly apt for Murdoch. See also the Appendix (p. 272).

13. She spoke of herself as 'poet *manqué*' to Bigsby in H. Ziegler and C. Bigsby (eds), *The Radical Imagination and the Liberal Tradition* (London, 1982) p. 217; as an 'engineer *manqué*' in the BBC Radio 3 programme 'Novels up to Now' broadcast 1 Aug. 1981. While such enthusiasms are being chronicled it should be added that to John Haffenden, in *Literary Review*, LVIII (Apr. 1983) 31–5, she acknowledged that she would also much have liked to have pursued a career as a Renaissance art historian, and as a painter: she paints as a hobby; the novels are both intensely visual, and '*seen*', and make much play with themes from Renaissance painting.

14. G. Beer, *Darwin's Plots* (London, 1983) pp. 40–3 ff.

15. Viktor Shklovski, 'Art as Technique', in L. Lemon and M. Reis, *Russian Formalist Criticism* (Nebraska, 1965) pp. 3–24.

16. Margaret Weldhen, 'Morality and the Metaphor', *New Universities Quarterly*, Spring 1980, 214–28.

17. Cited by Denis Donaghue, 'Mediate and Immediate', in *The Times Literary Supplement*, 3832, 22 Aug. 1975, 934–5.

18. Byatt, *Degrees of Freedom*, p. 38; M. Bradbury, 'Iris Murdoch's *Under the Net*', *Critical Quarterly*, Spring 1962, 47–54; it should be added in fairness that Bradbury finds the terms in which the crisis is rendered unsatisfactory. My suggestion would be that the 'unclear-ness' here, even in the first book, has to do with Murdoch's desire to show us that while moral change can occur, 'final truth' cannot be reached.

19. 'Novels up to Now' (see n.12), and 'M. Bradbury and L. Sage Interview Iris Murdoch', University of East Anglia Interviews, 20 Oct. 1976, unpublished, respectively.

CHAPTER 3: 'AGAINST GRAVITY': THE EARLY NOVELS AND *An Accidental Man*

1. M. Bradbury, ' "A House Fit for Free Characters": Iris Murdoch and *Under the Net*', pp. 231–46 in *Possibilities: Essays on the State of the Novel* (London, 1973).

2. Byatt, *Degrees of Freedom*, pp. 40–60.

3. Lionel Trilling, *The Liberal Imagination* (London, 1961) p. 221.

4. Byatt, *Degrees of Freedom*.

5. John Bayley, *The Uses of Division* (London, 1976) p. 18.

6. S. Weil, *Waiting on God* (trans. Emma Crauford) (London, 1959) p. 114.

7. Ibid., p. 115.

8. Baldanza, *Iris Murdoch*, p. 51.
9. Byatt, *Degrees of Freedom*, pp. 122 ff.
10. John Bayley, *Tolstoi and the Novel* (London, 1966).
11. E. Dipple, *Iris Murdoch: Work for the Spirit* (London, 1982) pp. 166, 349, *et passim*.
12. L. Sage, 'The Pursuit of Imperfection', *Critical Quarterly*, XIX, no.2 (Summer 1977) 67–87.
13. Bayley, *Division*, 84ff.
14. Radio 4, 'Interview with Iris Murdoch', for *Weekend* broadcast 18 Apr. 1982. See also Anon, 'Interview with Iris Murdoch', *Vogue* (American ed.), Mar. 1981, 329, 367.
15. Bayley, *Tolstoi*, p. 220.
16. S. Weil, *Need for Roots* (trans. A. F. Wills) (London, 1952) p. 114.

CHAPTER 4: EROS IN *A Severed Head* AND *Bruno's Dream*

1. Sage, 'Female Fictions', p. 72.
2. H. G. Gadamer, *Dialogue and Dialectic: Eight Hermeneutical Studies on Plato* (trans. P. C. Smith) (New Haven and London, 1980).
3. David Newsome, in *Two Classes of Men: Platonism and English Romantic Thought* (London, 1972) p. 13, points out that Platonism was in some sense the 'life-blood of Romanticism'. Pater's quarrel with Coleridge is discussed in Nathan A. Scott, Jr., 'Pater's Imperative – To Dwell Poetically', in *New Literary History*, XV (Aut. 1983) 1,93–115. The quotation from Pater comes from his *Plato and Platonism* (London, 1910) p. 195.
4. Julia Kristeva, *Desire in Language* (trans. L. Roudiez *et al.*) (Oxford, 1980) pp. 80ff.; G. S. Morson, 'Who Speaks for Bakhtin', *Critical Inquiry*, 10,2 (Dec. 1983) 225–44; Mikhail Bakhtin's *Problems of Dostoevsky's Poetics*, trans. and ed. C. Emerson, as vol. VIII in the 'Theory and History of Literature Series' (Manchester, 1984).
5. 'Force Fields' (review of A. S. Byatt's *The Virgin in the Garden*), in *New Statesman*, 3 Nov. 1978, 586.
6. Norman Vance discusses this in 'Iris Murdoch's Serious Fun', *Theology*, Nov. 1981, 420–8.
7. Bayley, *Romantic Survival*, p. 27.
8. See Terry Eagleton, 'John Bayley, Critic', in *New Left Review*, 110 (July–Aug. 1978), 29–40, for a Marxist account of this view of literary history.
9. In her interview at Caen, Murdoch said that Freud 'thinks that one must live in the ego and I wouldn't accept this, I would regard the ego as continuing into the superego and in a Platonic sense I think this is very good human psychology though not necessarily

good as therapy.' In interview with Rose she noted both how basic the Oedipus myth was to *The Italian Girl* – but also added that 'I'm not Freudian. I think Freud discovered a lot of things but I think that this whole business of sexuality and spirituality is very hard to understand'; and to her Russian translator Ivasheva she noted, crucially, 'Really I think I am in many ways anti-Freud. (I think love *transcends* sex in a way F. might not recognise).' She referred to it again in 'A Note on Drama', *Cue*, Sep. 1970, 13–40. I have explored Miss Murdoch's concept of Eros at greater length in 'Iris Murdoch and the Purification of Eros' (PhD thesis, London, 1984) from which some of the material in the present chapter is drawn.

10. L. Sage, 'The Pursuit of Imperfection', *Critical Quarterly*, xix, no. 2 (Summer 1977) 62ff.

11. S. Kierkegaard, *Repetition* (1843), cited in G. Josipovici, *The World and the Book* (St Albans, 1973) 327n.

12. Edmund Leach, *Lévi-Strauss* (London, 1970) ch 7.

13. Frye, *Secular Scripture*, p. 137.

14. George Steiner, in *Tolstoi or Dostoievski* (London, 1967) p. 204, points out that father–daughter incest fascinated Shelley, Landor, Swinburne, Hawthorne and Melville.

15. Lodge, *Modes of Modern Writing*, *passim*.

16. As early as *Under the Net*, Anna, perhaps quoting Hugo, tells Jake that 'Unsatisfied love is concerned with understanding. Only if it is all, all understanding, can it remain love while being unsatisfied'(40) – this is in a sense the message of *Symposium* and *Phaedrus*. Moreover early drafts of the novels at Iowa endorse the view that the Platonic Eros is a central concern. When at the start of *Under the Net* where Jake in the published text says that unlike Finn who has 'no inner life' he, Jake, would be thinking about 'freedom art, immortality', a verso note gives the alternative 'I would be thinking about love, art, death'; and Lefty in the Skinner's Arms refers familiarly to the *Theaetetus*; and when in *The Flight from the Enchanter* (written before the publication of *Under the Net*) Anna explains to her headmistress that she is leaving the school, an early draft makes her add 'to learn about things in philosophy, about goodness, about love'.

17. Bayley, *Characters of Love*, p. 5.

18. F. M. Cornford, *The Unwritten Philosophy* (Cambridge, 1950) p. 78.

19. Sage, 'The Pursuit of Imperfection', p. 63.

20 Sage, 'Female Fictions', p. 72.

21. Malcolm Bradbury first suggested this in *Possibilities*, p. 54. It should be added that in interview with Jack Biles (1978) Murdoch said 'By the way, there's nothing in that Lynch-Gibbon idea.'

22. F. Baldanza, 'The Manuscripts of Iris Murdoch's *A Severed Head*', *Modern Fiction Studies*, xv, no.3 (Aut. 1969) 417–28.

23. Edgar Wind, 'Amor as God of Death', in *Pagan Mysteries in the Renaissance* (London, 1958) ch.10, pp. 152–70. This book throws light on a number of Murdoch themes.

24. F. Kermode, 'Necessary Persons', review of *BD* in the *Listener*, 16 Jan. 1969, 84–5. It might be pointed out that Kermode, who makes some fun out of the novel's references to 'necessary' (presumably as opposed to 'contingent') persons, fails to observe that it is, in every case, *the artist Miles* who so classifies people; and that his is scarcely a voice the author asks us to endorse unquestioningly; any more than we endorse Jake's division of his world into 'necessary' and 'contingent' geography, which is ironised by Hugo's Nottingham address.

25. David Marquand, 'Anti-hedonism' in *London Review of Books*, 30 Sep.–3 Oct. 1984, 6.

26. F. Kermode, 'Necessary Persons'.

CHAPTER 5: THE SUBLIME in *The Bell* AND *The Unicorn*

1. Diogenes Allen, 'Two Experiences of Existence: Jean-Paul Sartre and Iris Murdoch', *International Philosophical Quarterly*, June 1974, pp. 181–7.

2. 'Novels up to Now' (Chapter 2, n.12) and UEA interview (Chapter 2, n.18).

3. A. S. Byatt, *Iris Murdoch* (London, 1976) p. 28.

4. 'On the Crest of a Wave', interview with P. Lewis, *Daily Mail*, 23 Nov. 1978. In the *Observer*, 26 Nov. 1978, Derwent May noted Miss Murdoch's 'stern and handsome bust of Poseidon' presiding over a water-tank for swimming in.

5. Anon (1981); see Chapter 3, n.14. See also Chapter 10.

6. Thomas Weiskel, *The Romantic Sublime: Studies in the Structure of Transcendance* (London and Maryland, 1976).

7. Paul Friedlaender, *Plato* (trans. H. Meyerhoff) vol. I (London, 1958) p. 146.

8. Samuel Monck, *The Sublime* (Ann Arbor, 1962).

9. Anon, *The Times Literary Supplement*, 16 June 1961, 9. In Longinus' *Sublime* the reader is 'scorched, *inundated*, blown down' (15.2) (my emphasis).

10. S. Weil, *Notebooks* (trans. A. F. Wills) (London, 1956) p. 384.

11. Notable exceptions were Peter Hebblethwaite in *The Month*, Oct. 1963, Christopher Derrick in *The Tablet*, 14 Sep. 1963, and Malcolm Bradbury in *Spectator*, 6 Sep. 1963. Most reviewers treated this book and *The Time of the Angels* as diseased attempts at Tolstoian realism.

12. *Listener*, 31 Dec. 1981, 817.
13. Trilling, *Liberal Imagination* (London, 1961) pp. 205–22.
14. As H. German pointed out, 'Allusion in the Early Novels of Iris Murdoch', *Modern Fiction Studies*, xv, no.2 (Aut. 1969) 361–77.
15. Dan Jacobson, 'Farce, Totem and Taboo', *New Statesman*, 16 June 1961, 956–7.
16. Philip Rieff, *The Triumph of the Therapeutic* (London, 1966) p. 4.
17. Frank Kermode, in 'The Novels of Iris Murdoch', *Spectator*, 17 Nov. 1958, describes Michael as an 'accumulator of disasters'.
18. *Listener* (see n.12).
19. I owe this anagram to Robert Scholes, *Fabulation and Metafiction* (Urbana and London, 1979), which contains a useful discussion of *The Unicorn*. Scholes sees the work as allegorical but misses the fact that the novel is by a Platonist. Effingham's moments of ascesis are dismissed, the sea of self-extinction, as Bradbury called it (see n.11), Max's philosophy, and the connexions between these, are all left out of account.
20. Scholes, *Fabulation and Metafiction*, pp. 64ff.
21. A. S. Byatt, in *Iris Murdoch*, does not, I think, give full weight to the fact that Murdoch's description of sado-masochistic relations between good and bad selves is intended as an image of ordinary everyday moral temporising and time-serving, rather than being a specialised ethical perversity. The concept borrows, incidentally, from Freud's *Civilisation and its Discontents* (London, 1930) p. 73, where Freud describes relations between a masochistic ego and a sadistic superego.
22. John Bayley, 'Larkin and the Modern Tradition', *Critical Quarterly*, 26, nos 1 & 2 (Spring and Summer 1984) 61–6.
23. As Malcolm Bradbury pointed out in *Possibilities*, p. 268.
24. R. T. Wallis, *Neoplatonism* (London, 1972) p. 61.
25. C. S Lewis, *The Allegory of Love* (New York, 1958) p. 44.
26. Wind, *Pagan Mysteries*, pp. 133ff.

CHAPTER 6: SELF-SUFFICIENCY IN *The Time of the Angels* AND *The Nice and the Good*

1. Mircea Eliade, *The Sacred and the Profane* (New York, 1961) p. 33.
2. Ibid., p. 24.
3. Edmund Burke, *A Philosophical Enquiry into the Origins of the Sublime and the Beautiful* (ii, sec. vii).
4. Angus Fletcher, *Allegory* (Cornell, 1964) p. 253.
5. As Dipple points out, *Work*, pp. 69ff.
6. In the 1982 Gifford Lectures Heidegger featured as a more

sympathetic figure and with due regard for his own interest in the
religious.

7. As Frank Baldanza points out in 'The Nice and the Good', *Modern
   Fiction Studies*, xv, no.3 (Aut. 1969) 417–28. Baldanza also points
   out the connexion between this and the preceding novel.
8. See, for example, R. Todd, *Iris Murdoch: The Shakespearian Interest*
   (London and New York, 1979).
9. 'Premium Books', in *New Fiction Society*, i (Oct. 1974) 8.
10. Bayley, *Tolstoi*, pp. 52ff.
11. See Erwin Panofsky, *Studies in Iconology* (1972) 87 for a useful
    discussion of this painting; and see Wind, *Pagan Mysteries*, ch. v,
    'Virtue Reconciled with Pleasure'.
12. *Philebus* 21DE, *Phaedo* 82AB; and see E. R. Dodds, *The Greeks and
    the Irrational* (London, 1951) p. 211.
13. A. S. Byatt, 'Kiss and Make Up', *New Statesman*, 26 Jan. 1968, 113–
    14.
14. Sage, 'The Pursuit of Imperfection', p. 64.
15. 'Characters in Love', *The Times Literary Supplement*, 25 Jan. 1968.

CHAPTER 7: *A Fairly Honourable Defeat*

1. Bradbury, *Possibilities*, p. 237.
2. Ann Wordsworth, in R. Young (ed.), *Untying the Text* (Boston and
   London, 1981): 'An Art That Will Not Abandon the Self to
   Language: Bloom, Tennyson and the Blind World of the Wish', pp.
   189–206.
3. Murdoch discussed this structure at Caen (1978) and with Bellamy
   (1977).
4. Swinden, *Unofficial Selves*, p. 253.
5. Northrop Frye, *A Natural Perspective* (London, 1973) p. 253. Iowa
   notes show Murdoch hesitating between *Don Giovanni* and *Fidelio*
   before choosing the former for Chapter 2, and hesitating between
   The Abduction from the Seraglio, *Fidelio*, and *Figaro* before settling for
   the second of these for Chapter 6. See also Chapter 1, n.4.
6. Wind, *Pagan Mysteries*, p. 115n.
7. D. H. Lawrence, Preface to *The Grand Inquisitor* (trans. Koteliansky)
   (London, 1930), collected in A. Beal (ed.) *Selected Literary Criticism*
   (New York, 1961) pp. 223–41.
8. Dipple, *Work*, p. 184, argues, for example, that despite two moments
   of moral vigour Tallis' goodness is defined by an attitude of 'generous
   waiting'.
9. For an account of the alternation of these moods in the annals of
   'metaphysical passion', see A. D. Nuttall's *Two Concepts of Allegory*

(London, 1967) pp. 120ff., a work which began as a B. Litt. thesis partly supervised by Miss Murdoch.

CHAPTER 8: *The Black Prince*

1. John Bayley, 'Character and Consciousness', *New Literary History*, v (Winter, 1974) 225–35.
2. Both A. S. Byatt, 'People in Paper Houses: Attitudes to "Realism" and Experiment in English Postwar Fiction', and L. Sage, 'Female Fictions' are in M. Bradbury and D. Palmer (eds), *The Contemporary English Novel* (London, 1979) pp. 19–41 and 66–87 respectively. Richard Todd, 'The Plausibility of *The Black Prince*', in *Dutch Quarterly Review*, XIII (1978/2) 82–93.
3. Wind, *Pagan Mysteries*, pp. 17ff.
4. As Anthony Quinton first pointed out in his review, 'Slings and Arrows', *Sunday Telegraph*, 25 Feb. 1973.
5. G. Pearson, 'Simultaneous and Quadratic', *Guardian*, 22 Feb. 1973.
6. Murdoch recounted at Caen (1978, p. 78) how she asked a friend to draw a head of the statue of Apollo at Olympia, but that, despite this picture of Apollo on the front of the book, British reviewers failed to understand Loxias' identity as Apollo. He is named as Luxius and 'Lycean' in Sophocles' *Oedipus Rex*, for example.
7. Wind, *Pagan Mysteries*, ch. XI, 'The Flaying of Marsyas', pp. 173ff.
8. Dipple, *Work*, p. 43. References to conversation with the author refer to an unpublished interview conducted in November 1983.
9. The same point is made at *SG* 103. In a letter to me Miss Murdoch has denied that Bradley's Christian name was intended to provoke a recall of either F. H. or A. C. Bradley. In interview with Jack Biles she acknowledged a private origin for his surname. 'I don't type, so I send all my material long-hand to a typist – and in this [philosophical] piece I constantly used the word "Reason" with a capital *R* . . . . The typist misread this on each occasion as "Pearson"! With extremely comical results, as you can imagine!'; earlier she said 'Bradley is a good name' and suggested a distant connexion, 'although the characters are totally different' with Bradley Headstone in Dickens' *Our Mutual Friend*.
10. *Treasure Island* was the first book Murdoch was aware of and she rereads it at intervals. See F. Raphael (ed.), *Bookmarks* (London, 1975) p. 125.
11. Pearson, 'Simultaneous and Quadratic'.
12. Byatt, 'People in Paper Houses'.
13. P. Ricoeur, *Freud and Philosophy* (New Haven and London, 1970) p. 47.

14. Ibid.
15. Todd, *Iris Murdoch: The Shakespearian Interest.*
16. E. Jones, *Hamlet and Oedipus* (London, 1949).
17. Freud discussed a female 'Oedipus complex' analagous to the male one. 'Things happen in just the same way with little girls, with the necessary changes: an affectionate attachment to her father, a need to get rid of her mother as superfluous', *The Penguin Freud Library*, vol. 1 (1976) p. 376. See also vol. 7 (1977) p. 327.
18. The draft for the novel at Iowa has a verso note by Miss Murdoch on Julian's last letter to Bradley: 'Love for Arnold dominates Julian's letter to Bradley.'
19. Frye, *A Natural Perspective* (1965) p. 38.
20. R. Todd, 'The Plausibility of *The Black Prince*', *Dutch Quarterly*, 1978/ 2, 82–93.
21. R. Todd, *Iris Murdoch: The Shakespearian Interest*, pp. 76. Her sympathy towards and understanding of every form of sexual expression is obvious throughout her work; the real human problems remain, whatever your sexual temperament. In *A Fairly Honourable Defeat* Simon and Axel's relationship is not merely (finally) the stablest in the book but the only one left standing at the end.
22. L. Trilling, *Beyond Culture* (London, 1967) p. 34.

CHAPTER 9: *The Sacred and Profane Love Machine* AND *Henry and Cato*

1. Barbara Johnson has argued that Platonism can be seen as 'another name for the history of a strongly stressed metaphysical binarity', in her translation of J. Derrida's *Dissemination* (London and Chicago, 1981) p. xxiv. Speaking on 'Now Read On', 27 Nov. 1971, on Radio 4, Murdoch suggested that 'Very often I find two characters coalesce into one . . . . Sometimes one does the other thing; one divides a character into two separate people and sets them going in opposite directions as it were.'
2. My account draws on E. Panofsky's *Studies in Iconology* (1972) pp. 150ff.
3. Ibid.
4. F. Dillistone, 'Christ and Myth' (interview with Iris Murdoch) *Frontier*, Aut. 1965, 219–21.
5. *Letters of Marsilio Ficino* (London, 1981), Liber IV, no. 26; vol. III, p. 55.
6. As A. S. Byatt pointed out on 'Critic's Forum', Radio 3, 11 Dec. 1976.
7. 'Negative (mystical) theology requires the abandonment and

indifference towards every explanation and discourse. In the cessation of all discourse this denial makes possible unity with nothing . . . ', John Jones (ed.), *The Divine Names and Mystical Theology* (Milwaukee, 1980) p. 5. See also Evelyn Underhill's discussion of 'ecstatic deprivation . . . emptiness . . . divine dark' in her *Mysticism* (London, 1930) p. 318.

8. Sage, 'Pursuit of Imperfection', p. 63. 'In being stuck with an unwanted icon he finally shares the fate of Henry, after all the contrasts.'

CHAPTER 10: *The Sea, The Sea*

1. In *An Accidental Man* Matthew is pursued by Gracie to the Peter Pan statue in Kensington Gardens; much of the action of *A Word Child* takes place near the statue, and the play is to be performed as an office pantomime. Rachel compares Bradley to Peter Pan in *The Black Prince*. It is a favourite play of Charles Arrowby's. At Caen, Murdoch commented at length on her interest in the play: 'It's a play about the subconscious mind and one's relationship to it.' Peter Pan figures throughout, also, for an immature spirituality.
2. As Dipple, *Work*, p. 116, points out.
3. M. Bradbury, 'The Semi-Isle', *New Statesman*, 25 Aug. 1978, 10; G. Annan, 'Murdoch Magic', *Listener*, 23 Aug. 1978, 250.
4. John Bayley's *Romantic Survival*, pp. 116–17, contains useful discussion of the poem.
5. 'Good, Evil and Morality', discussion between Iris Murdoch and Father Martin Jarrett-Kerr, *CR: Quarterly Review of the Community of the Resurrection*, no. 266 (Michaelmas 1969) 17–23.
6. Kaleidoscope, 22 Nov. 1978, Radio 4.
7. Speaking to Bigsby (1982), Murdoch said 'James has always been in love with Charles and this he more or less says at one point', adding that this was why James returned to see Charles, to release himself from his attachment. He fears that the feat of raising Charles will have enmeshed him once more but finds that the magic has 'broken its own spell or that he is going to be let off'.
8. See, for example, John Blofield, *The Way of Power* (London, 1970).
9. Angus Wilson calls it 'probably Kipling's most important book . . . one of the most remarkable novels in English', *Diversity and Depth* (London, 1983) pp. 108ff.
10. Speaking to Bigsby (1982), Murdoch suggested that 'I think paranormal things probably do happen, particularly in Tibet . . . . The reader has to lend credulity to the writer I think in a quite harmless sense, about [James] pulling him out of that pool and so

forth.' The 'tulpa' mistaken by Charles in James's flat as 'some sort of inferior tribesman I suppose' (446) is a psychological projection of a lama magically actualised for good purposes. It extends the themes of magic, religion, and the 'reality' of projections, since (see A. David-Neel, *Magic and Mystery in Tibet*) the 'tulpa' may be hard to dissolve.

11. 'The Statesman's Manual', in K. Coburn (ed.), *Collected Works of S. T. Coleridge*, vol. vi (London, 1967) p. 30.

12. I have discussed this in *John Fowles* (London, 1982).

13. The ontological proof has deep roots in Murdoch's thought. 'Plato's main idea' (*FS* 34), it is discussed at *SG* 55, 61, 63, and recurs as I noted in Chapter 4 in the novels. It is related to the inner world of faith, grace, belief, the rewards for moral assent and the ways these help create the world in which we make choices, 'The only proof of God is the ontological proof, and that is a mystery. Only the spiritual man may give himself to it in silence' (*U* 100) says the spiritual Max in *The Unicorn* to Effingham who, in the last chapter realises that 'the vision of the good forced into being as the object of desire' (268) he would leave to Max: he is too small for it. In many novels someone adverts to it. In *The Sacred and Profane Love Machine* Edgar says 'If it's true love it contains its object. There's proof of God's existence like that'(118). In *Nuns and Soldiers* Anne ponders 'Could she live now by the ontological proof alone? Can love, in its last extremity, create its object?'(62). One of Murdoch's 1982 Gifford lectures was devoted to a demonstration of how the proof might work, not for God but for Good; and in *The Philosopher's Pupil*, which satirises so many of its author's most cherished beliefs, it is derided: 'It's all done with mirrors like the Ontological Proof.... You can't have a real [response] so you fake one, like sending a letter to yourself'(192).

14. Longinus, *Peri Hypsous* 15.2, cited in Weiskel, *Romantic Sublime*, p. 5.

15. 'Novels up to Now', Radio 4, broadcast 1 Aug. 1981. See also Chapter 5 for discussion of this theme.

16. 'Crest of a Wave', *Daily Mail*, 23 Nov. 1978. See also Chapter 5.

17. In 'Existentialists and Mystics', in W. Robson (ed.), *Essays and Poems Presented to Lord David Cecil* (London, 1970), Murdoch questions the role of participatory theatre.

CHAPTER 11: CONCLUSION: *Nuns and Soldiers* AND *The Philosopher's Pupil*

1. To be fair to Linda Kuehl, in 'Iris Murdoch: the Novelist as

Magician/The Magician as Artist', in *Modern Fiction Studies*, xv, no.3 (Aut. 1969) 347–60, her point is that Murdoch's characters could possibly exist in Huxley's world but hardly in Tolstoi's or George Eliot's. Murdoch's characters seem to me quite as different from Huxley's as they are from George Eliot's.

2. James Bellamy, 'The Saint and the Artist: an Approach to the Aesthetics and Ethics of Iris Murdoch', PhD thesis, University of Wisconsin–Madison, 1975, p. 152.

3. Mikhail Bakhtin's *Problems of Dostoevsky's Poetics*.

4. T. Eagleton, 'Liberalism and Order: the Criticism of John Bayley', *New Left Review*, 110 (July/Aug. 1978) 29–40.

5. A description of structuralism I owe to correspondence with Miss Murdoch.

6. C. Ricks, 'A Sort of Mystery Novel', *New Statesman*, LXX (1965) 604; and *The Sunday Times*, 7 Sep. 1980.

7. In 'Thinking and Language', *Proceedings of the Aristotelian Society*, xxv (1951) 25–34, and also in many succeeding essays, Murdoch notes the special indeterminacy which is the leading characteristic of mental imagery.

8. Alasdair MacIntyre, 'Good for Nothing' (review of Dipple's *Work for the Spirit*), *London Review of Books*, 3–16 June 1982, 15–6.

9. Ibid.

10. Sage, 'Pursuit of Imperfection', p. 67.

11. Sage, 'Female Fictions', p. 73.

12. T. Eagleton, *Literary Theory: An Introduction* (Oxford, 1983) pp. 184ff.

13. H. O. Mounce, *Philosophy*, 47 (1972) 178–80, review of *SG*.

14. Bayley, *Romantic Survival*, p. 27.

15. Frank Kermode, 'Necessary Persons', *Listener*, 16 Jan. 1968, 84–5, 'if the best self of Bloomsbury has an heir, it is Miss Murdoch'.

16. V. Woolf, 'The Novels of E. M. Forster', in *The Death of the Moth and Other Essays* (New York, 1974) p. 169.

17. E. M. Forster, 'Virginia Woolf', in *Two Cheers for Democracy* (London, 1965).

18. MacIntyre (see n.8) argues that Miss Murdoch's novels risk seeing morality as 'in the end no more than an aesthetically engaging and compelling phenomenon'. Speaking to Father Martin Jarrett-Kerr in 1969 (Chapter 10, n.5), she noted 'I think a certain amount of one's thought about goodness is perhaps aesthetic in a way. That one is very much magnetised by the notion or symbol of goodness.' This is too large and important an argument to be fully addressed in a footnote. Leaving aside Murdoch's often-repeated and surely proper insistence that art and politics are different realms it might nonetheless be pointed out that the other-centredness her books can seem to praise is not, for her, a self-sufficing commodity, but is for use in the world. Lovejoy noted in *The Great Chain of Being*

(Cambridge, Mass. 1978) p. 28, that there was perhaps nothing so favourable to success in this world's business than a high degree of emotional detachment from it. From her first prose publication (Chapter 1, n.13), through *The Sovereignty of Good*, to the Gifford lectures in 1982, she has insisted on 'a descending as well as an ascending dialectic and [Plato] speaks of a return to the cave . . . so far as goodness is for use in politics and in the market place it must combine increasing intuitions of unity with an increasing grasp of complexity and detail' (*SG* 96).

19. 'Good, Evil and Morality' (Chapter 10, n.5).
20. C. L. Barber, *Shakespeare's Festive Comedy* (Princeton, New Jersey, 1972) pp. 250ff.
21. 'An artist's first job is to be a good artist, which may or may not involve attention to the contemporary scene. As an articulate citizen he also, of course, has the duty, perhaps especially important today, to take an active part in the politics of his country. But these are quite separate issues', *London Magazine*, Aug. 1968, 16.
22. Philip Rieff, in *The Triumph of the Therapeutic*, views self-effacement in this way and, in accord with much of the political Neofreudianism of the 1960s declares that 'It may well be the closing-time in the ascetic culture of the West' (209). The announcement now looks premature. The only cultures to make a hero out of the man who is the enemy of his own needs today may be socialist (and nationalist); and yet the moral bankruptcy of the West seems related to its inability to make any intelligible place for the spiritualisation of the instincts.
23. R. Taubman, 'Double Life', *London Review of Books*, 19 May–2 June 1983, 23.
24. See Appendix p. 272, for discussion of these points.
25. Sage, 'Female Fictions', p. 73.
26. Sage, 'The Pursuit of Imperfection', p. 68.
27. 'The Machinery of Pain: Romantic Suffering in Three Works of Iris Murdoch', *Renascence*, xxix, 2 (Winter 1977), 69–85.
28. Anon, *The Times Literary Supplement*, 7 Nov. 1958, 31–2.

Select Bibliography

For a full listing up to 1976 readers are referred to Thomas T. Tominaga, *Iris Murdoch and Muriel Spark: A Bibliography* (USA, 1976). John Fletcher's *Iris Murdoch: Her Works and her Critics, 1933–1983* (New York: Garland, forthcoming) will be an invaluable addition to Murdoch studies.

1. WORKS BY IRIS MURDOCH

(a) *Novels*

Under the Net (London, 1954).
The Flight from the Enchanter (London, 1956).
The Sandcastle (London, 1957).
The Bell (London, 1958).
A Severed Head (London, 1961).
An Unofficial Rose (London, 1962).
The Unicorn (London, 1963).
The Italian Girl (London, 1964).
The Red and the Green (London, 1965).
The Time of the Angels (London, 1966).
The Nice and the Good (London, 1968).
Bruno's Dream (London, 1969).
A Fairly Honourable Defeat (London, 1970).
An Accidental Man (London, 1971).
The Black Prince (London, 1973).
The Sacred and Profane Love Machine (London, 1974).
A Word Child (London, 1975).
Henry and Cato (London, 1976).
The Sea, The Sea (London, 1978).
Nuns and Soldiers (London, 1980).
The Philosopher's Pupil (London, 1983).
The Good Apprentice (London, 1985).

(b) *Plays*

Iris Murdoch and J. B. Priestley, *A Severed Head* (London, 1964).
James Saunders and Iris Murdoch, *The Italian Girl* (London, 1969).

The Three Arrows with *The Servants and the Snow* (London, 1973).
'The Servants', unpublished libretto for an opera by William Mathias (1980).
'Art and Eros, a Platonic dialogue', with 'Acastos' (forthcoming, 1986).

(c) *Philosophy, Criticism and Letters*

'Against Dryness', *Encounter*, xvi (Jan. 1961) 16–20.
'Art is the Imitation of Nature', *Cahiers du Centre de Recherches sur les Pays du Nord et du Nord-Ouest*, No. 1, Publications de la Faculté de Lettres et Sciences Humaines de l'Université de Caen, 1978.
Bookmarks (a brief description of her reading), ed. F. Raphael (London, 1975) p. 125.
'The Darkness of Practical Reason' (review of S. Hampshire, *Freedom of the Individual*), *Encounter*, xxvii (July 1966) 46–50.
'T. S. Eliot as a Moralist', in Neville Braybrooke (ed.), *T. S. Eliot: A Symposium for his Seventieth Birthday* (London, 1958).
'Epistolary Dialogues', *Soviet Literature* (1977, pt 2) 48–61, with Valentina Ivasheva.
'Existentialist Bite' (review of E. Knight's *Literature Considered as Philosophy*), *Spectator*, 12 July 1957, 68–9.
'The Existentialist Hero', *Listener*, 23 March 1950, 523–4.
'The Existentialist Political Myth', *Socratic*, v (1952) 52–63.
'Existentialists and Mystics', in W. Robson (ed.), *Essays and Poems Presented to Lord David Cecil* (London, 1970).
The Fire and the Sun: Why Plato Banished the Artists (Oxford, 1977).
'Force Fields' (review of A. S. Byatt's *The Virgin in the Garden*), *New Statesman*, 3 Nov. 1978, 586.
'Freedom and Knowledge', (Symposium) in *Freedom and the Will* (London, 1963) pp. 80–104.
'Hegel in Modern Dress' (review of *Being and Nothingness* by Jean-Paul Sartre), *New Statesman*, liii (25 May 1957) 675–76.
'A House of Theory', *Partisan Review*, xxvi (1959) 17–31.
'Important Things' (review of De Beauvoir's *The Mandarins*), *The Sunday Times*, 17 Feb. 1957, reprinted in *Encore: A Sunday Times Anthology* (1963) pp. 299–301.
'A Jewelled Occasion' (review of B. Brophy's *The Snowball*), *The Sunday Times*, 19 Jan. 1964.
'Knowing the Void', *Spectator*, cxcvii (2 Nov, 1956) 613–14.
'Let them Philosophise' (review of S. T. Coleridge's *Confessions of an Inquiring Spirit*), *Spectator*, 14 Dec. 1956, 873.
'Mass, Might and Myth' (review of Canetti's *Crowds and Power*), *Spectator*, ccix (7 Sep. 1962) 337–38.
Manuscript Collection, University of Iowa, No. MsC 212.
'Metaphysics and Ethics', in D. F. Pears (ed.), *The Nature of Metaphysics* (London, 1957).
'Midnight Hour', *Adelphi*, Jan.–Mar. 1943, 60–1.
'The Moral Decision about Homosexuality', *Man and Society*, vii (Summer 1964) 3–6.

'Mr. Gellner's Game' (review of Gellner's *Words and Things*), *Observer*, 29 Nov. 1959.

'Negative Capability', *Adam*, 284–6 (1960) 172–3.

'Nostalgia for the Particular', *Proceedings of the Aristotelian Society*, LII (1952) 243–60.

'A Note on Drama', *Cue*, Sep. 1970, 13–14.

'The Novelist as Metaphysician', *Listener*, XLIII (16 Mar. 1950) 473–6.

'Philosophy and Beliefs' (Symposium), in *Twentieth Century*, June 1955, 495–521.

'Political Morality', *Listener*, 21 Sep. 1967, 353–4.

'Premium Books', in *New Fiction Society*, no. 1 (Oct. 1974) 8.

'Rebirth of Christianity', *Adelphi*, July–Sep. 1943, 134–5.

'Salvation by Words', *New York Review of Books*, 15 June 1972, 4.

Sartre, Romantic Rationalist (London, 1953).

'Simone, Antoine and Anne' (review of De Beauvoir's *Memoirs of a Dutiful Daughter*), *The Sunday Times*, 17 May 1959, 15.

'Socialism and Selection' in C. B. Cox and Rhodes Boyson (eds), *Black Paper 3* (London, 1975) pp. 7–9.

The Sovereignty of Good (London, 1970).

'The Sublime and the Beautiful Revisited', *Yale Review*, XLIX (Winter 1959) 247–71.

'The Sublime and the Good', *Chicago Review*, XIII (Aug. 1959) 42–55.

'Thinking and Language', *Proceedings of the Aristotelian Society*, XXV (1951) 25–34.

Untitled review of De Beauvoir's *Ethics of Ambiguity*, in *Mind*, LIX (1950) 127–8.

Untitled review of J-P. Sartre's *The Emotions, Outline of a Theory*, in *Mind*, LIX (April 1950) 268–71.

'Vision and Choice in Morality', *Aristotelian Society Supplementary Volume*, XXX (1956) 32–58.

'Worship and Common Life', *Adelphi*, July–Sep. 1944, 134–5.

(d) *Poetry*

'Too Late'; 'John Sees a Stork at Zamorra', *Boston University Journal*, Nov. 1975.

'Agamemnon Class 1939', *Boston University Journal*, 25, 2 (1977) 57–8.

'Poem and Egg', 'The Brown Horse', 'The Public Garden in Calimera', *Transatlantic Review*, 60 (June 1977) 31–4.

'Motorist and Dead Bird', *The Listener*, 16 June 1977, 781.

A Year of Birds (with engravings by Reynolds Stone) (Tisbury, Wilts, 1978).

Four poems in *Poetry London Apple Magazine*, I, 1 (Autumn 1979) 38–42.

'Miss Beatrice May Baker' in *People: Essays and Poems*, ed. Susan Hill (London, 1983) pp. 114–5.

2. Criticism

(a) *Interviews*

Anon (1981) 'An Interview with Iris Murdoch', *Vogue* (American edn), March, 329, 367.

Anon (1958) 'Mainly about Authors', *Bookman*, Nov., 26.

Barrows, John (1961) 'Living Writers – 7', *John o' London's*, 4 May, 495.

Bellamy, Michael (1977) 'An Interview with Iris Murdoch', *Contemporary Literature*, XVIII, 129–40.

Bigsby (1982), in Ziegler, H. and Bigsby, C. W. E. (eds), *The Radical Imagination and the Liberal Tradition: Interviews with English and American Novelists* (London) pp. 209–30.

Biles, Jack (1978) 'An Interview with Iris Murdoch', *Studies in the Literary Imagination*, XI (Fall) 115–25.

Blow, Simon (1976) 'An Interview with Iris Murdoch', *Spectator*, 25 Sep., 24–5.

Bradbury, M. (1976) 'Iris Murdoch in conversation, 27 Feb. 1976', British Council tape no. RS 2001.

Bryden, R. (1968) (with A. S. Byatt), 'Talking to Iris Murdoch', *Listener*, 14 April, 433–4.

Caen (1978) 'Recontres avec Iris Murdoch', Jean-Louis Chevalier (ed.), Centre de Recherches de Littérature et Linguistique des Pays de Langue Anglaise, Université de Caen, France.

Davie, Gill (1975) 'I should hate to be alive and not writing a novel: Iris Murdoch on her Work', *Woman's Journal*, October, 64–5.

Dillistone, F. (1965) 'Christ and Myth', *Frontier*, Aug., 219–21.

Haffenden John (1983) 'John Haffenden Talks to Iris Murdoch', *Literary Review* LVIII, April, 31–5.

Hayman, R, (1970) 'Out of the Tutorial', *The Times*, 30 Sep., 13.

Hebert, Hugh (1972) 'The Iris Problem', *Guardian*, 24 Oct., 10.

Heyd, Ruth (1965) 'An Interview with Iris Murdoch', *University of Windsor Review*, XXX, 61–82.

Hobson, Harold (1962) 'Lunch with Iris Murdoch', *The Sunday Times*, 11 March, 28.

Jarrett-Kerr, M. (1969) 'Good, Evil and Morality', *CR: Quarterly Review of the Community of the Resurrection*, no. 266 (Michaelmas) 17–23.

Kermode, Frank (1963) 'House of Fiction: Interviews with Seven English Novelists', *Partisan Review*, XXX, 61–82.

Lello, R. (ed.) *Revelations* (London, forthcoming).

Lennon, Peter (1978) 'The Odd (but Triumphant) World of Iris Murdoch', *The Sunday Times*, 26 Nov.

Lewis, Peter (1968) 'Crying Blue Murdoch', *Daily Mail*, 30 Jan.

Lewis, Peter (1978) 'On the Crest of a Wave', *Daily Mail*, 23 Nov.

Magee, Brian (1978) *Men of Ideas: Some Creators of Contemporary Philosophy* (London) pp. 264–84.

May, D. (1978) 'Iris Murdoch's Best Seller in the Swim', *Observer*, 26 Nov.

Mehta, Ved (1961) 'Onward and Upward with the Arts: a Battle against the Bewitchment of our Intelligence', *New Yorker*, 37 (9 Dec.) 59–159.

Nettell, Stephanie (1966) 'An Exclusive Interview', *Books and Bookmen*, XI (Sep.) 14, 15, 66.

Purcell, H. D. (1977) 'Faust lives OK', *Books and Bookmen*, Nov, 52.

Rose, W. K. (1968) 'An Interview with Iris Murdoch', *Shenandoah*, XIX (Winter) 3–22.

Sutcliffe, Tom (1980) 'Interview with Iris Murdoch', *Guardian*, 15 Sep.

Taylor, Jane (1971) 'Iris Murdoch Talks to Jane Taylor', *Books and Bookmen*, April, 26–7.

(b)   *Reviews, Articles and Books*

Allen, Diogenes, 'Two Experiences of Existence: Jean-Paul Sartre and Iris Murdoch', *International Philosophical Quarterly*, June 1974, 181–7.

Baldanza, Frank, 'Iris Murdoch and the Theory of Personality', *Criticism*, VII (Spring 1965) 176–89.

Baldanza, Frank, 'The Manuscripts of Iris Murdoch's *A Severed Head*', *Modern Fiction Studies*, xv (Aut. 1969) 417–28.

Baldanza, Frank, 'The Nice and the Good', *Modern Fiction Studies*, xv, no. 3 (Aut. 1969) 417–28.

Baldanza, Frank, *Iris Murdoch* (New York, 1974).

Batchelor, Billie, 'Revision in Iris Murdoch's *Under the Net*', *Books at Iowa* (University of Iowa), VIII (April 1968) 30–6.

Bradbury, M., ' "A House fit for Free Characters": Iris Murdoch and *Under the Net*', in *Possibilities: Essays on the State of the Novel* (London, 1973).

Bradbury, M., 'The Romantic Miss Murdoch', *Spectator*, 3 Sep. 1965, 293.

Byatt, A. S., *Degrees of Freedom: The Novels of Iris Murdoch* (London, 1965).

Byatt, A. S., *Iris Murdoch* (London, 1976).

Byatt, A. S., 'People in Paper Houses: Attitudes to "Realism" and "Experiment" in English Postwar Fiction', in M. Bradbury and D. Palmer (eds), *The Contemporary English Novel* (London, 1979) pp. 19–41.

Conradi, Peter J., 'The Metaphysical Hostess', *ELH*, XLVIII (Summer 1981) 427–53.

Conradi, Peter J., 'Useful Fictions', *Critical Quarterly*, XXIII, no. 3 (Aut. 1981) 63–9.

Dillon, M. C., 'Why Should Anyone Refrain from Stealing', *Ethics*, LXXXIII, no. 4 (July 1973) 338–40.

Dipple, Elizabeth, *Iris Murdoch: Work for the Spirit* (London, 1982).

Dunbar, Scott, 'On Art, Morals and Religion: Some Reflections on the Work of Iris Murdoch', *Religious Studies*, XIV, no. 4 (Dec. 1978) 515–24.

Felheim, Marvin, 'Symbolic Characterisation in the Novels of Iris Murdoch', *Texas Studies in Literaure and Language*, II, no. 1 (Spring 1960) 189–97.

Fraser, G. S., 'Iris Murdoch and the Solidity of the Normal', in John Wain (ed.), *International Literary Annual*, vol. II (London, 1959) pp. 37–54.

German, Howard, 'Allusion in the Early Novels of Iris Murdoch', *Modern Fiction Studies*, xv, no. 2 (Aug. 1969) 361–77.

Goode, John, 'Character and Henry James', *New Left Review*, 40 (1966) 55–75.

Graham, Martin, 'Iris Murdoch and the Symbolist Novel', *British Journal of Aesthetics*, v (July 1965) 269–300.

Gregor, Ian, 'Towards a Christian Literary Criticism', *Month*, XXIII (April 1965) 239–49.

Gindin, James, 'Images of Illusion in the Work of Iris Murdoch', *Texas Studies in Literature and Language*, II, no. 1 (Spring 1960) 180–8.

Hall, J., 'Blurring the Will: The Growth of Iris Murdoch', *ELH*, XXXII, 2 (June 1965) 256–73.

Hall, William, ' "The Third Way": the Novels of Iris Murdoch', *Dalhousie Review*, xlvi (Aug. 1966) 306–18.

Hebblethwaite, Peter, 'Feuerbach's Ladder: Leszek Kolakowskie and Iris Murdoch', *Heythrop Journal*, xiii (April 1972) 143–61.

Hebblethwaite, Peter, 'Out Hunting Unicorns', *Month*, Oct. 1963, 224–28.

Hoffman, F. J., 'The Miracle of Contingency: the Novels of Iris Murdoch', *Shenandoah*, xvii, i (Autumn 1965) 49–56.

Hoffman, F. J., 'Iris Murdoch: The Reality of Persons', *Critique*, vii (Spring 1964) 48–57.

Hoskins, Robert, 'Iris Murdoch's Midsummer Nightmare', *Twentieth Century Literature*, xix (Jan.–Oct. 1972) 191–8.

Jacobson, Dan, 'Farce, Totem and Taboo', *New Statesman*, 16 June 1961, 956–7.

Jarrett-Kerr, M., 'Goodness Gracious' (review of *SG*), *Guardian*, 19 Nov. 1970.

Kemp, Peter, 'The Flight Against Fantasy: Iris Murdoch's *The Red and the Green*', *Modern Fiction Studies*, xv, no. 3 (Aug. 1969) 403–15.

Kermode, Frank, 'Necessary Persons', *Listener*, 16 Jan. 1969, 84–5.

Kermode, Frank, 'The Novels of Iris Murdoch', *Spectator*, 17 Nov. 1958.

MacIntyre, Alistair, 'Good for Nothing' (article-review of Dipple, *Work for The Spirit*), *London Review of Books*, 3–16 June 1982, 15–16.

Majdiak, Daniel, 'Romanticism in the Aesthetics of Iris Murdoch', *Texas Studies in Literature and Language*, xiv, no. 2 (1972) 359–75.

Obumselu, Ben, 'Iris Murdoch and Sartre', *ELH*, xlii (Summer 1975) 296–317.

O'Hearn, D. J., 'Iris Murdoch in the Role of Philosopher' (review of *SG*), *The Age*, 24 April 1971, 15.

Pearson, Gabriel, 'Iris Murdoch and the Romantic Novel', *New Left Review*, xiii–xiv (Jan.–April 1962) 137–45.

Pearson, Gabriel, 'Simultaneous and Quadratic' (review of *BP*) *Guardian*, 22 Feb. 1973.

Quinton, Anthony, 'Slings and Arrows' (review of *BP*), *Sunday Telegraph*, 25 Feb. 1973.

Rabinowitz, Rubin, 'Iris Murdoch', in G. Stade (ed.), *Six Contemporary British Novelists* (New York, 1976).

Ricks, Christopher, 'A Sort of Mystery Novel', *New Statesman*, lxx (1965) 604.

Sage, Lorna, 'Female Fictions', in *The Contemporary English Novel*, (eds) M. Bradbury and D. Palmer (London, 1979) pp. 67–87.

Sage, Lorna, 'No Trespassers' (review of *FS*), *New Review*, Sep. 1977, 49–50.

Sage, Lorna, 'The Pursuit of Imperfection', *Critical Quarterly*, xix, no. 2 (Summer 1977) 67–87.

Scanlan, Margaret, 'The Machinery of Pain: Romantic Suffering in Three Works of Iris Murdoch', *Renascence*, xxix (2) (Winter 1977) 69–85.

Scholes, Robert, *Fabulation and Metafiction* (Urbana and London, 1978) pp. 56–74, and *Structuralism in Literature* (New Haven and London, 1974) pp. 195–8.

Souvage, Jacques, 'Symbol as Narrative Device: an Interpretation of Iris Murdoch's *The Bell*', *English Studies*, xxxxiii, no. 2 (April 1962) 81–96.

Sullivan, Zohreh T., 'The Contracting Universe of Iris Murdoch's Gothic Novels', *Modern Fiction Studies*, xxiii (Winter 1977–8) 557–69.

Sullivan, Zohreh T., 'Iris Murdoch's Self-conscious Gothicism: *The Time of the Angels*', *Arizona Quarterly*, 1977, 47–60.

Swinden, Patrick, *Unofficial Selves* (London, 1973).

Todd, Richard, *Iris Murdoch: The Shakespearian Interest* (London and New York, 1979).

Todd, Richard, *Iris Murdoch* (London and New York, 1984).

Todd, Richard, 'The Plausibility of *The Black Prince*', *Dutch Quarterly*, 1978/2, 82–93.

Toynbee, Philip, 'For Goodness' Sake' (review of *SG*), *Observer*, 10 Jan. 1971.

Vance, Norman, 'Iris Murdoch's Serious Fun', *Theology*, Nov. 1981, 420–8.

Warnock, Mary, 'The Nice and the Good' (review of *SG*), *New Statesman*, 10 Dec. 1970.

Weldhen, Margaret, 'Morality and the Metaphor', *New Universities Quarterly*, Spring 1980, 215–28.

Winsor, Dorothy A., 'Solipsistic Sexuality in Iris Murdoch's Gothic Novels', *Renascence*, xxxiv (Autumn 1981) 52–63.

Wolfe, Peter, *The Disciplined Heart: Iris Murdoch and her Novels* (Columbia, Mo, 1966).

Index